INDIANA SERVICE CORPORATION
378
INDIANA CENTRAL LINES
378

FORT WAYNE AND WABASH VALLEY TROLLEYS

FT.WAYNE
84

FORT WAYNE AND WABASH VALLEY TROLLEYS

George K. Bradley, Author

Bulletin 122
Central Electric Railfans' Association

FORT WAYNE AND WABASH VALLEY TROLLEYS

George K. Bradley, Author

Bulletin 122 of Central Electric Railfans' Association

An Illinois Not-for-profit Corporation
Post Office Box 503 Chicago, Illinois 60690 USA

Library of Congress Catalog Card Number 82-71475
International Standard Book Number 0-915348-22-5

CERA Bulletins are technical, educational references prepared as historical projects by members of Central Electric Railfans' Association, working without salary due to their interest in the subject. This Bulletin is consistent with the stated purpose of the corporation: To foster the study of the history, equipment and operation of electric railways. If you the reader can provide any unknown information or are of the opinion that certain information is incorrect, please send your information, documented by source material where possible to: Curator of Corrections, Central Electric Railfans' Association, P.O. Box 503, Chicago, Illinois 60690, USA.

FORT WAYNE AND WABASH VALLEY TROLLEYS was designed and assembled by Zastrow Studios, Inc. of Thiensville, Wisconsin. Halftones are by Jim Walter Graphic Arts of Beloit, Wisconsin with typesetting by Zastrow Studios, Inc. of Thiensville, Wisconsin. The book was printed by Sorg Printing Company of Chicago, Illinois and was bound by John F. Cuneo Company, Melrose Park, Illinois.

Acknowledgements

FORT WAYNE & WABASH VALLEY TROLLEYS owes much of its success to the extensive list of people who were willing to contribute their time and resources. Several people played key roles in gathering and checking data. Foremost among these would be Roy Benedict whose hours of involvement are difficult to measure in his near tireless effort of supportive research as well as the reading and re-reading of each section for continuity and accuracy. Dr. Harold E. Cox and Dr. Reed Prugh made sizeable and valuable contributions to the rolling stock information. The field of public transportation provided years of experience information from Donald H. Walker, Neil Shober, Maurice Fox, Eric Kuhne, Mark DeHaven and George Nicolaides. John Stein, Chairman of the Fort Wayne Public Transportation Corporation (when I was Vice Chairman) made available the records still on the property. Earlier, E. A. Luhman of Indiana & Michigan Electric Company let me use the I&M photo and negative files which existed at that time (1963) and provided statistical data on passengers and revenues. The Allen County—Fort Wayne Historical Society through the late Roy M. Bates and others was a basic source. The Fort Wayne Public Library, especially Fred Reynolds, Robert Vegeler and Helen Colchin, provided easy access to records, papers, periodicals and inter-library loans. Other helpful data came from Stanley Chausse, John D. Knowles, Stanley Johnson, Paul Willer and W. F. Nedden. Bonnie Nalepa was the patient typist who made my notes readable.

William D. Middleton interviewed Samuel Insull, Jr. and made the transcripts available which were supplemented by my own conversation with Mr. Insull. Middleton also made his research on the "Windsplitter" interurbans available. Purdue and Lafayette information came from David W. Chambers, the Tippecanoe County Historical Association and Tom Alderson of the Greater Lafayette Public Transportation Corporation plus the author's own notes. Photos of Purdue University and Lafayette also came from these sources. The Lafayette, Logansport, Peru, Wabash and Huntington public libraries made history and newspaper files available as did the Cass County, Wabash County, and Huntington County historical societies. The Indiana State Library archives and the Indiana State Historical Society's records were also used as were the Brill records held by the Historical Society of Pennsylvania.

Bus data came from several sources and was carefully sorted out by John P. Hoschek and the Motor Bus Society. Many of the buses at Fort Wayne and Lafayette were purchased secondhand and the original owners were not always clear nor were the original numbers. Fortunately many of the serial numbers were available which made it possible to trace the buses and their owners. Many buses worked for three or more owners and tracing them is not an easy task.

Photographs came from a number of sources and several sizable collections. The largest number and widest variety of photos came from the diligent searching and constant aid of Herbert G. Harnish of Fort Wayne, the principal contributor to the Bradley-Harnish collection. Without the Herb Harnish effort this book would be much less than it is, not only in illustrations but in the information many of these photographs revealed.

George Krambles, John Humiston, Frank Butts, Gene Van Dusen, William Steventon (R. O. Dingley collection), Harry Zillmer and Malcolm McCarter were among the principal photo contributors. Others are noted in the credit lines.

Norman Carlson pulled the loose ends together and coordinated the author's efforts with others who were in a position to help. His aid has been a key factor in introducing other talents to the book, such as CERA's Max Zink. The outstanding cartography is another of Max's contributions.

The half-tone reproductions were handled by Jim Walter who took particular pains to bring out details in some of the old and rare but less than first class photos.

The layout, type style and book design was a pet project of the late Eugene Zastrow, of Zastrow Studios, Inc., my very good friend. It was Gene's plan to do the book in his studios in Thiensville, WI., north of Milwaukee. The book layout, type and art work was completed there and do reflect Gene's ideas as carried out by his long time associate George Houdek, and Suzanne Becker of the studio staff. They, and I, regret that Gene's sudden death deprived us of his keen artistic eye and denied him the chance to see the finished book.

Now some seven years after this "easy" task began, the book finally is completed.

George K. Bradley
October 1982

Introduction

In 1975, Central Electric Railfans Association decided to study the Indiana electric railway scene in greater depth than the broad brush coverage of its earlier Bulletins. FORT WAYNE'S TROLLEYS (by then out of print) was the suggested starting point. George Bradley, author of that book, suggested a much broader scope project based on the extensive Schoepf-McGowan traction syndicate properties as they were around 1910. The syndicate controlled most of the larger traction properties in Indiana, the giant Ohio Electric Railway and a number of sizable city street railway properties. All of the syndicate's interurban lines had some common relationships and an interface between the properties that allowed many of them to survive longer than most interurbans. Coverage of all of these will require several books as a long range CERA project. FORT WAYNE & WABASH VALLEY TROLLEYS is the first in this series.

FORT WAYNE'S TROLLEYS was the base point but it was soon engulfed in new and greatly expanded information, particularly the interurban lines and the smaller cities. The older work became the main frame of the new book. The formation of the Schoepf-McGowan Fort Wayne and other Indiana-Ohio properties into an interurban rail empire created situations where an action of one company usually affected several others. Control of companies and equipment was changed to fit master plans and competition was sometimes squeezed out. Unified control meant interline, through train, services in a partial integration of the syndicate's operations.

This set the stage for the eventual establishment of what may be the most unique and fondly remembered of interurbans—the Indiana Railroad. Samuel Insull's utility interests gained control of a number of key power and rail properties over a period of years resulting in consolidations and integrated power systems. The rail lines were, in 1930, brought together into the Indiana Railroad System under the Midland United Company as the Insull umbrella holding company in Indiana.

Fort Wayne enjoyed excellent city transportation from 1872 onward! The system was always kept up-to-date and the modernization of the twenties made the Fort Wayne property second to none and the envy of many. The system operations were slowly switched from streetcars to trolley coaches in the forties and then to motor buses in the sixties. Even in the difficult years of the late fifties and early sixties, a high quality service level was maintained. By 1968 ownership changed from the private to the public sector and the system was upgraded again. An excellent level of service with modern buses is available today (1982).

Elsewhere in the Wabash River valley, Logansport, Wabash, Peru and Lafayette had local trolley lines. Lafayette had an ill-fated street railway, from 1869 through 1873 (before Fort Wayne), which might have changed some future transportation patterns in Lafayette had it survived. Lafayette's second system started in 1884 and there has been continuous city transportation since, although there have been more difficulties and ownership problems there than in Fort Wayne. Both cities now have flourishing municipal transportation corporations providing local, tax supported, city transit.

Additional photo credits:

Title page spread: *The Ohio Electric 84 slows for the Fort Wayne and Findley rail crossing at Tillman's, east of Fort Wayne.* ***Dr. Reed C. Prugh Collection. End papers —front:*** *The new steel cars for the Northern Division-Lima line are presented in proud display at the Spy Run shops on August 15, 1924. All the cars sport bright red paint.* ***Bradley-Harnish Collection. End papers —back:*** *The new Wabash Valley Flyer, ready for service, sits on the ladder tracks at the Spy Run shops in 1926.* ***Bradley-Harnish Collection.***

Table of Contents

FRIEND'S ENTERPRISE
FASHIONABLE
CLOTHIERS
FRIEND'S ENTERPRISE
CLOTHING
REDLICK
BROS
SHOE
STORE

Citizens' Horsecars

CHAPTER 1

A fortunate location made Fort Wayne the commercial center of northeastern Indiana. The shortest portage between the Great Lakes and Mississippi Valley—via the Maumee and Wabash River—caused the Indian tribes to locate astride the portage, in their permanent village "Kekionga." These were followed by the forts built by the French, English and finally the Americans...under General Anthony Wayne. A town grew where only a fort had been and the serious needs of shipping and transportation were eventually met with the Wabash and Erie Canal. This waterway followed the easy, near waterlevel route of the Maumee River, the Fort Wayne portage, and then into the Wabash River Valley. The canal was followed by the railroads and growing commerce and industry as the city grew.

Within the "Summit City" (the nickname of Fort Wayne, the highest point on the old canal system) there was, by 1870, an urgent need for reliable public transportation beyond the limited reach of some private omnibus operators. The solution was simple and John H. Bass, Samuel T. Hanna, Stephen B. Bond and A. E. Bursley formed the Citizens' Street Railroad Company with a capitalization of $50,000 on September 8, 1871. Their representatives went to the City Council and gained permission to lay rails south on Calhoun Street from Main Street to Creighton Avenue, then west to Fairfield Avenue and also east from Calhoun, on Wallace Street, to Hanna Street. The principals, by no small chance, owned property and had industrial interests in the areas to be served by the two rail lines.

The contractors began, as soon as the City Council approved the project, on October 10, 1871, by laying their rails as fast as practicable considering winter conditions. They also ran a short stretch of track on Maumee Street (later called Chestnut and now Baker Street), east from Calhoun, where a car house and stable were erected to a design prepared by the City Engineer. Two horsecars were ordered from McNairy & Claflen Manufacturing Company at Cleveland. They arrived with the New Year of 1872.

On January 6, 1872, at 3:45 p.m., City Engineer Charles Brackenridge and company President John Bass, drove the first car over the lines to public applause of the city. A huge celebration was held at the Aveline House to toast the community progress. Most celebrants felt that Fort Wayne had arrived as a metropolitan area equal to any major city.

More cars came from the Cleveland builder. By the end of the year, the company had 18 horses, six passenger cars, a flat car and 3¼ miles of track. The car house area was extended south through the block from Maumee Street to Railroad Street. Another adjoining lot was bought east of the car house. Snow was a problem and in late 1873, a plow with a salting attachment was purchased for the flat car.

Two additional lines were built east and west on Main Street from Calhoun Street during 1872. The east line turned south on Lafayette to Jefferson Street, while the west line turned south on Broadway also terminating at Jefferson. A turntable was built in the middle of the Main and Calhoun intersection. The company thus avoided costly

Citizens Street RR Company 16 at Jefferson and Broadway in July 1890. ***Bradley-Harnish Collection.***

East Main from Calhoun Street, showing one of the Ft. Wayne Street Railroad's horsecars, probably from the second series. ***Bradley-Harnish Collection.***

special track work and provided an opportunity for the fast turnaround of cars. The same corner location was also the location of the company's office. Main and Calhoun was the center of the system and the transfer point for the system. By the fall of 1872, the east line was extended on Jefferson to Maumee Avenue.

Before the first year was over, the company's operations were a victim of a nationwide malady, "The Great Epizootic," an epidemic of influenza in horses. All large stables—everywhere—were excellent centers for the temporarily disabling disease and the Citizens' Company's stable was no exception. Service was irregular during November and December, with a complete suspension from November 23 to December 4, when the most horses were incapacitated.

During July, 1874, track was built west on Jefferson Street from Broadway to Garden Street and the new Fairgrounds. The east line was later extended by building north on Harmer Street from Jefferson to Washington Boulevard and then east on Washington to Glasgow Avenue. The additional distance required more cars and 35 horses operating over $5\frac{3}{8}$ miles of track. By January, 1876, one open summer car had been added, and the line was $6\frac{1}{2}$ miles in length.

As patronage increased, some additions were made to the equipment and those cars on hand were rebuilt. The records suggest

This highly ornate foundry type letterhead was a local printer's product.

OFFICE OF

Citizens' Street Railroad Co.,

J. W. PEARSE, Superintendent. N. E. Cor. Main & Calhoun Streets.

Fort Wayne, Ind., ... 188......

East Main Street from Calhoun in the 1880's. Two horses pull car 20 through the plowed street. ***Bradley-Harnish Collection.***

that time must have been fairly hard on the cars, as all were rebuilt in the early 1880's. A new 50′ x 120′ car shop building was a great aid in this effort. Two new box cars (as closed passenger cars were then called) were acquired in 1885, and one summer car was built by the company bringing the total to thirteen. By 1885, the company had rebuilt all but three of its eleven box cars, nine of which were in daily use.

On March 1, 1873, to raise the needed expansion capital, the Citizens' Company executed a $20,000 mortgage upon all its properties and rights. During the succeeding years, they neglected to pay off the mortgage and eventually defaulted on the original bonds. This was no oversight, because the principal owners were knowledgeable money men. The deliberate neglect ended, as expected, in court and a change of venue was demanded to move the case out of Allen County to avoid local prejudice and any hint of fast and loose money games. The case finally landed in Noble County Circuit Court later in 1873. The company was placed, as expected, in receivership with Mr. Sidney Lumbard, as receiver.

Prior to 1887, all the carlines were south of the St. Mary's and Maumee Rivers as the County Commissioners were reluctant to let the car lines cross the bridges. However, during the summer of 1887 the Citizens' Company, on petition of the receiver, and with court permission, was allowed to lay tracks over the Wells Street bridge to tap suburban Bloomingdale. The tracks started at Main and

The northwest corner of Broadway and Jefferson in June 1890. The Citizens' Street RR Company 14 is turning west onto Jefferson Street. Note the high-crowned hat of the conductor who is relaxing on the back platform. ***Bradley-Harnish Collection.***

Calhoun, went north to Superior (crossing the Nickel Plate Road tracks, next to that company's depot) and west to Wells Street. North of the St. Mary's River, the tracks made an abrupt northeasterly turn from Wells Street, crossed over to Cass Street passing by the Fort Wayne, Jackson and Saginaw Railroad station. The cars now reached all the railroad stations. The Bloomingdale line continued up Cass Street to Third Street where it turned west terminating at Wells Street. This new line followed the double tracking of the Calhoun line the year before.

The Court ordered the company sold to satisfy the outstanding claims and the receivership terminated. On August 18, 1887, the company was sold "at the Courthouse door" for $110,000 to John M. Bass and Stephen B. Bond. These gentlemen and Frank De Haas Robison formed the Fort Wayne Street Railroad Company on August 22, 1887, capitalized at $300,000. The three each held nine-hundred and ninety-nine, one hundred dollar shares. The remaining three shares were held by A. S. Bond and James M. Barrett, the company's attorney. Bass and Bond made a very handsome paper profit in selling their interests in the Citizens' Company to the new company. Most of this profit was in new company stock.

Frank De H. Robison represented Cleveland interests and Cleveland capital seems to have dominated the Fort Wayne lines during this period. Robison controlled the Superior Street Railroad Company and the St. Clair Street Railroad Company, two of the several city rail lines in Cleveland. He was also interested in sports, owning the Cleveland "Spiders" baseball team. (Fort Wayne's "Kekiongas" ball club was in the same National League circuit.)

During the summer of 1887, Mr. C. L. Centlivre of the C. L. Centlivre Brewing Company decided to build a car line through the Riverside area and north to his brewery. The area was not very well developed. It was outside of the city and the permission of the County Commissioners was necessary before any work could be done. They allowed the C. L. Centlivre Street Railway to build north on Spy Run Avenue, from the St. Mary's River bridge, to the brewery, but not to cross the bridge. The north terminus was at the

Centlivre car 5 on Spy Run Avenue. ***Bradley-Harnish Collection.***

Feeder Canal bridge some three blocks short of the brewery's beer garden. The new street railway had a three block gap from the Spy Run bridge to the other city lines, at Calhoun Street, when service started on August 14, 1887. Late in the summer of 1888, a new Spy Run Avenue bridge was opened and the tracks were extended on Superior Street to Calhoun.

The new Fort Wayne Street Railroad Company embarked on an expansion program. New cars were purchased from J. M. Jones' Sons, with fourteen coming during November for $950.00 each. By the end of the year the company was claiming 12½ miles of track, 20 one-horse cars, 10 two-horse cars and 132 horses.

During 1888 one completely new line and a number of major extensions were built. The West Main Line was built west, from Main and Broadway, to the city limits just beyond Leesburg Road. This line terminated at the gates of the well kept and spacious grounds of Lindenwood Cemetery. Cemeteries in all cities seemed to be good traffic generators and Fort Wayne was no exception.

By extending the tracks south on Broadway to Creighton and then east to the existing line at Fairfield the "Belt Line" was created. Creighton Avenue was, at that time, roughly, the southern boundary of the city. (The "Belt Line" name stuck although as the city grew it only encircled the southwestern commercial district of the city. "Belt Lines" existed in many cities with similar track patterns.) This line was the only circular line in the city and operated cars in both directions. Service was started on October 11, 1888. The Hanna Street Line, now called the Wallace Street Line, was extended easterly via East Creighton Avenue to Walton Avenue (now Anthony Boulevard) in early November.

The turntable located in the center of the city's main intersection became an irritating nuisance as each car had to wait its opportunity to turn or cross. The turntable was removed on November 15, 1888 and replaced with special trackwork allowing cars to turn or pass through with ease. Main and Calhoun was the principal transfer point for all lines and the "turntable corner" became the "Transfer Corner," a name carried to this day.

The Chestnut Street (formerly Maumee Street) central barn location was fairly crowded and the company now owned and used most of the property south of Chestnut through to Railroad Street. The Pennsylvania depot (then Pittsburgh, Fort Wayne & Chicago Railroad) was across Railroad Street. North of Chestnut the company's first brick stable had burned, in 1884, to be replaced by a block long stable that extended through to Brackenridge Street. A large sheet metal, six track car barn stood to the west of the stable. To relieve the congested central city area a new complex was built at the northwest corner of Washington and Glasgow. The East Barns were at the city limits and the new facilities were a model of efficiency when opened on November 30, 1888. The 68′ x 140′ building housed 100 horses, had the largest hayloft in the city and had what were described as "fire protection plugs" on all floors to protect against conflagrations. The idea of water outlets (perhaps with hoses) on all floors was considered as very advanced thinking. A sheet metal car barn was next to the stable.

One of the company's progressive attempts met with a complaint from the Fort Wayne Sentinel. In the Sentinel's February 13, 1889 issue the editor noted, "No sooner did the snow begin to fall this noon than the street car employees began to scatter salt broad cast on Calhoun Street. This is the way sleighing is spoiled on the main thoroughfare and businessmen cut off from their trade. How long will the authorities permit this outrage." (Ninety years later the papers sing the opposite tune.)

The cars no longer carried the company name painted on the side. Instead they appeared more like a billboard with the route name and streets served painted on the sides and ends. This system was inconvenient as it permanently attached a car to a particular route unless it was completely repainted. A later more practical and flexible system produced a four-sided destination sign. All of these cars carried a two-man operating crew, a driver and a conductor; the wages were low but the nickels continued to pour in.

Calhoun Street suffered from traffic congestion, so additional trackage was laid on

Car 33 on the Belt Line route was among the newer Ft. Wayne Street Railroad cars. This 1890 view was taken on West Creighton Avenue. ***Bradley-Harnish Collection.***

parallel Clinton Street from Main to Lewis, connected to Calhoun at Lewis, and extended east to Walton Avenue. This brought the Lewis Street line into being in 1890 without creating further clutter on Calhoun Street.

The Jenny Electric Company, Fort Wayne's pioneering electric light manufacturer had now become the Fort Wayne Electric Works and many people were very interested in the new electric marvels that were being produced there. Hardly a week would go by without Mr. R. T. McDonald's works turning out something new to the public. The associated Jenny Electric Light and Power Company, in 1883, was busy building a new generating station on Spy Run Avenue at Kamm Street. This was a steam station and a successor to the Fort Wayne Water Power Company which had planned to use the Wabash and Erie Canal's feeder canal and reservoir to turn a turbine type generator. This had been a miserable failure because of an insufficient and irregular head of water. The new company got its water supply from the St. Joseph River across Spy Run Avenue.

The large stables at the East Barns, believed to be safe, became a total loss in a fire that swept the building on December 22, 1890. The fire department responded swiftly to the call but the highly combustible straw and hay gave the fire too much of a head start. The building exploded into flames so quickly that 59 horses perished in the holocaust before help arrived. The adjoining car barn was not damaged being saved by the fast action of the firefighters. The loss was $25,000. A new but smaller stable replaced the old one.

Marmaduke M. M. Slattery of the electric works made a number of battery-power, propulsion experiments on bicycles and wagons and eventually got to the horsecar situation. Mr. Slattery was one of many inventors

Ft. Wayne Street RR car 18 heads north from Calhoun Street on the Bloomingdale line in the late 1880's. ***Bradley-Harnish Collection.***

throughout the country trying to improve street railway operations with electric power. Some used overhead wires, while others tried an underground conduit, but Slattery preferred storage batteries and he arranged to have a horse car fitted out with twenty-five, eight-pound batteries and one motor. Late on the night of November 11, 1891, to avoid startling any horses, this car was loaded with forty-six people. It made a trip on the Belt Line reaching speeds up to 12 miles per hour! The car was rebuilt with a second motor but was unreliable and the unimpressed street railway decided to stick to horses. Mr. Slattery, a young man with a brilliant mind, was in ill health and died shortly afterwards.

An untouched area known as the "Old Orchard" was acquired by a real estate firm and named "Lakeside." This area, immediately north of the Maumee and east of the St. Joseph River, was low and subject to flooding. This problem was partly solved with flood dikes and the digging of small ponds to collect run-off waters. These ponds were called "lakes," with Delta Lake the largest, and provided nice park grounds. As early as 1890 a carline was contemplated for the area but little was done until 1892. The Lakeside Street Railroad Company was officially formed in August with a capital of $50,000.

The new company was fostered by R. T. McDonald, who owned $49,900 of the authorized stock. He planned to build east from Calhoun on Columbia Street, cross the river and terminate at Delta Lake. The company immediately met organized opposition which, more than likely, was quietly fostered by Fort Wayne Street Railroad. They no doubt felt that two companies were enough and three a crowd. In a silent compromise, the opposition to the new Lakeside Street Railway ceased, early in 1892, although the Nickel Plate Railroad at first refused a crossing at Columbia Street. The other independent line, the Centlivre company, extended its trackage by building east on the Hicksville Road (now East State Boulevard) to Crescent Avenue and the newly established Driving Park.

East Washington (Glasgow Avenue) car barn with a group of drivers and car barn workers posing for a formal portrait. Superintendent L. D. M. Nutt is sitting on a stool at the left end of the front row. ***Bradley-Harnish Collection.***

MAIN ST. LINE
38

The Magic of Electricity

CHAPTER 2

Horses won the first bout with electricity but the management continued to think that a better motive power might be available. The trade journals were full of success stories of cable and electric railways in many cities. Cost savings could be achieved without two sets of horses plus their feed, care and housing. The electric streetcars were now thoroughly proven, they worked all day without complaint and were much needed in Fort Wayne.

With no fanfare, and in a series of rapid moves, the Fort Wayne Street Railway surprised the city with the magic of electrically propelled streetcars. In March of 1892, the company simply announced plans to spend $100,000 to electrify the system. The first move would be a large powerhouse at Clinton and Chestnut Streets adjoining the South Barns and the second step, a fleet of new streetcars. Rapid progress was made and three new electric streetcars arrived in June. These were unloaded at the Nickel Plate Railroad spur track near the East (Glasgow Avenue) Barns and towed to their new home in the remodeled barns. Representatives of the press were dispatched to cover this activity and they soon reported that more cars were arriving each day from the J. M. Jones Company of Watervliet, New York. These news stories of more than thirty new cars created much curiosity and speculation. At the same time a steady procession of new poles and miles of copper wire had arrived to be erected at a fast pace.

M. Stanley Robison, the company manager —and brother of Frank—ran one of the new open cars over the West Main-East Washington line on July 8, 1892. Electric power was obtained from the Jenny Electric Light and Power Company as the new Chestnut Street Station was not completed. The Short Electric Railway Company was contractor for the electrification and their 20 h.p., single reduction motors were used on the new cars. The new powerhouse went into service just in time to save the Jenny plant from overstrain. The Chestnut Street Station was a great attraction to youngsters who watched the huge flywheels of the Bass built, Corliss engines. These big, non-condensing, reciprocating steam engines drove three 200-kw and one 500-kw DC generators. The station originally used the abundant Indiana natural gas supply. When this fuel source failed it was changed to coal at a 50% increase in cost.

The company's horsecars disappeared at this change-over and all the contemporary news stories speak of "new" cars from Jones. Several of the cars look as though they had had a large-windowed center section spliced into them, thereby enlarging the car. This practice was quite common and some of the newer and better Jones built horsecars may have been returned to the builder for this alteration and strengthening.

Most of the company's twenty miles of track was rebuilt as part of the changeover. The old Bloomingdale line on Cass Street was replaced by a new, double track line on Wells Street—one block to the west—and extended northward to Huffman Street.

On August 19, the old company was sold to the new Fort Wayne Electric Railway Company. This new company was capitalized at $1,000,000 par value stock. Most of the stock remained in the same Fort Wayne hands. The electrification costs were met in a new mortgage to the Guaranty and Indemnity Company of New York. This was for $600,000 in bonds, all of which were issued.

At this time and over the next few years a number of practices were carried on that would be frowned upon in much later years. Barrett's firm did all of the legal work; much of the metal work was done by the Bass Foundry, and Frank Robison continually advanced large sums of cash to the company and was paid substantial interest on extended and new notes. Frequently the company paid interest on notes to Fort Wayne National Bank (John Bass) but nothing on the principal. The company was making money but spending

Calhoun Street north from Main about 1898. Car 38, one of the newest closed electric cars, is just changing ends prior to running in the other direction.
Bradley-Harnish Collection.

Horsecar 60 was given new life as the electric age approached becoming one of the cars rebuilt for electric use with a large center window section added on. This car is heading west on East Creighton Avenue. ***Bradley-Harnish Collection.***

it just as fast with the expansion. The basic expansion was completed on August 28th when the last of the company's horsecars returned to the barn.

The Lakeside Street Railway was an independent corporation but virtually was built by the Fort Wayne Electric Railway. During the early months of 1892, the Lakeside Company built east from Columbia and Calhoun, on Columbia, across the Maumee River Bridge and eastward on Columbia, in Lakeside, to Crescent Avenue. They hired their own crews to lay all trackage except the curve east of the river. The rails, overhead and all hardware were bought from the Fort Wayne Electric Railway. The company had a long standing dispute about crossing the Nickel Plate's tracks which was resolved so that service over the entire line began on August 24.

Obligingly, the Fort Wayne Electric Railway even sold the Lakeside Company four of their brand new Jones built cars. These were two 8-bench open cars, numbered 1 and 3 for $600.00 each and two box cars, numbered 2

Open car 57, heading west, looks brand new as it journeys over East Creighton Avenue. The "Hanna Street Line and All Depots" sign at the top of the car designated its route which began on the northwest side of Bloomingdale, passed all four rail depots in its north-south run through town, and traveled eastward on Hanna and East Creighton to its termination at East Creighton and Walton (now Anthony). ***Bradley-Harnish Collection.***

and 4, for $925.00 each. The relationship between the two companies remained very close.

The life of the employee was not always the easiest. The motorman and conductor were subjected to all types of weather, which, in itself, might not have been so bad, but often clean-up and other duties remained for the crews after the little cars rolled back to the barn. No one was overpaid and the clamor over wages was climaxed by a strike of motormen and conductors. Track crews were paid 15¢ per hour and the crew foreman was paid 33½¢ per hour as a typical example of the inequity the car crews recognized. The strike lasted from May 29 to June 3, 1893.

The motormen and conductors demanded a ten percent increase from thirteen and one-half cents an hour to a flat fifteen cents and a company statement that twelve hours constituted a working day. The company refused to negotiate and tried to continue service but the strikers resisted, did some damage and threatened to do more. The labor movement sympathizers were then threatened by the city law enforcement. Before things got too bad, the company relented and granted the employees' request.

The Centlivre Brewery owners were no longer interested in retaining their street railway operation particularly in view of the impending necessity to electrify. As a result the Centlivre owned line was sold to the Fort Wayne Electric Railway June 27, 1894 for $18,000. No service changes were made and the horsecars continued to run while the new owners sought franchise agreements from the city and county to electrify and extend the line. The permission was granted and the Spy Run Avenue line was electrified to the feeder canal bridge, by the brewery, by July 4 allowing swift service to the Centlivre owned parkgrounds. On August 9, the remaining, former Centlivre, horsecars were called in as electric horsepower replaced the last hay burners in Fort Wayne.

"It is the proud boast of Fort Wayne, that while in almost every city of the United States, including all the greater ones, horses and mules are still used to propel streetcars on some lines." This opening statement appeared under the heading of "Our Superb Electric Railway System" in the twentieth anniversary special issue of the FORT WAYNE NEWS, and gave a rather flamboyant description of the line in 1894.

"There are twenty miles of track in the system of the Fort Wayne Electric Railway company. It has fifty-seven new and commodious coaches, of the latest and most luxurious pattern known to manufacturers of street railway carriages, and twelve trailers. Mammoth sprinklers keep the track free from dust in the summer, and huge cyclone snow

Calhoun Street in the 1890's, north from Washington Boulevard. ***Bradley-Harnish Collection.***

Ft. Wayne Electric Works celebrates the Ft. Wayne Centennial in this view. One of the closed electric cars heads north on Broadway, stopping at the Pennsylvania Railroad crossing. This car has one open and one closed vestibule as the company began to comply with the state law requiring enclosed vestibules. ***Bradley-Harnish Collection.***

plows quickly remove the winter's snow. The introduction of electricity as a means of propelling streetcars in the city of Fort Wayne has solved the problem of rapid transit for our people. The cars are run as rapidly as is consistent with the safety of people using the streets for the purposes for which they are intended, and passengers have no cause to complain of delays or loss of time in passing from one part of the city to another.

The plant at which power is generated for the street railway system is a model in every respect. Located near the center of the system, it furnishes easily abundant power to transact all that is required of it, not only to meet every day demands but also to supply any exigencies that can possibly arise out of any unusual influx of visitors, or the necessity of carrying large numbers of our own citizens on any special occasion. The three huge engines of two hundred and seventy-five horsepower each, that drive the dynamos to generate electricity for the large system are the product of the great Bass Foundry of this city, and the dynamos are made by the Thomson-Houston Company, of which the Fort Wayne Electric Company is an important and rapidly expanding branch."

The arrival of the electric streetcar brought still another revolution to the city. Nearly half of the new fleet were eight-bench open summer cars which were designed for utility but soon proved to be very attractive to a pleasure seeking public. The open trolleys were a tremendous success and, in those days before the wheezing of the first auto had been heard, the trolley had many virtues of luxury and elegance. For a few cents anyone could ride through every section of town, enjoying the gentle sway and the breeze generated by the car's movement. Consequently an exciting new fad developed—the "streetcar party." Trolleys became interesting and glamorous when an evening dinner party was climaxed with a thirty mile, three hour ride through the city on a special car—and $5.00 was a cost which almost any group could afford. The company was only too happy to oblige and the following comments from the newspaper show how popular the fad became. On July 9 ten streetcar parties were held, on July 21 mention was made of fifty-three such parties in the past week and in August it

Ft. Wayne celebrates its Centennial. Open car 77 heads north on Calhoun, passing under one of the series of arches built over Main Street. This particular arch is the Anthony Wayne Arch at Wayne Street. **Robert Parker Collection.**

Nothing like a trolley outing...especially when it's a nice summer day on the Lewis Street line with car 13 of the Ft. Wayne Electric Railway and the fare is only 5¢! **Bradley-Harnish Collection.**

A seven-bench open car turns onto Calhoun Street. The decorations and crowd are for festivities of the 1895 Centennial. ***Bradley-Harnish Collection.***

was noted that "trolley parties have become the rage and half a score such parties take place each evening making a tour of all the city lines." One can easily imagine the laughter and gaiety radiating from an open trolley filled with young people. Truly the company had a new and unexpected source of revenue. The public was in love with the trolleys.

The citizens may have been happy and content, but the employees were not. In 1894, the management attempted to cut the wages to twelve and one-half cents an hour but finally dropped the idea. In 1895 the attempt was again made, in earnest, and the car men walked out. Service was maintained with Pinkerton detectives riding the cars. The Trade and Labor Council ordered all union members to boycott the cars. Public opinion was on the workers' side and again the company backed down, winning but one point in not re-hiring some previously discharged employees.

On November 11, 1895 articles of incorporation were filed for the Fort Wayne Consolidated Railway Company. Capitalization was doubled to $2,000,000. Fort Wayne Electric Railway was purchased December 4, 1895 for a consideration of one dollar. The sale conveyed all rights, franchises, properties and debts to the new firm. On the surface, to the general public, the old company ceased to exist as the new name appeared on the streetcars.

At this time the company had seven routes; No. 1 Belt Line; No. 2 Bloomingdale, Hanna Street and Walton Avenue Line; No. 3 Main Street Line; No. 4 Jefferson Street Line; No. 5 Spy Run Avenue Line; No. 6 Race Track Line, and No. 7 Lewis Street Line. (Lakeside, the eighth line, was still independent.)

One of the reasons for the increase in capital was to keep the vogue of trolley pleasure riding growing. The new firm felt that an excellent traffic generator would be an amusement park of large proportions. Everything would have to be in the best of taste and designed to attract all ages, groups and interests, and the desired location was available.

The Centennial arch at Lewis and Calhoun Street with open car 77 headed north. Today not only are the trolleys, rails and arch gone, but every structure visible has been torn down in a massive renewal project (1982). ***Allen County-Ft. Wayne Historical Society Collection.***

Splendid Robison Park 1896

CHAPTER 3

The Wabash and Erie Canal, 458 miles long, was the longest man-made canal in the world, but the entire canal operated for only a brief period. The upper end, near Fort Wayne, was already falling into disuse as a result of the railroads when the southern portion was completed. The highest elevation on the canal was reached at Fort Wayne with ascending locks in either direction.

The main canal westward from Fort Wayne to Huntington and eastward from Fort Wayne required a steady water supply with a sufficient head of pressure for the locks. To accomplish this, the canal builders had erected, in 1834, a dam seven miles northeast of Fort Wayne and just below a large horseshoe bend in the St. Joseph River. The impounded water was conveyed to the main canal by means of a feeder canal with a storage reservoir in Fort Wayne just south and east of the present State and Clinton street intersection. The big feeder dam was constructed of heavy timbers and debris and anchored to stone filled cribs. A guard lock kept the water level consistent. The deep water provided a pretty lagoon and swelled the river for several miles. The west side had high bluffs and groves of trees. By 1896, the dam was still in existence but in need of repair as was the feeder canal.

The management of the Consolidated company purchased 265 acres of the adjacent land, acquired the rights to the dam and canal, and announced a $300,000 development program in late 1895. On December 27, contracts were let for the building of a long double track line, using the feeder canal's west bank, and the purchase of twenty-five new open cars. Promotions for "Swift Park," (named for the former landowner) with a picture of the main pavilion on the back of all tickets, began as part of a continuous and active publicity program. Work commenced immediately on a feverish basis to try to complete the job by the next June.

The new rail line was a 4.83 mile extension starting from the canal bridge at the north end of Spy Run proceeding north on Clinton (then known as the Fort Wayne-Leo Road) up a light grade to Centlivre Park. From that point the line ran down the hill to the feeder canal and then northward to the park site. The line was built quickly as the broad canal banks provided an excellent and level right-of-way. Materials were hauled over the new line to the park ground to construct the park buildings. On May 30, 1896, the first open car ran to the park and back with city and company officials. The park was informally opened on June 13 to the interested and curious, but much work remained to be done to the buildings, grounds and double track car line. In deference to many requests from the citizens, the company changed the name of "Swift Park" to "Robison Park" in honor of the General Manager, M. Stanley Robison.

A spectacular Grand Opening was held on July 4 when over 35,000 people went out on the cars, a supreme test of the hauling capacity of the new line. Cars rolled on a two minute headway hauling two or three open trailers.

Cars 111 and 127 were two of the new nine-bench cars bought to open the new line in June 1896. The route, following the Feeder Canal, was far from straight, but scenery was more important than speed. ***Bradley-Harnish Collection.***

A mule-drawn, ex-horsecar serves as a mobile tower to string overhead wires on the Robison Park line. The track is barely in place and has no ballast and even less alignment. ***Bradley-Harnish Collection.***

Many special features, acts and attractions were included on this first big day to set the pace for years to come.

The management wanted a high-grade, family-oriented operation and allowed no intoxicants sold on the premises. They hired their own police force to enforce the park regulations and also saw to it that the primary entrance to the park could only be by the trolley. Later, beer drinkers could stop half-way up the river and cross over to the private Corner Rod and Gun Club which became Germania Park in 1910. A wooden, suspension footbridge crossed from the car line stop. The grounds of Germania Park are now part of the city's Shoaff Park.

The principal building was the big, main pavilion with four circular corner towers. This building was the center of park activities and usually flag bedecked to honor the various clubs that visited the park. It contained a cafe, dancing and party facilities and a huge electrically operated organ or Orchestron. This instrument could produce the general effect of a large and complete orchestra with sufficient volume to be heard in almost every area of the park. Water was supplied from a high stone water tower designed to represent a dutch windmill. Below the pavilion were the docks and boathouses. Several naphtha launches, about one hundred rowboats and a steamboat, the Clementina, operated from here. This continued until 1905 when the badly deteriorated dam was almost completely washed away, returning the river to its original level and restricting water activities to canoes and small boats.

Another dance hall was built near the center of the park where the car line looped around a large grass and flower plotted area in front of a trim depot and waiting room. Spur tracks provided extra car storage for the heavy traffic periods. A theater seating about nine hundred people was a popular attraction and placed Robison Park on the routine vaudeville circuit.

A rustic bridge connected this main area to the amusement area beyond a small bay. In

The Clementina accepts a sizeable crowd of paying patrons. The launch used this pier at the foot of the main pavilion as a starting point. ***Bradley-Harnish Collection.***

Crowd-eater 119 loads at the Robison Park Terminal late on a summer afternoon. The main pavilion is on the right. One of the park employed policemen can be seen leaning on a cane. ***Bradley-Harnish Collection.***

the bay, on an island, was the tall steel-towered circle swing. Just over the way on the high ground was a large roller coaster. Many lesser concessions and refreshment stands were in the roller coaster area and extended to the shoot-the-chutes which gave pleasure seekers a sixty-foot drop, one hundred and fifty-foot, mad-dash to the water.

The park had its own agents to attract patronage and they arranged excursions from all over the area to bring crowds of people to the park. Trips came from as far as Detroit and Indianapolis, and often in conjunction with the steam railroads.

At all times Robison Park presented a well groomed appearance, with beautiful lawns, gardens, and well-trimmed sidewalks. The big buildings as well as all lesser structures, such as bandstands, always appeared freshly painted. The rustic touch was carefully preserved yet everything was kept neat and tidy. Excellent grounds maintenance was always the objective of the large ground crews. All of these things made a day's outing a joyful and relaxing experience which was not soon forgotten as evidenced by the hundreds of people that still hold fond remembrances of the park. Many romances developed from an outing followed by the breezy ride home on the open car swaying down the moonlit river valley.

The Consolidated company was paying for these major improvements with some more borrowed money on top of previously borrowed money. This time a mortgage was executed with the Guardian Trust Company of Cleveland for $1,500,000 in bonds. The Cleveland money was probably arranged through Frank De H. Robison, M. Stanley Robison's brother. Frank Robison, quarreled with his fellow

The Robison brothers (particularly Frank) were avid sports fans and backed numerous sporting events. This car takes a special crowd of fight enthusiasts to a boxing exhibition during the first few days after the park's opening. ***Bradley-Harnish Collection.***

The Shoot-the-Chutes ride at Robison Park. ***Bradley-Harnish Collection.***

owners and took the Consolidated company to court thus placing it in receivership in September, 1896. M. S. Robison and J. H. Bass were declared co-receivers but Robison soon resigned and was replaced by Howell C. Rockwell. The receivership bounced around the court for the next three years in mass confusion.

Fort Wayne Electric Railway came back to life in the claims filed by the Guaranty and Indemnity Company. The bank demanded the old company be revived and placed in receivership and its bonds a first lien on the Consolidated company. These bonds were in default as were the Consolidated company's own bonds. Guardian Trust made a rapid appearance also claiming first lien. All these claimants came forward in a rush demanding their money.

The court had its hands full and finally handed down a lengthy decision on July 14, 1899. Everyone holding property belonging to the Consolidated company was ordered to return it. Robison held certain properties and Bass held the twenty-five new open cars. In the same decree the Consolidated company was ordered sold to satisfy all claims. Actually both Fort Wayne Electric Railway and Consolidated companies had to be sold and the Fort Wayne Electric Railway was finally terminated. The Consolidated company was sold to George H. Garretson of Cleveland. The Fort Wayne Traction Company was organized on October 26, 1899. The Consolidated property was transferred, for $1,092,000, to Fort Wayne Traction on November 8, 1899. In the purchase local ownership disappeared for nearly fifty years.

R. T. McDonald died on Christmas Eve, 1898 ending a most brilliant and spectacular career in finance and the electrical industry. It was through McDonald's efforts that the

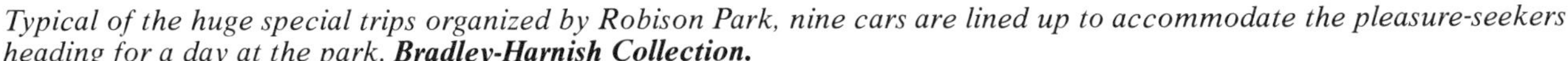

Typical of the huge special trips organized by Robison Park, nine cars are lined up to accommodate the pleasure-seekers heading for a day at the park. ***Bradley-Harnish Collection.***

The boat concession was a popular and profitable one. Here the entire fleet is neatly anchored awaiting the next crowd. ***Bradley-Harnish Collection.***

The naphtha motor-launch provided a small form of power boating for pleasure seekers. Its fuel, however, made it somewhat dangerous and an explosion of the naphtha was to destroy this launch before long. ***Bradley-Harnish Collection.***

Robison Park's roller coaster. ***Bradley-Harnish Collection.***

Fort Wayne Electric Works was still in the city. After it was sold to the Thomson-Houston Company, the new owners wanted to move the pioneering firm east. It stayed in Fort Wayne becoming the nucleus of the big General Electric complex there.

The Lakeside Street Railway, as part of McDonald's estate became a court problem. The line's dollar value was quite low and the estate refused to spend any money on it. The City Council ordered the Consolidated company to re-lay the tracks in accordance with a paving program. The Consolidated company, also in the courts, refused, taking the position that they only operated the line and were not supposed to maintain it. By July 12, 1900, the Knickerbocker Trust Company of New York sued to collect on the bonds which were now in default. Albert L. Scott, the receiver, was ordered to sell the company to the highest bidder. Fort Wayne Traction Company offered $25,000 for the company and bought it on December 31. This action unified all the street railway operations and a period of quiet and stability was expected. An entirely new phase was about to begin for Fort Wayne and its traction company. A whole quiet way of life was about to change, but no one realized it.

Ft. WAYNE
HUNTINGTON
WABASH
PERU
LOGANSPORT
Ft. WAYNE
HUNTINGTON
WABASH
PERU
LOGANSPORT
303

CHAPTER 4

New Century—New Challenge

At the turn of the century, the technology of the electric railway and electric power systems had progressed so much that the possibilities of fast, frequent, inter-city rail operation—beyond suburban lines—became evident. Most midwestern small towns and cities were served by steam railroads, but many little crossroads communities had only dirt road communication with the outside world. Local roads were rarely good but were sufficient for buggies and teams...in good weather. The steam railroad's fast trains did not stop at every town and the local trains that did make all stops were slow and few in number. As the new electric railway lines reached out from town to town, the magic word "interurban" came into use. The rise of the interurban electric railways was an economic phenomenom, spectacular and perhaps, for the investors, tragic. The interurban was most successful in the midwest where many companies operating several thousand miles of trackage were interconnected. Indiana and Ohio were the largest fields of activity. Initially, most interurban companies were local affairs with relatively little advance planning toward the integration of lines into any eventual semblence of order.

Fort Wayne was not the area leader in building interurban lines although a number of early, stillborn, proposed lines were projected in the early 1890's. In the next decade or so, over half a dozen paper traction lines appeared. Some companies actually did a little preliminary grading of a right-of-way or built a few small bridges before perishing in these early stages. Most were legitimate efforts begun by people who had little idea of railroad finance and costs. One of these was concocted by Mr. C. E. Everett who started on a line to Columbia City. This venture was harmless enough but he also proposed a ridiculous scheme to replace the Fort Wayne Electric Railway Company with a new company if the city would grant him an exclusive franchise. The whole idea was preposterous and was rejected. Another group started to work on a line to Hicksville, Ohio but ran out of money. Although these two cities were early targets for electric rail lines on more than one occasion neither city was ever served by an interurban rail line.

The upper Wabash River Valley had several potential centers for electric rail lines other than Fort Wayne. These included Huntington, Wabash, Peru, Logansport and Lafayette. By 1900, street railways were already in operation in both Lafayette and Logansport and both properties had been electrified before the Fort Wayne lines, yet the first interurban line was to appear elsewhere in the valley.

The Wabash River Traction Company (WRT) was the first successful interurban operation in the upper Wabash Valley and proved to be a curious oddity in many respects. Construction was started on the Wabash—Peru line, in March, 1901, on what proved to be little more than a rural trolley line...a midwest extension of the technology as perceived by the New England owners. The line was financed from New Haven, Connecticut where its home office was located. The same group owned the New Haven Car Register Company.

Mr. Frederick Coleman Boyd was chosen to come to the town of Wabash, put the line in business and then, if practical, to extend it. The initial—and only—streetcar line in Wabash started on Manchester Avenue at the northeast city limit, ran to Wabash Street, then south on Wabash Street across the Wabash River bridge to Columbus Street, southwest on Columbus to Vernon Street,

The Ft. Wayne & Southwestern 303 on the passing siding at Huntington not too long after the line had been taken over as part of the Ft. Wayne & Wabash Valley. The car has been rehabilitated and will soon be renumbered into the 200 series of interurbans. Another interurban is expected as can be seen by the station activity (people and baggage) to the rear of the car. ***John Rehor Collection.***

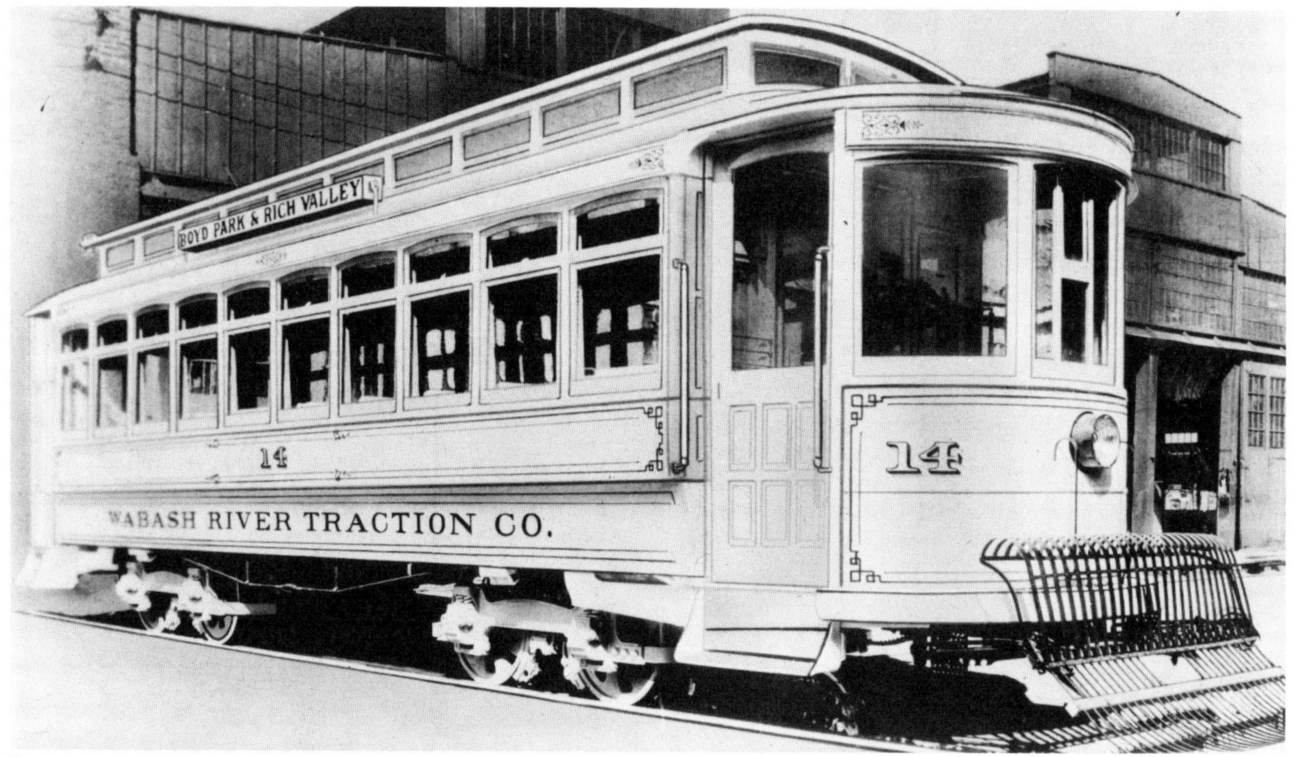

Wabash River Traction bought four city cars for the interurban line. They were slow and later were better utilized in city streetcar service. ***George Krambles Collection.***

south on Vernon to Pike Street and on Pike Street to the city limits. From this point the route ran southwesterly along Mill Creek Pike to Mill Creek, then northwesterly along and over the public highway and on private right-of-way for about one mile to the river. There the line crossed back over to the north side of the Wabash River by using a highway bridge, and ran north along the public road for a few hundred feet. Here, the line made an abrupt, almost right angle, turn to the west. This point was approximately midway between Wabash and the city of Peru. At the point where the line turned west and on the west side of the public road, the company built its powerhouse and car barn. East of the highway, a tract of land was purchased and laid out as a picnic grounds. The barn and park area became known as Boyd Park.

From Boyd Park, west to Peru, the Wabash River Traction acquired the right to use the abandoned Wabash and Erie Canal towpath. This route was followed to Peru where the line entered onto Main Street and ran, west, to the center of town. The total distance was 18 miles.

In Peru, the city fathers were very disturbed as they claimed Boyd had promised to build the company power plant and shop in that city—instead of at the mid-point location—in return for the right to use Main Street.

Ten cars were unloaded at Peru on July 10, 1901. Six of them were newly built by the American Car Company at St. Louis and were described as "four vestibuled and closed and two open." The closed cars were "new and modern cars that can be thrown open to such an extent as to make it almost the equal to summer cars. It seats forty passengers..." The cars were painted yellow. The remaining four cars were reported to have "come from New York" and may have been second hand units purchased in either New York state or through a New York based used equipment dealer. Some, if not all, of these cars were small, single truck open cars and at least two were not powered.

On July 26, 1901, car 16 operated from the Boyd Park car barn into Peru. Over the whole line, the first run was accomplished by open car 13 on August 12. The power supply was not quite adequate for city operation in Wabash, so runs up Wabash and Manchester Streets were delayed until August 17.

In December the company reported that two cars ordered for city service were held up in the rail yards at Worcester, Massachusetts. The two smaller, closed city cars, with longitudinal seats, arrived January 10, 1902. They may have been second hand cars. One each was assigned to Wabash and Peru to take over the local streetcar service.

The company now owned twelve cars and operated only eighteen miles of track, not a record, but certainly a lot of equipment for a small rural trolley line. Speed was not a factor in this operation and, when a special express service, was announced in March, 1902, the new time was 46 minutes or a leisurely 21 miles per hour.

In May, 1902, the Wabash River Traction owners set up a new company, the Wabash—Logansport Traction Company, with the apparent intention of merging the existing company into the new one and then extending the trackage from Peru to Logansport. As more ambitious goals were devised, it became apparent that everything east of Boyd Park had been built improperly. The interurban line was very much of the New England side-of-the-road character and was poorly built. Virtually no grading was done and this later made the running of through interurban cars nearly impossible.

The Fort Wayne & Southwestern Traction Company, the "Southwestern" route, made an almost simultaneous start with the Wabash River Traction Company. The Southwestern

The Southwestern owned one interurban freight car built by the Jackson & Sharp Company in 1901. **Bradley-Harnish Collection.**

Two big open cars came to the Wabash River Traction Company. Car 13 made the first run over the Wabash-Peru route. **M. D. McCarter Collection.**

was capitalized at $600,000 and called itself the "Canal Route" using the ideal but meandering canal banks of the Wabash & Erie Canal for its roadbed. The Southwestern gained control of the canal from Fort Wayne to Huntington and from Huntington to Wabash as well as options on the old canal beyond and to the west of Wabash. Ownership of the abandoned canal right-of-way had changed hands several times and had been proposed for a rail line by more than one of the earlier promoters. The Wabash Railroad, which had accelerated the canal's demise, was never more than a few hundred yards away from the Fort Wayne to Lafayette portion of the canal.

The city of Huntington landed the offices, shops and powerhouse of the Southwestern company by providing a cash subsidy to the company. Construction on the Huntington-Fort Wayne line started at several points between those cities during early 1901. Most of the trackage was along the canal right-of-way running from the Erie Railroad at Huntington to Taylor Street in Fort Wayne.

In Fort Wayne the company built its own entrance to the downtown via Taylor Street to Fairfield Avenue, then north on Fairfield to Brackenridge Street where the tracks jogged to the west, through a pair of tight curves to Fulton Street, (the trackage, because of street alignments, actually curved through and across Brackenridge), then north on Fulton to Pearl Street where the line ran east to Harrison Street. The Company's station was located in a store on the north side of Pearl Street. The interurban line crossed the Fort Wayne city lines at both Broadway and Main Streets. There were no track connections between the two systems.

The Southwestern's Huntington-Fort Wayne line was involved in considerable litigation over clear title rights to the canal towpath and, as a result of these problems, took longer than expected to build. The line was apparently built by a contractor's group as either a speculation or on a private commission from the McKinley interests who did not publicly appear until late 1901. The first interurban cars arrived July 29, 1901, in Huntington, under tarpaulins and on flat cars, at the Erie Railroad yards. A September 30 special trip, pulled by a steam engine, took a group of Fort Wayne businessmen over the line but ended short of Huntington as the underpass at the Erie tracks and route into the city were not completed until December 11. On that day the new cars, which had been parked east of the Erie tracks were moved through the underpass and into the new shop, under their own power. On that date the "Indiana" made the first run over the Huntington to Fort Wayne route.

The Huntington powerhouse was located adjacent to the shop and next to the Erie Railroad for easy delivery of coal. The 800 h.p. steam engine drove a large A.C. dynamo which fed electric current to the systems substations. The plant's capacity was more than enough for the line and its extension to Wabash built during 1902.

The Wabash extension, which opened in July, 1902, was not built without difficulties. Fred Coleman Boyd wanted Wabash exclusively for himself and the Wabash River Traction Company. When the Southwestern wanted to modify its entrance into Wabash they were met with repeated objections from Boyd. Boyd got so heated at one time that he announced that his company would build to Huntington in competition with the Southwestern. As a result, relations between the two companies were never very good.

The Southwestern's first five cars were built by Jackson & Sharp at its Delaware Car Works and carried names of states instead of being numbered. These first five cars were joined by four, new, interurban combination baggage and passenger cars, numbered 301-304. These were bought from the John Stephenson Company for the Wabash extension and arrived in July, 1902. All of these olive green-colored cars seated forty-six passengers.

The southwest corner of the Southwestern's Huntington powerhouse. The building was next to the Erie Railroad for easy coal delivery. The building was used as a generating station from 1901 through 1907. It remained in use as the sub-station and storage building for many more years. **Bradley-Harnish Collection.**

The Wabash Valley's 205 about 1905. Originally it was one of the state named Jackson & Sharp built, 1901 passenger cars. The 205 is seen at the Wabash station. ***Bradley-Harnish Collection.***

Above: *In 1902, four high-speed combination cars for Ft. Wayne & Southwestern Traction Company were built by John Stephenson Company.* ***At right:*** *The interior of the Southwestern 304 viewed from the baggage-smoker compartment.* ***Both photos —McGraw-Hill Publishing Co.***

504

The Wabash Valley Route

CHAPTER 5

A major and overpowering factor appeared in 1901 which had an important effect on all transportation in the upper Wabash Valley as well as a significant Indiana-Ohio traction impact. This factor was the Schoepf-McGowan Syndicate, which represented an enormous amount of Philadelphia capital. The combination included the Dolan, Morgan, Widener and Elkins group. These substantial financiers were joined by T. J. Levering and Col. J. Levering Jones, also of Philadelphia.

Two outstanding individuals were the name persons for this great syndicate. They were W. Kesley Schoepf, who was chairman of the executive committee of the Cincinnati Traction Company, and Hugh J. McGowan, who was president of the Indianapolis Street Railway. Both of these companies were owned by the Dolan and Morgan interests. McGowan had come from Randall Morgan's United Gas Improvement Company's Kansas City property. Schoepf had been successful in putting together the Cincinnati Traction Company as a unified property.

Schoepf and McGowan were efficient operators and clever managers. They proceeded to build what may have been the largest inter-related interurban and street railway empire.

The Schoepf-McGowan Syndicate acquired control of the Indiana Union Traction Company in 1902. This was the syndicate's first major move into inter-city properties. From this point on, the syndicate continued to grow until it controlled approximately 1400 route miles of interurban lines plus several city operations which included Cincinnati, Indianapolis and Fort Wayne.

The syndicate was well known to represent power and money, and to mask some of its moves it made excellent use of "front" men. These clever dealings of the syndicate to protect the financial backers' anonymity unfortunately makes part of the traction history of the Wabash Valley a bit clouded. Complete companies were projected, built and put into operation before people in the region became aware of the real owner and true source of the capital.

One "hidden" operation was the Indianapolis & Northern Traction Company, then building towards Logansport, headed by George McCulloch who was credited in the newspapers with being the sole financial and construction genius for the Indianapolis & Northern. In reality, McCulloch was a front man for Schoepf-McGowan. He created a small ripple when he announced the acquisition of the Logansport, Rochester & Northern Traction Company (LR&N) in 1901 by his associates. The LR&N had been incorporated in June 1899, ostensibly to build an interurban line north from the city of Logansport. The company had never gone further than the paper stage and was assumed by many to be another stillborn projected line...but it did have a projected route and a city ordinance permitting it to be built. In itself, the LR&N acquisition was not viewed with much concern by anybody. However, the Logansport situation took a sudden and interesting turn. The problem was that the Logansport Railway Company had a franchise supposedly granting it the sole rights to all streets in the city.

The Logansport Railway was the only actual electric railway operator in town. Not only McCulloch of the LR&N, but also Fred Coleman Boyd of the Wabash River Traction, coveted the streets of Logansport. Boyd's plans were to build his extension from Peru to Logansport and he boasted of his intention to build to Lafayette. He snapped up the Logansport franchise by buying the Logansport Railway. But McCulloch's backing was superior and he would prevail in the long run to win the city streets for the Schoepf-McGowan interests. After much maneuvering, which is detailed in a later chapter on the Logansport city system, the Schoepf-McGowan interests took over all of the Boyd properties in 1903.

Fort Wayne Traction moved to the syndicate camp on March 24, 1903 when the newspapers indicated the company had been purchased for the "Murdock Syndicate" for $1,513,000. The Murdocks of Lafayette were interested in gas, electric and street railway properties and were closely allied with Randall Morgan of the Schoepf-McGowan Syndicate.

The Southwestern, with its 45-mile Fort Wayne-Wabash line, went into receivership in 1903. From all indications the McKinley interests decided to concentrate in Illinois and wanted to get out of the Southwestern ownership. The McKinley ownership of this property has always been somewhat obscure, but the decision to leave this basically sound property available helped to set up a major new electric railroad system. The Southwestern was now available to any firm that was strong enough to acquire it. During the receivership, former general manager Samuel L. Nelson acted as receiver. The syndicate managed to quietly gain control of the company and Nelson was able to submit his final receiver's report on October 10, 1904. At that point, the Southwestern was officially an independent company again.

On May 29, 1903, an organization with the pretentious and formidable sounding name of Fort Wayne, Logansport, Lafayette & Lima Traction Company was incorporated. On that same day this new company acquired the Lafayette Street Railway. It also set up the vehicle for a series of major street railway and interurban purchases.

The new company simplified its name to the euphonious Fort Wayne and Wabash Valley Traction Company (Wabash Valley Route) on February 25, 1904. The principal personalities of the company were revealed as being from the Schoepf-McGowan Syndicate. Two days later, on the 27th, it formally took over five companies: Fort Wayne Traction Company; Wabash River Traction Company; Wabash-Logansport Traction Company; Logansport Railway Company; and Logansport, Rochester and Northern Traction Company.

The Southwestern arrived in the syndicate's hands by a round-about route which produced a very solid electric power base for the Wabash Valley system. Fort Wayne Electric Light & Power Company had come into existence in July, 1902. This was largely a group of New York investors who planned to build, own and operate a power and light system. On March 24, 1904, they bought the Jenny Electric Light & Power Company, the existing power company, in a one dollar merger. The newly merged firm was sold to the Fort Wayne & Southwestern on October 27, 1904, and the next day (legally transferred on the 29th) the Southwestern was sold to the Wabash Valley company. These were also one dollar transactions. Throughout these legal and corporate maneuvers the power company retained its identity. The general public was hardly aware of any change and, except for ownership and some policies and procedural changes, nothing was changed. The Schoepf-McGowan Syndicate interests were behind the entire move and, by early 1905, the power and traction company were one and the same. Part of an announced expansion included a huge million-dollar power station to be build near the Jenny company's existing Kamm Street plant on Spy Run Avenue.

When the Fort Wayne & Wabash Valley Traction Company was finally put together in February 1904, all of the previously collected companies were reorganized and merged

The private car "Lawton" of the Ft. Wayne & Wabash Valley Railway served as the company's office and business car.
McGraw-Hill Publishing Co.

Charles D. Emmons (1871-1933)

Charles DeMoss Emmons was born February 13, 1871 in Lafayette, Indiana. He devoted his entire life to the transportation industry and was the backbone for a large number of rail-related companies, including the Fort Wayne & Wabash Valley Railway Company.

After graduation in 1892 from the Western University of Pennsylvania (now the University of Pittsburgh) with a degree in civil engineering, he was associated with the engineering department of the Pennsylvania Railroad, east of Pittsburgh for nine years. Subsequently he spent two years (1901-1903) as superintendent of the Lafayette Street Railway in his hometown and then eight years (1903-1911) as general manager of the Fort Wayne & Wabash Valley Railway. It was his influence that forged and fashioned these lines into a strong system, well-equipped with excellent rolling stock for interurban service. He directed the building of the Ft. Wayne-Lima line. Under his direction, the four city systems were modernized and expanded. Interline "through" trains (including special limited trains) to Indianapolis were developed. His leadership established the standards of excellence that subsequent managers would emulate.

Thereafter, Emmons undertook new duties as general manager of the Chicago, South Bend & Northern Indiana Railway (1911-1916), and then as second vice-president and general manager of the Boston & Worchester Street Railway.

In 1918, he took charge of the Boston Elevated Railway, though he would leave the position the following year when elected president of the United Railways & Electric Company in Baltimore. In his capacity as directing head of the Baltimore company, he was drawn into their case before the Public Service Commission involving issues of valuation and fares. Throughout the long, drawn-out ordeal and despite the controversial issues involved, Mr. Emmons remained self-composed and gracious thus carrying the matter through to final settlement without cause for recrimination and without sacrificing the good esteem of the community. If there was any one characteristic which marked this man it was his innate ability to get along with others—being friendly without being familiar and forceful without being dictatorial.

Beginning in 1922, Emmons served a year as president of the American Electric Railway Association and became a member of the American Association of Engineers, the Maryland Academy of Sciences and the Baltimore Association of Commerce. He was also vice president of the New York Railroad Club. Mr. Emmons was highly regarded for his abilities and the public took every opportunity to show their esteem, such as selecting him as a trustee of the Savings Bank of Baltimore.

After serving the Baltimore rail company for ten years, Emmons became president of the Hudson & Manhattan Railroad (the underground railway between New York and New Jersey) on September 1, 1930.

C. D. Emmons died quite suddenly on February 2, 1933, shortly after midnight. He was retiring in his suite at the Waldorf-Astoria in New York when he suffered a heart attack and died within a few minutes. He was 61 years old.

Footnote: Information acquired from the author's notes and the Electric Railway Journal, McGraw-Hill Publishing Company.

Wabash Valley 202 and others were upgraded with new motors and trucks in 1905 to improve their speed and performance; then they were used on the new line to Bluffton. This is the first Wabash Valley station used at Ossian. ***Bradley-Harnish Collection.***

into the new company. The many names and personalities have, over the years, tended to confuse and blind researchers who did not possess a good road map. Many of the syndicate actions are not a matter of public record and it is only by chance that some of the information was unearthed.

The Wabash-Logansport extension was completed for Schoepf-McGowan interests by the Wabash-Logansport Traction Company (known as "The Picturesque Route"), which existed until February 1904. Four larger cars came with the new company. These cars were built by the Jewett Car Company. The first Peru-Logansport cars ran on the night of May 12, 1903 but through Wabash-Logansport trips required a change of cars at Peru because of power difficulties.

The Wabash Valley had found the Wabash River Traction to be in good physical condition (within the limits of its design). The Southwestern's condition was somewhat different. Its rolling stock was in a deplorable state and had been for some time. It was carelessly run and some trackage was not well maintained. The first time a "yellow" Wabash River Traction car (actually #28, a Wabash-Logansport Jewett-built car) passed over the line, it became stuck on the "S" curve from Fairfield to Fulton Streets over Brackenridge Street. This piece of trackage became well known as the "notorious Brackenridge curve." The WRT's yellow cars with the long-wheelbase Peckham trucks had to slow to an inch-by-inch crawl. (This Taylor-Fairfield-Fulton route was not used after November 1904 and was torn up in June 1905.) In test runs the Southwestern's green cars went to Logansport to see if these cars could go over the route (this was in May 1904, before the Southwestern officially merged into the Wabash Valley).

When the Wabash Valley took over the operation of the Southwestern, they found two of the passenger cars were sitting in the shop partially stripped to keep the others running. Several cars had at least one shorted-out motor or other defects. Faster schedules were put into effect—but the Wabash River Traction's cars had to be pressed into through service, and they could not meet the schedules. The bigger Southwestern cars were far more comfortable and had much better heaters. The smaller cars were kept in service because as fast as one Southwestern car was repaired and put back in service, another broke down. The winter of 1904-1905 brought much abuse to the Wabash Valley line from its patrons. The fact that the little Southwestern 44-footers, which were little more than three years old, were so run down proved a Huntington newspaper comment that the "Southwestern was run on the premise of the greatest amount of returns for the least amount expended."

Along with the mechanical repairs, the Southwestern cars had the "Canal Route" monogram painted out. The letterboard area, above the windows, was painted red with the names of the cities served painted in silver letters. The company's paint shop was moved to Huntington from Fort Wayne in December 1904. Eventually all nine of the Southwestern's passenger cars were painted in the Schoepf-McGowan Syndicate's olive green (Pullman green) and renumbered. Extensive rehabilitation of these cars took place in 1905 with the lower-numbered cars receiving new trucks and electrical gear. Car 202 exceeded the 65 mph mark in a start to stop run of nine minutes over a rebuilt stretch of track near Roanoke.

In the spring of 1905, one of the Wabash-Logansport Traction Company's Jewett-built

The company emblem used an indian good luck sign. The names of the cities served appeared on the arms of the swastika emblem.

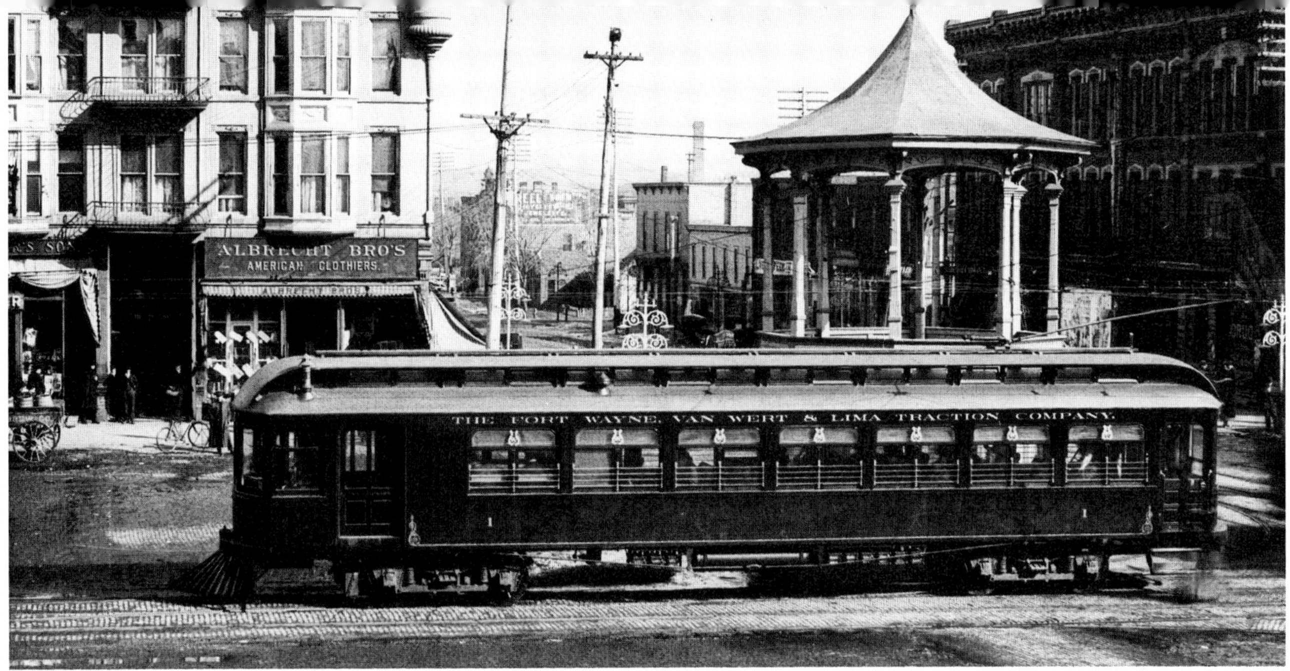

Ft. Wayne, Van Wert & Lima's new car #1 at Lima in late 1905. This was one of the early large interurban cars built by Cincinnati Car Company. ***George Krambles Collection.***

cars was brought to the Fort Wayne Baker Street car shops and transformed into a gem of a private car named "Lawton," for Fort Wayne's Spanish-American War hero, General Henry F. Lawton, killed in the Philippines in 1899. According to the **Journal-Gazette** the car was "fitted with tapestries, easy chairs, tables, observation ends and other conveniences. The car is finished in natural woods and is decorated in olive green and gold." It made its first long distance journey on July 8, going to Wabash and back. The Lawton was assigned to General Manager C. D. Emmons and played an active role in moving Wabash Valley officials and visitors for many years. It also traveled all over the midwest via other interurban lines.

The interurban main line from Fort Wayne to Logansport suffered from the routes laid out by the early companies. Immediately after the formation of the Fort Wayne & Wabash Valley system in 1904, it became obvious not only that the rolling stock was inadequate, but also that the route itself would have to be improved before any fast through operation could succeed. An immediate improvement was a new Wabash to Boyd Park line north of the river, along the canal route, which was completed in July 1904. This shortened the through route, eliminated unnecessary street running, and removed the need to cross the Wabash River twice. The fact that the north side route was on the canal tow path owned by the Southwestern (not officially in the consolidation at that time) further illustrates the Wabash Valley's unofficial ownership influence. East of Wabash the Southwestern's route, which also followed the canal towpath very closely, was not conducive to high speed operation. A number of tight curves were eased and some straightening was successfully completed but, for a line that lay largely in a river valley, the trackage meandered right and left, following the old canal. If nothing else, the old "Canal Route" trackage was fairly level with a minimum of grades.

The electric power supply was another problem. All of the companies operated their cars with nominal 600-volt direct current at the trolley wire. The oldest of the interurban lines, Wabash River Traction, generated at this voltage. The power plant at Boyd Park thus fed directly east to Wabash and west to Peru. After the Logansport extension of 1903, Boyd Park also generated 13,200-volt alternating current. The high-tension line at this voltage fed substations at Peru and Logansport where the power was converted for the trolley. The Peru substation had a one-way feed west over the new line and could maintain trolley voltage fairly well. To the east of Peru was another story because that city was at the far end of the original direct feed. With that relatively inefficient system the line voltage chronically fell well below the nominal level. Until this imbalance could be corrected, the company elected not to attempt through Wabash-Logansport runs. The Southwestern (like the Logansport extension) fed power to its cars via high-tension lines. In this case the transmission was at 16,000 volts with substations at Largo, Roanoke and Fort Wayne as well as direct feed from the powerhouse at Huntington.

At this time all of the interurban routes which were to become part of the Wabash

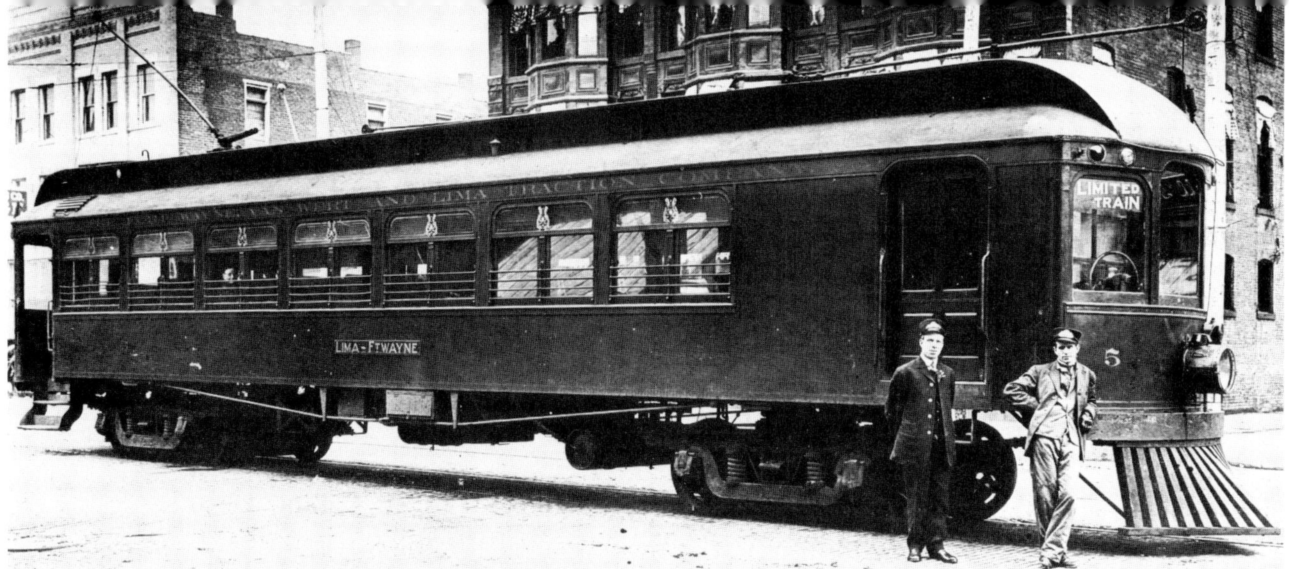

Car 5 of the Ft. Wayne-Lima route was among the first of a fairly standard design 55-foot interurban built by Cincinnati Car Company. ***George Krambles Collection.***

Valley system formed a chain west of Fort Wayne. A line to the east, connecting into Ohio was an obvious idea. The Fort Wayne, Van Wert & Lima Traction Company appeared in 1905 after what appeared to be several false starts. Two companies of the same name were created in 1902 to build the "Lima" line with one building in Ohio and one in Indiana. Both companies had planned routes but the Indiana company was planned first and its route, in Indiana, was indirect and low speed in operation. The route was extended from the Lewis Street car line, in eastern Fort Wayne, passed under the Wabash Railroad and then followed the north side of what is now called New Haven Avenue to the town of New Haven. The line then proceeded eastward before turning south to what became U.S. 30 (the Lincoln Highway) and followed the south side of the roadway for several miles before it went onto its own right-of-way. The line crossed the Findlay, Fort Wayne & Western Railroad at Tilman's (actually only a location name) at grade because this unfortunate steam railroad rarely ran more than one train a day. The "Lima" line's route turned southward following, in part, county roads to Monroeville, Indiana. Before entering this town, the tracks crossed over the Pennsylvania Railroad main line by use of a trestle approach and steel girder bridge. The land in this area is flat and there was no natural approach available. On the south side the line turned abruptly eastward into Monroeville. From Monroeville eastward most of the line closely paralleled the Pennsylvania Railroad. This portion was well constructed and contained long stretches (up to 10 miles) of straight trackage. Substantial combination passenger stations and substations were located in Elida, Middlepoint and Convoy, Ohio and at Monroeville and New Haven, Indiana. Each car carried a phone and one pole in twenty had a jack for a plug-in. (This 2,000 feet meant that no car was ever more than 1,000 feet from a phone plug.) Most of the Ohio side trackage was completed first but it was not placed in service because the line was Fort Wayne-based. Experimental service was tried on the Fort Wayne to New Haven portion on September 19, 1905.

Construction of the Fort Wayne, Van Wert & Lima was credited to a Fort Wayne businessman, Henry C. Paul. It soon became evident that more than Mr. Paul were involved when the "Lawton" was used for the first through trip on September 29, 1905. The Monroeville overpass was just completed allowing the through trip. The Lawton was able to hit 65 mph on some of the long tangent stretches. The new electric line was officially opened on November 1, using new, large-type 55-foot interurban cars built by the Cincinnati Car Company (this car builder was owned by the Schoepf-McGowan Syndicate). It was soon revealed that the Lima line belonged to the Schoepf-McGowan Syndicate and General Manager Emmons stated that it would be run as part of the Wabash Valley System. This plan was later shifted when the syndicate began putting together the Ohio Electric Railway. The 65 mile Lima line was leased to Schoepf-McGowan's new Lima & Toledo Traction Company on March 1, 1906 and to the Ohio Electric on August 31, 1907. Unfortunately, no attempt was made to improve the circuitous 19-mile Fort Wayne to Monroeville route.

The Indianapolis & Northern Traction Company completed its Indianapolis-Peru line on December 6, 1903 and leased it to Indiana Union Traction Company. When the Wabash Valley was put together in 1904, Schoepf-McGowan had an Indianapolis-Fort Wayne route. Passengers changed cars at Peru because the Wabash Valley did not have cars enough for a through service and the bigger Union Traction cars could not, initially, get around some of the tight bends in the Wabash-Peru segment. One of the Lawton's early trips was from Fort Wayne to Indianapolis.

The Lima line's first three cars arrived in Fort Wayne in late August 1905, and as soon as one was equipped and ready, it was given a trial run on the route at least as far as Peru. The Wabash Valley and Union Traction announced that cars of this type would be placed in through Indianapolis-Fort Wayne service in the near future.

Meanwhile the countryside some miles south of Fort Wayne was being laced with interurban lines. The Muncie, Hartford & Fort Wayne Railway, an independent company, built an interurban line north from Muncie, where it connected with a Union Traction line from Indianapolis. The first car from Muncie reached Hartford City on January 24, 1903. The company built northward to Montpelier by May 10 of that same year. Bluffton was reached on December 1, 1903, but that was to be the north end for some time. With less than five thousand people, it was a terminus that meant little.

This existing 42-mile route, if it was extended, would reach Fort Wayne and invade the territory of the Wabash Valley company. Recognizing that sooner or later this would happen, the Wabash Valley, after some of its company consolidation was complete, decided to keep the other company out. To do so, the Wabash Valley incorporated the Fort Wayne, Bluffton & Marion Traction Company, on April 25, 1905, to close the 25-mile Fort Wayne-Bluffton gap. As this company began building south, the Muncie, Hartford & Fort Wayne was galvanized into a leap to the north.

The Fort Wayne crews had the advantage and went southward rapidly following the Nickel Plate railroad to Kingsland. At that point the line turned eastward, crossed what is now Highway 1, and turned south on the east side of the road. As this crew built southward, they met the rival Muncie crew pounding down rail at an equally rapid pace, northward, on the west side of the road. It was a hot and absurd race and both companies were prepared to build right past the other before a truce was declared. The trackage north of Bluffton was turned over to the southbound company and the tracks made a second crossing of the road at the meeting point. Until the last interurban car was run on this route, these two unnecessary and treacherous grade crossings existed.

Schoepf-McGowan owned the stock of the Fort Wayne, Bluffton & Marion. The company was sold and deeded to the Wabash Valley on December 30, 1905. This creation of an underlying company was a handy way to raise new capital through large bond issues without upsetting the financial structure of the parent company. Operation of the new Bluffton line commenced on March 1, 1906 with the cars entering Fort Wayne over the Broadway streetcar line.

No long-distance through service was planned for the new Bluffton line. The first cars were the former Southwestern cars which had been upgraded and speeded up to provide better service. Cars, connecting at Bluffton for the ride to Muncie were very similar, with some being sister cars to the Southwestern's Stephenson-built cars. Later in the summer of 1906, two large 55-foot interurban cars, identical to the new Lima line's cars, were ordered. These arrived and were placed in service—one on September 4 and the second on October 6.

The Muncie, Hartford & Fort Wayne was leased to the Union Traction Company on June

The 302 was the second of the two cars bought for the Wabash Valley's Bluffton line. **George Krambles Collection.**

The 303 (as it was originally built for the Lafayette & Logansport Traction Company) stands at the Peru passenger terminal. This car was considerably altered after the Kingsland accident. **M. D. McCarter Collection.**

27, 1906. This offered a second syndicate-controlled joint operational route between Fort Wayne and Indianapolis. However, larger new cars, which sat taller than smaller cars, couldn't be run through on this route because a public highway bridge was used by the interurban at Hartford City and that bridge had a low clearance. This blocked any through operation of the new Wabash Valley cars.

The syndicate ownership and control of a vast amount of interurban track mileage set the stage for many through services and the so-called "lightning palace" cars. Special "Limited" Fort Wayne to Indianapolis (via Peru) trains, with parlor-buffet facilities, were placed in service as a joint Wabash Valley-Union Traction operation on May 1, 1906. This route already had some through car service, but the new cars were designed to offer a level of service that would be first class and easily competitive with the nearby steam railroad services. Four of these big palace cars (numbers 501-504) were furnished by the Wabash Valley and only two (297-298) by the Union Traction Company. A seventh, identical car was built as number 101 of the Lima & Toledo Traction Company for Fort Wayne-Lima limited service which started in June, 1906. This luxury fleet was the wonder of the interurban industry and the cars were carefully described in the trade journals. The Wabash Valley, proud to show off the cars, ran special trips for Midwest interurban rail officials including a late March preview trip to Indianapolis in a heavy snow storm. The various officials, the press and the public declared these cars to be "magnificent."

The buffet service soon proved to be unprofitable and special food services were

Among the best designed wooden cars, the "Kenilworth" (501) was the first of seven identical 61-foot palace cars. ***Above:*** *At left the buffet and smoking compartment and at right the regular passenger section.* ***Both photos —McGraw-Hill Publishing Co. Below:*** *The exterior of the "Kenilworth."* ***George Krambles Collection.***

The magnificent "Talisman" (504) at the Indianapolis Traction Terminal, was the fourth of the great palace cars built by the Cincinnati Car Company and placed in service in May 1906. It became one of the pool cars supplied by the Wabash Valley to the Indianapolis-Peru through limited runs. These cars carried porters to serve the buffet patrons, but the service was considered unprofitable and was of short duration. Nevertheless, these cars were used for over 25 years. **Bass Photo Studios.**

dropped. Several attempts to reinstate light refreshment service were made but none lasted for any extended period. After the Hartford City bridge was rebuilt, these cars were also used on the shorter Fort Wayne, via Muncie, Indianapolis through route.

A major gap in the Wabash Valley chain remained unfilled which left the Lafayette city lines separated. This was remedied by the formation of the Lafayette-Logansport Traction Company in 1906. Building this line took longer than the theretofore usual practice: the line was not ready for operation for a year. One of the differences with this line was time, as the company was not pressed on a deadline or in a race to beat some other party. The route was superior to the trackage on the canal-bed right-of-way. The abandoned canal was again available but was a remote and out-of-the-way route. Instead, the new line followed a very direct and nearly straight route between the two cities and closely paralleled the Wabash Railroad. There were few towns along the way, with Delphi, the county seat of Carroll County, being the largest. The roadbed was substantially constructed and several sizable bridges were included on the route with the largest crossing Wild Cat Creek. Another feature was the avoidance of railroad grade crossings with only one at Clymers. The other railroads were crossed by underpasses. Street running outside of the terminal cities was at a minimum and at Delphi, counter to general practice, the interurban ran through the town on a private right-of-way a few blocks south of the court house square. This line was the Wabash Valley's best trackage but it was expensive to build and may have been, in retrospect, an error. This was also excellent trackage for higher speeds and was the "hot" line for motormen. The Lawton made a number of fast runs over this line on business and inspection trips. General Manager Emmons had started his career on the Lafayette city lines so he had good reason to visit the western terminal city of the Wabash Valley.

Because of the long new 114-mile main line and the fact that the company was committed to interline through service with its biggest and best cars, the lack of sufficient good interurban cars was evident. Five large passenger cars and two freight motors were purchased as part of the equipage of the new line. They were actually intended for system use but conveniently charged to the new company. Local service between the two cities started on July 1, 1907 with through Fort Wayne-Lafayette service started on October 1, 1907.

The Lafayette-Logansport Traction Company was leased to the Wabash Valley on March 1, 1908 but remained as a separate underlying entity owning the line and the cars bought in its name. The public never knew the line by its true name because it was controlled by the Wabash Valley and usually that line was mentioned. The cars carried the parent company name and, only at first, carried a small L&L Tr. Co. legend to identify them.

DANGER
KEEP OFF
DO NOT WALK OR
TRESPASS ON THIS
RAILROAD
T & C I Ry Co.

Four More Interurban Companies Arrive

CHAPTER 6

THE TOLEDO & CHICAGO INTERURBAN RAILWAY

To the north, a much-ballyhooed line known as the Toledo & Chicago Interurban Railway Company was looking over the sparse possibilities of northeastern Indiana. The prospects looked quite slim and the promoters, wanting something tangible for the stockholders of the proposed east-west route between the cities named, elected to build a branch line called the "Fort Wayne Division." The supposed branch was all the company ever managed to construct. It was the first line in the area that used alternating current on the trolley wire. Car number 1 made the first trip to Fort Wayne on "May Day" 1906 with regular service beginning on May 10. The tracks extended north to Garrett, then meandered in two directions to Waterloo and Kendallville. This huge half circle of trackage anchored at Garrett provided an interesting operation and scheduling problem for the duration of the line's existence. After struggling, unsuccessfully, to take passengers from both the Grand Rapids & Indiana (GR&I) part of the Pennsylvania lines and the Fort Wayne, Jackson & Saginaw (FJ&S) part of the New York Central lines, the firm fell into receivership in February 1908.

The route ran north from Fort Wayne along the east and then the west side of the Lima Road to Huntertown and then ran across country to the northeast. This stretch of trackage contained a large gravel pit operation and eventually had two steam railroad connections. The southern interchange was with the NYC lines, and at Butler Center the company intersected and interchanged with the Pennsylvania lines. There was no connection with the Baltimore & Ohio R.R. in Garrett. A block south of the B&O yards the interurban's well known wye and station were located. This was the regular three-way meeting point for trains.

The western route from Garrett achieved a B&O railroad crossing by the simple expedient of running under the line through a bridge the B&O had built over a stream. Both the railroad and farmers opposed this idea as it partially blocked the stream flow. As expected, it was a normal flood point. The interurban then followed an abandoned B&O alignment west to Avilla and then ran north to Kendallville. From the powerhouse, at Bixler Lake, the cars ran westerly to South Main Street and their terminal, far from the center of town. The cars were turned on a large loop east of the station and then backed into the station.

The easterly leg, from Garrett to Auburn, was the first built and started operation in late 1905. It followed the public highway, on the south side of the B&O, toward Auburn and crossed over three rail lines at Auburn Junction where the NYC's FJ&S lines and the Pennsylvania's Vandalia line crossed the B&O. The interurban ran on the public streets of Auburn, turned to the north and followed the highway on private right-of-way to Waterloo. In Waterloo the cars turned on a

At the left: A very dapper gentleman boards a Toledo & Chicago car at a country crossing, but he had better pick up his gladstone bag and umbrella first! The wooden pole in the foreground has split and has been reinforced...there is a hatchet in it too. Why? ***Bradley-Harnish Collection. Below:*** *Toledo & Chicago's first car was built as a double-end car, but was soon changed to a single-end car.* ***George Krambles Collection.***

T&C's 7 on the Garrett, Avilla, Kendallville run. ***Bradley-Harnish Collection.***

T&I 51 pulling, borrowed and elderly, Union Traction 237. This car was used during the 1906 construction period. ***Bradley-Harnish Collection.***

At left: *Typical resourcefulness produced this T&I construction locomotive, hardly more than an off-center outhouse on a motorized flat car.* ***Above:*** *Toledo & Chicago home built work motor, working a ballast train in 1905. Construction methods were rather crude on many interurban lines.* ***Both photos —Bradley-Harnish Collection.***

Above: *It's 1906 and the first interurban enters Auburn, Indiana. DeKalb County Courthouse can be seen in the background.* ***Lefthand photo below:*** *Spring floods often threatened to stop the interurbans and swollen creeks flooded nearby fields and overran the interurban tracks. The cars ran under the B&O railroad through a bridge built across a small stream (in the photo, the bridge is to the right of the approaching car).* ***Both photos —Bradley-Harnish Collection.***

Above: *T&C freight motor 50 shoves coal cars at the Kendallville powerhouse.* ***Below:*** *The Hartford City Fire Department outing required more than one car. This lead motor car is pulling trailer car #2 to accommodate the overflow.* ***Both photos —Bradley-Harnish Collection.***

wye next to their station. This station was only a block from the New York Central's main line and FJ&S station, but was separated from them by a fence. There was no street crossing of the NYC at this point and the steam road did not favor the electric line's presence. In later years, when the FJ&S no longer offered regular passenger service, a convenient hole appeared in the fence allowing an easy, but not quite legal, access to the two stations.

Ft. Wayne & Springfield Railway Co. car 1 as equipped for AC operation at the Ft. Wayne terminal. **Bradley-Harnish Collection.**

THE FORT WAYNE & SPRINGFIELD RAILWAY COMPANY

The Fort Wayne and Springfield Railway Company began, in 1903, a slow, struggling battle to build southeast from Fort Wayne. Financial backing was slow to appear and the line was built in bits. Farmers along the way contributed labor and material in return for the promise of convenient transportation for themselves and their produce. The company first ordered cars in 1904 but had to postpone the orders. By the summer of 1905 the grading was complete, but little track was laid. The line finally started service on February 1, 1907, with the tracks constructed on private right-of-way along the west side of the Fort Wayne-Decatur highway for most of its length. The office and two-track car house and shop were located north of Decatur, as was the powerhouse. The three passenger cars and a baggage car were based there. The line was relatively flat with only one major bridge over the St. Mary's River, north of the powerhouse and car barn. There was only one rail crossing, with the GR&I, near Monmouth.

Above: *Ft. Wayne & Springfield Ry. 50, a bit worse for wear, sits on the shop entry track.* **Frank E. Butts Collection.**
Below: *Ft. Wayne & Springfield freight motor at the Decatur shop and power plant. These cars briefly used the unique and rare bow trolley.* **George Krambles Collection.**

Ft. Wayne & Springfield Railway Co. car 2 and the Decatur shop crew. ***Frank E. Butts Collection.***

Ft. Wayne & Springfield Ry. car 3 at Decatur, Indiana in 1915 serves as an imposing backdrop for a formal portrait. ***Frank E. Butts Collection.***

The road had the distinction of being one of the few 6,600 volt, single-phase alternating-current systems in the country. The high voltage permitted the road to be operated from one powerhouse without substations or feeders to the catenary overhead. Insulated changeover stretches were used to change to 500 volts a.c. in Decatur and 550 volts d.c. in Fort Wayne. The cars experimentally used, for a brief time, a front end bow-trolley collector. Standard, but well insulated, trolley poles were used on both single-phase lines.

Unfortunately, the use of alternating current rail applications was in its infancy and presented many new motor problems as opposed to the simpler d.c. motors which had evolved on streetcar lines and the earlier interurbans. Oddly enough, Fort Wayne had two of the few a.c. lines built, and each had a different voltage. The Toledo and Chicago used 3,300 volts while the Fort Wayne-Springfield used 6,600 volts.

Above: *Ft. Wayne & Springfield Ry. crew with cars 2 and 3 at the Decatur barn on March 29, 1913.* ***Below:*** *Ft. Wayne & Springfield Railway Co. 60 was a 2-8-0 steam locomotive used to build the line and later for freight service. Here it is shown with a load of sugar beets.* ***Both photos — Frank E. Butts Collection.***

MARION, BLUFFTON & EASTERN TRACTION COMPANY

Two other area interurban companies of importance to the Fort Wayne/northeast Indiana area were the Marion, Bluffton & Eastern Traction Company and the Bluffton, Geneva & Celina Traction Company. Though not entering Fort Wayne, both played a significant role in the area's transportation pattern and had an overall impact on the Fort Wayne company.

The Marion, Bluffton & Eastern Traction Company (MB&E) was incorporated in Indiana on May 6, 1905. While it had contemplated continuing northeast from Bluffton to Decatur, Indiana, and on into Ohio, it never took any action to do so. A route 32 miles long connected the two cities named in its title. Much of the road was straight, with two relatively long track tangents, although in order to reach several smaller communities it did not follow a direct route between the two terminal cities.

By March 1906 grading of the roadbed between Marion and Van Buren was completed; this portion of the road was opened for business on August 1. The remainder of the line was finished on December 1; operation over the whole route began on December 15, 1906.

The construction was done, and initial operation was managed, by the Bluffton & Marion Construction Company. The line was turned over to the railway management on July 1, 1907. The Moore-Mansfield Construction Company later sued for payment of some construction costs; it is not known whether this was a successor or a different contractor. The quality of construction is questionable, since the Indiana Railroad Commission ordered tie replacements and reballasting.

The railway was progressive in rolling stock management. Almost in the beginning, company employees invented a trolley pole clamp which was placed on the trolley bases of the line's cars. It held the shaft of the trolley pole firmly to the base, but it could readily be released by a lever which rotated a cam, freeing the pole. This device reportedly made it so easy to change a pole without tools out on the road, that crews routinely replaced defective poles rather than bringing in the car with the trolley harp sliding along the wire in case the trolley wheel was lost or broken. Operating with a broken trolley wheel or no wheel could do severe damage to the overhead wires.

In 1908, passenger service was operated between Marion and Bluffton every two hours. The service required two passenger cars, meeting on each trip at Warren, as the running time was 75 minutes each way. The company had over three times as many cars as needed in normal daily service. The extras were for spares, expected passenger increases and special moves.

From Marion a financially unrelated interurban railway, the Kokomo, Marion & Western Traction Company, was constructed westward to Kokomo. The two companies cooperated in the construction of a freight house in Marion. Through operation of passenger cars between Kokomo and Bluffton began on September 12 or 26 (sources differ) of that year. The interline operation was seemingly short-lived as it is not mentioned in January 1910 timetables.

A power station was listed among the early assets, but by March 1909 the power was being purchased from Marion Light & Heating Company.

A head-on collision occurred near Marion at 3:15 PM on July 7, 1912. A light open motor

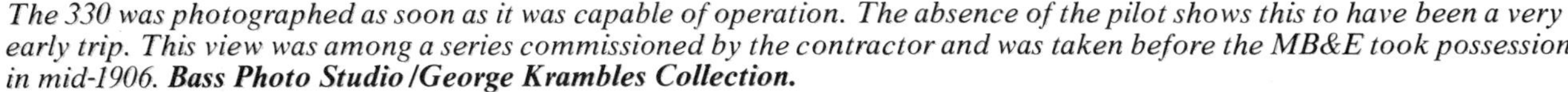
The 330 was photographed as soon as it was capable of operation. The absence of the pilot shows this to have been a very early trip. This view was among a series commissioned by the contractor and was taken before the MB&E took possession in mid-1906. **Bass Photo Studio/George Krambles Collection.**

Above: *Marion, Bluffton & Eastern Traction's 325 is the victim of this costly mistake at the Cloverleaf-Big Four crossing in Marion, Indiana about 1910.* ***Below:*** *On July 7, 1912 light, semi-open car 350 collided head-on with car 330. Four persons were killed and sixty injured.* ***Both photos —Frank E. Butts Collection.***

passenger car and a heavy interurban combine were involved. Four persons were killed and 60 injured. Together with interest on the trust deed, the resulting claims exceeded the road's financial ability.

The MB&E went into receivership on July 24, 1912 with the Union Savings & Trust Company of Marion as receiver. The future of the MB&E would now change and it would not grow any larger.

MB&E 325 was one of the short cars used on the Marion and Bluffton route. The whistle on this car was a unique, special installation. ***Frank E. Butts Collection.***

BLUFFTON, GENEVA & CELINA TRACTION COMPANY

Another interurban electric railway—perhaps the most unusual, little-known and financially unsuccessful one in northeastern Indiana—operated between Bluffton and Geneva. Although it was small, impoverished and short-lived, remarkably much documentary evidence of its existence appeared in publications of national scope. Because it was somewhat unusual and not always orthodox in its operation it is included in this book with what would appear to be more emphasis than is justified.

The territory between Bluffton, Indiana and Celina, Ohio, a short distance east of the Ohio state line, had no east-west railroad, although it was bisected by a north-south line, the Grand Rapids & Indiana Railroad Company. Berne and Geneva were of comparable size, having populations in 1900 of less of 2,000 each. Monroe was much smaller. All were located in Adams County.

The Bluffton, Geneva & Celina Traction Company was incorporated in Indiana on March 4, 1907 with capital of $30,000. The corporate officers included Louis C. Justus as president at first. He was a local interurban promoter and had been one of the original directors of the Marion, Bluffton & Eastern Traction Company (MB&E). He died as a result of the train collision September 21, 1910, on the neighboring interurban line of the Fort Wayne & Wabash Valley Traction Company.

The company office was maintained in Bluffton on South Johnson Street, where quarters were shared with the MB&E.

In Bluffton the railway was to use Washington Street. County roads were to be used in other places. However, a later report said that the line was entirely on private right-of-way outside cities. Only the portion of the route between Bluffton and Geneva, 18.50 miles, was being actively pursued.

The Wabash River follows a reasonably direct route between these places. The interurban was routed along the existing county roads near the south bank of the river most of the way between Bluffton and Linn Grove, two-thirds of the distance to Geneva. Along this section the railway listed Vera Cruz as a stop—a case of puffery since that town was across the river, about one half a mile from the line. Beyond Linn Grove the alignment was another story. The railroad went south for over three miles, gaining separation from the river and climbing perhaps ten feet. A minor road was paralleled for part of this distance, but most of the way the track followed a section line where there was no other thoroughfare. Then it turned abruptly east and proceeded about four miles to Geneva. This diversion increased the length of the line by a mile or so, but it permitted the railway to avoid a hilly region where the county roads climbed hills of thirty or forty feet.

At Geneva, the line entered town from the west on Butcher Street. A wye at Butcher and Washington Streets turned the cars, which headed east beyond the wye toward High Street, then backed around the corner and south on Washington Street to a stub-end at Line Street. The traction cars never ran into brick-paved Line Street past the stores nor reached the Grand Rapids & Indiana Railroad depot. The interurban station was established along with a restaurant on the ground floor of a two-story frame building on the northeast corner of Line and Washington Streets.

The entire route of the interurban either directly followed, or roughly paralleled gravel-surfaced roads which were reasonably weatherproof and satisfactory for all but the heaviest wagons. However, transporting freight loads was still a slow process. A few automobiles were already in use in the area. However, the area held a high concentration of Amish who did little travelling unless required by church or business—and then they preferred a horse and buggy. These facts did not augur well for the success of the railway, especially as a passenger carrier.

Tracklaying began August 17, 1909, in Bluffton. By mid-November the track was finished to Vera Cruz. Rail was completed all the way to Geneva on January 2 of the following year, problems from early winter weather notwithstanding. The completion was a big event in town.

The use of self-contained motor cars had been considered, but electrification by 600-volt d.c. overhead trolley was settled upon in 1909. Power was secured at Bluffton from the MB&E and distributed through a single portable substation with no fixed substations at all. The portable was initially located at Linn Grove—giving a seven-mile stub feed to the end of the line at Geneva, a condition that must often have resulted in low voltage.

On November 13 or 15, 1909, a passenger car was handled between Bluffton and Vera Cruz by a steam construction locomotive. The line had no cars of its own at the time; presumably the car was borrowed from a connection.

Revenue service to Geneva began on April 7, 1910. A single passenger car provided service every three hours, with five departures

Bluffton, Geneva & Celina's only car was the 400.
Charles Hess Collection.

from Geneva between 7:50 AM and 7:50 PM. While this was infrequent service for an interurban, it was more than the three trains each way on the town's railroad, and of course the intermediate points had no other mechanical transportation at all.

On July 1, 1910, the BG&C was leased to the MB&E. Through cars were planned. The lease was short-lived, being relinquished on the first day of 1911. However, the MB&E continued to control the BG&C, and the two roads shared their operating management.

Surveying and some grading were done in the spring of 1910 beyond Geneva. Again in the 1911, 1912, 1913 and 1914 seasons there was intention to build the railway here. Various routes to Celina were surveyed. Some reports have suggested that the death of company president Louis C. Justus in the autumn of 1910 influenced the curtailment of the railway's plans. However, some years after his death the BG&C was still actively contemplating extension, as set forth above.

The premier and only passenger car of the BG&C was its motored two-compartment passenger-baggage "combine" built by the Jewett Car Company. The company also owned one powered box motor car, two trailer box cars and five ballast cars. Completing the roster was the portable substation.

A daily freight car (a box motor) was run from the early days of service. The potential for less-than-carload freight in the railway's largely agricultural area was undoubtedly as limited as the potential passenger traffic. In any event, the line preferred carload freight as a profit source.

That traffic was entirely in cars interchanged with the steam railroads. Few Midwestern interurbans provided an outlet for railroad-interchange freight as more than an incidental part of their business. In most cases the railroads refused interchange or granted it with great reluctance. But the BG&C was a happy exception. Its handling of railroad cars began upon establishment of an interchange with the Clover Leaf Route (the Toledo, St. Louis & Western Railroad, a predecessor of the Norfolk & Western Railway Company) at Bluffton, apparently on the line of the MB&E, which paralleled the Clover Leaf. As the MB&E and the BG&C both ran on Washington Street, Bluffton, freight cars could apparently be handled straight through town by the two electric roads. The Cincinnati, Bluffton & Chicago Railroad (a steam short line, since abandoned) established interchange in 1913 with the two interurbans. Subsequently the Lake Erie & Western Railroad (Bluffton's other steam railroad and another component of today's Norfolk & Western) followed suit.

About half of the carload traffic of the two electric lines (MB&E and BG&C) consisted of general commodities, principally coal inbound and hay and grain outbound. About 1915 the BG&C installed a switch to the Bluffton municipal electric light plant. Outbound traffic on the BG&C originated at Newville and Linn Grove, where there were grain elevators drawing business for a distance of several miles.

The other half of the two interurbans' carload freight, about 800 cars during five summer months annually, was crushed stone from a quarry of the Erie Stone Company at Bluffton. This was received from the railroads after a short switching move and delivered to consignees at country sidings of the interurbans.

The MB&E and BG&C interurban lines used railroad-owned freight cars. The box motors owned by each road were equipped with railroad-type knuckle couplers (then rare on interurban roads) and train air brakes for handling freight cars. Movements of three to seven cars at a time were customary, with certain grades presenting limitations. On level track the motors could each handle as many as ten loads. The BG&C could stand by itself for now...but not for long.

CHAPTER 7

Service, Facilities, Electric Power... and a New Plan.

These were the great days for the interurbans. The cars had a majestic glamour and magic appeal for young and old alike. Cars of five distinct interurban companies were in constant attendance at the Fort Wayne terminal. Long and racy limited palace cars or short and stubby local cars; all well-maintained, carefully painted, complete with bright gilt lettering and trim, created an impressive array in the station. Limiteds and locals nosed slowly onto Main Street where they shoved the few automobiles out of the way with complete disdain. The big cars trundled their way to the city limits. As the cars left the streets, the motorman opened the controls and it was all power and full speed as the interurbans counted on making their best time while running on their own open tracks. Few people will ever forget the loud toot of the whistle and the flurry of dust as another country grade crossing was left behind. The big cars of the Wabash Valley, Union Traction and Ohio Electric always excited the imagination of both passengers and casual observers.

A whole way of life was changing and the Midwest was growing in a new way. The city dwellers could travel easily, quickly and conveniently from their home town and do it at low cost. Small rural communities, dependent largely on themselves for years, now found the cities close at hand. Farm produce was easily moved; the people, likewise. Plentiful autos and hard surfaced roads were still in the future but people were beginning to move. Trips that had taken a whole day or several days or were never taken at all were reduced to hours or one day. It was no wonder that everyone took to the interurban railway. Unfortunately, even greater freedom of mobility would be its great undoing, but no one could see ahead. However, Henry Ford and the mass produced, cheap Model T were just around the corner.

The Southwestern's original cars were too small for the average passenger loads. Some were rebuilt for further use. The 320-series interurban cars were built at the Chestnut Street Shops from the small 44-foot cars and were originally very similar in appearance. All three of these 63-foot cars had new trucks, motors and controls. Subsequent rebuildings brought about substantial variations in the three. The big cars were very popular with the company and, along with the big 500-series cars, were the favorites for most Fort Wayne-Lafayette assignments until Indiana Railroad put surplus steel cars in their place in 1931. These big wooden cars were among the finest of the builder's art. They were regularly modernized and excellently maintained.

During the early years, before through interline services became routine, the visit

The 308 was one of four 55-foot cars built for the Wabash Valley in 1909. They were essentially the same as the earlier cars, but were mounted on Curtis trucks. The Electro-Technic Band poses for a semi-formal portrait.
Bradley-Harnish Collection.

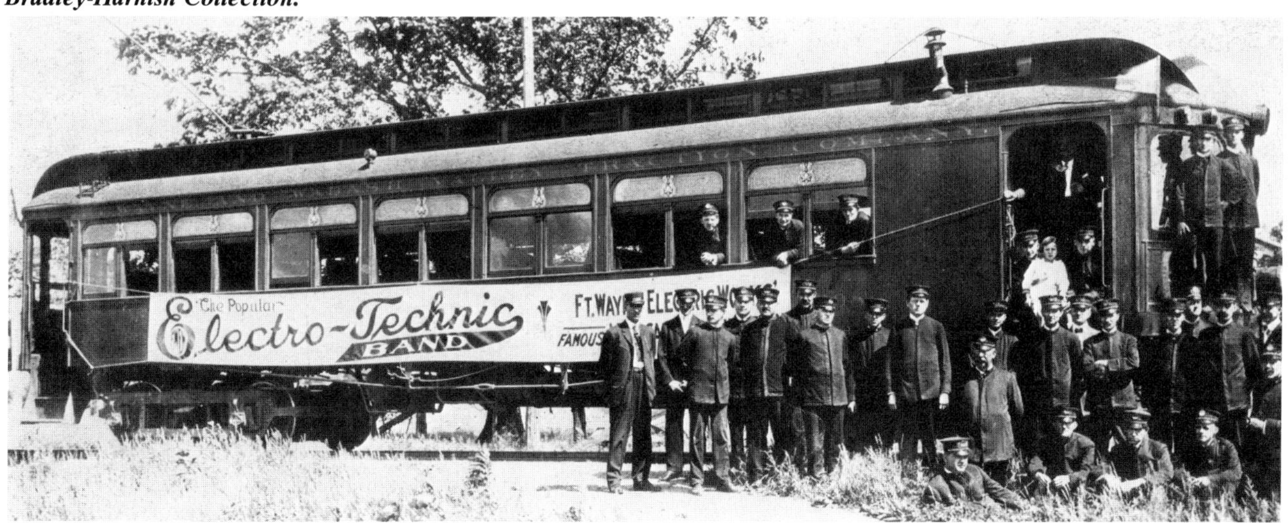

The 321 was the first of the 63-foot cars built from the smaller Southwestern cars by the Wabash Valley. 321 is shown on a special trip for the Electro-Technic Band of the Ft. Wayne Electric Works. This band was a popular attraction of the day. ***Bradley-Harnish Collection.***

Above: *Ft. Wayne & Wabash Valley Traction car 320 (at Peru), one of the 63-foot cars built by the Wabash Valley in 1910 at the Ft. Wayne shop.* ***Tippecanoe County Historical Association Collection. Below left:*** *The Logansport car barn from the southwest corner.* ***M. D. McCarter Collection.***

of a foreign company car brought newspaper rumors of new car designs. The 500-series of limited cars was actually ordered in early 1905 in a somewhat shorter version. The Wabash Valley trackage was, at that time, not in shape for such big cars and the order was postponed for a year.

Limited train services were a varying off-again—on-again operation on the Wabash Valley Lines and the Union Traction. These also included special package express services. Services were stopped and started. The

Above: The Huntington shop (from the south side), built by the Southwestern, was a well-equipped facility used for maintenance, new construction and painting. ***Below:*** *The Kendallville barn of the Toledo & Chicago was a four-track brick and frame building which continued in use until the 1930's.* ***Both photos —Bradley-Harnish Collection.***

Fort Wayne-Lafayette and Fort Wayne-Indianapolis (via Peru) buffet services were replaced in February 1909 by establishing lunch rooms in stations or assuring the availability of convenient lunch facilities. The expense of the service and the desire to make better use of the car space was the excuse for the change.

Only a few months later new limited services were established on May 16, 1909, with ten, through, limiteds over both the Peru and Bluffton routes from Indianapolis to Fort Wayne. At the same time new through local trains via Bluffton were established. (The first through service with the larger cars had started on September 11, 1907.) The second route to Indianapolis was the shorter of the two routes and served more large cities than the Peru route. In time it became the more important route.

Various buildings were needed for each of the several companies. There were duplications of facilities and a mixed-bag assortment in the companies collected together in the Wabash Valley lines. Each of the firms had to have a car barn and an electric power generating plant. Some of these facilities were used for years by the subsequent companies. In most cases the smaller power stations were uneconomical and were closed as fast as the line was consolidated with the bigger company. All but the Lafayette plant were closed by 1907.

In Lafayette the company acquired a substantial power station and a large car barn. The barn had light repair facilities for city cars. Both were used as long as the system retained its control over the property in Lafayette.

The Logansport facilities were changed several times. The earlier facilities are detailed in a later chapter. A joint passenger and freight station, for both the Wabash Valley and Union Traction, was established at Fourth and Market Streets.

On the east side of the city, the Wabash Valley built two substantial concrete, steel and brick buildings which housed the east side waiting station, offices, shops and substation. The outside ends of these buildings were closed and access to the three tracks was made by a transfer table located in the middle. The design was a miniature of a large-city car barn design, for use in congested areas, although the Logansport location was anything but crowded. The shop area had one pit track for light repairs to city cars. The storage yard had five tracks and a loop for turning single end cars.

The Huntington plant was the best equipped interurban facility on the system and the shop was better than the Fort Wayne car shops. The Southwestern's shop and powerhouse were located between First Street and the Erie Railroad. The powerhouse was closed after 1907, and the better machinery taken to Lafayette, but the building was retained for the power distribution substation and storage. The slate-roofed, brick, car house shop building covered an area of 13,680 square feet with the lumber shed adjoining it. The shop had

The 322 was the last of the big 63-foot cars built by the company. Planned by the Wabash Valley management, 322 was finally completed by the Ft. Wayne & Northern Indiana Traction Company. ***George Krambles Collection.***

The Spy Run Avenue powerhouse upon completion in 1907. The building, of a new design and arrangement, was soon rivaled by the municipal city light plant. ***Bradley-Harnish Collection.***

been built, along with the power station, as the center point location home base for the Southwestern line largely because of a cash subsidy from the city of Huntington and some centralization economies. The shop was designed to handle all major repairs and consequently had four pit tracks and a complete machine shop. Interurban car rebuilding, repairs and painting were continued here for many years. As a car house it was in the wrong place for practical operations (as planned) being in the center of the proposed line instead of one or the other ends.

Kendallville was selected by the Toledo & Chicago in anticipation of the building of a long east-west line as the site of the company's main power station. A large and handsome powerhouse was built on the south side of town, near Bixler Lake, to generate the 3300-volt alternating current to power the cars. Nearby stood the four-track brick and frame car barn. Repairs and rebuilding were done here until, in later years, it was found to be cheaper to have the work done by the Fort Wayne company.

The Lagro station/power substation was typical of the well-constructed brick buildings on the Wabash Valley lines. ***Bradley-Harnish Collection.***

Wabash River Traction had constructed a large four-track car barn and powerhouse along the river, between Wabash and Peru at an isolated and remote location a couple of miles south of the little community of Rich Valley. This spot was named after Fred Boyd and to the east of the car barn was the Boyd Park picnic and amusement park area. This park site was a popular attraction but it was impractical for an operating base. The big car barn was among the better buildings on the system but was even more poorly located than the Huntington barn which was at least close to people. After it was not needed for a power generating station, that portion of the building was used for the substation equipment and materials storage. The barn served a useful purpose as a storage depot for surplus cars although it seemed more remote after the 1911 closing of the public side of Boyd Park.

Along with Boyd Park, other parks had been acquired in both Lafayette and Logansport. Spencer Park, near the Eel River, east of Logansport, contained about eighteen acres of grounds used primarily for dances, picnics and ball games. Tecumseh Trail Park, north of

The Kendallville powerhouse (looking east) when new in 1906. The car barn is on the right. The track in the foreground leads to the Kendallville station. ***Bradley-Harnish Collection.***

The new coal-handling facility at Kendallville powerhouse came about as a result of demands for increased generating capacity. ***Bradley-Harnish Collection.***

Lafayette along the Wabash River, was very popular with its large dance pavilion and picnic grounds. None could remotely compare with Robison Park.

Mayor Hosey of Fort Wayne was much opposed to the traction company's monopoly on electric power. He spearheaded a drive throughout 1906 to build a municipal power plant with funds originally levied as early as 1898. The power plant question created a serious controversy and there were frequent comments from Col. J. Levering Jones, president of the Wabash Valley, in opposition to the city plant. A special election was held in November 1906 and construction on the city generating station was begun in 1907. The City plant was opened in 1908 in direct competition to the Traction Company. Charges and countercharges were hurled back and forth between the traction company and the city for years. The gap between the two opposing views never closed. (The competition ended, in 1974, when City Light was leased to the power company.)

The Schoepf-McGowan Syndicate members failed to anticipate the huge potential market for electric power. The collection of small power plants within the city included Fort Wayne Traction's Chestnut Street station and the Jenny Electric Light and Power Company. None of the four interurban power plants was remotely adequate, so the Wabash Valley built the very large and efficient Spy Run Avenue power plant. The big Spy Run station was started up on March 1, 1907, and became the central electric power generating point for the entire area. The station was a new design, attracting widespread engineering interest. Several articles were printed in the leading engineering and traction journals.

Large central power stations had been advocated in the industry for economic reasons. A large plant could generate in large units of electricity, operate more efficiently from the standpoint of making steam and be run by relatively fewer people. Steam driven turbines were far more efficient than the earlier generators belt driven from large reciprocating steam engines. The big Spy Run Avenue plant replaced the nearby power station built by the Jenny company in 1883 and the city trolley line's Chestnut Street station and both were closed down. The outlying small stations at Huntington, Boyd Park, and the two at Logansport were also replaced. The Lafayette power plant continued to supply power to the Lafayette city system and the west end of the interurban line.

With plenty of economical generating capacity and with high voltage long distance transmission capability, the electric railway was now firmly in control of electric power sales and distribution for a large section of the state. The name Fort Wayne & Wabash Valley Traction Company, with no reference to electricity, masked the company's greatest potential and its greatest long range asset. The power plant's load was, in 1907, about two thirds railway and one third commercial. However, the commercial demand was continually growing while the rail side remained nearly static in magnitude. The Wabash Valley was the largest Schoepf-McGowan property that included a major electric power generating

Above: *The Boyd Park barn (east front) looking west from the main line and east of the north-south county road. The north end (right) was used for power generating until 1907. The sub-station remained in the building.* ***Below:*** *The Boyd Park barn (west front) looking east. This view was taken in the 1920's.* ***Both photos —Bradley-Harnish Collection.***

utility. Regrettably, when the later Kingsland wreck forced a choice, the syndicate elected to keep other railway companies, which did not have equally strong electric utility components, and let go of the Wabash Valley through reorganization.

In 1910, the Fort Wayne & Wabash Valley Traction Company came through with one of the typically grandiose schemes conceived during this wide-open period of interurban consolidations and expansions. The officials who ambitiously analyzed the company proposed the acquisition of the Fort Wayne & Springfield Railway Company; the Toledo & Chicago Interurban Railway; the Marion, Bluffton & Eastern Traction Company and the Toledo & Indiana Traction Company. The Wabash Valley family would then include almost all of the interurban lines in the territory it served with electric power. Three of these companies were in, or on the verge of, serious financial difficulties.

The Toledo & Indiana Traction Company, which had just come out of receivership, was not one of the Fort Wayne area companies. Rather it was a northwest Ohio operation with original plans to build into Indiana from Toledo. It had a 56 mile line from the heart of Toledo to Bryan, Ohio, a scant 29 miles from a possible connection with the Toledo &

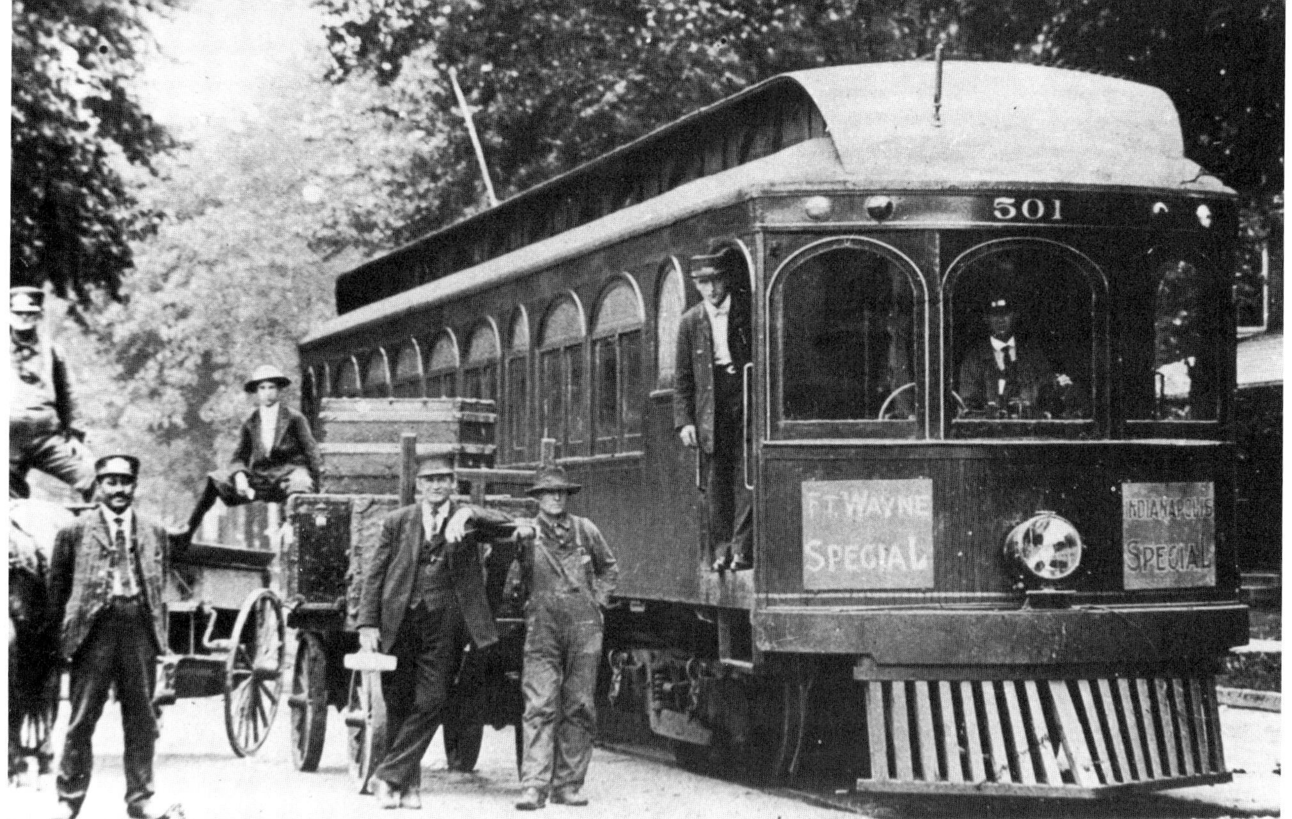

The 501 still running as a parlor-buffet car loads trunks and other baggage on the Ft. Wayne-Indianapolis run. **George Krambles Collection.**

Chicago Interurban Railway at Auburn, Indiana. Combined and joined, this would have provided a well-built 225-mile, through, trunk line from Toledo, Ohio to Lafayette, Indiana. Even more important, it provided, via the syndicate connecting lines, to Indianapolis over two north central Indiana routes.

Another extension was planned to Columbia City, nineteen miles along the Pennsylvania Railroad west of Fort Wayne. This was a route often discussed as a potential interurban route. The Fort Wayne & Winona Traction Company was incorporated on June 15, 1910 by associates of the Schoepf-McGowan Syndicate with the intention of selling or transferring the new company in name or in complete form to the syndicate. The company was chartered to reach not only Columbia City but beyond to Warsaw. None of this projected line was built and no interurban ever reached Columbia City, one of the few northern Indiana county seat towns that never saw electric rail service.

Such a large scale plan, if it were carried through, would have produced one of the largest and most powerful midwest interurban empires—and it almost did. All the preliminary negotiations were completed, financing arranged, and, to make certain, careful studies were made of the entire cost of the extensions to the last tie and spike needed. Certain rehabilitations of the lines to be acquired were also figured and additional rolling stock estimates considered.

The new organization and consolidation plan with its careful estimates was to be known as the Fort Wayne & Wabash Valley Traction and Terminal Company. This dream was kept under careful consideration awaiting the "right" moment and was finally presented in October, 1910. By then the right moment had gone by and the dream was now a nightmare.

Ohio Electric's 93 on the Ft. Wayne-Lima run was built for the Schoepf-McGowan's Ohio Electric combination of lines by the Cincinnati Car Company. **Dr. Reed C. Prugh Collection.**

TION COMPAN
R KINGSLAND, IND. SEPT. 21,'10

Kingsland—End of a Dream!

CHAPTER 8

Interurban lines often had mishaps. Minor derailments were not uncommon. In town streets or at rural crossings a car might strike a pedestrian or demolish a vehicle. Careless pedestrians presented a continued problem in the early days of the interurbans. Speeds were misjudged and the unfortunate victim found that a big interurban passenger or freight car did not stop quickly in an emergency situation. Streetcars suffered the same problem and most companies were required to add clumsy safety devices to the front of the cars. These "fenders" were supposed to scoop the unlucky victim out of harms way.

Rural trespassers presented another problem as the right-of-way offered convenient pathways across the country. Several attempts were made to stop offenders with one being carefully reported in ELECTRIC TRACTION WEEKLY in January 1909. "...the Ft. Wayne & Wabash Valley Traction Company, Ft. Wayne, Ind., is making a special crusade against trespassers upon its right-of-way, and as one method of warning those who have no business to be on the tracks, the company has hit on the novel scheme of supplying all motormen with a number of big red envelopes containing the following notice:

'Warning—All persons are forbidden to use the tracks or any portion of this company's right-of-way for footways or thoroughfares. The practice is dangerous and unlawful. All persons so doing are trespassers and will be prosecuted. The company is not liable for accidents or injury to trespassers.'

'Ft. W. & W. V. T. Co.'

When a motorman sees somebody on the tracks, he slows up, and either tosses or hands out one of the large envelopes. The trespasser naturally reads the contents and is impressed thereby. This is an excellent idea for it not only warns the trespasser but also further relieves the company of liability for accidents to persons on the track."

The management must have supposed that literate trespassers carefully opened the envelope, read the warning and thanked the company for such a timely warning. The company thought "nine out of ten offenders" would "read the warning on the enclosed sheet and take heed of it." One wonders about the many illiterate vagrants and tramps who, after turning the envelope over and looking at it from various angles, wondered why the company was throwing away such nice, new, big, red envelopes.

Sometimes a big interurban would catch up with a small city car that had made the mistake of stopping too quickly. Shop records show scattered reports of repairs to city cars munched or nipped by an interurban. Minor derailments were not uncommon. Occasionally the interurban cars themselves would meet head-on with a thundering smash that left twisted steel and heaps of kindling wood strewn about. Worse still was the possibility of the entire mess catching fire from an upset heater stove.

Such a smashing occurrence happened on September 21, 1910, north of Kingsland on the Wabash Valley's Bluffton Division where Union Traction's car 233 rolled northward (as Train 56) filled with its usual passengers plus pleasure seekers bound for the Fort Wayne Fair. Southbound Wabash Valley Car 303, on that fateful day, was running toward Bluffton as an extra train and was empty with the exception of its crew. It was to return from Bluffton with more fair patrons.

Train 56, from Muncie, had departed Bluffton on time and had just made the routine change from a Union Traction to a Wabash Valley crew at Villa, north of Bluffton (Bluffton station was the routine change point but Train 55 southbound was a couple of minutes late). The Wabash Valley crew of motorman Charles Van Dine and Conductor E. A. Spillers, took over on Train 56. The Union Traction crew took over Train 55 and headed south, back into Bluffton. It was approximately 12:03 p.m. and Train 56 was on time. Van Dine had a written order (Order No. 31) to meet extra Train 303 at Siding 106. The order was clear enough to Van Dine who had already made two duplicate runs that morning. Van Dine frequently worked as a dispatcher and was a regular motorman so he knew the rules and schedules.

On the other hand Car 303 (Extra Train 303) was in the hands of Benjamin T. Corkwell, motorman and Delford Wilson, conductor. The Bluffton Division train dispatching was done from the Bluffton interlocking plant (Wabash Valley-"Clover Leaf" now Norfolk & Western) and transmitted, by phone, to trains starting from Fort Wayne.

Infamous Kingsland wreck, Kingsland, Indiana, September 21, 1910. Forty-one were killed. ***All photos —Bradley-Harnish Collection.***

Wabash Valley dispatcher, W. H. Friemeyer, issued his train order No. 30 to the crew at the Fort Wayne station. Normally both the motorman and conductor were to repeat orders back to the dispatcher but traffic into Fort Wayne was heavy, Wilson had some work to do, and Corkwell had made the Bluffton-Fort Wayne run as motorman on Train No. 56 so he could be assumed to be familiar with regular train schedules.

Order No. 30 was simple enough and carried only two brief instructions, "Extra car No. 303 and Train No.... Extra Car No. 54 will meet at Siding No. 101." and "Extra Car No. 303 will report at Siding No.... Bluffton. Will run extra to Bluffton. Time 11:40." Siding No. 101 was just outside Fort Wayne and west of the St. Mary's River bridge. No. 54 was a northbound Wabash Valley freight motor. Order No. 30 also listed the crew of Corkwell and Wilson who were supposed to know the Wabash Valley train operating rules. These rules were fairly standard throughout the industry as most electric lines followed a code similar to the steam railroad operating rules. Extra trains were required to be off the main track clearing all scheduled trains by five minutes unless they had a meeting order or any order that specified other meeting arrangements. The 303, therefore, was to clear Train 56 by at least five minutes regardless of where the 303 happened to be. However, Friemeyer, in Order No. 31 anticipated that Extra Car 303 would easily make siding 106 and ordered

Train 56 to meet Extra Car 303 at that siding. This might be considered a minor discrepancy but was a simple holding order advising Train 56 that Car 303 would probably be at Siding 106 and, if not, a phone call to the dispatcher would advise Train 56 where the 303 was actually waiting and a revised order would be issued.

Van Dine's car, Union Traction No. 233, was not a regular on the Bluffton-Fort Wayne line because it was smaller, slower, and seated fewer people than the usual cars such as the Wabash Valley's 300-series cars. However, Van Dine had run the 233 before, was familiar with it, and later reported the car and equipment had been in good condition. The standard train stop was made at the Erie Railroad crossing about a half mile north of the village of Kingsland and, with a wave of clearance from Spillers, 233 moved northward, slowly picking up speed. It was 12:12 and Train 56 was due at Siding 106 at 12:16 p.m.

Dispatcher Friemeyer received a phone call from Corkwell at Siding 101 indicating completion of the ordered meet with No. 54. Corkwell did not call again although Friemeyer later stated that he expected to hear from him at Siding 105, at Yoder, based on time available. Friemeyer became concerned when he didn't hear anything although motormen were often slow to call in when safely out of the way. He called Yoder and learned that 303 was not there so he called Ossian, further down the line, just missing Extra Train 303. The big car had stopped in Ossian long enough for Wilson to pick up some matches. It then rolled southward leaving Ossian at approximately 12:13 p.m.

Siding 106 was about a mile south of Ossian. Extra Train 303, based on known times, would have been there by 12:15 p.m. at the latest. Since the necessary five minutes were not going to be available, Corkwell and Wilson should have stopped at Siding 105 some four miles back, where Friemeyer had expected them, and reported in. This would have allowed Train 56, upon finding no meeting train at Siding 106, to phone in and receive a revised order calling for a meet at Siding 105 and permission to proceed with safety. This is what should have happened. It didn't, and Siding 106 stayed empty. Corkwell and Extra Train 303 raced past at between fifty and sixty miles per hour.

Ahead of Van Dine's northbound car a grove of large trees obscured a long "S" curve. What he could not see was the southbound Extra Train 303 roaring into the north end of this blind curve. Corkwell and Wilson were heading for Siding 107 and took the corner as fast as permitted. Seconds later the air was filled with a resounding, earsplitting crash. The smaller car was telescoped more than halfway by the heavier car. The 303 sat higher than 233 and its floor slid over the lower floor crushing everything in its path and pushing baggage, seats...and bodies to the rear of the doomed car. Forty-one people were instantly killed or succumbed later from the disaster. The two Wabash Valley train crews were injured but survived although just how is not clear. Only Corkwell suffered injuries requiring hospitalization.

The wreck scene was a tragic mess and there were as many different stories as there were survivors. Several are a matter of record and some must have been agonizing. Dispatcher Friemeyer, losing touch with the cars must have realized what was happening, kept searching and finally, in despair, asked the Ossian agent if he had seen Train 56. Getting a negative reply he asked him to phone the Erie Railroad tower operator. This man reported the wreck to the agent who passed the news to Friemeyer.

The tragedy of the dead and injured reached almost every person in Bluffton where the victims had many relatives and friends. Several prominent persons, among them Mr. Louis C. Justus of the Bluffton, Geneva & Celina Traction Company, were killed. This was not just a local accident: the Kingsland wreck ranks as the worst and most tragic wreck in all interurban railroad history.

In the aftermath, the wreck was cleared away. The remains of the 233 were burned on the spot while the 303, with its crushed front end, was towed home in the dark and stored out of sight until it could be rebuilt. The road was restored to order and traffic again passed.

The disaster at Kingsland was only one of several accidents occurring in Indiana during this same period. Only three days later, on September 24, a similar accident occurred north of Tipton on the Union Traction's line. In this case a southbound freight train crashed head-on into a northbound passenger car, killing six passengers. The southbound train, according to reports, was nearly three miles south of what should have been the meeting point. These accidents brought about a detailed study by the Railroad Commission of the State of Indiana.

Actually several investigations were made of Wabash Valley's accidents by local, state and company bodies. What happened and who was to blame at Kingsland was not really fixed... at least no one went to prison. There was little question that Corkwell and Wilson erred. The only reasonable explanation is that Corkwell either completely forgot the northbound Train 56 or just didn't look at his watch. Wilson first claimed that he had orders to proceed to Siding 107 but could produce no record of any such order. This story was ignored by the investigation as only a cover of little value.

The state railroad commission ran a full investigation of the individuals involved. Corkwell and Wilson had checkered employment records but they met contemporary hiring standards. Corkwell had been fired by the Union Traction Company and came to Fort Wayne to operate city street cars on December 27, 1909. He was promoted to interurban operation on the Bluffton Division on April 1, 1910 and regularly ran, among other trains, Train No. 56. Wilson had worked for the Wabash Valley from October 8, 1909 to March 26, 1910 as an interurban conductor. Wilson quit and then was rehired on August 17, 1910 to work the city lines. He had returned to interurban service only the day before the accident. Reportedly, he had nearly failed a written rules examination. On the other hand, Van Dine, Spillers and Friemeyer had very good records and were considered competent employees.

The Wabash Valley's hiring standards and employee records were checked and it was found that Corkwell and Wilson were anything but exceptions to normal standards. Over an extended period preceding the accident, at least fifty motormen and conductors had either quit or been fired following serious rule infractions including drunkenness, ignoring train orders and the overrunning of meeting places. The Bluffton line, like most others, had no signaling system, depending alone on competent carrying out of written train orders. Later requirements demanded block signaling on the heavy traffic lines.

Throughout the rest of 1910 there was much speculation about what would happen to the Wabash Valley. The company started paying off the damage claims of survivors and relatives. By early 1911 rumors were afoot that the company would reorganize. New eastern financial interests were reported to be looking over the company.

At the February 16, 1911 Directors' meeting held in Philadelphia, it was announced that 90% of both classes of stockholders had agreed to a recapitalization at $15,000,000. The company name was changed to Fort Wayne & Northern Indiana Traction Company. Later in the month it was revealed that three-fifths of the wreck claims had been settled out of court. The total expected claim loss was estimated at $300,000. Additional funds were to come from Tucker, Anthony & Company of Boston, and Barney & Company of New York. Randall Morgan also indicated he would put up more money, but he seems to have been the last of the Philadelphia financial group to remain interested. For all practical purposes the Wabash Valley reorganization ended the Schoepf-McGowan Syndicate influence on the property.

Randall Morgan may have had a better appreciation of the long range potential for electric power than his fellow syndicate members. He maintained a minority interest in the new company for several years. It was largely

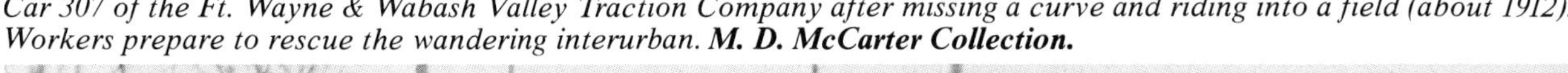

Car 307 of the Ft. Wayne & Wabash Valley Traction Company after missing a curve and riding into a field (about 1912). Workers prepare to rescue the wandering interurban. ***M. D. McCarter Collection.***

Another example of inattentiveness. The Wabash Valley car's motorman was not looking for the Union Traction line car and the line crew didn't expect the through train on the Indianapolis-Peru line. ***Bradley-Harnish Collection.***

through Morgan's concern that the Terre Haute, Indianapolis & Eastern built and maintained a solid electric power base that kept that company solvent in the twenties long after it might otherwise have slipped into receivership.

The Wabash Valley sale transaction gives some idea of interurban financing. The Wabash Valley had $6,000,000 common and $1,500,000 preferred stock, $8,900,000 bonds and about $1,000,000 of floating debts. The new Fort Wayne & Northern Indiana company announced $4,000,000 each of common and preferred stock and $15,000,000 of authorized refunding bonds. The Wabash Valley was taken over subject to all its indebtedness. Upon payment of $17.50 per share, the old company's preferred stockholders could obtain $1,500,000 of preferred stock with the new company. New common stock in the amount of $2,622,200 went to the old common stockholders. The $17.50 per share fund was turned over to the new company. A banking syndicate (presumed to be Tucker-Anthony) got $125,000 of the fund plus $344,300 in new common stock for underwriting the sale of $1,000,000 bonds, $1,000,000 in preferred and $1,000,000 common stock. The sale was supposed to yield $1,500,000 in cash.

Colonel Jones remained President and Emmons stayed on as General Manager. A new Union Station, to replace the Pearl at Harrison station, was announced to be located in the block bounded by Main, Pearl, Webster and Maiden Lane although it was finally located further to the west between Webster and Ewing streets. By the end of March the directorship had changed somewhat to reflect the new owners and Robert Watson, of New York, suddenly arrived in Fort Wayne to assume the role of vice-president in charge of the new development plan.

On April 27, 1911, it was announced that the capable Charles D. Emmons was going to South Bend to be General Manager of the Chicago, South Bend and Northern Indiana Railway. Watson was the active head of the new Fort Wayne company and he apparently could not get along with Emmons. Emmons was very popular and the Schoepf-McGowan people took care of their own as the South Bend company was in the Murdock family's hands. (Emmons became General Manager of the Boston Elevated in 1918 and in 1919 was elected president of United Railways & Electric Company of Baltimore, Maryland.)

The new company, now separated from the syndicate's interlocking plans, had no further interest in the great consolidation and expansion plan. The great dream had been shattered in one split second near the village of Kingsland, and the plans were shelved where they quietly gathered dust. The slogan "Wabash Valley Lines" remained as a reminder of the old company. Firmly organized, seemingly leaving trouble behind, the Fort Wayne & Northern Indiana seemed ready to meet new and great potential opportunity. It just did not happen that way.

The Troubled Teens

CHAPTER 9

The struggling Marion, Bluffton and Eastern went down in defeat. In October, 1913, the Marion Trust Company, Indianapolis, brought suit to foreclose. The company was reorganized emerging on July 1, 1914, as the Marion and Bluffton Traction Company. "Eastern" disappeared from the title as the new company tried to make a paying proposition of what it had.

The Bluffton, Geneva and Celina faced a more serious prospect. As a planned Indiana-Ohio connecting link, it would have run in the wrong direction (from northwest to southeast) for practical traffic flow, when a southwest to northeast line such as the proposed Auburn-Bryan line was needed. The line remained in its short form with very light passenger traffic and not enough freight business. The company deteriorated into a sad condition. Receivership came in 1917. In October, 1917, it was sold at a receiver's sale to Thomas Flinn. Flinn said the line was insolvent and he would scrap it. Operation continued into early 1918 to move the grain from the elevators. The track was then torn up.

The two alternating-current lines to the north and the south of Fort Wayne also underwent some changes. The Fort Wayne & Northwestern Railway Company succeeded the Toledo & Chicago in a reorganization on April 14, 1913. It was sold for the upset price of only $550,000 to the principal bondholders at a receiver's sale held in Fort Wayne. The 3300-volt A.C. system may have been justified by the long main line which the Toledo & Chicago had planned to add. But for what had actually been built, the new company realized that 600-volt direct current, the standard trolley voltage, was more suitable. The existing cars were reequipped with new motors and controls which made them much lighter. Schedules were easier to maintain because direct current motors were better adapted to rapid acceleration after the frequent stops needed in local interurban service. The new company was modestly successful for a number of years.

The weak Fort Wayne & Springfield also did the expected and collapsed into receivership in 1912. It continued to be run by the Court-appointed receiver.

During this heyday period of the interurbans, changes and improvements continued on the Fort Wayne city lines through the purchase of new cars and extensions to the local trolley lines. The car shop area on Chestnut (Baker) Street was also expanded in piecemeal bits. West of the old powerhouse four metal clad sheds had been erected for car repair and material storage. The first shed (next to the powerhouse building) was the original stable and barn. The western shed, which was torn down (and not replaced) had four pit tracks. As a result much work had to be done out-of-doors, regardless of the weather. This conglomeration must have presented the most adverse working conditions, although one entire group of city cars and several interurban cars were built in these facilities and extensive rebuilding regularly carried on. Unfortunately the whole collection of buildings, at best, made a very poor appearance and must have given Pennsylvania Railroad passengers arriving at the neighboring railroad station, a rather rude shock for their first impression of the city.

The Broadway line was extended south to the Bluffton Road Bridge in 1903 when Fort Wayne Traction embarked on its improvement program. The same year the new South Wayne line was created by laying rails south from Creighton to Organ Street, now Kinsmoor. South Calhoun was extended to Pontiac and east on Pontiac to Walton. The Lewis line was extended east to Wabash Avenue and Maumee. The Huffman line succeeded the

Line car 41 and track crews prepare to place the new span of the Wild Cat Creek bridge rebuilt in 1917.
Bradley-Harnish Collection.

The Toledo & Chicago cars got more than a new company name in 1913 when the power system was changed from AC to DC. The cars got new motors and controls as a result which made them much lighter. ***George Krambles Collection.***

*The old Chestnut Street (Baker Street), Ft. Wayne complex —**Above left:** Chestnut Street looking west from the door of the repair shop toward the trainmen's building (ex-stables) and the open-end car barn with seven tracks. The area behind the fence is for material storage. **Above right:** Interior of the old powerhouse repair shop with Union Traction car 429. **At left:** Chestnut Street looking east from in front of the car barn. The building to the right of the telephone pole is the carpenter shop. The two lead tracks, to the left of the telephone pole, enter the inspection shop area (one building with a flat-roof wing). The two distant switches enter the repair shop (ex-powerhouse). The track extends to Clinton Street, but does not enter it; across Clinton Street can be seen the Pennsylvania shops (locomotive construction facilities).* ***All photos — Bradley-Harnish Collection.***

Bloomingdale line through the building of new tracks on Huffman Street, west of Wells to Jessie Street.

As each interurban line arrived extensions had been made to the street railway to provide a proper entrance. The line to Bluffton merely hooked onto the end of the Broadway line. The Toledo and Chicago connected to the city system near Wells and Sixth Streets. The Lewis line was again extended east on Maumee to Warren and south on Chestnut (a different Chestnut Street than where the car barns were located), over private right-of-way. This provided an entrance for the Lima line. The Decatur line entered the city over South Calhoun Street.

During the era of the Fort Wayne and Northern Indiana, many of the turn-of-the-century streetcars were showing their age by their old style. Maintenance costs and problems increased correspondingly. The front door entry system with the conductor near the motorman was introduced and this "nearside" style of car was adopted for the city lines, in 1913. Twenty-six new cars were purchased to meet the new operating plan and to replace some of the system's oldest cars. These new single truck cars were quite long with most of the overhang in front and did not ride well. The extreme length of the front platform produced a wobbling gait. These cars were purchased through the use of Equipment Trust Certificates. It appears that the FtW&NI was a pioneer in the use of equipment trusts for electric railway cars.

Little new trackage was built but "wyes" were constructed at the end of most lines to turn the new single-end nearside cars. The only major new track work during the Fort Wayne & Northern Indiana period was an extension of the South Wayne line to one block south of Rudisill completed in 1916. The city trackwork was rapidly falling into disrepair, through over-age and light rail, and becoming incapable of carrying heavier traffic.

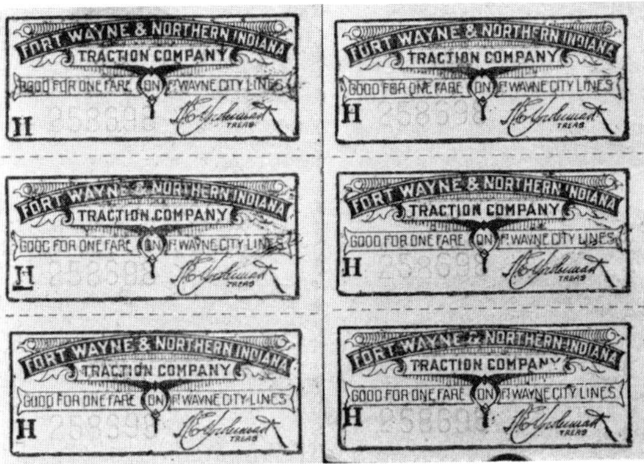

An Ohio Electric 92-94 series car (about 1913) in an odd location facing south on the north track of Calhoun Street. The car is backing and the switch has been thrown to turn it east on Main Street where a crossover will allow it to proceed westward to the station. A movement of this type was awkward at best in 1913 when few cars were on the street; it would be prohibitive today. ***Bradley-Harnish Collection.***

The Allen County Courthouse from the Transfer Building, showing the central Main and Calhoun intersection about 1913. A two car train from Decatur is heading north on Calhoun, ready to turn left (west) onto Main Street. It's Ft. Wayne Fair time (late summer). The courthouse, fully restored, is used today as the Courts Building of the City-County Complex. ***Bradley-Harnish Collection.***

Main Street bridge (Lafayette) after the 1913 flood, from the west bank of the Wabash River showing the spans precariously canted due to the damage of the central bridge pier. ***Tippecanoe County Historical Association Collection.***

A view of the temporary streetcar bridge across the Wabash River following the 1913 flood which took out the Main Street bridge. The pile driver unit is setting freshly cut trees as piers. ***Bailey Collection / Tippecanoe County Historical Association.***

The spring of 1913 actually started the series of events that would make the "teens" an unhappy time for the Fort Wayne & Northern Indiana. The 1913 Flood was the area's worst general flood of this century and the interurbans and street railways all suffered. There was a lot of rain and a fast runoff, more than in many years, and it was uncontrollable. The Wabash Valley lines did not suffer as much as some companies but they took a pounding.

The Fort Wayne-Springfield line had its usual run of luck. The St. Mary's River at Decatur unexpectedly rose six feet on the night of March 24 and flooded the power plant. While the power was off, the car barn was also flooded. As on most interurban lines, no night service was scheduled, so all the cars were partly inundated. It took several days to dry out the cars' motors. As an alternating-current line, the company could not borrow cars from its connections even if any could be spared. Flood damage repairs prevented full operation for nearly two weeks.

The Marion-Bluffton was briefly stopped by a power failure. Also, a one span 50-foot bridge at Liberty Center was damaged. It was quickly restored.

The Fort Wayne-Bluffton line of the FtW&NI was out of service because of two small washouts from March 25 to March 29. The Fort Wayne-Huntington portion, largely along the canal rather than the river, was only mildly affected with the only difficulty in the western Fort Wayne flood plain along Taylor Street. From Huntington to Logansport about 35 miles of trackage was inundated. In some places it was eight feet under the raging waters. Operation was suspended on March 24. This portion remained closed until March 31, when the line was re-opened to Wabash. The next day it was opened to Peru and the day after to Logansport.

At Logansport much of the downtown district, where the Eel River meets the Wabash, was under as much as eight feet of water.

The line west to Lafayette crossed to the south side of the Wabash River via the roadway of the Third Street bridge. Two 124-foot bridge spans went down during the flood. This affected the whole line to Lafayette as no cars were west of Logansport when the bridge went down. The Wabash Railroad took an interurban car over their line to a connection

with the interurban. Partial service from north of Lafayette to the west end of the Logansport bridge began on March 28. This car could not get all the way into Lafayette as there was another major break where 380 feet of the Wild Cat Creek trestle was swept out by the flood. This was quickly replaced by a temporary rebuild using the old materials.

The Logansport-Lafayette section was virtually closed except for a shuttle car, for several weeks.

One span of the Main Street bridge over the Wabash River at Lafayette also went down in the flood, cutting West Lafayette and Purdue University off from the city. The gas and electric company in Lafayette was flooded and forced to stop. The traction company picked up the extra electric load, which put a severe strain on the power system. The traction plant was also out for several hours when water reached the boilers.

Restoration was costly. The company had to pay partial costs for rebuilding the city-owned bridges in both Logansport and Lafayette. The temporarily rebuilt Wild Cat Creek bridge was adequate for most service but by mid-1917 it had to be permanently reconstructed. The total project was huge. The east approach of 795′ and the west approach of 375′ were earth fill. Three 100′ deck girder spans and one 181′ steel truss span completed the crossing. When this was done the Lafayette-Logansport portion was again the best constructed and fastest operating portion of the

Ft. Wayne's Wells Street bridge (1910) never carried two tracks and was a bottleneck. A work motor car is heading inbound and running against traffic. **Bob Parker Collection.**

Wabash Valley lines—but the least promising for passenger traffic.

At the same time the flood clean-up took place, the interurban company began the installation of new signals on the Huntington to Logansport portion of the main Wabash Valley line. Part of the Fort Wayne to Hunting-

At work on the Wild Cat Creek bridge—at left a line car and crew put the finishing touches on the new central span; below the span is ready to slip into place. **Both photos—Bradley-Harnish Collection.**

The 301, on a Ft. Wayne-Lafayette local run, stops at the Wabash station. ***Bradley-Harnish Collection.***

ton line was already protected at this date. The signals were in compliance of an order issued by the State Railroad Commission following the investigations of the recent wrecks. By 1920 this block signal system had expanded to 49.4 miles of General Railway Signal Company's absolute permissive type light signals with track circuits. Two highway crossing flashers had been installed to protect both motorists and the interurban cars. Five sets of hand block signals were also used for orders to trains. Oddly enough none of these installations were on the Bluffton line where the Kingsland wreck had occurred. The only improvement in that operation had been the moving of train dispatching to the Fort Wayne station and making it a single position to insure better administration of train orders. At Bluffton the dispatcher had also been responsible for the interlocking plant.

In addition to the signals, the interurban lines had four major interlocking plants. The interlocking plant at Fox Station was east of Lagro and protected a level crossing of the Wabash Railroad with a steep approach from both sides for the interurban cars. A two story frame building with a Saxby Farmer machine used 16 levers and had home and distance signals protecting both roads. The Kingsland plant was much simpler with hand operated derails and track circuit controlled signals on the Erie Railroad. The Bluffton interlocker had a one story structure, an eight lever Saxby Farmer machine and home and distance signals on both the electric and steam roads (Toledo, St. Louis & Western-"Cloverleaf"—now Norfolk & Western). The major plant was the Clymers interlocking plant protecting a three way crossing of the Wabash Railroad, Vandalia Railroad and the FtW&NI with each crossing the other two. The machine at this location contained 72 functions and was maintained by the Wabash Railroad. The FtW&NI paid a sizable portion of the investment in, and the operation of, the plant. (Another set of interlocking plants was located on the Fort Wayne & Northwestern with one at Butler Center and another at Auburn Junction. The first was a fairly simple crossing but also controlled an interchange with the Vandalia. The second covered a junction of four rail lines and was a joint operation with the other lines (the B&O being the principal company).

In 1917, the company began operating a motor bus line in Fort Wayne. The 1½ mile line connected the end of the Huffman Street line with the West Main Street line, at Runnion Avenue. A new car line for this residential area was too expensive. Four sixteen passenger Studebaker buses were purchased for $1,465 each. They were painted the standard sand yellow color of the street cars. It only took two buses to run the line but the untested motorbus idea made the company buy not one, but two, spares. The buses were one-man-operated without the usual conductor. The drivers got a premium wage for motorbus driving. The bus operation, however, was not profitable and lasted only a short time.

Another serious problem was the labor force. During mid-1915 an attempt to unionize was made and the company fought the move. From September 27 through September 30 most Fort Wayne city service was stopped by a strike of 180 car men. There was some violence and the men had the support of the Mayor. Legal maneuvering went on for weeks

In 1917, city bus 33 on West Main Street was the first attempt to use motor buses in Ft. Wayne. ***Bradley-Harnish Collection.***

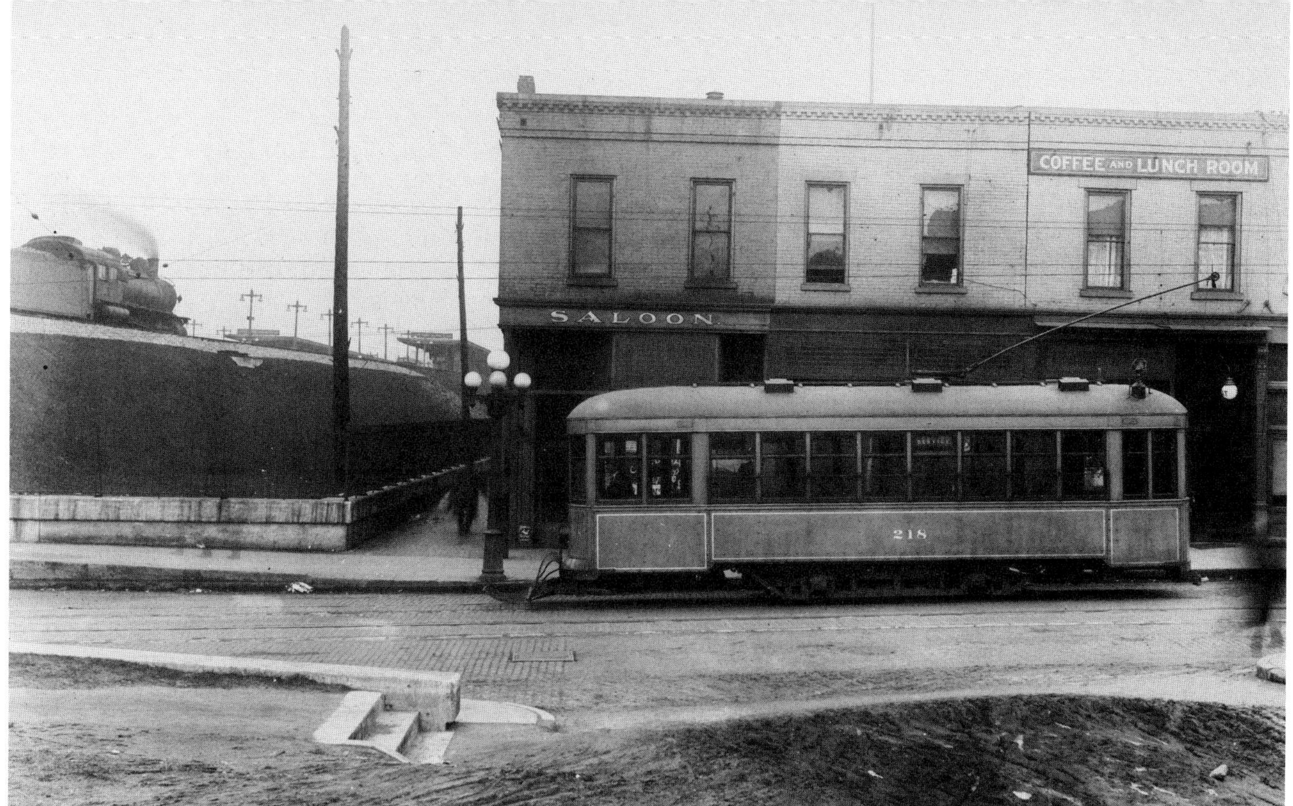

New "nearside" type car 218 heads south on Calhoun Street in 1913. The car is heading into the underpass of the Pennsylvania RR elevation. A fast-moving passenger hurries toward the new Pennsylvania station with an E-Class Atlantic (left) heading the train. ***Bradley-Harnish Collection.***

and was not finally settled until May 1916, although service had been upset for only the first few days.

The Fort Wayne strike ended just in time for the Logansport City Line's two man crews (motormen and conductors) to go on strike. The company had eliminated two man crews and was running most of the city cars with one man for several months as a necessary economy measure. Sympathizers joined the strikers and a riot occurred on the evening of July 18, 1916, the first day of the strike.

Throughout the 19th no cars were run and the mob element commanded Logansport's downtown. Things quieted down on the 20th, cars were running in the day and, by the 24th, cars were running at night with two policemen on each car. The memory of this unpleasantness lingered for years.

The Decatur line continued its checkered career from the 1912 receivership, through the flood and numerous attempts to settle affairs until December 2, 1915 when it was sold at public sale by the court. On July 1, 1916 a group composed largely of people associated with the Fort Wayne & Northern Indiana took control. Samuel W. Greenland, General Manager of the Fort Wayne company, operated the new Fort Wayne & Decatur Traction Company. Here, as on the other AC line, the new company name reflected actual achievements rather than obsolete hopes for great expansion. The company became a testing ground and it was rebuilt and reequipped. As a separate operation many ideas could be tried for the benefit of the Fort Wayne company—with separate money.

The 6,600 volt, 25 cycle, alternating current, single phase system, along with the Decatur powerhouse, were marked for replacement. Also, the heavy 90,000 pound cars which had never had strenuous use were set aside for salvage. A new 1200-volt direct current power system was installed which used the old catenary overhead with a rotary converter placed in a new substation built at the midpoint of the line. A step-up substation was built just south of Fort Wayne to feed power purchased from the Traction Company. The step-up station was not yet in service when the old powerhouse burned, leaving the line with no power and no operations for five days.

The line thus had its second relatively unusual power system. Because of the late development of 1200-volt equipment, that voltage was used on only a few lines although, for interurban service, it was technologically superior to the 600-volt DC which was practically an industry standard.

New cars were another experimental move on the Fort Wayne & Decatur. They were designed by Arthur W. Redderson, Superintendent of the Motive Power for the Fort Wayne & Northern Indiana who came to Fort Wayne in 1914 from the Chicago Railways Co. The new cars were built by St. Louis Car

Company. The 48-foot cars weighed 59,000 pounds and were an early step toward lighter weight interurban cars. The trucks were of the heavy Baldwin 73 design with four Westinghouse motors. The cars used 50% less current and set the stage for further car designs. The overall rehabilitation of the Fort Wayne-Decatur line was a nominal success.

During 1917, two positive steps were taken by the Fort Wayne & Northern Indiana. Ten new double-truck city cars were purchased by the system in 1917. These were assigned to heavy traffic lines in Fort Wayne as they were much better riding than the single truck cars and the large capacity meant two new cars could do the work of three small cars. In an era of rising costs the better utilization meant one less two-man crew. To the public, the company was presenting a fairly strong image in these new cars even though some schedule headways were lengthened.

Robert M. Feustel was named as president of the company on January 9, 1917 succeeding James M. Barrett. (Barrett had taken the top spot after Colonel Jones left in 1912.) Feustel, a Fort Wayne native, had established an outstanding reputation as a consulting engineer and railroad expert before his appointment as president of the FtW&NI. However, the company was in financial trouble and in a shaky position.

It was for this reason that Barrett, and others put the knowledgeable and experienced Feustel in the presidency. His abilities would be needed to solve the problems of the company. Barrett remained as company legal counsel, a position he and his firm had held for years. Sam Greenland continued as vice president and general manager. (Greenland stayed with the company until 1925 when he moved on to St. Louis and a successful career as head of the St. Louis Public Service Company.) All four of the small city properties were, and had been, operating at a deficit. The Wabash and Peru lines were not expected to do better than break-even but the Logansport and Lafayette city lines were supposed to be profitable and they were not. Logansport had had its labor problems and also had too much old track work as a legacy of the three-way battle to capture the street railway. The Lafayette Street Railway Co. was a special problem. It had been acquired as the earliest part of the

The Ft. Wayne-Decatur modernized with a new car design. The bodies came from the St. Louis Car Company and were mounted on new car trucks at Spy Run shop during the summer of 1916. ***Both photos —George Krambles Collection.***

Wabash Valley System and had a high bonded indebtedness. By 1918, the Lafayette property was in poor physical shape with much of the trackwork worn out. The local system had been heavily assessed for the new Main Street bridge. Unregulated jitneys were grabbing a high percentage of the Lafayette-West Lafayette business. Most of the rolling stock was old. Seven single truck Brill nearside cars had been bought in 1913 for the lines and these were supplemented by other cars from Fort Wayne. All the original cars had long since been scrapped.

Feustel, throughout 1918, conducted an exhaustive study of the system realizing the rail and power company utility was slowly slipping toward bankruptcy. He presented the opinion that the capitalization was faulty to the point where a fair return could not be earned on portions of the line. The underlying Fort Wayne & Wabash Valley, the Lafayette & Logansport Traction Company and the Lafayette Street Railway Company presented high fixed charges and bonded debt which were an unnecessary burden on the company. The system depreciation reserve account was excessively high. General operating costs of both the rail and power utility were on a slow, steady increase. It was also felt that nearly $1.4 million in improvements was needed.

The company went into receivership on February 8, 1919, in a suit filed by the Evans Coal Company. Feustel was named receiver and faced the problem of undoing the mess. As receiver, he started a much needed equipment rehabilitation program and eventually added more than sixty new single truck one-

The Decatur line also bought a new freight motor in 1916. This view was taken in the Spy Run yard in August 1928, almost a year after the line had been abandoned. Ft. Wayne-Lima 43 (in the background), like the 110, would be reconstructed for other uses. ***Bradley-Harnish Collection.***

New cars pepped up the business on the Decatur line. The pride of the employees also improved as is apparent in this view at the Decatur station. ***Frank E. Butts Collection.***

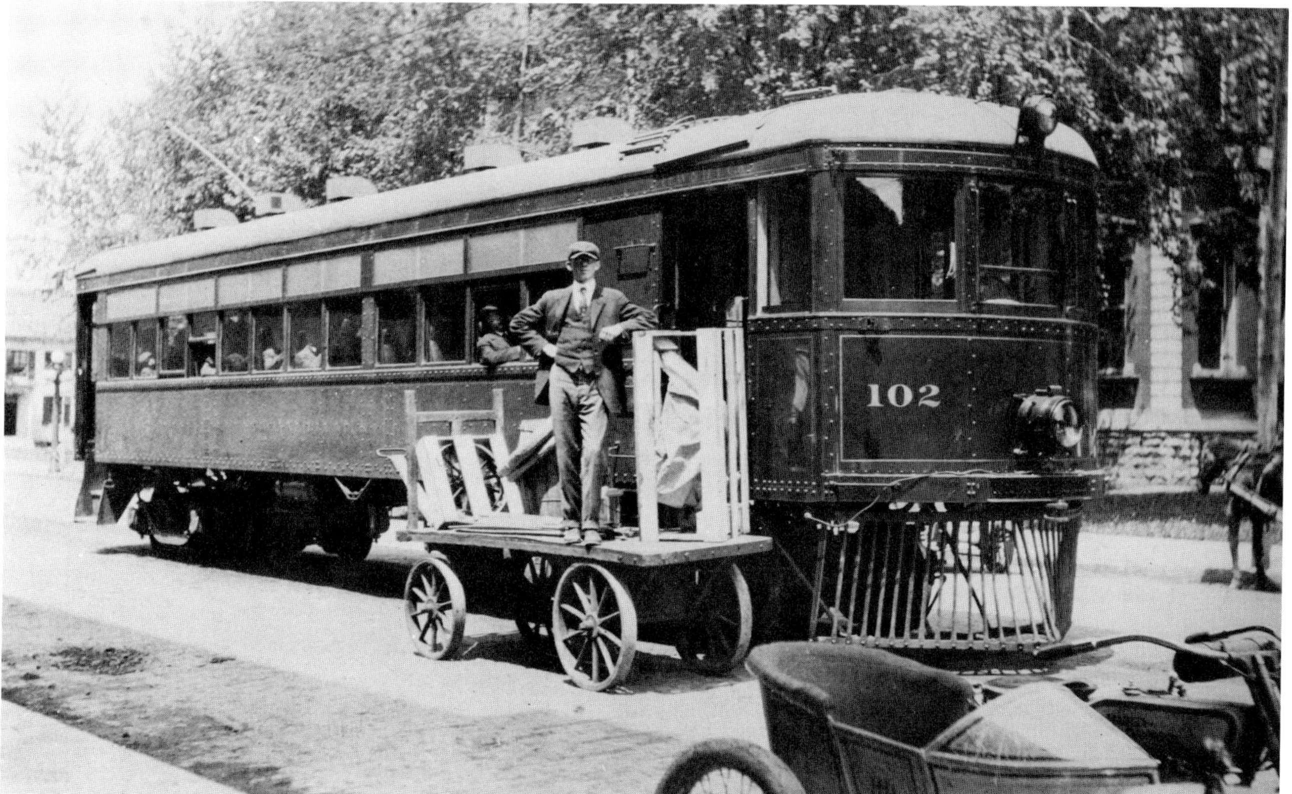

man cars of an advanced design displacing many old single truck cars. Some of these new cars went to Logansport to successfully rehabilitate that system and bring it back into the black. Conversion to one-man operation in Fort Wayne was completed by the end of 1919. This was partly accelerated by a shortage of car men. The public accepted the idea even though there were some operational problems in the early days of one-man operation.

Although the company wanted to get rid of part of the system, the only possible spin-off was the Lafayette Street Railway Company. The Lafayette City Lines was one of the four major pieces which made up the company rail system.

The company properties were divided in three main divisions based on the underlying companies. The Lafayette and Logansport Division included the main line from the center of Logansport to Schuyler and 18th Street in Lafayette. This long Lafayette-Logansport interurban route was no real asset; however, the electric light, heat and power plant system in Delphi and Carrol County, as well as five of the best 300 series passenger cars and two express motors belonged to that underlying company. These could not be cast away.

The portion described as the Wabash River Division included all the lines and properties of the old Wabash River Traction Company from the north end of Wabash through to the west end of Peru. The original south side line from Wabash to Boyd Park was still very much in place but was apparently used only occasionally and for seasonal service. Boyd Park, as a recreation park, had been closed in 1911 and the property sold. The barn and substation were still in use. Five remaining Wabash River Traction cars, still in existence, were also the property of this division.

The largest portion was the Fort Wayne Division which included all the completely merged companies and their property. This meant the Fort Wayne City Lines, the Fort Wayne to Wabash line (ex-Southwestern), the Wabash to the Boyd Park barn northside route (built by the Wabash Valley), the West Peru to Logansport trackage, the Logansport City Lines, and, in Lafayette, the T.H.I.&E. entry on Main Street from Kossuth to Earl and the Battleground line extension north from the Soldier's Home. The Bluffton line and Robison Park line were also included. Most of the rolling stock, including all the remaining single-truck open cars now numbered 357, 359 and 600-638, belonged to the Fort Wayne Division.

Lafayette, at the far end of the system, was left out because a mortgage executed by the Lafayette Street Railway Company, dated June 1, 1893, to secure a $225,000 bond issue

A Union Traction steel 400 in the old canal bed at the Lagro Wabash Valley-Wabash RR interlocking plant. This car unfortunately ran through the de-rail protection at the Wabash crossing and dropped down the steep embankment. ***Bradley-Harnish Collection.***

Newly arrived 240 was the first of the new 1917 double-truck city cars for Ft. Wayne use. The cars were built for use by two-man crews, but would be converted for one-man operation in only three years. **Bradley-Harnish Collection.**

was still outstanding. This fourth part of the system was a liability the Fort Wayne & Northern Indiana could not afford in any reorganization and planned to avoid.

During the corner-cutting period of this reorganization, Robison Park fell an untimely victim of economy. Unfortunately the park was served by a long rail line that ran profitable service for only four months of the year. Car service was provided year round with only four daily trips during the off season, made by a double truck closed car to buck the snow. Although the park continued to be a leading attraction, people began coming by automobile and trolley riding dropped. Declining revenues were not enough to meet the continued cost of first class maintenance or to meet the rehabilitation expense that would be coming in the near future, especially when the company went into receivership. There would also be no new open cars to replace the aging two-man, open cars. President Feustel issued a simple statement to the press that the park would not open for the 1920 season. This was the final word following a series of veiled threats to close the park as that line lost money. All of the park facilities, including rides, concessions and buildings were dismantled and nature slowly took over the site. The park line tracks were torn up back to Parnell Avenue, in the first retrenchment of the Fort Wayne rail lines.

The tiny remainder from Spy Run Avenue and State Blvd. to Parnell was called the Centlivre Short Line (#13). Later, the tracks on North Clinton were taken up and, in part, moved down to the Feeder Canal bed so that the line curved onto its own right-of-way as it swung by the brewery. North of the brewery it was reduced to single track. The line served the "Riverview" residential area which was expected to grow. This line was not a money maker. It could continue to exist as long as the trackage needed no major maintenance.

The Fort Wayne and Northern Indiana Traction Company was sold at a foreclosure sale, December 29, 1919, to a representative of the Bondholders Protective Committee. The receivership continued until April, 1923, when the receiver filed his final report. The four-year receivership was, at that time, the longest in the history of the Fort Wayne courts.

Three "nearsides" and an interurban car on Broadway in 1917. Traffic was slowed by a General Electric employee's Victory Bond parade. **Bradley-Harnish Collection.**

SPECIAL
2 4
376
376
376

CHAPTER 10

The Indiana Service Corporation

On January 15, 1920, a bright new star appeared on the horizon when the Indiana Service Corporation (ISC) was incorporated. Within a few days the Bondholders Protective Committee accepted a proposal to deliver the physical assets of the Fort Wayne and Northern Indiana Traction Company to the ISC in a stock exchange. The Lafayette City Lines were left out, and that system went to its bondholders. However, from March 1922, until abandonment March 13, 1923, ISC was saddled with the isolated three mile stretch to Battleground. At the same time the Wabash Valley Utilities Company, another power company, was delivered to ISC. The new corporation officially assumed control May 1, 1920, with Feustel as president. With a clean slate, ISC began to push a vigorous new program throughout the twenties.

The ISC set about in a strong and confident manner to renew and strengthen all aspects of the property: interurban lines, city lines, and power facilities. The street railway and interurbans were always kept as a separate operating segment from the power facilities of the company. Electric power, the other "half" of the utility, had for some time overshadowed its early ancestry as only a part of the traction lines. The interurban properties went through some exciting changes during the 1920's.

The fleet of eighteen heavy wooden motor cars was continually rebuilt to bring them up to more modern standards. The big, 61-foot, ex-palace cars were among these. Five of the old 40-foot, ex-Southwestern, trailers had come in the sale but only the 82 and 83 were kept in rail passenger service.

Feustel was very interested in the Arthur Redderson-designed cars in use on the Decatur line. Newer truck and control designs were now available that could make this attractive design even more practical for future uses.

The Fort Wayne, Van Wert and Lima Traction Company, which had been operated under a lease, came back to life on January 24, 1921, as an independent company following the collapse of the Ohio Electric Railway and its breakup into various original companies. As a part of the dissolution agreement, the former leased and subsidiary companies were to get back their equipment or substitutes. The Lima line was to receive eight cars but only six were still in existence, so two, big, 60-foot, classic, Cincinnati-built cars were sent along. Although in fair condition, none of the reacquired cars had been modernized and they were expensive to operate by 1920 standards on the somewhat marginal route.

In mid-1922 a big Lake Shore Electric Railway car appeared in Cleveland's Public Square signed for the through Lima run with an additional front window sign, reading "Fort Wayne." Departing at 7:30 a.m. the big car would arrive in Fort Wayne at 3:30 p.m. after a run of 222 miles over four connecting rail lines. Through service was arranged by Indiana Service Corporation. The original plan envisioned a continuous through run to Indianapolis via the Union Traction Co., but that company would not agree to changes in their schedule to accommodate the service. The Cleveland-Indianapolis run would have required a twelve hour run over a 345 mile route and an all-time record long distance run.

In 1924 ten new lightweight interurbans arrived. Six of the new lightweights went to the FWVW&L as 90-95 and the remaining four went to the ISC. Pictured here is FWVW&L's new car 92. ***George Krambles Collection.***

The twenties brought new steel cars, but the older wooden cars continued in regular service. Two 300 series cars are operating in a multiple unit and pulling trailer 82. ***George Krambles Collection.***

Above: *A proud display of the new steel cars for the Northern Division-Lima line taken at the Spy Run shops on August 15, 1924. All the cars are decked out in bright red paint. The 90's were in heavy use, but the 323's had been orphans and were out-of-service since the May 1924 Roanoke collision.* ***Below:*** *The new limited trains of the ISC were taken to all points on the line in special trips to show off the new two-car parlor trains that would make the through, limited-stop Wabash Valley runs.* ***Both photos —Bradley-Harnish Collection.***

The result of not paying attention to orders—car 306, on the left, was not supposed to be on the main line when the Wabash Valley Flyer came through on May 19, 1924. Car 322, on the right, rammed through half of the 306 (which was empty) on the west edge of Roanoke. ***John Rehor Collection.*** *The next day the cars were pulled apart (photo at left) and a decision was made on salvaging the interurbans. 322 would be salvaged and reconstructed as freight motor 53, but 306 was considered more than a 50% loss and so was stripped of useable parts and destroyed on the site.* ***George Krambles Collection.***

The Cleveland-Fort Wayne run was a unique through run but it was not practical and the Lima-Fort Wayne portion was soon separated.

The Lima line had been in the hands of receiver Henry C. Paul since February 1, 1921. Paul had originally built it for the Schoepf-McGowan interests and it was returned in its original state with little improvement. Almost one and a half million in mortgage bonds were outstanding and in the company reorganization the old bondholders were offered less than one-third of their bond value. A new company, the Fort Wayne-Lima Railroad Company, was organized on December 10, 1926 and took over the property from the receiver on April 1, 1927 for $150,000. New issues replaced the older issues.

While these transactions were taking place the actual operations were directed by ISC officials. Cost reduction was mandatory and Redderson went to St. Louis Car Company for an improved design, medium weight, car. Improved techniques allowed a design, at 51,000 pounds, that was nearly 8,000 pounds lighter, although four feet longer, than the Decatur line cars of 1916. Ten, new design, cars were ordered and these began to arrive in April, 1924. Six were lettered for the Lima line and four for the ISC. All were painted a brilliant red with gold trim. The six Lima line cars, (90-95) went into immediate service and virtually eliminated the need for the old wooden cars. The new cars also proved to be popular, fairly fast, and much less expensive to operate.

The four ISC cars (323-326) were placed in trial service on the Wabash Valley route and on some through runs to Indianapolis. Both the ISC and Union Traction were investigating new car purchases and, although the Union Traction had ten heavy, standard, steel cars,

Above: *ISC's big steel interurbans were the acme of development of their car type. They were fast, comfortable and relatively smooth riding. At least one of these cars is still in use over 55 years later.* ***To the left:*** *Car 379 on one of the demonstration trips is stopped on the tow path at the abandoned Lagro locks of the old Wabash & Erie Canal.* **Both photos —Bradley-Harnish Collection.**

the two companies had not decided on what to buy. Lightweight cars, less costly to operate, appealed to both companies. An announcement in the Electric Railway Journal of May 17, 1924, stated that Union Traction was contemplating construction of ten new cars of the model developed by Redderson for ISC.

Two factors changed this lightweight car viewpoint when both companies suffered serious accidents involving their heavy wooden cars. The Union Traction's head-on collision at Fortville, on February 2, 1924, cost thirteen lives. Hard on the heels of this came an ISC accident.

On the evening of May 19, 1924, a westbound local passed an eastbound extra passenger train which was waiting in Mahon siding, about a mile west of Roanoke. To the local conductor's surprise, he noticed the two-car extra train, back out onto the main line. The crew of 306 and 307 had misread their orders and the extra train headed east, toward Roanoke, where they collided head-on with car 322, running as the Wabash Valley Flyer, the crack Fort Wayne-Indianapolis limited train. Five were killed and one died later from the accident. The 306 was destroyed.

The ISC and Union Traction recognized that mixing small, low floor, cars in among the large, high floor, cars in regular service could lead to even worse consequences if another such accident should occur...and no one wanted a repeat of the high floor-low floor Kingsland accident. Neither company could afford a total replacement. The Union Traction then purchased a series of fifteen standard, heavy, steel cars, comparable to their existing ones, and ISC's new 323-326 went into storage.

Extensive mainline interurban rehabilitations were made to the ISC in 1926. Five of the finest (and heaviest) all-steel interurban cars ever built and two deluxe parlor-buffet cars were placed in service on such fast through runs as the "Wabash Valley Flyers." They also took over the other limited runs to leave only the better wooden cars for local

The 309 was photographed on December 24, 1925 fresh from the shops. ***Below:*** *The 309 poses in its new (though short-lived) paint scheme of brilliant red with gold trim.* ***To the right:*** *An interior view of the 309 shot from the forward baggage compartment, showing the standard smoker section with the passenger section beyond.* ***Both photos —Bradley-Harnish Collection.***

Below: *351 (formerly 501) was carefully rebuilt and modernized...it was partially steel-plated to match the appearance of the newer steel cars, the arch windows were covered and it was painted in the bright red with gold trim. Though the car looked "like new" posed here on Pearl Street, December 24, 1924, the improvements were only cosmetic and would not be repeated. This car met a tragic end on June 3, 1925, destroyed in a head-on collision with Union Traction 409 near Kokomo.* ***Bradley-Harnish Collection.***

trips. The remaining old equipment was stored for specials and emergency use.

The Fort Wayne & Northwestern Railway Company had slowly slipped into a quiet decline. They closed their Kendallville power plant in 1922 and bought power from the ISC. By May 1924, negotiations were underway to sell out to the ISC for $472,200. This was completed by August when ISC officials assumed the officer and directorships of the Northwestern. The last corporate meeting was held on November 3, 1924, although the company continued to exist and was not dissolved until September 21, 1936. The four orphan, lightweight cars (323-326) were then put to work on the ISC's new "Northern Division" replacing the old, heavy cars late in 1924. Since they would be the only passenger cars on the line any accident would involve similar cars.

The Marion and Bluffton Traction Company in 1925, was reported in the trade journals as having been sold to a group of Gary men headed by Charles W. Chase, who represented the Insull interests. On February 10, 1925, Chase was named President of the new company. Samuel Insull, Jr., President of Midland Utilities was among the announced owners.

At a meeting held July 20, 1925, at the Peoples Gas Building in Chicago, notes and an equipment trust for two cars, to cost $32,000, were authorized. They were announced as lightweight 45-passenger cars, including a

The Ft. Wayne Traction Terminal was a busy place most of the time. ***Above (left photo):*** *Typical action at the Ft. Wayne Traction Terminal shows that all types of people passed this way including some whose identities remain a well-kept secret.* ***Above (right photo):*** *Cars from all over the state came to the terminal; a THI&E car is on the west track after coming in on a special. Car handling crews begin breaking up the special with trailer 82 about to be uncoupled.* ***Below:*** *The terminal from Main Street. In the near row are ISC 320, FWVW&L 45 and ISC 325. The second line holds an ISC 300 series car, ISC 354 and a 325 series car.* ***All photos —Bradley-Harnish Collection.***

smoking compartment, mounted on Brill 77-E-1 trucks, to be built by the G. C. Kuhlman Car Company and to be numbered 1 and 2. They would have been very nearly identical to the new Gary Railway cars. Apparently Midland Utilities had a falling out with Kuhlman as subsequent Gary cars and the two M&B cars were built by the McGuire-Cummings Car Company.

The Marion and Bluffton Traction Company was sold to the Indiana Service Corporation, on July 27, 1927, for ten dollars. (In the purchase ISC also acquired a light and power business.) The company was formally dissolved on September 17, 1928. With this action

The Pearl Street freight depot during the FW&NI era. This depot was improved, but continued overcrowding caused its demise and replacement by a new freight depot. **M. D. McCarter Collection.**

The Commerce Drive freight terminal was opened in 1928 and became an immediate success and center of much activity. ***Above:*** *The new freight terminal viewed from the east.* ***Below:*** *The freight terminal viewed from the west. ISC freight motor 50 is visible—this is the only known view of this car.* **Both photos—Bradley-Harnish Collection.**

Above: *Freight motor 53 (later 853) pulls ISC 167, 168, 166, THI&E 243 and two unidentified box cars on May 11, 1925. This freight motor was rebuilt from passenger car 322, the one salvaged car from the 1924 Roanoke collision.* ***Bradley-Harnish Collection. Below:*** *The ill-fated ISC 853 (formerly 53) was again the victim on August 21, 1929 at France siding on the Lima line. This time, though, it was virtually destroyed and only the trucks and frame were salvaged to make up a new 853.* ***Dr. Reed C. Prugh Collection.***

all the interurban lines in the Fort Wayne area were finally under the control of ISC.

The Fort Wayne-Decatur line ceased operation on August 9, 1927. A local group, in a suburban area known as Gardendale, proposed to run the 2.5 mile stretch of track south from the end of the city car line on South Calhoun Street to the substation at Philleys. They supposedly worked out an arrangement with ISC and were to start service at 6:00 a.m. on August 10. Something happened and they never started. On August 18, the ISC announced that no cars had run since the ninth and that dismantling operations had begun.

Not only a railway operator, Indiana Service Corporation continued to purchase power companies and also to acquire a number of bus companies operating intercity lines. In 1927, ISC operated over twenty intercity motor coaches. Services were offered to South Bend, Warsaw, Peru, and Marion, Indiana and also to Coldwater, Michigan. Some of these supplemented rail service but were not considered as a replacement. The phenomenal growth and expansion of ISC can be attributed to the Insull utility interests which gained control January 1, 1925. Well over 200 miles of track were included in the rail-power system's operations.

In downtown Fort Wayne the interurbans shared special trackage with the city lines. This included, besides the line on Pearl Street, two large loops using Harrison, Columbia, North Clinton and Main. West of Webster Street and between Pearl and Main a three track terminal served the interurban cars and intercity buses. Two converted houses served as office and station buildings. The passenger terminal facilities were adequate, but certainly far from impressive.

Electric freight service received better treatment. The Wabash Valley lines had recognized freight potential and participated in the

Eastbound freight motor 56 with one trailer runs through the Wabash RR interchange east of Lagro. ***M. D. McCarter Collection.***

Marion & Bluffton's 202 at the Paris, Illinois plant of McGuire-Cummings. The 201 and 202 were sufficient to hold the regular schedules on the line with a few old wooden cars for spares and extras. ***George Krambles Collection.***

The surplus Ft. Wayne-Decatur 103 was redesigned by Arthur Redderson into a useful one-man car. The reconstruction work was done as an experimental/pilot project at the Spy Run shop. ***Above:*** *The "reborn" car was photographed on Broadway near Illsley.* ***Below:*** *The interior of the newly modernized 327 had bucket seats and introduced a new standard of comfort to the ISC.* ***Both photos —Bradley-Harnish Collection.***

Central Electric Railway Association interchange and joint traffic arrangements. The C.E.R.A. and its affiliated groups also worked out joint passenger arrangements and through fare rates.

Fort Wayne's first electric freight service was handled from the Pearl and Harrison station. In 1906, a complete freight terminal was built west of Harrison on Pearl Street. In the smaller cities freight was usually handled through the local station. The 1906 freight station became a very busy and crowded place

The success of the 327 brought the quick conversion of the 323-326 to one-man operation. ***Above:*** *The 325 has just rolled out into the sunlight from the Spy Run paint shop ready to go into service on the ISC Northern Division.* ***To the left:*** *The 325 after remodeling had an all new interior with tiger-stripe, plush bucket seats in the forward passenger section. The smoker section with all leather seats was in the rear beyond the lavatory (right rear).* ***Both photos —Bradley-Harnish Collection.***

as cars from many distant traction lines were always waiting for loading or unloading. The business continued to grow and grow—rocketing beyond the capacity of the terminal. For years the freight facilities were congested.

ISC recognized freight as a valuable adjunct to the survival of the interurban and took steps to improve the situation. Old passenger cars were reconstructed into freight motors to speed the movement of freight cars. The old terminal was abandoned and replaced with a new terminal on the near north side. This was located on a newly built street with double tracks down its boulevard center. The Commerce Drive terminal was far superior to the old freight facility and much better appearing than the passenger facilities. The improved handling methods, the new building and the carefully planned layout were widely hailed in the leading traction journals. Not only was service improved and speeded through efficient handling, but additional steps were planned. In 1928, tracks were built from the back of the Spy Run plant, west across North Clinton, to the interurban's Northern Division. This line had an interchange track with the New York Central and an underpass under that steam line. Other trackage was planned to run west from the freight terminal along the NYC and Nickel Plate to the west city limits near Lindenwood Cemetery. Use of this bypass would eliminate crossing the Wells Street bridge and reduce street running to a minimum. Other special rights-of-way were secured, in part, on the west side for these bypasses. High voltage transmission lines were also to use the land for the enlarging power business. No tracks were ever laid on this land.

While the 1920's were kind to ISC, the Union Traction had not been as lucky, with the real future of the interurban industry peeking through. The big Union Traction fell into receivership on the last day of 1924. The company whose trackage and best cars were once the epitome of good maintenance, put much of

The beautiful reincarnation of passenger car 310 as freight motor 47 emerges from the Spy Run shop in July 1927. ***Bradley-Harnish Collection.***

its resources in main line passenger equipment, while the freight equipment standards fell far behind those of its economically strong northern neighbor. Consequently, ISC crews soon grew to dread the thought of finding a joint operation train made up of UT freight equipment. This reversed an earlier picture, when everyone envied UT's pioneering of all-steel passenger cars and well maintained service equipment. ISC's cars seldom failed, but UT's had developed habits of breakdowns which snarled traffic. Often, a freight train would arrive with one or more shorted traction motors under the big "freight motor." Control shorts produced numerous stories of freight motors wandering away from where they were parked. Other short circuits created minor fires which threw a scare into the train crew, although ISC was not immune to car fires. ISC cars usually had "Golden Glow" incandescent headlights, whereas UT still used arc lights which were tempermental with a habit of flickering out at dark and inopportune points. An ISC crew finding themselves on UT property at the end of a run would go to great lengths to hide or lock up their precious headlight. These precautions saved the lamp from being "borrowed" by UT personnel. Arc headlights, and, on the line, plug-in telephones were considered unnecessary nuisances.

A great deal of time, money and engineering went into the interurban rolling stock during the mid and late twenties. New ISC steel cars joined the five, bigger, heavy wooden cars on the Wabash Valley route. Along with the 375 series cars the company reintroduced limited parlor trains and two special cars 390-391—were added at the same time. These were the same length and also powered. They introduced a new standard of quality which was more for show than profit.

All the 375 series cars were capable of hauling big loads at good speeds. For example, in a series of Purdue Christmas 1927 Holiday specials, the fastest Lafayette-Fort Wayne run, the Highball Special, using #376, made the run in 2 hours 57 minutes, one hour faster than regular limited runs. Students made good connections with other rail lines at Fort Wayne. The speed average was 38 m.p.h.

During early 1928, the four-year-old lightweights, 323-326, came in for some changes as

ISC's new 324, pictured at the Spy Run Avenue yards, would service the Northern Division. ***Bradley-Harnish Collection.***

Above: *A full crowd of "passengers"—mostly ISC employees—demonstrate the comfort on the parlor cars where seats could be moved for passenger convenience. Some of these seats have out-lived the cars by over 40 years and are still in use at Ft. Wayne PTC, though their comfort is questionable.* ***To the left:*** *The 390 and 391 parlor cars carried a complete railroad style diner kitchen for preparation of light refreshments as well as full meals.* ***Both photos —Bradley-Harnish Collection.***

the Feustel-Redderson interests were pursued. The action resulted from the decision to use one man cars on the Northern Division to further reduce costs. The three surplus Decatur line cars (101-103) helped spark this interest as the company searched for some way to use them. The 103 was selected and thoroughly rebuilt. The back became the front and a folding entrance door with enclosed step was substituted in place of the former left rear vestibule entrance. The right rear entrance was plated over and a new operator's station placed there. The baggage compartment was now in the rear. New Commonwealth trucks, new controls and motors were bought for 103 which emerged as number 327. The job was so well done that it was difficult to recognize the car as being a former sister to 101 and 102.

The 323-326 received like treatment. All got new twin bucket-type seats and the seating was reduced to 48 from 50. These cars also got

ISC freight motor 55 with a five car freight train at Ardmore siding on Taylor Street in Ft. Wayne (August 1926). ***Bradley-Harnish Collection.***

four 60 h.p. motors giving the car a new top speed of 55 m.p.h. All were painted in the yellow-tan with green striping and lettering. The five one-man cars were officially placed in service on August 23. The last of the old wooden cars, usually used as a spare, were now retired. Another advantage was the cost reduction of one-man operation on the lightly traveled Kendallville-Waterloo lines.

This very successful rebuilding and one-manning was copied by many companies including the later Cincinnati & Lake Erie which had some newer but very similar two-man mid-weight cars. The pattern was later used by Indiana Railroad to convert many heavy steel cars. Car 324 was sent to Cleveland for the American Electric Railway Association convention display. The trip was made on the afternoon of September 21, 1928 and took seven hours and forty-five minutes. Two ISC operators took the car, picking up a pilot operator for each "foreign" company. The car ran as a second section of a Lake Short Electric limited train from Fremont to Cleveland. The 324 had some clearance difficulties getting into the subway entrance and crossing the lower level of the Superior Street bridge in Cleveland. Run onto the special tracks outside of the Municipal Auditorium, the excellent, innovative, rebuilt car was much admired by A.E.R.A. members.

Some of the old wooden passenger cars were surplus and were reconstructed for other uses. The 310, for example, was reconstructed into #47, a handsome freight motor to improve freight service. Cars of this type were used on "The Lindbergh Freight," a typical fast freight operation from Indianapolis to Detroit. The 318 miles were covered overnight at an average speed of 22 m.p.h. using the lines of the Union Traction to Bluffton, ISC to Fort Wayne, Fort Wayne-Lima Railroad to Lima, Lima-Toledo Railroad to Toledo, and Detroit United Railway beyond to Detroit.

The "end of the run" at the Ft. Wayne freight terminal for the crew of Ft. Wayne-Lima freight train 33. ***Bradley-Harnish Collection.***

CHAPTER 11

The Spy Run Plant

The sale of electric power in the early Wabash Valley's day had been a convenient source of extra revenue and a captive power supply for the all-important railway utility. To the officials of the company in those early days it was only the tail of the dog. Over the years the power business and its profits consistently rose while the fortunes of the helpless interurban empire sank lower. By the mid-twenties the tail was thoroughly wagging the dog.

The new and modern Spy Run Avenue powerhouse had been built south of the old Jenny Electric Light and Power Company plant, and across Kamm Street. It was opened in 1907 and subsequently enlarged in 1913, 1917 and 1925. This central generating station served forty-four communities, the four city lines and five interurban routes. Time and new long-distance transmission technology passed it by. By the early 1950's the plant was shut down, placed on a stand-by basis, and finally torn down in 1962-63.

Additional land was acquired north of the old powerhouse and this area used for material storage. The draining of the feeder canal and storage reservoir left a large low area in the rear of the property. When the city built the new Rudisill School, the old school building behind the powerhouse was sold to the traction company. This building was used for several purposes, including a paint shop and bus garage. The ex-school grounds were largely used for coal storage.

The former Kamm Street power plant building was used as a car storage barn until it burned September 11, 1918 with a loss of three cars. The destruction of the old building brought about the possibility of a significant change. The Indiana Service Corporation determined to concentrate its railway operating facilities in a modern complex of several buildings incorporating offices, shops and eventually replace the downtown barns. During the twenties they built a physical plant that could be rivaled by very few traction companies and certainly not surpassed by any company of equal size. The city agreed to vacate Kamm Street to the company to facilitate this expansion.

The first new building was built, in 1923, on the destroyed car storage building site. The first floor housed a paint shop, inspection pits, washing equipment and light service department. Shop offices were on the second. The building faced Spy Run Avenue and was north of the powerhouse. Several smaller buildings of lighter construction were put up, west of the powerhouse, for garaging the motor buses and service vehicles. A large car yard was constructed north of the new Inspection-Office building with a long series of ladder tracks entered from Randolph Street which was the north boundary of the property. This was a change in operation as cars were now stored in the open instead of housed inside or at least under cover. At the Randolph Street entrance a small building called the

At left: *The first steam power plant in Ft. Wayne was located in this building at Spy Run Avenue and Kamm Street. The Jenny Electric Light & Power Company operated it before it was replaced by the Chestnut Street power plant. The building was used for car and materials storage. This view shows the east side of the building on Spy Run Avenue.*
At right: *The Kamm Street barn from the northwest showing the "L" shape of the one time powerhouse. Work car 17 is from the 101-108 series of city cars.* ***Both photos —Bradley-Harnish Collection.***

Farebox House was erected. It contained a large vault for the lockboxes brought in from the arriving cars. Exit from the yard was made onto Spy Run Avenue.

In the earlier years, most of the open cars had been stored on a narrow strip of land on the east side of the Spy Run Avenue opposite the powerhouse and between the street and river. The open cars could either be run downtown or out to Robison Park as needed. This trackage was removed and a landscaped park area was created.

In 1925, plans were made for the dry pond section. It was filled in and a large 185′ x 207′ shop building constructed. This excellently equipped building became the system's main shop building and handled all repairs, rebuilding and new construction. Painting was later moved to this building. Eight tracks entered the building which had its own yard and ladder tracks to serve it. The two story Engineering Building, to the south of the shop was also completed in 1925 as a companion building in the complex. The Engineering Building housed the engineering staffs for the rail and power systems. This completed the spacious, well laid out and integrated physical plant for both power and rail facilities.

Almost coincidental with the opening of the new shops, the Huntington Shop was destroyed in a spectacular fashion. The old shop burned in a severe electrical storm on June 24, 1927. Lightning not only set the building on fire but also destroyed the phone lines. By the time help was summoned, it was too late to save the building.

The poorly located Glasgow Avenue barn remained on the company books for many years, long after it was closed. The buildings were razed and the property sold during the twenties.

The Spy Run Avenue facilities replaced Baker Street for repair work except for some light service work. In 1928, 31 base, 5 tripper and 19 industrial streetcars operated from the South Car House (Baker Street). At this same time 25 base, 6 tripper and 15 industrial cars operated from the North Car House (Spy Run). These 101 city cars handled over 61,000 passengers each day with full service run for twenty hours out of twenty-four. By 1930, streetcars were gone from Baker Street. The power people stored trucks at the old site. The earliest depression years made it practical to close and eliminate any remaining operations at the dilapidated Baker Street facilities. The old powerhouse building on Baker at Clinton survived until late 1977 and was last used as a new car show room.

A number of substations were built to feed power to various users. At the Webster Street Substation current was reduced for railway,

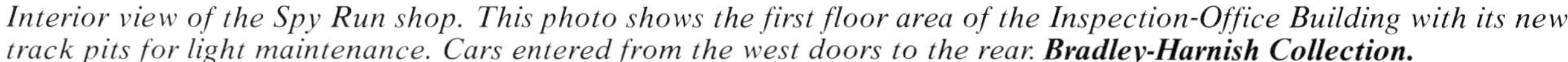
Interior view of the Spy Run shop. This photo shows the first floor area of the Inspection-Office Building with its new track pits for light maintenance. Cars entered from the west doors to the rear. ***Bradley-Harnish Collection.***

This 4-track Inspection-Office Building was built in 1923 on the site of the old Kamm Street barn. At the same time, the 24-track, north car yard was built to relieve the Baker Street congestion. ***George Krambles Collection.***

Above: *The rear (west end) of the Inspection-Office Building.* ***Bradley-Harnish Collection. Below:*** *The east front of the 8-track shop building, pride of the ISC and envy of many companies.* ***George Krambles Collection.***

Shots of the Spy Run shop. The ***photo above*** *was taken with three Ft. Wayne-Lima cars (48, 95 and 47) in for service.* ***Bradley-Harnish Collection.*** *The* ***middle photo*** *shows the methods employed to temporarily energize cars to be moved within the truck shop. Note the insulated pole to hook over the trolley wire.* ***George Krambles Collection.*** *The* ***bottom photo*** *shows steam derrick car 1119 and freight motor 52 south of the Inspection Building about 1923. This was formerly Kamm Street vacated to ISC.* ***Bradley-Harnish Collection.***

The former Huntington powerhouse was used as a substation and storage building. This view was taken looking east from the front of the shop. ***Bradley-Harnish Collection.***

The Engineering Building was the last of the major new buildings in the Spy Run complex. ***Above:*** *The building is seen as completed.* ***George Krambles Collection. Below:*** *The foundations for the building are being laid while the new shop facility nears completion.* ***Bradley-Harnish Collection.***

Scenes within the Spy Run yard. The ***top photo (below)*** *shows part of the car yards north of the Inspection-Office Building. Car 225, pictured here in the center, was a one-of-a-kind rebuild. The* ***bottom photo (below)*** *shows assorted car types in storage including an ISC 300 series car and several Ft. Wayne-Lima 41-43 series and 44-46 series cars. The foreground ramp was used to unload cars.* ***Both photos —Bradley-Harnish Collection.***

Above: *The McKinley Avenue yard in the late twenties, showing work equipment and surplus wooden interurban cars. The three cars in the left foreground are of the 300 series.* ***Bradley-Harnish Collection. Below (top photo):*** *An overall view of ISC's Spy Run shop and yard in 1926.* ***George Krambles Collection. Below (bottom photos):*** *The remains of the Huntington shop after fire destroyed it on June 4, 1927. The view on the right was taken looking north; this twisted steel and rubble had been a useful shop facility before the fire. The remains of passenger trailer 81 are in the far corner.* ***Both photos —Bradley-Harnish Collection.***

The Waterloo station was on a "wye" at the east end of the Northern Division. This view is from the north with the N.Y.C. railroad behind the photographer. ***Bradley-Harnish Collection.***

light and power. On McKinley Avenue a large substation was built to feed power to the western and southern interurbans, plus light and power in the area. Adjacent to it was the McKinley Avenue Yard with one building to house the yard office and the track and overhead departments. All ties, bricks, paving materials and poles were stored here. This location was convenient to the two main interurban lines and removed the need for hauling these materials back and forth through the city. The old wooden interurban cars were later stored in the McKinley yard and it eventually became the scrapping center for city and interurban equipment. Its usefulness dwindled with the passing years and the demise of the interurbans. McKinley Avenue yard was closed and sold in the mid-forties with the substation retained for streetcar, trolley bus and commercial power.

Two other building and equipment assortments came to the ISC in the acquisition of the Fort Wayne & Northwestern (the ISC Northern Division) and the Marion & Bluffton Traction Company. The facilities were brought into the control of and continued in use under ISC with the exception of the Kendallville powerhouse which had been closed down in November, 1922. Power then came from the Spy Run Avenue power plant.

The powerhouse was located on what is now the grounds of the East Noble High School complex. It has been removed as was the four track car barn that also stood on the site. The car barn remained in use into the early 1930's and was used as a storage barn

The Vandalia interlocking plant on the Northern Division south of Garrett. Car 225 was taken from service in 1928 and used to replace the earlier wooden tower (above) as part of this plant. ***Bradley-Harnish Collection.***

Auburn station on the Northern Division. ***Bradley-Harnish Collection.***

Yoder substation and passenger station. ***Bradley-Harnish Collection.***

New Haven station on the Ft. Wayne-Lima line. ***Bradley-Harnish Collection.***

Kendallville station looking west. Car 303 is picking up a trailer box car (300 series cars rarely were used on the Northern Division; however Northern Division passenger cars did not have rear drawbars). ***Bradley-Harnish Collection.***

Remains of the Boyd Park barn after the March 21, 1916 tornado. ***Above:*** *The view was taken from the south. The "wye" in the foreground remained after the south side Wabash-Boyd Park route was torn up.* ***Bradley-Harnish Collection. Below:*** *A view from the west shows a plow standing to the left and the Wabash River Division line car holding up part of the roof.* ***M. D. McCarter Collection.***

for spare Northern Division cars. The location was remote even to the small town of Kendallville.

The Fort Wayne & Northwestern had four substations. The Kendallville substation was in the powerhouse and remained active after the power plant was shut down. The other three were built of yellow brick in 1914 when the power system was changed. In Auburn the passenger station building contained the substation. At Vandalia the substation was located next to the wood passenger station and interlocker tower just north of the Vandalia Railroad crossing. (The combination station and interlocker was replaced first by city street car 225 and then a newer smaller frame building.) At Wallen the substation was shared by the passenger station.

Passenger and freight facilities were located in each community. The Huntertown station

The Bluffton car barn (at Harrison, in Bluffton) was a substantial five-track barn and the home shop for the MB&E. ***Bradley-Harnish Collection.***

was brick (built in 1912). The Garrett station was an old two story frame building. The little Avilla station was built of wood in 1914 and was so small that in 1916 the company claimed its value at $25. The Kendallville passenger and freight stations, built in 1909, were one story frame structures. The Waterloo station was a one-story frame building.

The Marion & Bluffton had two substations. The Van Buren substation was brick and frame and the Liberty Center substation was concrete block and frame. At Marion the company owned a freight station. The station at Warren was brick and frame. Station facilities were shared at other locations. The Marion and Bluffton did have a large brick and frame, five track, car barn officially listed as "Harrison" although it was located just west of Bluffton. The building was the M&B's home base and had complete shop facilities. This car barn, however, had little value beyond storage after the later 1920's.

One other stray property was the old Boyd Park complex of the Wabash River Traction. The building survived the adjoining park by thirty years. Built as a power plant and shop, it contained only the substation and car storage after 1908. Spare city cars for Wabash and Peru were kept there as well as the west end open cars and surplus interurban cars. On March 21, 1916 a tornado did severe damage to the west end of the building. Part of the walls collapsed and the damaged roof fell and destroyed several cars. The building was valuable enough to be rebuilt and continued in use until the early 1930's.

SOUTH WAYNE
4
511
EXIT
AT
REAR
511

Fort Wayne 1920-1931

CHAPTER 12

Indiana Service Corporation had to meet the responsibility of rebuilding and reequipping the Fort Wayne City Lines. Major rail improvements made between 1918 and 1925 included the purchase of 130 new cars which handled all the base service. These sturdy cars, of both the single and double truck variety built to ISC's specifications, were far superior to the lightweight Birney car variations built for many medium sized city properties. No other city of comparable size could boast, in quantity, streetcars equal or superior to those in Fort Wayne. The new cars closely approximated the features suggested in an "industry" designed "standard" car. The only criticism that could be leveled at this excellent car fleet was that, in order to standardize, the same basic design was used for several years without incorporating some of the innovations that were developed during this period.

ISC also had to rebuild and extend the city trackage. Some of the rails had been in place for over thirty years. Many lines were constructed of patchwork, with rails of varying heights and weights imbedded in deteriorated paving. In carrying out this work, the company promoted good public relations with informative signs and press releases. Whenever a major street rebuilding job was carried out, prominently placed signs were set up along the way explaining that ISC was rebuilding a certain number of blocks at a specified cost, always followed with "just to give you better streetcar service." A huge electric sign downtown carried ISC's trademark, the unique script phrase "Traction-Light" which was the name commonly used by local residents in reference to the company.

Services and improvements were "sold" to residents in a good public relations program. This included the new attraction of the dollar weekly pass which allowed unlimited rides. Fort Wayne was the second city (Racine, Wisconsin was first) to introduce the weekly pass. The weekly pass was used for over thirty years.

Clinton Street, between Main and Lewis, was relaid with double track in 1920. A few years later the city widened Clinton by reducing the parkway on the east side by about ten feet. This created a serious problem for the streetcars, as the tracks were well off center. The southbound track was in the west side traffic lane and northbound track in the center of the street. This widening project had been undertaken to remove part of the motor vehicle traffic from the congested, parallel Calhoun Street. The move was a success, from this standpoint, but meant that passengers alighting from northbound trolleys had to be fleet of foot to reach the sidewalk in safety. To avoid serious pedestrian accidents, a series of safety islands (the only ones built in the city) were constructed for the use of the northbound cars.

The first new track work commenced in 1921 with the complete rebuilding of the tracks on Wells Street and the extension of the Huffman line south on Franklin to Third and west to Runnion. This extended line became the Third Street line. However, Huffman trackage was not renewed and much of the new track was single track. Next, in 1922, the Lakeside line was extended east to Kensington Avenue. These were the last sizeable single track extensions.

Placing new rails on West Main. Work motor 22 and a flat car are at work; methods employed were thorough but slow. ***Bradley-Harnish Collection.***

Above: *The double-tracking of Creighton Avenue (west from Calhoun) in 1924, showing one of the excellent and informative public relations signs placed by ISC during the 1920's.* ***Below:*** *Track reconstruction at Main and Clinton Streets in 1920. This work forced an East Washington car (282) to crossover and run east on Main Street on the westbound track. This entire area has changed with the City-County Building occupying the area now (only the fire hydrant remains).* ***Both photos —Bradley Harnish Collection.***

Work moved forward at a quickening pace in 1923. Many of the existing lines were completely rebuilt with double-track to accommodate heavier traffic and tighter schedules. These included Pontiac, from Calhoun to Anthony; South Wayne, from Creighton to Kinsmoor; Calhoun, from Pontiac to Rudisill, and West Creighton from Calhoun to South Wayne, which was finished in 1924. The Pontiac line was extended three times: to Plaza Drive in 1923, to Alexander in 1925, and to Queen Street in 1927. Single track with turnouts was eliminated on these lines.

Broadway, in 1924, was extended south from Bluffton Road to Rudisill and East State was double-tracked from Spy Run to Pleasant Avenue just west of the switch for the State School coal yard. A long freight spur was built north from the Taylor line to serve the mushrooming Dudlo Manufacturing Company. City cars also used this trackage, at shift changes, to carry the employees.

Early in 1923, a long siding was built south from the Lima line, along what became Bueter Road (now Coliseum Blvd.), as part of the agreement made by the ISC to provide street railway service to the newly completed International Harvester works. Lewis line city cars used the Lima line interurban to the Bueter

Safety Zones appeared on Clinton Street as a result of the widening of the street which left the car tracks off-center. These safety islands were used at the high traffic areas of Berry, Wayne and Washington Streets (for northbound cars only) to avoid serious pedestrian accidents. ***Bradley-Harnish Collection.***

A city car turns west onto Huffman from Wells Street. Interurban cars (north to Garrett) entered Wells from the right; the Wells Street waiting station is partly visible. Southbound interurbans could crossover to the south track at the switch in the foreground. ***Bradley-Harnish Collection.***

The 1923 reconstruction on Pontiac Street. ***Above left:*** *Pontiac, east from John Street, showing the thorough methods used in track reconstruction in the 1920's—including the temporary track laid on the right.* ***Above right:*** *Westbound car 202 stopped on Pontiac at Anthony Boulevard as workmen prepare to rebuild the intersection. This car acted as a shuttle from this point to the end of the line.* ***Below left:*** *Work motor 52 with ballast cars working on Pontiac west of Anthony Boulevard.* ***Below right:*** *The intersection of Pontiac and Anthony. This intersection contained an awkward jog from Pontiac Street, which was smoothed considerably in the reconstruction. Here a portable cement mixer is at work.*
All photos—Bradley-Harnish Collection.

City car 212 (a rebuilt "nearside" type) runs around the new track work on Pontiac Street, September 25, 1923. The car is delayed by the electric track welder which took power from a hook placed on the overhead trolley wire. A group of children on their way to the James Smart Elementary School gather to watch the operation. ***Bradley-Harnish Collection.***

Looking east on Pontiac from Weisser Park Boulevard in August 1923. The city car is on the new trackwork, which is unpaved, and the temporary construction track is still in place. ***Bradley-Harnish Collection.***

Above: *Laying double-track on South Calhoun in front of South Side High School (1923). Work car 19 is just north of Oakdale Drive.* ***Below:*** *Oxford Street, about 1929, was the last new car line built by ISC. Here 449 heads west on Oxford. The new concrete poles can be seen along the curb line.* ***Both photos —Bradley-Harnish Collection.***

All photos above *— The 1925 reconstruction on the West Main Street line.* ***Top photo:*** *West Main looking east toward Camp Allen Drive and the St. Mary's River bridge with motor 52 and gondola 1005. Loose dirt is being dumped on the street in preparation for rebuilding the bridge approach.* ***Middle photo:*** *Two city cars with a work train between—only the temporary track is in place.* ***Lower photo:*** *Single-trucker 276 runs around work motor 22 on the temporary track. The car is operating the Route 8, West Main-East Washington line.* ***Photo at left:*** *Among the many items of special equipment used in track reconstruction was a Kerwin rail grinder shown here on the West Creighton line near Hoagland Avenue with a circular saw attached for cutting up tree branches. The grinder served also as a belted power source.* ***All photos —Bradley-Harnish Collection.***

Production line methods were used in the construction of steel-rod reinforced, concrete poles at the McKinley yards. These poles were widely used in Ft. Wayne though they were not strong enough for intersections where there was considerable and heavy overhead wiring, especially when double wires for trolley coaches were added. ***Bradley-Harnish Collection.***

Road extension. In 1925, the East Lewis line was extended south on Edsall from Chestnut to Raymond by a winding route and then east to the Harvester works, where a large loop was constructed at Bueter Road. This new line was planned to serve the growing new East End industrial complex and replaced the temporary Bueter Road siding. West Main was double-tracked and the Taylor line rebuilt in the same year.

State Street was again extended in 1926 when it was double-tracked east of California and extended to Randalia. The line still had some long stretches of single track. This was the year of least activity during the twenties.

Nineteen twenty-seven saw activity grow at a new pace as the East Washington line was completely rebuilt. The South Wayne line was extended to Maxine Avenue, where the street widened to boulevard proportions with a center parkway. Rails were laid in the street crossings as far south as Pettit in anticipation of laying tracks in the boulevard center, but the line was never extended. An isolated set of double track work was laid in the new Lafayette Street underpass, from Brackenridge to Murray, but was never connected to any line and never used.

A completely new line, Oxford, was built in 1928. The tracks were built south on Warsaw from Pontiac and then east on Oxford Street to Anthony to serve a newly developed residential area.

As industries moved into the east-end area the company felt the need of a second line to serve the workers. The Pontiac line, with the aid of a new underpass at Wayne Trace, was extended east then north to the Lewis line at Raymond. This second line to the Harvester loop was completed in 1930.

Work motor 21 pushes crane car 1140 on Warsaw Street during the 1928 building of the Oxford line. The concrete poles, widely used in Ft. Wayne, were made by the company. ***Bradley-Harnish Collection.***

Rebuilding of the track work at Baker and Calhoun Streets brought out the portable crossover track assemblies. Northbound car 510 is moving onto the crossover as 409 (now on the right side) rolls off. The motor man on car 400 patiently waits to head south. ***Bradley-Harnish Collection.***

Some of the city lines were extended at the expense of dying interurbans. The demise of the Decatur line brought an extension of service to the Calhoun line. It was extended to Cornell Circle where the interurban trackage had branched off onto private right-of-way. A short section of the Lima line was used for a short time to provide freight and passenger service to the Inca Manufacturing Company (Phelps Dodge Magnet Wire Corp.).

The last major trackwork was completed during 1931 and 1932. Calhoun Street was relaid with new rails from Main to Wallace. A number of unused crossovers were removed and the Baker Street turnout rebuilt. This brought most of the trackwork up to modern standards. All of this city trackwork used "T" rail as ISC and its predecessors never used special flanged streetcar rails. The standard "T" rail did not hinder interurban car wheels with larger flanges.

North from Calhoun and Wallace where the East Creighton turned east. The rail was replaced late in 1931 in some of the last track restoration efforts. The switch for this corner was electrically operated. ***Bradley-Harnish Collection.***

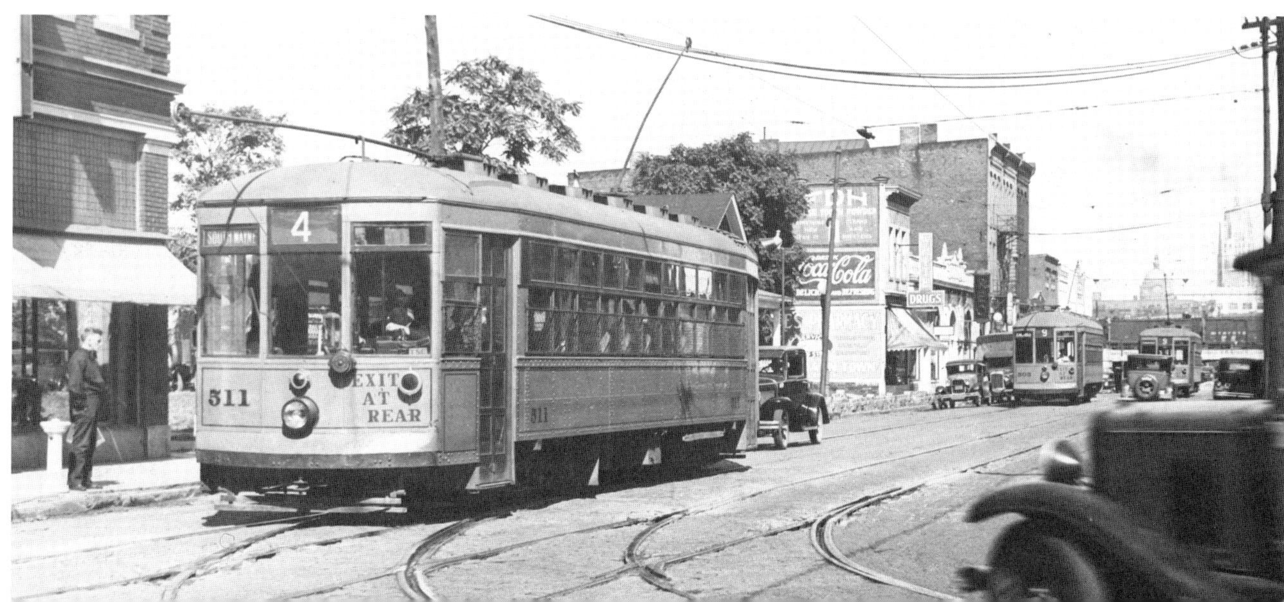

SALE
325

CHAPTER 13

Indiana Railroad...the "magic" interurban

On July 2, 1930 the course of the Indiana Service Corporation was drastically changed although it would not be immediately apparent. On that day Midland United Company bought the Union Traction Company. This was the climactic step in a series of acquisitions by the Insull interests. The extremely complex chain of events affecting the electric utility properties of two holding companies began in the preceding decade.

During the 1920's the Insull utility interests acquired control of several major Indiana public utilities, giving them a firm hold on the electric power service in many large communities and sizable rural areas. The principal companies were Interstate Public Service Company and the Indiana Service Corporation. These companies were not interconnected. Geographically interspersed with them were several electric utility companies controlled by the American Public Utilities Company. Three of the power companies acquired by Insull were also in the electric railway business. The various rail and power systems were a geographic hodge-podge of overlapping service territories, yet there were several major Indiana areas they did not serve.

Insull's initial Indiana consolidation organization was the Public Service Investment Company (incorporated on June 22, 1924) which became the Midland Utilities Company on August 19, 1924. Midland Utilities obtained control of the Chicago South Shore and South Bend Railroad, Gary Railways and the Indiana Service Corporation and several utility properties. From a railroad viewpoint this consolidation might have contained the germ of a master rail combination but none of the three were physically connected and they were about as different in character and operation as any three properties could be. They ranged from the roadside interurban and street railway of Gary to heavy railroad standards of the South Shore. Each of the three was modernized to standards that fit its particular type of service.

A further step in the overall consolidation occurred on December 26, 1928 when Midland Utilities Investment Company was formed. This new company changed its name to Midland United Company on August 29, 1929. It acquired immediate control of all the common stock of the Midland Utilities Company.

The Midland United Company's president (later Chairman) was Samuel Insull, Jr. Although only in his mid-twenties, he was given this choice plum due to his father's faith in him and because of the excellent management team available to him. This team included Samuel E. Mulholland (NIPSCO), Charles W. Chase (Gary Railways) and Robert M. Feustel (ISC). Feustel was selected by the elder Insull, to be the executive vice-president and then president of the Midland United Company succeeding Sam Insull, Jr. He was also the chief executive officer of most of the companies in the Midland United group. The primary business of Midland United was electric power production and distribution.

The eventual plan for the Indiana Railroad probably grew out of a 1929 trip Sam Insull, Jr. and Feustel took from Fort Wayne to Indianapolis for an inspection trip of the Interstate Public Service Company. En route they had a good look at the Union Traction Company's problems in providing interurban service. Already in receivership and operating at a deficit since 1924, Union Traction was obviously in deep financial trouble and could not keep operating efficiently. However the Union Traction had a lot to offer Midland United beyond a deteriorating electric railway property.

Its subsidiary, Traction Light & Power Company, supplied power to fifty small communities and many rural customers along its interurban routes but not to key cities such as Anderson, Muncie and Marion. This power subsidiary was a valuable asset and it made money. Union Traction's longer main rail lines were not losing money as operating units but the shorter branches were either marginal or

Night at the Ft. Wayne terminal in April 1936. The 325 sits on Track 1, ready for a trip northward to Garrett. ***Ralph A. Perkins.***

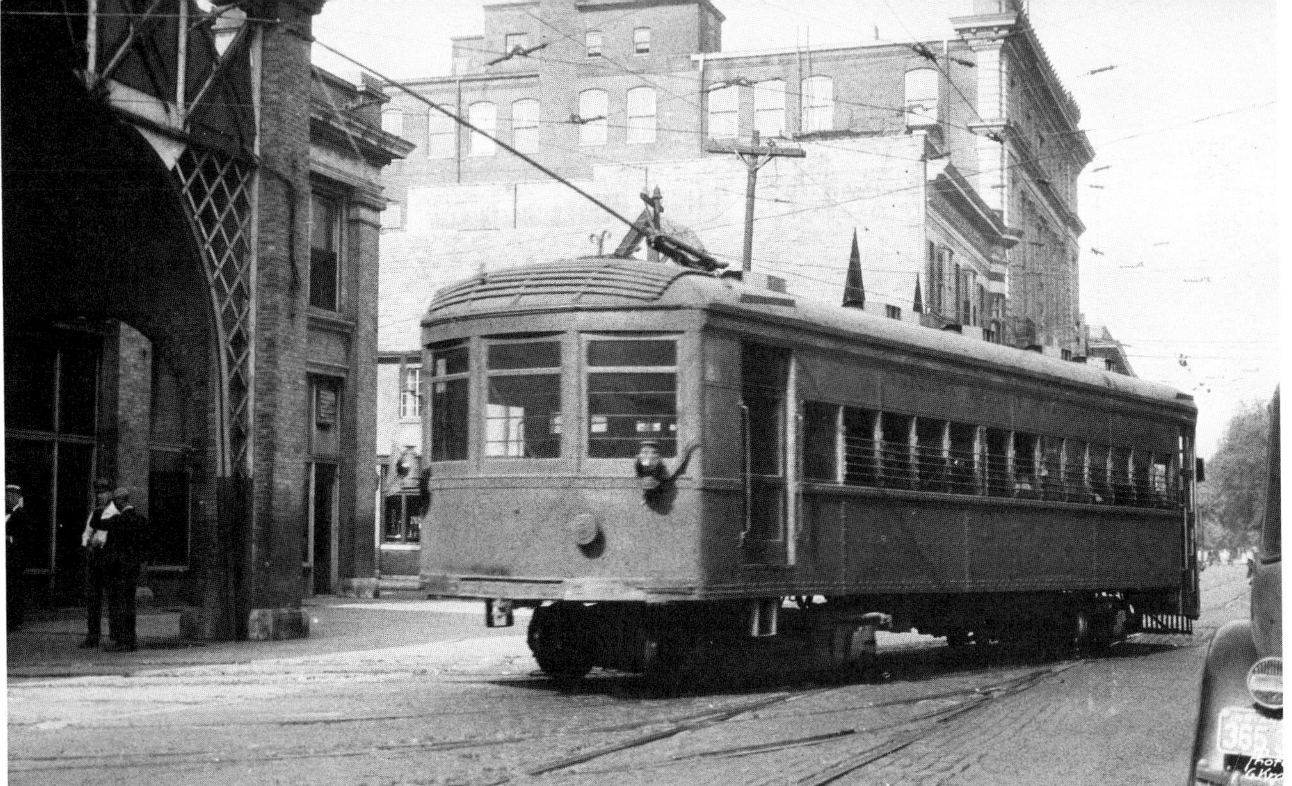

Indiana Railroad brought the 327 to Muncie to run the New Castle line soon after this former Union Traction line came into the IRR. ***George Krambles Collection.***

deficit operations. The company had gone into receivership in 1924 because, even though the net operating revenue was in the black, it could not meet the interest on the bonds of underlying companies.

Although the details are not a matter of public record, Midland United did approach the court appointed receiver, Arthur W. Brady, during 1929 with a view to acquiring ownership of the Union Traction's profitable assets. This would include the power company subsidiary, some of the rail lines and the power lines that went with them. The other rail lines would be completely abandoned.

Brady petitioned to end the Muncie-Union City line and the Anderson-Middletown line. All were abandoned on February 28, 1930. At the same time, abandonment proceedings were started on the Kokomo-Logansport and Wabash-Marion lines. These two were abandoned on September 15, 1930. All of these lines had been marginal or deficit operations.

In June, 1930, Midland United entered into an agreement with the committee representing the bondholders of the Union Traction and its underlying properties. Approximately 60% of the outstanding bonds were purchased. Reportedly, Midland paid $2,829,000 for $14,201,000 principal amount of the traction company's first mortgage bonds. The bondholders, not stockholders, held the real control of the Union Traction and its underlying companies as they did with many other interurbans. These individuals and banks had to be offered an amount that they would accept or they would oppose the whole sale. Buying out all or the greater majority assured a smoother transaction in acquiring the physical properties of the Union Traction.

On July 2, 1930, the Traction Light & Power Company was purchased on behalf of the Midland United Company itself. Midland United Company purchased the mainline properties (but did not accept certain leased railway property) of the Union Traction Company on behalf of a new company known as Indiana Railroad. Both were bought at foreclosure for $3,923,110.

The Indiana Railroad, a magical subsidiary of Midland United, was rapidly organized in 1930...and a better, more descriptive name for this Camelot of electric railways could not have been conjured by the greatest magicians. Feustel and Insull had created what is possibly the best known and least understood of interurbans. However, its corporate shell was much older, having started life July 20, 1920 as the Gary Connecting Railroad. In 1925 the Gary Railways Company purchased the Gary Connecting Railroad which then ceased to be an operating company. The shell was available and was put to use by changing its name to Indiana Railroad. Robert Feustel was named president of the new company. Henry Bucher (an ISC vice-president) was placed in charge of the railway department through which the

Robert M. Feustel (1884-1932)

Robert Max Feustel was a native of Fort Wayne, Indiana born in 1884. For many years, he was a dominant figure in the field of electric transportation, valuation and organization—often considered the foremost authority on these subjects. He was largely responsible for the plan under which the electric railways in Indiana were united as the Indiana Railroad System. And he participated in a number of historic and famous cases for the transportation industry including those of the Philadelphia, Pittsburgh and Boston rapid transit systems; the Canadian systems; and innumerable mid-west and western systems.

Mr. Feustel graduated from Purdue University in the Civil Engineering class of 1905 and joined the Fort Wayne & Wabash Valley Traction Company as an assistant engineer. His genius for appraisal and his uncanny ability to strip any situation of extraneous detail were soon apparent, and brought him other assignments such as assistant chief engineer in the formation of Wisconsin's Railroad Commission—the first commission of its kind in the country. After three years serving the Wisconsin body, Feustel became chief engineer for the Illinois Railroad Commission and began laying groundwork for procedures which would dictate standards for subsequent commissions to follow.

Feustel left his activities with railroad commissions to become a consulting engineer, devoting all his time to this endeavor until 1917 when he was named president of the Indiana Service Corporation at Fort Wayne. Mr. Feustel was well paid as head of Indiana Service Corporation, though he remained free to take on independent consulting work for other properties with additional fee compensation. His consulting activities, plus his heading of a major Indiana public utility, brought him into close contact with Samuel Insull and his associates. This led to ISC being purchased by Midland Utilities Company which enlarged Feustel's responsibilities in Indiana electric utilities matters.

Later, Samuel Insull Sr. was interested in finding ways to get more time for his son, Sam Jr., to operate as vice-chairman of several of the elder Insull's numerous companies; consequently Sam Sr. approached Feustel asking what he would want in compensation to expand his own responsibilities and devote full time to the Insull properties. The salary discussed was quite high (it would make Feustel the fourth highest paid executive among the Insull group). Sam Sr. and Feustel met for about half an hour on the matter and emerged together with Insull saying simply, "All right Junior, go ahead; good luck gentlemen."

Sam Insull Jr. and Robert Feustel became great friends working closely in the many Indiana projects that came under the umbrella of Midland United Co. They understood each other and Sam Jr. truly admired the quickness and ease demonstrated by Feustel in their business dealings. As an example, Insull Jr. often recounted his first meeting with Feustel in 1926, when in the midst of a difficult purchase negotiation, Feustel calmly passed him a note with "the" suggestion that led to the consummation of the purchase.

Feustel's untimely death on May 8, 1932 was officially listed as the result of acute nephritis, though it was actually the result of a peculiar form of cancer which in only 18 days progressed from the base of his spine to his shoulders. Junior Insull was with his wife, mother and father when the news of Bob Feustel's death was phoned in to them. His mother said, "Sam, I have never before seen Junior so broken up by anything."

The Insull family and business associates were not alone in feeling the loss of this man as probably no other individual in private life in Indiana was better known and respected than Robert Feustel. At the time of his death, this well-known personage was president and chief executive of the Midland United Company; president of the Chicago, South Shore & South Bend Railroad; president of the Indiana Service Corporation, and head of the Public Service Company of Indiana and the Indiana Railroad—all operating electric railway lines in Indiana.

Footnote: This information came from a Samuel Insull Jr. note to the author, the Electric Railway Journal, McGraw-Hill Publishing Company; and newspaper accounts in Fort Wayne.

operation of the other electric railways in central and southern Indiana controlled by the Midland United Company would be coordinated, unified and closely managed. These included portions of ISC, the Northern Indiana Power Company and the Interstate Public Service Company and comprised an interurban railway network which the Insull interests hoped would be economically sound. The entire operation, Indiana Railroad itself plus these other rail lines, was classed as the "Indiana Railroad System." There were no formal leases for the "system" operated utility properties. All the accounting was handled by the respective companies, as before, to record profit and loss tallies for the various lines. Indiana Railroad handled passenger and freight revenues, returning a certain portion to each line, based on ownership. It was a somewhat loose "gentlemen's agreement" but it succeeded.

The Indiana Railroad System could draw on a wealth of good middle and top management people who went on to the payroll of the new Indiana Railroad. Many of these people came from the ISC—the interurban engineering force in Fort Wayne was virtually wiped out. Staff reductions produced economies for the utilities. Indiana Railroad not only profited from having the better rail property people available but they enjoyed an added plus in sharing corporate officers. Most Indiana Railroad officers were officers of the other utilities and did double duty, serving both companies. The "pooling" of talents brought the services of many skilled and highly qualified people to the Indiana Railroad. The shared management meant that the several interurbans could be operated under the direction of one central supervisory organization. Coordination of services and schedules for the benefit of riders and shippers was one of the expected results.

Samuel Insull, Jr. in a 1979 interview dispelled the myth that Midland United had plans to link its various interurban lines in the Chicago area with the Indiana Railroad System. There never was such a plan. In Insull's words, such an idea "was not considered on the passenger side."

The THI&E, the other large mid-Indiana interurban system, was not under Insull control. It had been in financial straits although solvent. In anticipation of an earlier attempted merger it had borrowed more than $2,000,000 in short-term notes. This strain pushed the company into receivership with Elmer W. Stout, President of the Fletcher American National Bank of Indianapolis named receiver on April 21, 1930.

Several attempts were made to complete a purchase of the THI&E properties. This was a very complicated process because the THI&E was a complex mass of owned and leased properties which included both a sizable interurban rail operation and several city operations, including Terre Haute, and electric power facilities. The electric power holdings of the company were also more attractive than the electric rail facilities. Finally, on June 23, 1931, an agreement was completed. In the sale the Midland United acquired the electric power facilities which were transferred to another company and retained some of the main line electric interurban rail and city street railway properties.

In both the Union Traction and the THI&E purchases, Midland United, separated the rail and power facilities as much as possible. This placed the Indiana Railroad on its own as a separate company operating its own rail lines as well as the "system" rail lines owned by Midland's power companies. Also, unusual among interurban railways, Indiana Railroad had no outstanding bonded debt and the only stock was held by Midland United. Midland, however, advanced large sums of money to the company. Indiana Railroad would survive on its rail operating earnings without having these earnings paid to bondholders, thereby wiping out the chances of the lines showing a profit. This was a simple financial operating method and would demonstrate whether the Indiana Railroad could survive.

On the electric power side, Public Service Company of Indiana (formerly Interstate Public Service Company) gained ownership of Traction Light & Power which Midland United had separated from the Union Traction properties.

In the division of the THI&E, both the power and the rail facilities around Terre Haute were assigned to Terre Haute Electric Company, Inc. This whole company was leased to Public Service Company of Indiana. Its retained rail lines, the Terre Haute city lines and the interurban line to Brazil, were operated for them as part of the Indiana Railroad System.

On those parts of the THI&E east of Brazil, Midland United separated the power and the rail facilities. The power business went to Public Service. Midland United assigned the ownership of the Indianapolis-Brazil, Indianapolis-Richmond, New Castle-Dunreith interurban and the Richmond City Lines of the THI&E to the Indiana Railroad. Like the former Union Traction properties, these were owned directly by the Indiana Railroad.

The various acquired or controlled street

railways were handled in three different ways. City street railways were owned at Marion, Anderson, Muncie and Richmond (Marion was sold in 1933). In the system operations, Indiana Railroad managed the power company-owned street railways at Logansport, Peru, Wabash, Terre Haute, Jeffersonville, and New Albany. The Fort Wayne city lines were retained by and controlled by Indiana Service Corporation.

With the organization plans out of the way, the Indiana Railroad began setting up its operating plans. The August 1, 1930 change-over (nearly a year before the THI&E acquisition) provided the public with very little show. Even the schedules were almost the same. However, the interurban routes were fewer as the Indiana Railroad pared down to what Feustel and others thought might still be viable operations. Connections with the Ohio interurbans still existed via Richmond-Dayton and Ft. Wayne-Lima.

Unified control meant that all of the rolling stock could be utilized as most practical. One of the few visible changes was a cosmetic change as some ex-THI&E and ex-Union Traction cars had their old corporate names painted out and the new Indiana Railroad name added. Public Service and ISC cars were not changed, when they came into the "system," and continued running in their original paint and lettering although sometimes routed to different lines. Red, green, yellow and orange cars carried the system name or were used by the system. Fortunately, at this time, there were few numerical conflicts so the ownership lettering did little to upset anything. The assortment of big cars could not readily fit into Feustel's plans for a high-speed modernized interurban system although it would still be necessary to use most of the steel cars for some years. The wooden units were rapidly retired. The heavy, parlor car trains didn't fit either and their last regular runs were made on December 11, 1930. ISC's two parlor cars, only four years old, went into dead storage.

Indiana Railroad had three car design philosophies to consider and evaluate for the new cars that would be needed to excite the public and attract riders. The available designs included the Marion & Bluffton's two lightweight interurban cars which, like those in use on the Gary Railways, were really overgrown streetcars. The two cars were relatively slow and not especially comfortable. The other car style already in use on the ISC property was the Redderson designed 323-series cars. These cars had been very successful, especially since the 1928 rebuilding for one-man operation and the equipping of them with new and comfortable seating. The cars could run up to 55 m.p.h.

ISC 325 repainted for Indiana Railroad at the Ft. Wayne Traction Terminal. ***George Krambles Collection.***

and were smooth riding. They had also turned operations of the Northern Division of ISC into the profit column.

The third design could be borrowed from the recently modernized cars put in service on the Cincinnati & Lake Erie Railroad Company. Its new lightweight cars were very fast and they offered a comfortable ride. The cars had been an instant hit with the riding public. C&LE car 128, a lightweight coach-parlor unit, was brought over the Fort Wayne-Lima line on August 6, 1930 to Fort Wayne where it was carefully inspected by the ISC car design engineers, including Arthur Redderson, as this team plus a few others would design new cars for the Indiana Railroad System. The 128 continued its late Fall trip by making a test run to Indianapolis via Bluffton. The car was run as an "extra" to check clearances and to see how well it would perform on this Indiana Railroad System mainline route.

In Indianapolis, the 128 picked up Sam Insull, Jr., Robert Feustel and other Midland United officials the morning of August 7. The Midland party went north over the old Union Traction line to Peru, then west to Lafayette over the ISC lines. The Logansport to Lafayette portion gave the operator a chance to make some high speed runs over the long, level trackage. The 128 then returned over the line to Peru and continued on to Fort Wayne. The car then went back to the C&LE over the Lima line.

The following year another C&LE lightweight was run in regular Fort Wayne-Bluffton service for several days to study times in preparation of the new schedules for the new Indiana Railroad cars.

The lightweight cars performance had been impressive. The C&LE cars rode little better than the ISC 323's but with four 100 hp motors, as opposed to the 323's four 65 hp motors, the C&LE cars had more rapid acceleration plus a higher top speed. The lightweight high speed idea looked good. With this in mind Indiana Railroad proceeded with its own plans to design their own lightweight, high performance cars.

Thirty-five high speed cars were ordered in a split order from two builders. Fourteen of the new cars, numbered 50-63, were built by American Car & Foundry at Jeffersonville, Indiana. These cars were deluxe, coach-lounge in design. Twenty-one cars, numbered 64-84, were built by Pullman-Standard Car Manufacturing Company's Chicago plant. The Pullman-built cars were of a coach-baggage configuration. The two car groups were very similar in appearance and virtually identical in performance. Unique to most lightweight cars, these cars were equipped with multiple-unit controls and could operate in trains of up to three cars. The total cost of the 35 cars was approximately $980,000 ($28,000 per car).

Indiana Railroad's new cars began arriving in July 1931 and were readied for service at the Anderson shops. Some were sent to Spy Run Shop for inspection by the local shop crew who would have to do some maintenance on them. The cars were also put on the line to test every aspect of the operation and to see how well they performed. Speed tests were also run to determine where the cars quick acceleration could be put to good use. The Midland chiefs took a similar spin to the 128's trip in one of the new cars. Once again the long tangents between Logansport and Lafayette provided some opportunities for fast running.

The cars aroused curiosity and in the interest of gaining good publicity several were put on public display in a number of on-line cities. All the Indianapolis-Fort Wayne, via Bluffton, and the Indianapolis-Louisville trains were handled by the new lightweights and the schedules were immediately improved. With a fleet of thirty-five new cars, it was now possible to segregate the lightweight cars from the older, higher and heavier passenger cars, thus reducing the potential for disaster in a collision of dissimilar cars.

Service on the Marion & Bluffton line of the ISC was abandoned by Indiana Railroad on August 16, 1931. The slow lightweight cars, although one-man, were of no further use to the Indiana Railroad and were kept in reserve at Spy Run yards.

The important connecting Fort Wayne-Lima Railroad Company slipped into receivership on June 30, 1931 largely because it owed a $65,000 power bill and had operated at a net loss in 1930. On June 30, 1932, the ISC-managed line ceased operation altogether and approximately 100 people had to look for work.

On the night of May 21, 1932, the interurban line from Peru to Lafayette was also abandoned. This meant the end of some of the best midwest interurban trackage. This was the first major portion of the Indiana Railroad to go and the trackage was barely 26 years old.

ISC 323 series cars went all over the Indiana Railroad system even though three cars always remained on the Northern Division. The 326 is at the Terre Haute car barn in 1934. ***R. V. Mehlenbeck /George Krambles Collection.***

At the left: *During a summer's day in 1936, 323 nears the end of its journey turning east onto the street at Waterloo. The NYC Ft. Wayne-Jackson rail line is in the background.* ***Above:*** *Freight motor 845 is on the north end of the Waterloo "wye," ready to return to Ft. Wayne in April 1936.* ***Both photos —Ralph A. Perkins Collection.***

The ISC 323's continued to hold down the Northern Division runs. The "wye" at Garrett was the normal meeting place for three cars. The 324 has just come from Ft. Wayne and is heading toward Kendallville while 325 is heading east toward Auburn and Waterloo. The 325 is riding on a test pair of standard C-50-PL plate frame trucks. ***Glenn Nicely Photo /George Krambles Collection.***

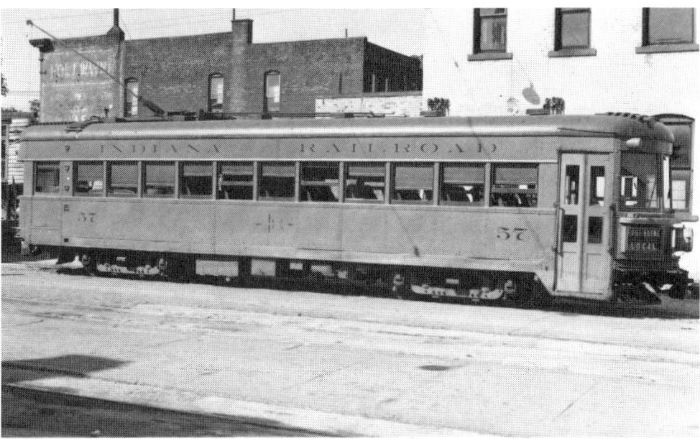

Above: *IRR 54 on the "wye" at the Bluffton station.*
Below: *IRR 58 passes the interlocking signal on the approach to the Wabash RR crossing, August 20, 1938.* ***Both photos — Van Dusen-Zillmer Collection.***

Above: *IRR 57 at the Ft. Wayne passenger station in 1938.*
Below: *IRR 58 at Big Four underpass, Wabash, Indiana (August 20, 1938).* ***Both photos — Van Dusen-Zillmer Collection.***

Below (top left): *IRR 91 (the former Northern Indiana Rys. 352) on track 6 in the Spy Run yards awaiting its next run.*
Below (top right): *IRR 98 (formerly Northern Indiana Rys. 359) stands at the Ft. Wayne passenger terminal in 1936.*
Both photos — Van Dusen-Zillmer Collection. Below (bottom): *The 375 pulls out of the Ft. Wayne Traction Terminal in 1940 heading east on Pearl; it will either be run onto the old freight terminal trackage or head to the Spy Run shops.* ***George Krambles Collection.***

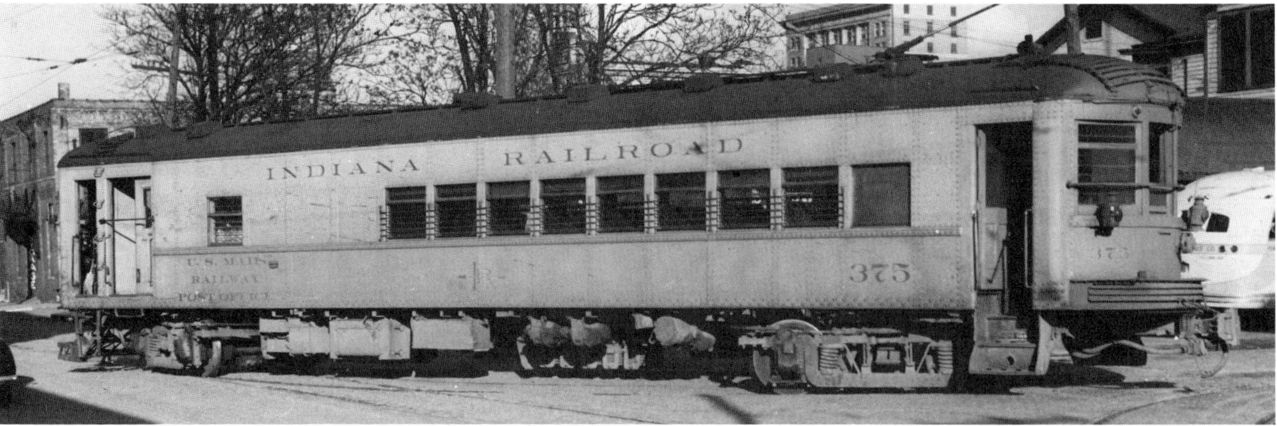

The line had been under Indiana Railroad supervision for less than two years and the loss of this 55-mile main line—the largest single abandonment—foretold of things to come.

In each case, as Indiana Railroad terminated operations of a property other than its own, the responsibility for the property was returned to the utility company that owned it. Each company would then tear up the line and recover its remaining scrap value. The owner's recovery was often very little. For example, the Fort Wayne-Lima line was sold, on July 5, 1933, for $95,000 which was not even enough to pay the indebtedness of the receiver or his attorneys' fees.

Indiana Railroad also pared its properties on owned parts of the system. By the end of 1932, the two Fort Wayne routes, the east-west lines (Terre Haute-Richmond), and the Louisville line were all that was left radiating from Indianapolis.

Midland United had gone to great length to put together a company that could operate as at least a break-even operation. It would seem apparent that the public was given a chance and the policy was stated in a use or lose the service manner. The Peru-Lafayette line, like the others that were abandoned, was a money loser of sizeable proportions and could not be retained.

One interesting facet of the Midland United Company control of several electric utility operations was the ability to "balance" systems. The ISC, the smallest of the three major Insull Indiana companies, had a long, strung-out, power system that followed the interurban routes. The main base was the Spy Run power plant, the sole generating plant on the system. ISC lay somewhat between Northern Indiana Public Service Company (NIPSCO) and Public Service Company of Indiana with the latter reaching far north into the state. Trades, switches and purchases of electricity sales territory among the several companies, which might not have occurred if they had remained rivals, allowed each company to concentrate its territory so that customers and generating plants were closer together. ISC had little to trade but NIPSCO and Public Service traded

Above: *Ft. Wayne-Lima 91, much in need of paint, at the Lima station in 1932 shortly before the line was abandoned.* **Below:** *Westbound IRR lightweight 58 crosses the Wabash RR near Lagro, Indiana on a "rail fan" trip in August 1938 shortly before the line was abandoned.* ***Both photos—George Krambles Collection.***

several fringe properties which made both much stronger companies. However, in all of these dealings, the rail lines were not traded. For that reason alone, ISC retained its power business in the Wabash Valley as far as Delphi.

On May 8, 1932, ISC and the Midland United Company lost a giant when 47-year-old Robert Max Feustel died after a brief illness, first diagnosed as acute nephritis, but what was apparently a virulent, fast-spreading and inoperable cancer. At the time of his death he was president of Midland United Company (estimated value $300,000,000), Indiana Railroad, Public Service Company, Chicago South Shore & South Bend Railroad, vice-chairman of NIPSCO and general manager of the Fort Wayne-Lima Railroad.

June 28, 1933, General Electric Company filed for receivership of the Indiana Railroad over a $328 bill. It was soon revealed that the line owed current obligations of over $210,000. Governor Paul V. McNutt appointed Bowman Elder, as receiver and the magic fizzled.

Indiana Railroad's receivership presented a host of new problems as the friendly "system" relationship was now gone and lease agreements had to be arranged to continue the central supervision by the receiver. The utility company lines in use were leased in October, 1934 along with the better rail equipment. Many cars designated for the Indiana Railroad, and in many cases renumbered, were returned or just never used.

Bowman Elder tried to run the Indiana Railroad to its best advantage and attempted to get it back into a solvent position. His job was made much more difficult and the character of his charge was changed by two major events. The first was a June 9, 1934 bankruptcy petition by Midland United. The second, a real blow to the company's future, resulted from the United States Congress' passage of the Public Utility Holding Company Act of 1935 which would cause the eventual liquidation of holding companies and force them to divest themselves of their rail properties.

In an attempt to cut costs the company began conversion of the better steel cars for one-man operation. A group of relatively new and modern lightweight cars, built for the Northern Indiana Railways and operated from South Bend, were purchased in 1935. Operated on the Indianapolis-Fort Wayne, via Peru, line, they were regularly seen at the Fort Wayne terminal.

Later this line became a test ground when Indiana Railroad buses and trucks succeeded the rail service on September 6, 1938. This had been a relatively successful line, although a money loser, and it offered a good testing ground of trucks and buses running over public highways in substitution for rail cars running on a fixed and expensive rail plant. Elder was pleased with the results and ISC offered no objection to the abandonment of its Fort

IRR 458 was ISC 379 converted to a one-man car. Modified in 1936, both the 379 and 378 (IRR 457) were used for only two years before being retired in 1938. ***George Krambles Collection.***

Five ISC differential dump cars in trail behind a freight locomotive on the Indiana Railroad lines in Kokomo in 1937. ***George Krambles Collection.***

Wayne-Peru trackage. Routes to Terre Haute and Louisville soon joined the ranks of abandoned rail facilities.

On February 14, 1940, petitions were filed to abandon the true main-stem, the Indianapolis-Fort Wayne via Bluffton line along with the New Castle branch. These were the only remaining passenger rail lines. Elder stated, at that time, the main line had lost $51,332 and the Muncie-New Castle line had lost $17,883 in the first nine months of 1939, and that the system had been running at increasing annual losses since 1936. The plan was to substitute buses and motor trucks for rail service as soon as possible.

The Securities & Exchange Commission, on November 1, 1940, initiated proceedings, under the Public Utility Holding Company Act to simplify the Midland United's corporate structure. This action expedited the end of the Indiana Railroad as a rail property and accelerated Midland's interest in disposing of the property to comply with the SEC.

On January 18, 1941, Indiana Railroad ran its last full schedule of trains on its remaining lines. (The last cars pulled in during the wee hours of the 19th.) Camelot's last passenger train had run.

The Fort Wayne arrival of the last Indiana Railroad interurban car ended the era of long distance electric railway passenger service which had begun with so much promise less than forty years earlier. In the generally accepted view of that time (1941), the interurban railroad was old-fashioned, inefficient and uneconomical and had no magical glitter. Motor buses were inexpensive, fuel was cheap and plentiful, and a motor bus and truck company paid few taxes. Based on these assessments, alone, the companies had good reason to switch to buses. Buses and trucks also had the advantage of newly built highway routes which offered more direct and frequently faster routings.

Following the abandonment, Indiana Railroad returned the ISC leased property to the company. Leased cars had been returned with ISC's number 377 being run empty into Fort Wayne on January 19 as the last Indiana Railroad operation on ISC tracks. Over the next few months, following receipt of permission to abandon the trackage, ISC crews tore up the Bluffton Division.

The ISC's Northern Division had not been leased to the Indiana Railroad in 1934, but it had remained in the joint timetable and Indiana Railroad ran the passenger trains. The line's principal freight traffic was coal for the Spy Run power plant and the utility kept the line for itself. Passenger service and freight north of the Pennsylvania Railroad interchange at Butler Center (about one mile south of Garrett) was abandoned on February 15, 1937. Trackage from about one mile north of Butler Center (near the south edge of Garrett) was torn up while the rest remained in ISC freight service and continued to operate with ISC's own equipment. After 1941, ISC kept one line car and two freight motors for this service.

An IRR freight train crosses the Bluffton Bridge leaving Ft. Wayne on January 11, 1941. ***R. O. Dingley Photo / W. A. Steventon Collection.***

A northbound lightweight has just crossed Engle Road in Indian Village, then the southern edge of Ft. Wayne (July 28, 1940). ***R. O. Dingley Photo /W. A. Steventon Collection.***

IRR 69 heads south on Broadway in Ft. Wayne (south of Creighton Avenue) November 21, 1940. ***R. O. Dingley Photo / W. A. Steventon Collection.***

IRR 69, southbound to Indianapolis, runs Broadway and Creighton in Ft. Wayne on November 21, 1940. The new trolley coach overhead is already in place. ***R. O. Dingley Photo /W. A. Steventon Collection.***

Above (left photo): *IRR 62 at Waynedale in 1940. In January 1941 the last car would run off into the distance on this line, and only a few years thereafter, this entire rural setting would be built-up.* ***Above (right photo):*** *IRR 60 enters Ft. Wayne on the new Bluffton Bridge late in the evening of January 11, 1941.* ***To the left:*** *By 1940 the Ft. Wayne station saw buses joining the high-speed interurbans.* ***All photos — R. O. Dingley Photo /W. A. Steventon Collection.***

Line motors 827 and 826, both in the new ISC maroon and cream paint scheme, work at dismantling the Bluffton line in the spring of 1941. This was to be 827's last assignment. ***Bradley-Harnish Collection.***

The Northern Division's line haul rail freight operation (usually daily, except weekends) continued until August 25, 1945. The freight and switching service which required only one 2-man crew produced enough revenue to retain the line that long. Maintenance was minimal and no large sums were expended on the line. After 1945 only the local switching of coal to the plant, in Fort Wayne, remained.

The interurban era was really closed in 1941 with the end of the passenger service. Few people paid much attention to the electric freight service and most were not even aware of the existence of the Northern Division freight only operation. The freight service was a convenience and a small source of revenue. Passenger service was not profitable.

The interurban, light rail concept, was sound enough but it was a victim of progress and its own inflexibility. They were utility owned and unpopular, in later years, because of the losses incurred. Managers didn't want to alibi for these losses which reflected on the company as a whole. The worse things got the more reluctant the companies became to spend any money, if they had any money, to spend. Indiana Railroad was somewhat unique because the owners decided to try and salvage something. Under some sort of tax-free, public subsidy program the higher density lines—and these were few—might have lasted longer.

Northern Division Freight

All photos by John F. Humiston.

A day on the ISC Northern Division with switch motor 817 (August 23, 1941); passenger service had been gone for four years and freight service would last for just four more years. There were several sidings on the line receiving and delivering cars to the ISC. The principal use was the transfer of coal trains to the ISC power plant.

Westbound 817 leaves the back of the Spy Run plant (photo 1) and crosses Spy Run Creek. The right switch lead goes to the NYC and the other under the NYC to the Northern Division trackage east of the NYC.

Photo 1

Photo 3

In the third view, 817 is just north of the Vandalia (Pennsylvania Railroad) crossing next to the "tower" with the brick substation in the background. This is the third tower (the second having been streetcar 225) to control the crossing and "smash paddle" on the signal pole. Trackage, seldom used, continued on for some distance north of here.

In the second view, motorman Baltimore stops the northbound 817 on the West State Boulevard bridge using the later diesel locomotive-operating method of long hood forward.

Photo 2

Photo 4

Looking north toward Garrett (photo 4) just south of the Vandalia RR crossing. This is Cedar Siding, milepost 18.3, and the interchange between the electric and steam rail lines. The 817 is picking up six loaded coal cars.

Back in Fort Wayne, photo 5 shows 817 moving onto the Home Siding off the Northern Division main line with the lead to the Spy Run plant in the foreground.

Photo 5

Photo 7

Looking west in the seventh view, 817 has returned and just cleared the switch from the lead track preparing to move ahead on the Home Siding to pick up two more coal cars. The far track, to the right, was the Northern Division main line which still ran westward for three blocks to the junction at Wells Street.

After August 25, 1945, switching services came no further west than Clinton Street and the interchange lead track to the NYC.

Even though interurban passenger service north of Fort Wayne ended in 1937, the New York Central continued its daily passenger service north to Hillsdale, Michigan.

In photo 6, 817 shoves two loads of company coal eastward under the NYC.

Photo 6

Photo 8

Photo 8 shows gas-electric M202, a railway post office-baggage car, with trailer MT9 (formerly Michigan Railway interurban electric motor car 803) northbound at the Fort Wayne NYC station in August 1941.

109
S. CALHOUN
P14
CALHOUN
RUDISILL
540
4

Fort Wayne 1932-1947

CHAPTER 14

The "thirties" opened on an optimistic note with many people expecting the country and world to bounce back from the crash of 1929. It didn't happen that way and a variety of adjustments were made.

A new car line had been planned for the rapidly developing West State Boulevard area. This area of new homes was to be served by motor buses as a regular city bus route until traffic warranted an extension of the car lines. New trackage was to be built north from Wells and Huffman to West State and then west to Runnion Avenue. In anticipation of the extension, the center of West State remained unpaved, awaiting the never laid rails. The end result was the city's first regular feeder bus line.

No major track construction was carried on after 1931 as revenues sank. The Depression saw a rapid decrease in riding and expansion plans were ended. Actual balance sheet losses were incurred in only 1932, 1938 and 1940, and these were not large losses. A balance between profit and loss was kept by deferred maintenance and corner cutting.

The real beginning of the last chapter for the streetcars occurred in the one minute stoppage of all Fort Wayne streetcars, at 2:30 p.m. May 10, 1932 in memory of company president Robert M. Feustel, the relatively young utility genius who had died two days before, casting much of Indiana in a pall of gloom. Feustel, was better known in the state than perhaps anyone else in private life... unique because he usually avoided the public eye. Governor H. G. Leslie (a fellow Purdue University graduate), Purdue's president Elliott, many prominent Purdue graduates from the business and government ranks, dozens and dozens of Fort Wayne and Indiana citizens, plus many prominent figures from the utility industry (including Samuel Insull and Samuel Insull, Jr.) attended the funeral service of the native Hoosier on Tuesday, May 10.

The Insull utility empire which had brought Fort Wayne the highest standard of public utility service was in difficulties as the grip of the depression tightened. The Insull utilities were financially over-extended and several groups (both political and financial) secured Samuel Insull's resignation from all of his utility and holding companies on June 6, 1932. Midland United and Midland Utilities were forced into reorganization although ISC and the other power utility companies comprising the holding company's properties remained solvent.

John N. Shannahan was named to head the Midland United and he also became the chairman of the company on January 1, 1933. Morse Dell Plain, a Northern Indiana Public Service Company veteran, became ISC president and the ISC headquarters were temporarily removed to Hammond where Midland had consolidated its offices. Dean Mitchell briefly headed ISC before Shannahan was declared president. Both Dell Plain and Mitchell headed NIPSCO in succession. Control of the ISC came back to Fort Wayne at the end of 1934. During the transfer period, local operations were handled by Samuel E. Mulholland, who had headed the NIPSCO and predecessor gas company operations for years. (When ISC and NIPSCO were part of Midland in the twenties, Feustel and Mulholland had adjoining offices, first in the Fort Wayne Traction Terminal and then in the Utility Building.)

Shannahan, came to the Midland and ISC from the Omaha & Council Bluffs Street Railway. He filled several posts in the Midland group that had been vacant since Feustel's death. Shannahan was over sixty and had been in the railroad and utility business since the 1890's. He had enjoyed an excellent reputation, had been president of American Electric Railroad Association (AERA) and was considered to be a fine manager. In his new post, however, he was the appointee of the

The war is on and the prime mover of Ft. Wayne people is public transit. Streetcars and trolley coaches operate together to form a solid line of transportation on Calhoun Street north near Washington Boulevard. ***Bradley-Harnish Collection.***

The 448 heads south on Calhoun at Berry on a quiet 1937 Sunday. The Allen County Court House is in the background. ***George Krambles Collection.***

new controlling owners who had wrested the control of the Insull utilities from friendly midwestern interests. The new owners, largely eastern financial interests, may have had some effect on the course Shannahan chose. It was not a popular course and Shannahan took control with a firm hand. His attitude at this point contradicts his previous success and makes for interesting speculation as to what caused this change. He was not an innovator and acted in a very conservative manner mostly on behalf of the electric and gas utilities in his control. He suddenly had little apparent use for the electric railway properties. He became very unpopular in the public press and antagonized both Fort Wayne Republican and Democrat politicians by some of his actions. This may have resulted from his being an outsider.

Shannahan made his first serious blunder in February 1933 by demanding that the city give the ISC some protection or assurances for the future. He announced a $50,000 loss for 1932 (the books show this to have really been only $33,495) and that he would consider abandoning the streetcar service. His high handed attitude and manner disturbed merchants, industrialists and the city council who were used to buoyant, optimistic and reasonable talk from Feustel. Shannahan's threat set in motion a city attempt to take over the ISC and merge it with City Light that rattled along for years finally ending in a referendum in November 1944. The fight cost both the city and utility considerable time and money. It was totally unnecessary. By the end of 1935, W. Marshall Dale, who had joined ISC in 1930, succeeded Mulholland as operating head. Shannahan died in August 1938 and Dale was named president to succeed him the next month. Both Shannahan and Dale tried to get as much as possible out of the ISC on both the power and rail utility sides. In doing so they aided Midland, the owner, maintain a solid position and preserved the stockholders' investment.

They did very little to better the physical property and neither the power nor rail facilities were improved. The aging Spy Run power plant could not supply all the power needed so more and more was bought from inter-connected electric utilities. Little by little ISC became less of a power producer and more of a power distributor through high tension line tie-ups with several other companies. Actually this course seriously weakened

The East State-Lewis #6 line was still fully streetcar operated in 1937 when the newly-painted maroon and cream 532 crossed Berry Street on Calhoun. This was the most colorful and best design balanced paint scheme. **George Krambles Collection.**

ISC as a viable electric utility. In many respects, the municipal City Light operation was much stronger, but City Light's proceeds usually went everywhere else in the city except back into the physical and operating plant, so City Light gained little on ISC.

Little track work was done and only some double track on the Columbia Street bridge (never completely used, as the cars used only the north track) and a one block rebuild on Lewis between Calhoun and Clinton were the only additions. The double track on Lewis resulted when, in 1936, the city was finally able to complete a long awaited project for a Clinton Street underpass at the Pennsylvania-Wabash track elevation. The Indiana State Highway Department participated in the work as several Federal and State routes were to be routed over Clinton Street, one of the city's few north-south through streets.

The Highway Department had established almost impossible standards for State High-

The #13 Centlivre short line ran through a virtual "jungle" on the old Feeder Canal-Robison Park right-of-way. It's no surprise that few people knew the #13 line was ever there. ***R. O. Dingley Photo /W. A. Steventon Collection.***

The #13 Centlivre line started here on Spy Run Avenue just north of East State; car 436 awaits transfer patrons before making its run. This second "short line" ended with little fanfare in March 1940 and was hardly missed. ***R. O. Dingley Photo /W. A. Steventon Collection.***

449, the newest single truck car, leisurely services the #12 Jefferson line on a wet and snowy day. The 12 was one of the "short lines"—only seven blocks long; it fed passengers to the Broadway line and required but a single car to provide the service. ***Bradley-Harnish Collection.***

way roadways containing streetcar tracks and the prohibitive cost forced many street railways throughout Indiana to convert to buses. The off-center Clinton Street car tracks fell prey to these standards as they would have to be completely rebuilt. The Lewis Street line was routed into Calhoun and the Clinton tracks came up except those between Main and Columbia.

The #12 Jefferson "Short Line" used one single truck car which ran on Jefferson from Broadway westward for a half mile to Garden Street. In Fort Wayne, "Short Line" referred to an outlying route, not providing service into the business center. This was one of the oldest routes and became the first car line converted to buses. "Feeder bus" became the replacement bus term for streetcar "Short Line." The Jefferson conversion on May 16, 1939 saw a Fargo-built bus replace the streetcar. The bus provided a more direct, non-transfer route from Garden Street directly to Calhoun Street in downtown Fort Wayne.

Shortly afterward, on March 3, 1940, the little-known #13 Centlivre Short Line, a feeder that served few people, was abandoned. This obscure little rail line ran from a crossover on Spy Run just south of State Blvd., northward on the old Robison Park line's trackage to Parnell Avenue. It was replaced by two company bus lines—"North Clinton" and a new bus route called "Parnell Avenue."

Among Marshall Dale's early steps was a decision to make improvements to the transit system and make it more attractive to patrons in hopes of bettering ridership. Much of the operating streetcar fleet was comprised of the 275 and 400-series single-truck cars. Those in regular use had been repainted from sand yellow to the new maroon and cream color scheme (as had most of the 500 series double truck cars) during 1936 and 1937. This had

Top photo (left): *The 443 has just arrived at Kensington Avenue on Columbia ready to change ends and head back on the #7 line.* ***Top photo (right):*** *An inbound car on the Lakeside line in 1940 passes Delta Lake on its Columbia Street run.* ***Both photos—R. O. Dingley Photo/W. A. Steventon Collection. Bottom photo:*** *Inbound car 512 heads north on the #6 Lewis line and successfully negotiates the gauntlet track under the Wabash Railroad on a Sunday in May 1940.* ***John F. Humiston Photo.***

The 542, in the trolley coach initiated paint scheme, poses to present the "new look" for ISC in 1941 which was a modification of the maroon and cream. The paint scheme was less attractive but was more utilitarian, especially with the entire doors painted cream (they opened outward) to be more visible for motorists. The company name again appeared on the cars after nearly thirty years. ***Bradley-Harnish Collection.***

Car 441 heads north on Calhoun Street on a busy, rainy night. ***Bradley-Harnish Collection.***

Northbound 511 on Clinton Street between Main and Columbia on a wintry day. This route was one of the two downtown loops for turning cars. The "route 2" sign on this car seems unique as there had not been a route 1, 2 or 3 in many years. ***R. O. Dingley Photo /W. A. Steventon Collection.***

been a necessary improvement, but it was only cosmetic as much regular maintenance had ceased. In the case of the 275's and 400's any disabled car was sidetracked and replaced with a good car from the abundance on hand. The man selected to supervise the improvement program was the newly appointed (1940) Assistant Railway Manager, Donald H. Walker, who came from the Indiana Railroad.

The best solution seemed to be the trolley coach, relatively new but proven in service in many cities. For an electric power company the trolley coach seemed an economical and natural vehicle. The lightest, and least direct routes were also those handicapped with most of the stretches of single track operation. Track extensions or double-tracking of rail lines at this late date would have been out of the question. But, duplicate trolley bus overhead for each direction seemed a much more manageable expense.

A revised franchise agreement allowed the conversion and rerouting of several lines. Twenty-eight new, J. G. Brill-built trolley coaches were placed in service on July 7, 1940. Streetcars were taken off the #6 East State-Lewis, #7 Lakeside-East Creighton and #9 East Washington-South Calhoun routes and the rail facilities for the most part were dismantled. A portion of the Belt Line, regularly used to serve the Broadway General Electric Company complex was also equipped for trolley coaches.

In the Walker supervised changeover, most of the trolley bus lines followed the old routes. Some of the kinks and bends were straightened out by direct routing on the East Washington and East Creighton lines. The downtown rail loops were also equipped with double wire and continued in service. All car and coach lines were through routed, but the loops were still useful for short turns and special movements. Main and Calhoun remained the chief intersection of the city. The rail crossing was short one curve of being a full "grand union crossing." The new trolley coach overhead was complete, allowing a coach to proceed in any direction from any approach. It was one of only two such installations of its kind in the U.S. The public acceptance of the new trolley coaches was excellent as they were comfortable and their greater acceleration and maneuverability got them through traffic quickly and quietly.

Rails were left in place to reach the four high schools. This included about ten blocks on Calhoun south of Pontiac, to reach South Side High School, and one block on Lewis to reach Central High School and Central Catholic High School. North Side High School could still be reached by the remaining East State Blvd. trackage retained for freight. Student passenger volume was too large for the number of available buses. Consequently school trippers and sports events required the streetcars.

Below: *The "Transfer Corner" for streetcars at Main and Calhoun remained the chief intersection of the city even as trolley coaches began to take over. This complex rail crossing was short one curve of being a full "grand union" crossing for streetcars. The trolley coach overhead at this corner made it possible for a coach to proceed in any direction from any approach. This was one of only two such installations of its kind in the USA.* ***Bradley-Harnish Collection. At the right:*** *Car 523 on Calhoun Street is outbound on the #9 Calhoun line just south of Pontiac Street.* ***R. O. Dingley Photo / W. A. Steventon Collection.***

Portable Substation 1000 stands duty on the International Harvester loop at Shady Brook and Raymond Avenue in 1941. Close scrutiny reveals the substation's operator reclining in the shade, testimony to the difficulty of the job. ***John F. Humiston Photo.***

Car 542 leaves the International Harvester loop heading west on Raymond Avenue on the weed overgrown #5 line, Saturday, August 23, 1941. The entrance to the loop on Redwood Avenue is to the right just behind the car and ISC's Portable Substation 1000 is about 5 poles to the rear. ***John F. Humiston Photo.***

Above: *Car 541 and 531 serving as "special cars" on East State Boulevard wait to load near North Side High School. After this line was converted to trolley coaches, only the East State trackage to the State School remained.* ***Bradley-Harnish Collection. Below:*** *These old single truck cars were retired after the 1940 introduction of trolley coaches and they were stored at McKinley Avenue yard. They would be stripped of electrical components and useable parts, and most would be burned for scrap metal.* ***R. O. Dingley Photo /W. A. Steventon Collection.***

The Taylor Street line had been served by two single-truck streetcars running from Broadway to Ardmore in Short Line service. Simultaneously with the trolley coach installation, Taylor was converted to motor buses and the tracks on the outer portion, beyond McKinley Avenue, were ripped up. The inner portion trackage was used to reach the McKinley yard for scrapping purposes. With all of these changes, the last of the 400-series, four-wheel, streetcars were removed from service. The remaining, heavy traffic lines, were served by the 500-series double truck cars.

In January, 1941 after the last interurbans were gone, the company was in a position to replace the balance of the rail lines and streetcars with trolley coaches. The necessary franchise was obtained on September 3, 1941 and an order for forty 44-passenger trolley coaches was placed with the J. G. Brill Company. However, by September the war winds were heating rapidly and Fort Wayne industry began to gear up. ISC soon felt that streetcars would not be immediately replaced. December 1941, and the war, ended all thoughts of the substitution, at least as planned.

It also became evident that the equipment in operation would not suffice until the new trolley coaches could be delivered. Fifty-three of the 500-series cars were still on the property although the remaining eight members of the 1917 group had been considered surplus and were not in good repair. The eight were quickly rehabilitated and placed in service. The company had nine motor buses for the feeder routes. Three 1931 Fargo buses had been retired and half scrapped but they were still on the property. Out of the pieces one complete bus was reassembled and put into use on a line near the Spy Run Shop so that it could be pulled in quickly if it failed. All motor buses were in use and there were no extras even though there was some bus relief when the company restored rail service on the inner portion of Taylor Street. At the same time car service was restored on the remaining portion of the East State and South Calhoun lines.

By March 1942, 53 streetcars, 28 trolley coaches and 10 motor buses were in peak ser-

Top photo: *The Spy Run car yards were modified for the new trolley coaches and outdoor storage tracks 5 through 12 were removed leaving eight lanes for storage. There were only four trolley coach overheads, one for every two lanes, which presented an interesting but effective use of less overhead wire. Coaches still parked side by side and shared the common overhead.* ***Bottom photo:*** *ISC's Spy Run plant in 1941. In the conversion tracks 1 through 4 (inside the Inspection-Office Building) plus tracks 5 through 12 have been removed for the trolley coaches. Tracks 13 to 20 were used for the active streetcars and were "through" tracks. Stub-end tracks 21 through 28 were used for storage with the sweepers kept on track 28. The pattern for the trolley coach installation can be seen. This layout remained the same until 1946 when tracks 13-16 and 25-28 were taken up. The rest were removed in 1947. The three "surplus" Fargo buses are next to the motor bus garage. Line car 826 is in the material yard to the right rear of the shop building.* ***Both photos —Bradley-Harnish Collection.***

In 1941 the #8 line became West Main-Oxford. Car 533 is at the end of the West Main line. **R. O. Dingley Photo / W. A. Steventon Collection.**

Accidents did happen—524 was southbound on Broadway when it split a switch at Creighton Avenue. The rear track turned left blocking both auto and rail traffic. **R. O. Dingley Photo /W. A. Steventon Collection.**

The 520 changes ends at Calhoun and Rudsill in 1940 shortly before this line was converted to trolley coaches. These tracks remained in place, and service on Calhoun this far south was restored during the war years. **R. O. Dingley Photo /W. A. Steventon Collection.**

It's a busy 1940's day in downtown Ft. Wayne with pedestrian and vehicle traffic at its peak. This area today (1982) is totally changed, although Calhoun Street remains the central bus artery. **Bradley-Harnish Collection.**

vice. There were now no spares of any type of vehicle! All inspection and repair had to be done outside of rush hours or schedules would be curtailed. It was an operating nightmare for, in 1930, when traffic levels were comparable, the company was using 110 streetcars and had spares available. Now the grand total, of all vehicles, was only 91! This was close to a panic situation and ISC petitioned the Office of Defense Transportation (O.D.T.) to insure the release of at least thirty, if not all forty, of the new trolley coaches. Most of the new wiring was in place.

The trolley coaches were finally released by the O.D.T. and delivered, arriving in mid-1942, just as the system was ready to come apart.

The equipment availability had been amazing, everything considered, because of a policy pursued from the time of the first trolley coach conversion. As the single-truck cars were scrapped, all of the good motors had been salvaged and used for maintenance and replacement on the double-truck cars whose days were also believed numbered. No motors had been overhauled since 1937 and routine dipping and baking had been deferred. Burned out motors were scrapped. Armature failure was high by mid-1942 and all the spare motors had been used. The situation was saved by the arrival of the additional trolley coaches and by December, 1942 eight streetcars could be allowed to leave the daily schedule for shop work and repair. The passenger load had now gone from 18,377,795 in 1941 to 34,130,150 in 1943. The peak year was 1944 when 36,249,538 passengers rode.

As a part of the plea to gain the forty new trolley coaches, ISC requested permission to substitute the new vehicles on the long #5 Third Street-Pontiac line. Two very valid reasons were offered. The single track rails on Huffman Street were the worst in the system and would have to be rebuilt. The Third Street line had three single track portions, which, with a few blocks on the reclaimed Taylor line and two blocks on the Belt Line, were the last such bottlenecks in the system. Third Street, as a trolley coach line, could reach more people because the outer end of its route had a huge loop over several streets. Also the Wells Street bridge, which the trolley coach route bypassed was not considered safe for heavy vehicles and its wartime replacement was very improbable.

The Third Street end of the #5 line was abandoned as a rail line. The #5 line became a trolley coach operation, but the Pontiac end was retained for rail service with some streetcars used for heavy traffic periods. However, most were short turn trippers changing ends on Pontiac at the Alexander Street crossover. After this early 1943 change the system settled in to meet the war traffic strain. Total transit vehicles available totaled 131 and most were kept busy. Because of the odd balance of traffic at various hours on the various lines, the four streetcar lines had occasional trolley coach service as trippers switched from line to line to meet the wartime-inspired, staggered industrial working hours. Riders had to keep a watchful eye to read signs and route numbers or be passed.

The 552 swings from Main Street to Broadway outbound on the #4 line; St. Joseph Hospital is on the right. This was also the line for interurbans on both routes to Indianapolis. ***Bradley-Harnish Collection.***

Midland Utilities, which held 98% of the ISC common stock, and its parent Midland United Company had been in reorganization since June 9, 1934. NIPSCO and ISC were the

War workers from the Broadway General Electric plant anxiously wait to board the crowd eaters on a wet, snowy day at the shift change. The second car is running the #11 Belt line. ***Bradley-Harnish Collection.***

Top photo: *523 heads north on Calhoun at Baker Street on a rainy June 6, 1947. The wartime revived #10 Taylor line used the Belt line route on Broadway, Creighton, Calhoun and Main, besides using Taylor Street from Broadway to McKinley Avenue.* ***T. H. Desnoyers Photo /George Krambles Collection. Bottom photo:*** *During the November 1946 strike the idle streetcars and trolley coaches sat in the Spy Run yards.* ***Ft. Wayne & Allen County Indiana Public Library Collection.***

After 1945, this trackage over the Spy Run Avenue bridge was used only for moving cars from the shop to the downtown; passengers, however, could catch a ride to and from the shops on cars running this route. ***G. E. Lloyd Photo / George Krambles Collection.***

The 524 and three trolley coaches pick up workers at the Broadway General Electric plant. The overhead sign indicates this as a "War Victory Stop" for northbound cars. ***Bradley-Harnish Collection.***

two principal utility operating subsidiaries (the CSS&SB entered bankruptcy in 1933 and reorganized in 1938). It was assumed by many that Midland was in a hurry to clean up its affairs and dispose of its properties. The city of Fort Wayne anticipated an early action and the administration planned to acquire the ISC facilities for City Light. The reorganization moved along slowly.

A city sponsored referendum for authorization to buy the electric utility, was scheduled for November 7, 1944. The ISC management, as elected officers of the common stockholders of Midland Utilities, could not engage in the battle. ISC employees did join in the fray and actively opposed the sale with great

Car 541 on the Pontiac line crosses the Nickel Plate tracks (New York, Chicago and St. Louis Railroad) on Calhoun Street with the station on the right. ***John F. Humiston Photo.***

success. One of the issues was the city's lack of interest in the transit facility which they said they would sell to any interested party. This attitude apparently did not sit well with the general public and part of the labor sector. Whatever the reason, the city failed to acquire ISC for City Light.

The end of the war removed the emergency needs and eight more streetcars went into the second hand market. Rail operations on the Pontiac line were abandoned from Warsaw Street to the end at Harvester loop in April 1945 as service requirements for the streetcar trippers ended. The end of the Northern Division line-haul freight service, on August 25, 1945, provided an opportunity to dispose of all but two pieces of work equipment. One switching and one freight motor were saved for the remaining switching services on Spy Run and East State. The Centlivre Brewery (a customer since 1913), City Filtration Plant (the newest customer in 1931), and the State School were the last customers for interurban freight.

Sunday, September 9, 1945, was a quiet day on all streetcar routes when, for the first time in seventy-three years, except for two service-stopping strikes and the Great Epizootic, not a streetcar operated. Full schedules were operated that Sunday, and every Sunday thereafter, with buses. Fewer cars were seen on week days, unless one passed the Spy Run yards where many of the forty-five somewhat tired streetcars rested quietly. Most of the vehicle miles were operated by trolley coaches and motor buses. Streetcars still clanged forth to run the #10-Taylor Street line, which since 1942, had included the Belt Line, and to fill the rush hour gaps on the four streetcar/trolley coach lines.

Labor problems cropped up in 1946 and the company and union could not agree. An operators' strike started Sunday morning, November 10, 1946, and no vehicles were run. The transit

The 541 sits on Broadway just north of Rudisill Boulevard, June 6, 1947—just three weeks before the end of rail service. ***T. H. Desnoyers Photo /George Krambles Collection.***

tie-up lasted until the morning of November 20. Even though riding dropped as automobiles became available and patrons left as a result of the strike, the company still did not have enough equipment to retire the streetcars. Ten more trolley coaches came in 1946, but the nearly exhausted motor buses—some dating back to 1940—were still in use. Upon the arrival of the new trolley coaches streetcars were virtually eliminated from the Broadway, South Wayne, Oxford and West Main routes.

Fifteen Twin Coach-built motor buses arrived in the spring of 1947. These, and the older motor buses, by now eleven in number, were enough so that the Taylor Street car line could be replaced. Until 1947, except on Sunday, there were not enough motor buses to replace the regular Taylor Street car service.

On the evening of June 27, 1947, ISC Transportation Vice-President Donald H. Walker shook hands with honorary conductor Frank Carbaugh and sent the last car on its way. Carbaugh had been a conductor on the first day of electric operation and asked to ride the last car. He was the first conductor on a city car in over twenty-five years. The ceremonies were brief and few people appreciated the fact that an era had closed. Later that night, with little fanfare, car #543 rumbled back to the Spy Run yard, for the last time, as seventy-five years of rail passenger service came to a close.

Corporate changes had seen Dale resign as President in 1945 to be succeeded by C. V. Sorenson, a former NIPSCO man. Midland was preparing to wind up its affairs and a new series of ISC common stock was issued and sold to American Gas & Electric (AG&E) on June 30, 1947. Unlike the other Midland properties which regained their independence, ISC had the misfortune to be sold off by one holding company to another utility holding company.

Photo at right: *500 series cars and their replacements, the trolley coaches, stand together at the Spy Run yards in July 1947, a few days after the last streetcars were run.* ***Van Dusen-Zillmer Collection. Below:*** *The Taylor Street line was the only "all streetcar"—all day long—line after 1946; the #4 and #8 lines continued to use streetcars also but only during rush hours. New Twin Coaches were on their way to Ft. Wayne on this June 6, 1947 day, and this scene at Broadway and Taylor soon would be history.*
T. H. Desnoyers Photo /George Krambles Collection.

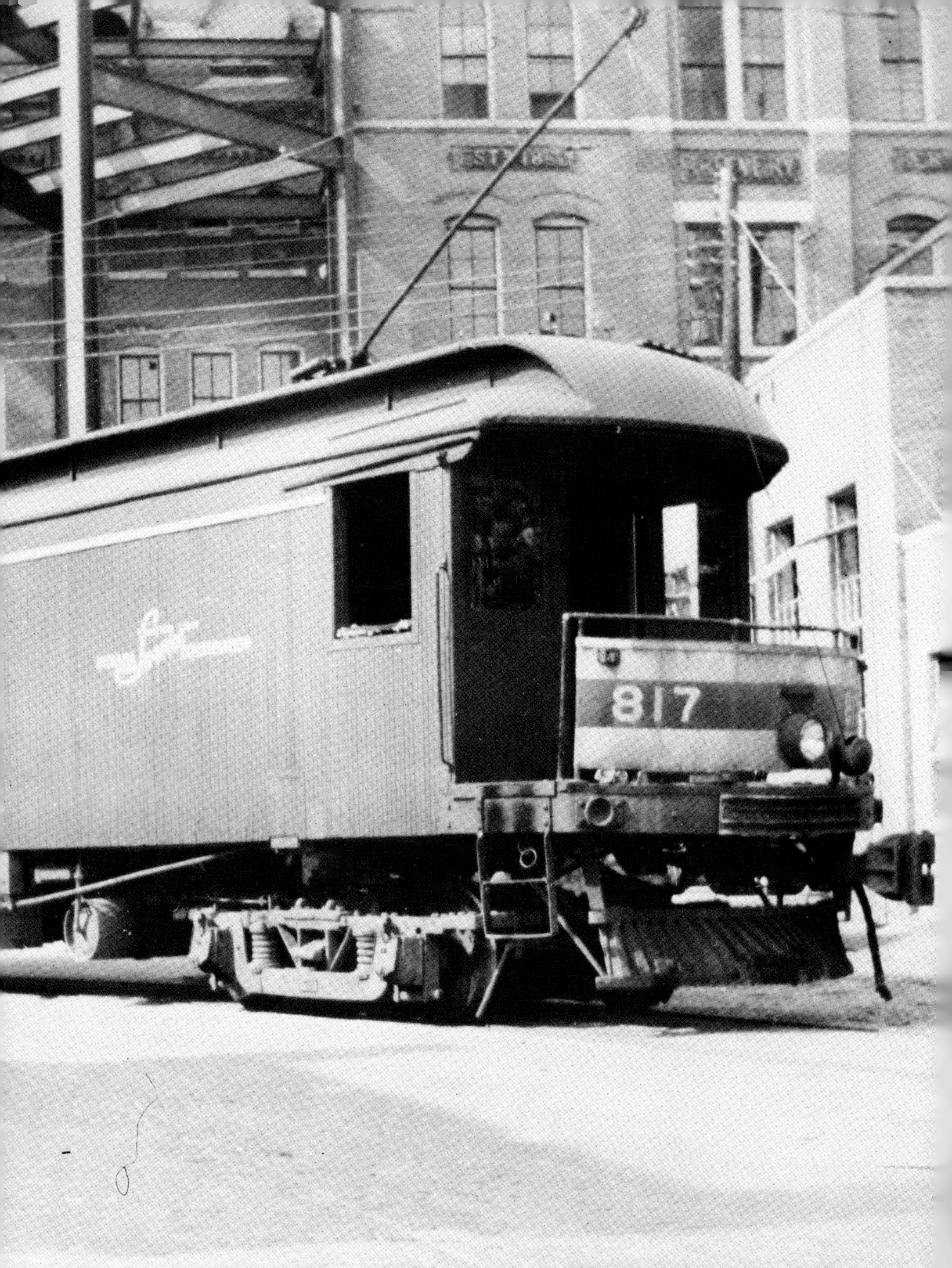
817

Fort Wayne 1947-1982

CHAPTER 15

In the ISC sale by Midland to AG&E many of the old Midland personalities resigned from the board to be replaced by representatives of the new eastern owners. The President of AG&E was made the Executive Vice-President of ISC. The Indiana & Michigan Electric Company, another AG&E property centered around South Bend and a main power supplier to ISC, was picked to absorb the ISC. Late in 1948 Indiana Service Corporation disappeared, forever, into the I&M.

One of the terms of the sale of ISC was the sale of the passenger transit facilities. Freight, particularly coal transport, would be kept by the power company. In January 1948, ISC had announced that they would sell the transit facility to the highest bidder. Several national bus operators came to look around. They offered no guarantees and one well known operator let it be known that Fort Wayne would be a satellite property with a resident company man as a manager. The trolley coaches would probably be replaced by diesel buses at an early date.

This unattractive prospect was countered by a group of local businessmen headed by Donald H. Walker who obtained local financial support. Fort Wayne Transit, Inc. (FWT) was a Fort Wayne corporation set-up, "Local Transportation—Locally Owned and Operated." FWT agreed to pay $805,000 for the system which included 78 trolley coaches and 26 motor buses. The local ownership, far more attractive to the citizens than the disinterested outsiders, passed to FWT on May 1, 1948. A new era began and local ownership returned after a half-century absence.

The Road and Equipment Valuation of Fort Wayne Transit was $2,301,030 for the transit property and $122,785 for the switching property. The switching property included certain facilities not used for transit operations but used by Indiana & Michigan for freight switching services. The switching property was considered to be fully depreciated.

Fort Wayne Transit leased and continued the shop facility on Spy Run Avenue, although they located their office downtown. One of the inherited commitments of FWT was the removal or covering of old rail still left in the street as part of the trolley coach franchise. Some of the rail was still in use by freight trains on Spy Run and East State. FWT by contract, agreed to maintain the track, overhead and the repair work on the two freight motors for I&M.

During 1951, I&M wanted to get out of the railroad freight switching business and petitioned the Public Service Commission for permission to end rail service. The State School was willing to use trucks as was Centlivre. The Filtration Plant still needed a rail spur, so a new connection to the NYC Railroad had to be built. The last rail runs on the street were on February 29, 1952. This allowed Fort Wayne Transit to retire the switching property and complete the paving obligation. However, electric operation had not ended as old #817 still hauled coal cars across Clinton Street, from the New York Central to the Spy Run power plant. The tiny remnant lasted until October 1, 1952 when Judson Kline, the motorman, retired. On that day the obsolete electric rail operation was retired. The power plant was also heading toward standby status. Regular coal deliveries became a thing of the past.

Fort Wayne Transit added several series of Twin Coach motor coaches. Five bought in 1950 were adapted for propane fuel. This move proved to be very successful so all the Twin Coaches were converted to propane gas; efficiency went up and maintenance cost came down. Five more propane Twin Coaches were delivered in May, 1951 and the last of the old small buses were retired. The East Washington trolley coach line was caught up in a one-way street program and was converted to motor buses in 1953. The company now had a surplus of trolley coaches and a shortage, again, of

motor buses. The situation sent the company into the second-hand market. They sold the newest trolley coaches to Indianapolis and bought seven Twins from Wheeling, West Virginia.

Construction was started, in late 1953, on a new office-garage complex located on Leesburg Road in western Fort Wayne. This new plant was completed in 1954 and consolidated all the company's operations. A new substation building (with old equipment) was built for I&M who had retained the power conversion facilities. The modern and complete garage and office replaced the leased Spy Run shop operations where servicing had been continued in the old interurban shop building as well as the downtown offices in the Purdue Center Building. This was a major optimistic step for a medium size company that was experiencing the national decline in ridership.

In early 1959, with no fanfare, wires were removed from the South Calhoun trolley coach line. Shortly afterward Fort Wayne Transit began to receive a number of used Twin Coach motor buses from Buffalo. Later, that same year, wires were removed from the Lakeside, East Creighton, State and Lewis lines. The public became aware that some major changes were being made by the transit company. In March of 1960, the Third Street and Pontiac lines were also changed to motor buses leaving four trolley bus lines. During this period about twenty-five of the older trolley buses were scrapped. In June 1960, the remaining lines were changed to motor bus and electric power ceased to be the prime mover in Fort Wayne.

Several factors brought on this conversion, but the principal one was the necessity to extend several lines. The needed wire extensions would have been very expensive and would have committed the company to the purchase of newer trolley buses, a luxury few privately owned transit companies could afford. The explosion of the city's boundaries would have made route selection very difficult with fixed facilities. Another problem was the 600 volt D.C. power which I&M now insisted on terminating for no good published reason. The transit company was the last customer for this voltage and the antique converting equipment was declared uneconomical and arbitrarily ended in one of the power company's unilateral actions. A plus, of questionable value, was the income from the salvaged trolley coach facilities and the elimination of the overhead department.

Finding no customers for the last of the used trolley buses, Fort Wayne Transit decided to scrap them. (By this date many newer second hand trolley buses were also on the second hand market.) Unfortunately no one had had the foresight to preserve one of the street cars for historical purposes. This oversight was much regretted by the Allen County-

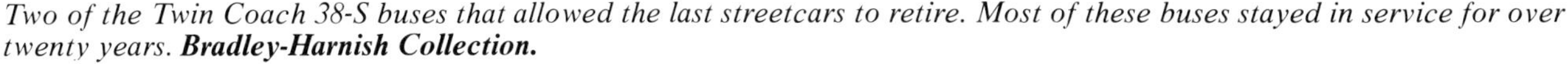
Two of the Twin Coach 38-S buses that allowed the last streetcars to retire. Most of these buses stayed in service for over twenty years. **Bradley-Harnish Collection.**

Above: *The 817 is pictured on the unique, new track entrance into the Centlivre Brewery. The enlargement of the brewery, completed in this view, changed the old track pattern which dated to the days of the #13 line (the brick pavement in the foreground shows the old rail pattern). For freight service, principally the delivery of carloads of grain, the tracks were moved to the north side. These tracks on Spy Run switched to the north edge of the street (just north of State Street), ran a few feet and then swung back out into the center of the road to make a gentle curve into the new brewery entrance.* ***To the left:*** *The 848 sits on the only remaining track in the Spy Run shop yard by late 1951; this track ran between the shop and the engineering building. By this time, the 848 rarely was used except as a relief car for the 817. Painted dark green when it served I&M, the car no longer carried name, number or trim paint.* ***Both photos —Bradley-Harnish Collection.***

Twin Coach 41-S #38 was adapted for propane fuel which proved to be very efficient and less expensive than gasoline in these motor coach engines. ***Bradley-Harnish Collection.***

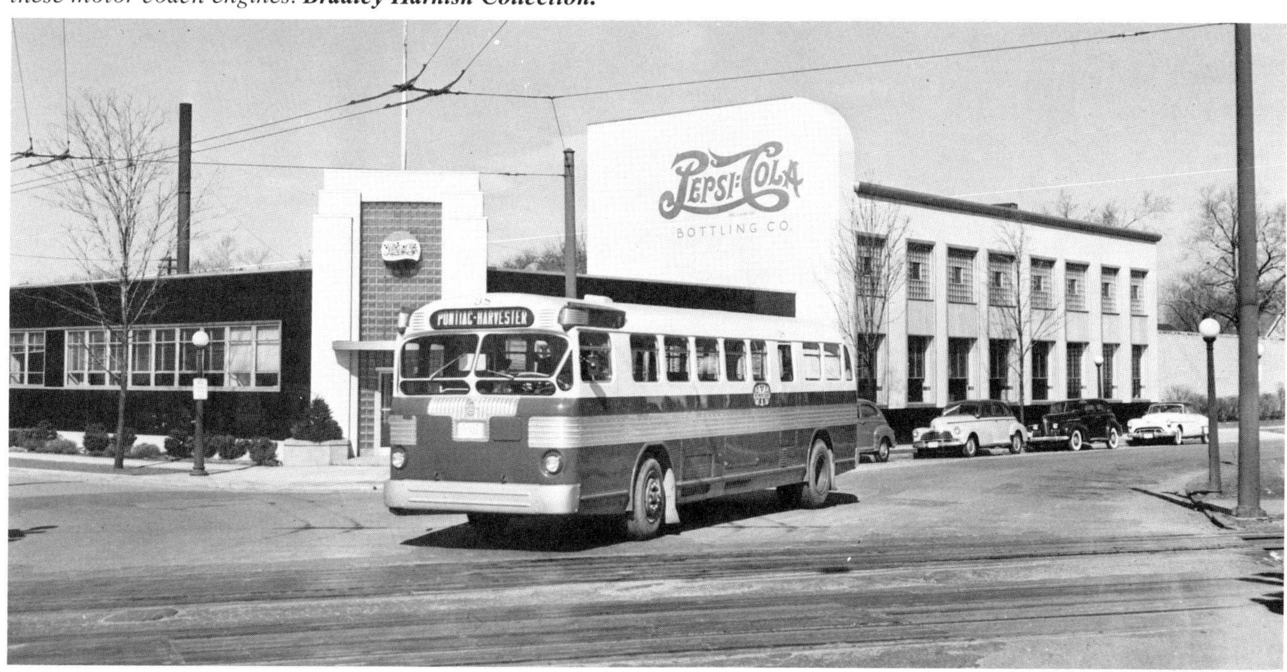

Completed in 1954, Ft. Wayne Transit's new office and shop facility on Leesburg Road was among the most modern in the industry. It allowed the company to unify at one location, moving its offices from downtown and its shops from the space leased on Spy Run Avenue. Here the new facilities are viewed from atop a nearby grain elevator. It's an off-peak period and over 25 trolley coaches are in the ready line-up. As the number of motor buses was increased, two more buildings similar to the white one (left rear) were added to provide indoor, minimum-heat storage. Ft. Wayne PTC uses these facilities today. ***Bradley-Harnish Collection.***

Fort Wayne Historical Society. Walker offered one of the trolley buses to the Historical Society, and the Fort Wayne Junior Chamber of Commerce offered to prepare it for display purposes in the park next to the museum. The Park Board politely declined this offer as they felt it had no immediate appeal and that it might become a distinct liability. Consequently, the forward-thinking Historical Society and Jaycees stored this remaining vehicle, the last in Indiana (Indianapolis had ended its trolley coach operation in 1957), for two years before transferring it to the National Museum of Transport in St. Louis.

Fort Wayne Transit had gone to the used bus field again, this time to Detroit, to replace the last trolley coaches with more Twin Coaches. The company now had over 100 motor buses including some General Motors diesels also from the used bus market. Declining ridership meant that added income was vital for survival. Contracted school bus service was a source of new revenue. Transit Truck & Body Repair, Inc., a separate subsidiary, used the transit company's facilities allowing the mechanical force to be kept at full strength. Even this was not going to be enough to keep going with full service and Sunday bus operations were ended.

In 1960 the transit company suffered its first operating deficit, recovered and then repeated it in 1963. Transit Truck's revenues saved the day. Considering the general state of privately owned transit systems it was surprising that the company remained in a solvent position. Declining revenue and increasing costs, largely due to operating and maintaining old buses, caused another loss in 1966 for Fort Wayne Transit which was again rescued by Transit Truck. The next year was worse and even with the subsidiary's added income the 1967 overall net loss was nearly $40,000. Clearly something had to be done.

Fort Wayne Transit, Inc. continued to provide local service as long as possible but Walker found the situation nearly impossible as a result of 1967 losses. After the state passed enabling legislation, the city created the Public Transportation Corporation (PTC) in September, 1967, but did little else. In the face of this, Walker announced in January 1968 that Fort Wayne Transit, Inc. would cease operations on June 15, 1968. The city then took action and the first PTC Board

Donald H. Walker (1900-)

Best known in Ft. Wayne as "Mr. Transit," Donald H. Walker actively headed local streetcar and bus transportation for over 28 years. For eight years he served as vice-president—transportation, for Indiana Service Corporation; after he became president of Ft. Wayne Transit, Inc. (until it was succeeded by the Public Transportation Corporation in 1968).

Walker was born in Indianapolis in 1900. He enrolled at Indiana University in 1918 but soon left to join the Marines. After a short hitch (coinciding with the end of the war), he returned to college. This time he enrolled at Purdue University graduating in 1924 with a degree in Civil Engineering. On Friday, the 13th of June, 1924, he began his transit career as Division Engineer at Terre Haute for the Terre Haute, Indianapolis & Eastern Traction Company (THI&E). The company soon transferred him to Indianapolis in a similar capacity.

When Willard Graves, the rail system's Chief Engineer, died suddenly, Walker became the acting Chief Engineer. Soon after, the THI&E appointed him Chief Engineer and he held the position until 1931 when Midland United bought the THI&E and assigned its rail properties to the Indiana Railroad. The IRR named Walker Superintendent, Maintenance of Way. In this post, he frequently found himself faced with disposing of abandoned rail lines and unwanted city street trackage. Many communities, caught in the grip of the depression, could not fund paving projects, so rail removal posed a real problem. Walker managed to resolve the dilemma in some cases by suggesting the use of WPA labor to remove the rail and repair the street. The community could then sell the scrap rail for cash and reap some benefits.

By 1940, little remained of the Indiana Railroad, and Don Walker joined Indiana Service Corporation being appointed Assistant Railway Manager by ISC's president, Marshall Dale. Later Dale named him vice president—transportation with the specific charge to convert the system from streetcar to trolley coach and motor bus operation. Walker projected a two-year changeover, but the onset of World War II postponed the plan and at the same time created numerous transport problems of its own. Under his direction, the company successfully overcame its problems and provided good public transit throughout the war years with a mix of streetcars, trolley coaches and motor buses.

In the post war sale clean-up of ISC activities, the last streetcars were retired (1947) and the transportation system was put up for sale. Convinced that local ownership and management of the city's transit system was important, Walker set out to enlist the support of local businessmen and bankers for the company's purchase. His availability for the transit company presidency and the retention of capable ISC transit personnel swayed many to Walker's way. They formed Ft. Wayne Transit, Inc. and on May 1, 1948 successfully purchased the city transit system. The result was an ambitious company that maintained a high level of bus service even in the face of losses (appearing in the 1960's) that brought on the end of many other transit companies. And while many cities of similar size became mere statistical satellites for national bus operators, Ft. Wayne remained an independent. Under Walker's direction, the company built improved facilities, innovatively maintained good will and developed a profitable subsidiary (Transit Truck Body and Repair, Inc.) which helped to keep FWT going until the Ft. Wayne PTC was organized, and they took over buying the company in 1968. Don Walker continued as FWT president to "clean-up affairs" during 1969. He then retired ending 45 years of continuous public transit involvement.

Don Walker was a significant figure in Ft. Wayne always active and visible in civic groups and public service efforts. Called "Mr. Transit" by the community at large, he is widely recognized in the field of public transportation. He has served as president and/or director of numerous transport organizations including the Indiana Bus Operators' Association and the American Transit Association. In retirement, Mr. and Mrs. Walker reside in Pompano Beach, Florida where they still keep up a busy pace.

In November 1960, Ft. Wayne Transit's president, Don Walker, turned trolley coach 157 over to the Allen County-Ft. Wayne Historical Society for preservation. This was the last trolley coach in Indiana. Later it would be sent to the National Museum of Transport at St. Louis. ***Bradley-Harnish Collection.***

held its first organization meeting on March 1.

Typical of such boards, the first PTC board was strictly political containing businessmen, a truck line operator, a car dealer, etc. with one thing in common—none of them had any experience in public transportation. Certainly their last bus ride was not of recent memory. Unfortunately, for several years, subsequent board members were frequently selected on the basis of similar qualifications, or, if you please, the complete lack of them. Some Board members after their appointment, have made valuable contributions to the PTC. More recent appointments have included some individuals who have taken a very active and constructive interest in company affairs.

The PTC board hired the American Transit Corporation of St. Louis to run the system. They sent in a resident manager who was described as "experienced." Fort Wayne

As part of PTC's "Let us be your car" promotion, two of the GMC buses were cleverly painted to resemble automobiles. This bus bears a vague likeness to a "woodie" station wagon; the other was painted to resemble an Auburn roadster. Here, the company's promotional director, Eric Kuehne, admires his "car." ***Bradley-Harnish Collection.***

Transit continued operating until PTC took over on July 19, 1968, and the $585,000 purchase price included 70 motor buses, the Leesburg Road office and shop and other transit facilities. The transition was fairly smooth. Fort Wayne Transit legally wound up its affairs and dissolved on July 17, 1969. Don Walker also wound up his over 45 year career in public transportation which had started on the Terre Haute, Indianapolis & Eastern Traction Company in June, 1924 as a fresh graduate from Purdue.

During 1968 and 1969 twenty-six new G.M. buses were added to the system as federal funds, available to public systems, became available. Twenty of these have the hardest seats ever used on any public transportation vehicle in Fort Wayne history. Twenty more buses arrived in 1970 with softer seats.

The managers sent by ATC made some classic blunders. One of the first was a revision of the schedules which moved downtown arrivals to the hour instead of a few minutes prior to the hour. The old schedule had allowed riders to get to work a few minutes before the hour. The schedule was later tinkered with some more. Each time riders became disgusted and deserted the buses. Another ATC management idea was a rearrangement of the routes and a mass reassigning of the route numbers which had stood for nearly fifty years. The second resident manager died in 1970 and was not replaced as PTC did not want to renew the contract. Localized management was finally recognized as the best solution.

PTC went to the open market and hired their own General Manager in 1971. Tom Black brought good experience and knowledge to the system and tremendous progress has been made since that time although not without some problems. Innovative ideas and better community awareness have become a part of

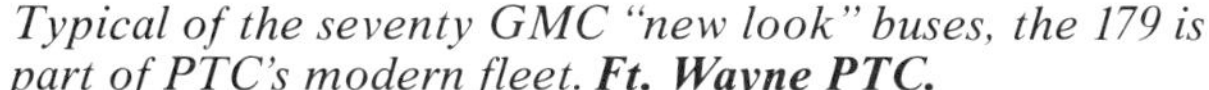

Typical of the seventy GMC "new look" buses, the 179 is part of PTC's modern fleet. ***Ft. Wayne PTC.***

The 104 is a 1981 GMC T70604. Twenty-eight of these 35-passenger, advanced design buses are in use. ***Ft. Wayne PTC.***

the program. Expanded services and route extensions have been made.

On January 6, 1972, public transportation entered its second century. Unlike the 1872 opening which was marked by celebrations, the 1972 day passed virtually unnoticed.

In some apparent dissatisfaction Black resigned and left PTC. The Board of Directors in a moment of weakness tried to solve a dilemma by establishing a three-headed general managership. The intent had been to retain some of the better operating people and to see who could do the right job. The problem solved itself when one of the three left and the other two became the General Manager and Assistant General Manager. The two were Mark DeHaven and Neil Shober. DeHaven resigned in 1979 only a short time after Shober retired (after over forty years). DeHaven's best contribution was putting the bus fleet into excellent condition with the entire fleet being "new look" General Motors buses. The oldest were the two bought by Fort Wayne Transit in 1965. All of the older diesels were sold and replaced by 1976. PTC then had 69 modern buses. The base fleet of modern G.M. buses is well-maintained and all but two are air-conditioned.

The advantages of city ownership and federal grant money allowed the local system to totally modernize even though it did not earn its keep from the farebox...and at the price of new buses few if any private companies could afford any. However, under the next manager, Leslie White, the PTC acquired 28 of the newest GMC buses. White left in 1981 and was succeeded by Bob Schreier.

Public transit in Fort Wayne entered 1982 ...110 years of continued service to the community by ten successive companies.

W. MARKET

Logansport, Wabash and Peru City Lines

CHAPTER 16

LOGANSPORT CITY LINES

The main line interurban route reached six county seat towns as it ran from Fort Wayne down the Wabash Valley. These smaller cities were Huntington, Wabash, Peru, Logansport, Delphi and Lafayette. All but Huntington and Delphi had local streetcar lines. Huntington seems to have had sporadic service, in the earliest days, on the cross town line, which really did not serve the heart of the business area. In Delphi, the interurban line did not use the streets. It was different in the other four cities...and they each had an interesting story.

The five city streetcar lines were kept as separate entities by the company's central accounting department. As separate accounts all fixed charges, revenues, equipment, depreciation, etc. could be charged to the respective City Line and a profit or loss record maintained.

In all of the cities, except Peru, the interurban was treated as a "foreign" company and rentals were paid to the respective City Line accounts as the "home" company. In Peru, where the city cars used the interurban trackage, exclusively, the Peru City Lines were classed as the foreign company and the interurban, oddly enough, was considered the home company.

Logansport, the Cass County seat at the junction of the Eel and Wabash Rivers, was the center of a rich agricultural area, a canal city and a major railroad junction point. For this reason Logansport grew early, reached a peak and then grew very slowly. But in 1882 it was a boom town ready for a street railway.

The Logansport Street Railway Company was incorporated in 1882 with the principal owners being the Jaques family of Urbana, Illinois. The first mule cars ran, on May 20, 1883, over a single route which used Broadway from a loop comprising Second, Market and Fourth to the company barn at 18th and Broadway. Later, a loop across the river, using the Market and Third Street bridges provided service to West Logan. The company was quite successful. A tragic loss occurred late on the night of May 20, 1891, when the frame car barn burned and the course of the company was drastically altered. Twenty-eight mules and eight of the company's nine cars perished in the holocaust. Only the lone car making a late night run survived. This single car provided a very restricted service for several months while the company changed over to electricity.

New cars, overhead wires, a generator and other items were secured as quickly as possible and the line was back in operation by October 1, 1891. A new brick powerhouse was built at 18th and Broadway. There was no time to rebuild the tracks so they were bonded and remained at the four foot narrow gauge. There were at least nine new electric cars and three trailers which are usually credited to have come from St. Louis Car Company. These cars were both open and closed cars. The total number of cars eventually grew to eight closed and six opens.

The company also acquired a new name on July 3, 1891, Logansport Railway Company, and new owners Mr. Samuel Spencer of New York became the President, and Spencer Park was named for him. The one mile extension of the Broadway car line had been extended by J. T. McNary, the manager, and the park was to have been called McNary Park. Service was seasonal. The local fairgrounds was also a part of the park.

Ownership changed hands again and the railway became the property of George Marott of Indianapolis. By 1901, the property had had little improvement, reportedly now to have eleven cars (only six sets of motors) and was supposedly in poor physical condition. However, Marott and his street railway had a valuable item in their franchise, which gave them sole rights to all the streets in the city. There was a legitimate potential rival in the Logansport, Rochester & Northern Traction Company, a projected interurban which was given construction permission, by Ordinance, on July 11, 1899. McNary, no longer associated with the streetcar company, was the acting

Ten-bench open car 352 had enclosed ends—a not too common design for open cars. The car and crew pose at Spencer Park. ***Bradley-Harnish Collection.***

Logansport Street Railway's company barn at 18th and Broadway during the 1880's. Cars 3 and 7 are each pulled by a pair of mules. The barn burned in a late night fire on May 20, 1891 with loss to all but one car; 28 mules perished in the blaze as well. ***Bradley-Harnish Collection.***

President of LR&N. The LR&N seemed to be an empty scheme and no threat to Marott as nothing had been built.

By 1902, the Logansport Railways' control of the streets was challenged by Fred C. Boyd of the Wabash River Traction Company who wanted to build an interurban line from Peru into Logansport via the canal tow path. At the same time the seemingly lifeless LR&N suddenly made a renewed appearance and, though thought to be in default, the company suddenly took on a new life from the "McCulloch interests." George McCulloch was locally known as the head of the Indianapolis & Northern Traction Company building toward Logansport from Indianapolis.

Taken to court, the Logansport Railway was told that they could only claim rights to those streets where they had actually built a streetcar line. The new Wabash-Logansport Traction Company wanted to go ahead with its tracks on Erie Street and the LR&N wanted to build on Fifth and High Streets.

This is where the fun began, as a route on High Street would parallel the Logansport Railway Company's Broadway line, only two blocks to the south, and would also touch Spencer Park. This High Street trackage bothered the Logansport Railway, but the Boyd forces were equally disturbed because a line east on High Street and then continued across country would go straight to Peru over a higher, but much shorter, route than the meandering low-level canal line. The LR&N was supposed to build north, not east. As it turned out, no interurban line ever did go north out of Logansport.

Boyd, in April 1902, bought the narrow gauge Logansport Railway from Marott and then tried to capture the city streets for himself. He succeeded to the extent that, through one manner or another, he lined up a majority of the city council and reportedly purchased his way into the editorial pages of one of the city's three newspapers. He soon found out that the upstart LR&N had some powerful financial backing, good attorneys and the support of many citizens as well as the power of the **Logansport Morning Journal.** Boyd's next counter was to claim that, if left alone, he would complete the Peru line, rebuild the local lines, and build a line to Lafayette. He was soon to learn that the LR&N was no debating society, but was a strong and capable action group with George McCulloch just fronting for the Dolan, Morgan, Widener syndicate.

The LR&N, on May 1, put several crews to work on Fifth Street and on High Street from Fifth to Twenty-Fifth. This occurred during one of the legal battle breaks and the Fifth Street trackage was swiftly completed. The pro-Boyd, **Logansport Daily Reporter** was mystified by what was going on and overlooked the behind-the-scenes activity. **The Reporter** noted the LR&N was supposed to be an interurban and doubted the legality of the operation of local streetcars. They also realized that the company would forfeit its franchise if they were not in some sort of operation by July 1, 1902. **The Reporter** did a good job with the news but their pro-Boyd stance is obvious. They noted for example, that the franchise required a brick, fireproof, powerhouse. The LR&N neatly avoided that issue by buying a High Street lot next to the Columbia Brewing

After the May 20, 1891 disaster at the Logansport Street Railway's barn, the company was forced to take rapid action toward electrification. Closed car 1 heads east of Broadway from Seventh Street about 1896. ***Bradley-Harnish Collection.***

Company and piping steam from the brewery to a newly built brick and frame generating plant next door.

By mid-June the LR&N was busy building its northern (Michigan Street) route on Sixth Street and laid track across the Sixth Street bridge. The City Council continued its pro-Boyd stance even though the politics had taken a change on May 3. In the election the Democrats acquired control of the council and the Mayor's seat but the terms would not begin until September. In the meantime, the old Council continued to fight for Boyd. Boyd's Erie Street line continued to be built.

The Logansport Pharos took the more neutral reporting stand and saw what was happening before most others. **The Pharos** reported the "new" LR&N cars which began arriving on June 18 and noted that they were not really new but had been thoroughly rebuilt. Six, (three closed and three open) had arrived by June 27. Three of the cars were not motorized at that time. **The Pharos** also noticed that George McCulloch was connected with the Union Traction Company and that J. T. McNary and the LR&N seemed to be part of this allied group. The newspaper felt that Boyd was not representing large interests and showed resentment of his attitude.

The LR&N had ten cars on hand by June 28, 1902 and made several trial runs with the first regular service (free) begun on June 29 at 1:00 p.m. McNary offered to set up transfer privileges with the Logansport Railway where their lines crossed. Boyd refused to accept or issue transfers. The LR&N was firmly in place before its July 1 deadline with both the Michigan Street and High Street lines in operation.

On July 11, Boyd finally got the Erie Street line running. A second-hand car, supposedly bought second-hand from Cincinnati, painted the Wabash River Traction yellow, provided the service.

In early August, the LR&N took another advantage of a break in Court fights to push from 25th and High Streets into Spencer Park in direct, parallel, competition with the narrow gauge Logansport Railway. The battles continued with the outgoing city council granting Boyd exclusive possession of the city streets. Such a grant flew in the face of public desire. This was particularly so as the public held a mass meeting to protest Boyd's lack of concern, and the failure of the company to accept a transfer privilege.

Little seven-bench open car 6 at Spencer Park about 1901. ***E. Belknap Collection.***

The make-up of the city government changed somewhat on September 1 as the new mayor took office. A one-month time delay in confirming the August pro-Boyd ordinance produced an interesting turn. The next time the ordinance was brought up, in early October, there was no record of the earlier action in the minutes and, as the minutes were "incomplete," the ordinance was declared illegal. There was no longer a majority of members to support Boyd and his strength was broken. The McCulloch forces and the **Logansport Morning Journal** were victorious. The **Journal's** active and strong fight against Mr. Boyd's talk and little action was a major factor in the LR&N victory.

As the dust settled on the mess it appeared that the Logansport Railway had 6.16 miles of track to the LR&N's 6.00 (the Boyd trackage on Erie Street was included in the Logansport Railway total). The LR&N led in equipment with six 18-foot closed and ten open cars (all opens were trailers) to the Logansport Railway Company's eight closed, six open and one work car. All but two of the Logansport Railway Company's cars were powered. The single car on Erie Street was replaced by a new car, which was built in St. Louis, in early November 1902.

The Wabash-Logansport Boyd interests also realized that their case elsewhere was also hopeless. Even if the public did not know, the company recognized the huge capital resources they faced. They secretly sold all of their Wabash, Peru and Logansport interests on February 14, 1903, to the "McCulloch interests" for a reported $1,000,000. The public announcement was made in the **Logansport Morning Journal** on April 23, with the paper congratulating McCulloch and indicating good riddance to Boyd. McCulloch, himself, sold his interests to the Schoepf-McGowan Syndicate in September, 1903.

The lines of the Logansport Railway were standard gauged during September, October and completed on November 21, 1903. In each case the tracks were completely renewed to bring them up to current standards. The company's standard "T" rail with paving blocks between and on either side of the rails was used. Much of the removed rail on Broadway was the original horsecar line rail. The

Broadway east from Third Street in Logansport, 1907. Two Union Traction passenger interurban cars are parked at the Logansport station blocking four city cars while a freight motor sits on the eastbound track. Use of city car lines for interurban terminal facilities frequently caused such traffic jams. ***Bradley-Harnish Collection.***

Erie Street line and the newer LR&N tracks were also brought up to company standards. This trackage, although practically brand new had, in many places, been laid in too much haste and had an improper foundation. The west side loop seems to have been broken at this time and the line split into separate rail lines. After this effort and excitement of the competition the Logansport City Lines settled down to business. The only extension of the lines was the new Burlington Street line built in 1907 to provide an entrance for the interurban line to Lafayette. This route crossed the Third Street bridge over the Wabash River and provided local service to residents south of the river.

During the rebuilding one of the old cars, number 20, had been given a new standard gauge truck. It was used to carry passengers to and from work on the end of the line that had the new track. Passengers had to transfer to an older car to continue part of the way. As the need for the old closed cars ended, four or more were sold or rebuilt to other than passenger uses. The main equipment was the LR&N 18-foot closed cars. There were also four 22-foot cars. The five seven bench Logansport Street Railway cars were standard gauged and kept in use. The LR&N eight and nine bench open cars rounded out the summer car fleet. In 1904, in keeping with a pledge to improve the service, the Wabash Valley system acquired a group of large window cars from Cincinnati Car Company. Eight of them were assigned to Logansport. These cars were kept at the new 26th and Erie Street car barn which replaced the older facilities at 18th and Broadway and the LR&N's hastily built barn on High Street east of the city limits.

The 1913 flood created near havoc at Logansport with both the Eel and Wabash Rivers out of their banks and running rampant. City streetcar service was discontinued from March 24 to March 29 when the power failed. Logansport's traction power came from Lafayette (the Broadway and 18th power plant was closed in 1903 and the High Street local power plant was closed before Spy Run opened) and the strain on the Lafayette plant left no spare power for use in Logansport. Power could not be transmitted from Fort Wayne. The local municipal plant was in its own difficulties and could not be called upon for any help.

When the river was at its peak there was eight feet of water in the interurban station. The Third Street bridge, used by Lafayette interurban and the Burlington Street city line lost two spans. The overall clean-up and restoration of service was costly.

Financially the lines were making a small profit until 1913 when they took a severe drop. One-man operation was introduced in early 1916 in an attempt to cut costs. Some of the employees went on strike on July 18 demanding a 5 percent pay increase and recognition of the union.

The subsequent events were no credit to the city of Logansport as mobs of labor sympathizers (Logansport was a railroad town with a sometimes unstable and rough labor element) rioted during the night of July 18. The streetcars were stopped, and a policeman and a civilian were shot during an attack on a line car which came in to repair a damaged high tension line. The condition prevailed throughout the 19th with the lawless element in control. Apparently most interurban schedules were maintained. Striking linemen diverted power from the Union Traction interurban line to the city car lines and the rioters ran the cars up and down the lines derailing and wrecking some. By the 20th things settled down and the crowd tired of venting its wrath on the city cars. Full city car service was running by the 24th with policemen riding at night.

The company reached an agreement with the city to put the trackage in good order and to furnish new cars. City officials remembered all the attention they had received from the railway company a dozen years past and did not like being just a part of the tail on the Fort Wayne kite.

Some route changes were made. Trackage remained in High Street from Sixth to Twenty-

Ten new cars were bought for Logansport use in 1918. In this view, the 298 heads east on Market at Third Street about 1925. ***Bradley-Harnish Collection.***

Car 145 stands in Logansport after a minor accident with another vehicle. ***John Rehor Collection.***

fourth (the outer end to Spencer Park was already gone) but was no longer in use. The west side loop had earlier been broken by removal of trackage on Wilkinson Street. The Miami route, the former north side of the loop, was extended one block beyond Wilkinson to Madison. The short branch on Sycamore Street from Miami to the Vandalia Railroad station was torn up. In a few years the former south side of the loop on West Market Street was curtailed. A bridge construction project ended the West Market line because no new rails were put down on the bridge. The isolated West Market trackage was left in place but not used.

Ten new cars, 290-299, identical to the new Fort Wayne single-truck cars, went to Logansport, although it would appear they were given older style Curtis trucks initially.

Revenues began to decline in the late twenties with small losses being recorded. After 1930, although the city lines and cars were run by ISC, Indiana Railroad operated the interurbans. The former Union Traction interurban line between Logansport and Kokomo ceased operation on September 15, 1930. Indiana Railroad, in 1932, next proposed ending the Peru-to-Lafayette interurban service. The fate of the Logansport City Lines was sealed. ISC was not interested in an isolated streetcar system that had lost money since 1930 and one which would require track rehabilitation. As the city had a municipal power plant, there was no electric power business in Logansport to keep ISC interested or for the city to use as a trump card. The city service was abandoned, without bus substitution by ISC, on April 29, 1932. (A later bus company provided local service.) The interurban line kept on using Erie Avenue and Burlington Avenue until Indiana Railroad stopped its service on June 22, 1932. Cars and anything of value were taken to Fort Wayne or Peru.

WABASH CITY LINES

Wabash was selected by a group of New Englanders as a good jumping-off point for an interurban company, the Wabash River Traction Company. Its opening in 1901, already recounted, was the start of electric railway service in the city. The only city line crossed town from a stub end at the northeastern city limits, at the Pioneer Hat factory on Manchester, to the southwestern edge of the city. Local service started August 17, 1901. Interurban service continued over the line, westward, to Peru, Indiana.

The city's second electric railway, the Fort Wayne & Southwestern Traction Company, began regular services on August 10, 1902. It extended its Fort Wayne-Huntington line westward to Wabash. The line used Water Street to South Wabash Street, the business center of town. The business district was safely located on the side of the valley above the Wabash River. It also began laying tracks west from Wabash Street on West Market Street and then stopped. Fred Boyd of the Wabash River Traction Company opposed the Southwestern and even threatened to build a competing line east to Huntington, the midpoint city of the Southwestern. The competition for territory was mutual because the Southwestern's tracks on West Market posed a threat to Boyd.

Still a third company arrived in town from the south. The Indiana Northern Traction Company opened on December 2, 1905. It tied into the city trackage on Columbus Street. This railway, a Union Traction predecessor connecting Wabash with Marion, Indiana, should not be confused with the Indianapolis & Northern Traction Company, a similarly named line into Peru and Logansport, which was also part of the Union Traction family. The Marion-Wabash line remained a regular work-a-day operation until September 30, 1930. Neither it nor the Southwestern ever operated city cars in Wabash, although they were glad to accept local passengers on the interurban cars.

The Wabash city line, as it evolved, extended from the city limits on the northeast to the city limits at Mill Creek Pike on the southwest and included two passing sidings. One was south of the river at the top of the Columbus Street hill; the other was on South Wabash Street, north of the Wabash River bridge. Two long, hard grades were required to climb out of the river valley. The south side section was not only steep but full of turns. The little system was truly very poorly planned.

One-man car 180 heads up the hill on Wabash Street at Market Street in the mid-twenties in Wabash. These deck roof cars were replaced by newer 200 series cars. ***Bradley-Harnish Collection.***

The interurban cars, run every half hour, were large double-truck city-type cars not suited for small-town service. Starting in January, 1902 a small single-truck car was used for city service. The big cars also picked up city passengers. After the Wabash Valley system took over, most of the large city-style cars were sent elsewhere (some stayed behind for the south side Wabash-Boyd Park line) and various Fort Wayne single-truck cars were sent out to Wabash to provide city passenger service. Typically good cars, but not the newest ones, were assigned. The last group used in Wabash was the rebuilt 202 series. For a time two cars were assigned to Wabash although one may have been nothing more than a spare car.

The city experienced more changes in routing than most trolley towns of comparable size. The original interurban line west to Peru used a wandering route on the south side of the river. In July, 1904, it was supplanted for interurban cars by a new north side line all the way to Boyd Park. The new route used the West Market Street tracks which had originally been laid by the Southwestern company. The old south side country road route survived until 1920 for trips between Wabash and Boyd Park, but it does not appear to have been used for any regular scheduled service. The portion within Wabash remained in city service even after that.

Another change came during the thirties when an alternate east-west route was completed in the summer of 1931 to get the Indiana Railroad trains off Water and Market Streets and straighten out the routing. The new route had fewer turns and hills and the grade was constructed to serve as an emergency flood dike. The work was done using unemployed relief workers and the help and cooperation of the city. The elevated road bed, one foot above recent high water levels, protected several large areas occupied by local industries. Culverts and drains were built so they could be sealed. ISC started work in December 1930. A new freight and passenger facility was also built. The change, and the end of the local streetcars, eliminated all the paved street operations in Wabash.

The city operation became a part of the Indiana Railroad System in 1931 although still owned by ISC. In July, 1931 the company petitioned to suspend the local car service and abandon those lines not needed by Indiana Railroad interurbans. The last city cars were run August 31, 1931. The Indiana Railroad System (locally still an ISC operation) as a concession to the local officials, agreed to run a local bus in exchange for the streetcar service. Bus service was no more successful than the streetcars and was withdrawn by ISC, through Indiana Railroad, on April 1, 1933.

PERU CITY LINES

The Peru city operation was the smallest of the five streetcar properties in the ISC chain. Streetcars in Peru were a sideline of the interurban rail operations. The city, for its size, had more local service and for a longer period of time than many Indiana cities. Peru was a steam railroad junction point and because of its location on these rail lines, its position along the north side of the Wabash River and its proximity to being almost directly north of Indianapolis, it also became an interurban rail junction. The ISC tracks ran through the town on an east-west route on Main Street. The line had a two block double track portion in the center of the city and passing sidings on the east and west end. From the center of town the Union Traction's line ran South on Broadway to Indianapolis and the Winona Interurban Railway ran northward, also on Broadway, to Warsaw and Goshen. The ISC had the longest city street operation because Peru is much longer east and west than north and south. The Union Traction had very little street running.

The Wabash River Traction Company was the first electric line in Peru which was well known as the "Circus City" because the city was the wintertime headquarters for several circus companies. The circus would be both good and bad for the WRT and its successors as the population fluctuated with the circus season. It also created a situation of frequent circus parades which tied up traffic on the main streets. It was a somewhat different traffic generator and problem than encountered by most city rail systems.

The WRT started construction in March, 1901 and by later that Spring work crews were busy in Peru, Wabash and points in between constructing track, buildings and other facilities. The first group of cars for the WRT arrived in Peru on July 10. These were unloaded and moved to the Boyd Park barn location. The first of the yellow cars operated into Peru on July 26, 1901. This was Car 16. The first run between Peru and Wabash was made on August 12 using the large open Car 13. Local service started the same day with cars running from the east city limits to the center of town. Good service was promised, by Fred Boyd of the WRT, to sooth the ruffled feathers of the Peru city officials who claimed Boyd had promised to locate his company's car shop in Peru in return for the franchise to use the streets. This broken promise of Fred Boyd, one of many, was used against him in the later Logansport controversy over who was most likely to fulfil promises in that city. Boyd promised better local service and did improve that service when a "new" city car was placed in service on January 19, 1902. This, and a sister car for Wabash, came from Worcester, Massachusetts and was either a new car or a reconditioned used streetcar. To Boyd's credit there was always an abundance of cars for Peru city service and this availability continued through the later owner companies.

In 1903, a sister company of the WRT called the Wabash-Logansport Traction Company was put together by Boyd. This line built westward from the center of Peru to Logansport and the line was completed on May 12, 1903. The power changeover problem originally encountered by the Wabash-Logansport Traction Company occurred at the west city limits of Peru. Prior to that time the Peru city cars, two were now in use, ran the full 1.8 mile stretch of trackage from city limit to

Car 214 goes down the Wabash Street hill on August 31, 1931—the last day of streetcar operation. ***Van Dusen-Zillmer Collection.***

Wabash Valley 133, about 1910, at the Chesapeake & Ohio Railway crossing on West Main Street in Peru. ***M. D. McCarter Collection.***

city limit. The Wabash Valley System bought the two companies in February, 1904. The consolidated operation presented little change that was visible to the local citizens. The arrival of a second interurban company, from the state capital, was more visible. This was the Union Traction line, from Indianapolis, and it was completed on July 30, 1904. The jointly operated freight terminal was built on the Union Traction line south of Main Street.

The Winona Interurban Railway arrived on the scene in May, 1907. This company was built in segments and the Peru to Chili portion was separated from the northern end for some time. The Winona built tracks into the center of town and connected with the other two companies at Broadway and Main. This trackage was used for a local streetcar operation from the heart of Peru to suburban Oakdale just a short distance outside of Peru, as well as for the interurban passenger cars and interchange freight cars. Usually one single truck car equipped to pull trailers was in use. Several trailers and an extra motorized car remained in Peru most of the time. These may have been parked on a spur track on Seventh Street.

The ISC and its predecessors usually assigned two city cars to Peru. They usually sat out-of-doors at the west end of the city unless they were sent to the Boyd Park barn. Cars were routinely sent back and forth over the interurban line from Peru to Fort Wayne. These long runs of the small, slow, city cars were usually made at night. As newer equipment became available in Fort Wayne, both Peru and Wabash got the best of the displaced cars. The cars were usually in very good condition and well maintained. Cars used in Peru did not need destination signs as there was only one place to go. Peru received cars from the 170-series at first then by the twenties got cars from 176-201 series, followed by the rebuilt 202-220 series and finally the newer single-truck cars from the 290-299 series. These former Logansport cars were in use when service ended.

When the Peru-Lafayette interurban was abandoned in 1932 the Peru West Main Street trackage was retained for the exclusive use of the city car (only one car was in use by that time). The Indiana Railroad System interurbans continued to run over the East Main Street tracks. ISC still controlled the city lines but they were managed through the Indiana Railroad System until the Indiana Railroad bankruptcy in 1933. This put the Peru line back in ISC's hands. The city operation was not a money maker and this lone ISC city line outside of Fort Wayne was a nuisance. ISC petitioned to end the service. The last city car was run on December 8, 1934 with no replacement service offered. The West Main trackage was abandoned at that time.

The Winona line offered city streetcar service on its north side line for many years and apparently on a continuous basis. Birney cars, bought second hand from Detroit, were used in Peru and Warsaw after 1924. The end of the Winona's city service came prior to or on September 30, 1934 when the Winona abandoned its passenger service and most of the trackage not used for freight service (the exception was the Warsaw city operation). This meant that the Winona's trackage south of Wabash Junction into Peru was abandoned.

The Indiana Railroad cars continued to run through Peru until September 10, 1938 when interurban passenger and freight rail service over the leased line was abandoned. ISC then tore up the tracks for the salvage value.

Peru was considered "Circus City" as it was the winter home for several major circus companies. On parade, one of the great circus wagons rolls south on Broadway with an eight-horse hitch. Car 188 patiently waits amidst other vehicle traffic. ***M. D. McCarter Collection.***

SPECIAL
52
52
52
SHOE
UILDERS

Lafayette City Lines

CHAPTER 17

LAFAYETTE'S FIRST STREET RAILWAY—(1869-1874)

Lafayette had the first street railway in the upper Wabash River Valley but it was less than a success for several reasons. Its history was a rather sad affair and ended in a discordant note of a family squabble. It should have fared better.

Colonel John Ball was the originator of the company in July 1868 but there is some question as to whether it was an actual corporation. In August the stockholders of the company were assessed to pay on their subscribed stock to demonstrate the company meant business. The company plan was taken to the City Council and an ordinance authorizing the construction and operation of certain passenger railways upon certain streets was approved on September 8, 1868. The street railway was granted a 25 year franchise. Active operation was to begin on June 1, 1869 unless an acceptable delay was duly presented. The ordinance contained several routine sections which eventually helped to kill the street railway. These included proper grading, the maintenance of the track work, the required paving by boulder or brick between the rails and on two feet on either side, that the company could forfeit its rights through failure to provide service and that the Council had the right to remove the rails if the company did not perform.

The only time that the company's official name is mentioned is in the ordinance, "Street Railroad Company of Lafayette." Mr. Israel Spencer was the president of the company and with the franchise problem settled the company went to work. Three routes were specified in the ordinance but with certain amendments some routing was modified. Iron rails were shipped from New Albany, Indiana and Mr. C. B. Pratt of Louisville, Kentucky was named contractor for the railway. On September 21, the Lafayette **Daily Journal** reported that the workers were "laying a square or two per day" and making the curve from South to Ninth Street. Other crews were at work on the second route laying track on Sixth Street between Ferry and Brown Streets.

Several segments of tracks were completed but the pace slowed and eventually stopped. The rails, since they were not in use, were covered with dirt to allow the free passage of vehicles and to prevent any damage from heavy wagons. A report then came along indicating that Mr. Pratt owed local firms for materials and work. Worse yet, he was alleged to have left town. The company representatives, to maintain some order, denied this and said some arrangements had been worked out. The debts were settled and Mr. Pratt may have been tracked down and pursuaded to give back some money. As the 1868-1869 winter came on, the street railway activity stopped. Nothing happened in the spring and on May 15, 1869, a notice was posted in the **Daily Journal** offering for sale "the roadbed, track, turnouts, stable and lease of the ground on which the latter stands, together with unpaid subscriptions to the stock of the company aggregating $3,809.50."

Throughout the summer of 1869, the City Council threatened to tear up the tracks because of the apparent default. Late in October the tracks were cleared. On November 10, 1869 reports indicated that Colonel Ball had bought out most, if not all of the other interests, and the street railway would be completed and put into operation, albeit an abbreviated form and with some modified routes. On November 30 the **Journal** reported the arrival of the first streetcar. It was described as nice, dry and clean. A second car followed soon after. These were double end horsecars and, from later accounts, appear to have been heavy. Who built them or whether they were new or second hand is a mystery.

First runs, with bonafide paying passengers, were made on December 11. There were two routes with both suppose to reach Linwood, just north of the Lafayette city limits. The "lower line" was described as the "North Ninth Street Line" and ran through the more level area of the town. This line commenced at Main and Fourth Streets, ran north on Fourth to Ferry Street, east on Ferry to Sixth, north on Sixth to Brown Street, east on Brown Street to Ninth Street, north on Ninth to

The 52 in July 1937 on Ninth Street. ***Van Dusen-Zillmer Collection.***

Tippecanoe Street and then east to Thirteenth Street. The line was then supposed to be run north to the city limits. At Fifth and Ferry Street, the company maintained a flagman to protect the cars from the Monon Railroad trains that ran through the city in the center of Fifth Street. The second line was usually described as the "South Street Line" and started at Third and South Streets. (This location is frequently referred to as "the Bramble House," a hotel located on the southeast corner of Third and South Streets.) The South Street Line proceeded east on South Street to Ninth Street, north on Ninth to North Street, east on North Street to the Valley Depot (Wabash Railroad), where it went northeast to Thirteenth Street, then north on Thirteenth Street to Union Street.

The company stable and car house building were located on the northeast corner of Union and Thirteenth Streets. A second lot was also acquired for an additional car shed. Only the South Street Line reached the stable. The other line terminated two blocks north. At this time —December 1869—the two lines were not connected.

Two new streetcars arrived by train, on the Wabash Railroad, on January 17, 1870. The only note is that they were built in "the East." They were one-man operated and of the "bob-tail" type. Fares were collected by depositing coins into a patented, self-depositing, fare apparatus at the car front. The back was enclosed with a door that covered the step and well. The cars were green and white and lettered "West Division-Linwood" and "Public Square" on each side.

Before the new cars could be used, turntables for turning the single-end cars had to be installed. One was placed at Tippecanoe and Thirteenth and the other at the Public Square (Fourth and Main). On January 28, 1870, car 1 went into service with car 2 in use on the next day. The cars passed on Brown Street, about mid-point, at the only switch. Cars on the line were run from 7:00 a.m. to 9:00 p.m. They sat on Tippecanoe Street overnight and the horses were walked the two blocks to the stable.

This line, North Ninth, was fairly successful but the South Street Line was not. The South Line apparently did not serve a well populated area of people that would ride the cars. Yet, Colonel Ball was looking for some way to put the line back into operation after briefly closing it down in mid-January for a month. The first idea was to connect the two by building track on Fourth Street between Main and South Streets. This didn't happen.

The next step taken by Colonel Ball was to correct the embarrassment of not being able to get the North Ninth Street cars to the car barn. A heavy snow on March 15, 1870 stopped the cars...and most of Lafayette. The public was sympathetic. Trading on this, Ball announced a planned connection of the two upper ends of the lines by building a track southward from the turntable at Tippecanoe and Thirteenth to the car barn on Union and Thirteenth. This would be only two blocks and one block of Thirteenth was hardly more than an alley. The property owners protested. At this same time, two new cars were reported to be on order and to be delivered soon. Noting this and with general support, the City Council gave the company a one year go ahead to use Thirteenth Street. The connection was quickly completed.

Two more bob-tail cars arrived on April 8, 1870 and these were lettered as either "Junction and Greenbush Cemetery" or "Junctionville and Spring Vale Cemetery," (both names appear in the newspaper) and were numbered as 3 and 4.

On April 16, 1870 a new, longer route was put in operation. This was an extension of the South Street Line by building south on Third Street from South Street to Greene Street where a turntable, at the Purdue Agricultural Works, was located. This area was close to the junction of the four rail lines that served Lafayette, hence the name "Junctionville." On May 6, 1870, Judge John Purdue and a group of "old settlers" took a special excursion sponsored by Colonel Ball who put four cars at their disposal. Each car seated 18 or 19 of the old settlers and they rode from Junctionville (and the Purdue Agricultural Works) up the South Street Line to Union and Thirteenth and then on the North Ninth Street Line back southward to Fourth and Main...a circuit of the entire system.

Was the street railway a success? At this point the company was also officially sold at a sheriff's sale to perfect the title and remove the old claims. The two new owners were Edward H. Ball and Henry S. Mayo. The company's office was on Fourth, just north of Main Street. The six cars were pulled by both horse and mules. One route made some money.

The other route was, at best, marginal. However, the business was not truly successful.

Much of what followed is a bit clouded by the limited recording of the happenings as day-to-day items were not always chronicled in the local papers. The South Street Line did not pay expenses and was used only occasionally, if at all, after 1871...and then for special events. The City Council forced the company to put the system in shape again in the summer of 1872.

The North Ninth Street line maintained regular service on a twenty minute schedule with the first car in the morning leaving Thirteenth and Union at 6:40 a.m. and arriving at Public Square (Fourth and Main) in time for a return trip at 7:00 a.m. The last car left the square at 9:20 p.m. according to a September 14, 1872 schedule which showed this as the only operating line. Special events during the summer of 1872, for the July 4 fireworks, and P. T. Barnum's circus used extra cars to reach the circus lot near the Wabash Railroad depot and 10th Street. The company, in the following year, was criticized for loading a car with 59 passengers and expecting two horses to pull the heavy load.

On March 16, 1873, an insurmountable calamity befell the street railway when Henry S. Mayo, president of the Second National Bank, died—Mayo had become the sole owner of the street railway on June 26, 1872, and since he left no will, it became part of a large and somewhat disorganized estate which had a large number of heirs, all of whom wanted what they felt was "their" share of the property. Edward H. Mayo, the banker's son, seems to have been the court appointed executor of his father's estate.

Dr. Glick, of the City Council, on May 20, 1873, asked that South Street Line, not now in use, be taken up. Mayo opposed this but Glick did get the track on Third Street torn up starting on June 5. A new dress of gravel was placed on the other tracks.

The squabbling heirs left a court recorded legal trail to follow as the estate was dragged around for over a year. At least it left a written record of what happened. The Street Railroad of Lafayette (also called Lafayette Street Railroad) was considered as a unit in the estate including buildings, tracks, horses, cars, franchise, et. al. and was something that could not be broken up. Also, little or no money could be spent on the lines because of the loud howls of many relatives and claimants grabbing for "their" money. The street railway was an unfortunate and unwanted orphan as it didn't—apparently—make much if any money. E. H. Mayo asked the Council for permission to close down the line in September 1873. He also hoped to find a buyer as no heir wanted it. Service was stopped on September 9, and then restored on September 15 with the cars still running in November.

The cars may have been operating in the spring of 1874 but the Council from March onward continued to attack the poor operation and maintenance of the line. E. H. Mayo made promises which he probably would like to have kept but could not. The court had had the railroad appraised for sale. The appraisal on October 31, 1873 was interesting and revealing as the list showed only three of the original six cars. The cars plus seven horses and their equipment and the franchise were valued at $10,000. The two lots, stable and barn were valued at $3,000. On May 4, 1874, E. H. Mayo reported to the court the property remained unsold for want of bidders and stated no one would pay $13,000 for the property. He asked for a reappraisal. On May 29, 1874, a new appraisal was returned to the court at $5,500. It still didn't sell.

The street railway was by now no longer running. The Council felt that it was important that Lafayette should have a street railroad yet the citizens, according to the Council, opposed it. The **Journal** noted that Lafayette was the only city of its size that will not sustain a street railroad.

The Council solved the estate's problem, in part, by announcing, in August 1874, that they would exercise their ordinance rights and tear up the no longer used rails. The rails were taken up during August, September and October 1874. On November 4, 1874, the **Journal** reported the street railway was a thing of the past. The rails had been shipped to an Indianapolis rolling mill for rerolling into new shapes. The land and building could now be sold by the estate. The remaining three cars were most likely sold to another property. Thus came the sad end to what had started as a success story, a railway that might have survived its problems and was finally crushed by the lack of a will.

Ten years would pass.

LAFAYETTE STREET RAILWAY
1884-1922

The desire for local street railway service came up again in 1883 and the construction was authorized by the City Council. An ordinance, adopted on March 5, provided for a twenty-five year franchise for a single-track line that would be powered by either horses or mules. The new line, to qualify, was to be completed and operating by May 1, 1884.

On March 13, a new company, the Lafayette Street Railway Company, was organized with an initial capital stock authorization, of $25,000. The five principals were Charles M., Frank D., and Freeland B. Caldwell, William Chambers, and James O. Lake; F. B. Caldwell was the first president of the new company.

Trackage was laid on Main Street starting at Third, east to Ninth Street, north to Salem Street, east to Tenth Street, north to Hartford Street and east to Twelfth Street. Two short branch lines were built, one on Ferry Street to the Wabash Railroad depot and the other on Third and South Street, to reach the Big Four and Lake Erie and Western depots. This one-route line was an interesting parallel to the original 1869 line and served the area north of Main Street but with a somewhat different and more direct route. The stables were even located in the north end. This time the stables and barn were located at Tenth and Hartford Streets.

Main Street was the city's principal commercial street and North Ninth Street was a fine residential area so the company would serve a practical route. No thought, then or ever—for that matter, was given to building a line south to the junction area. The new company seemed to have paid heed to the errors of its predecessor. The new line was ready and operating on the May 1, 1884 deadline.

The horsecars were built by J. M. Jones' Sons. Six cars had appeared by 1886. These double-end cars seated twenty people. The cars were run over 2.25 miles of line and the company boasted 40 horses. By 1888, the company had begun using mules and claimed 14 horses and 14 mules.

Chauncey, now the city of West Lafayette, authorized the street railroad to extend the Main Street car line west from the Wabash River bridge. The company also had to secure county permission to lay tracks across the bridge. This new line, built in early 1888, ran over the Main Street levee, up the steep State Street hill then west to Grant Street. Grant and State was the southeast corner of Purdue University. The long car line, the only one, was known as "Linwood, Main St. & Purdue University."

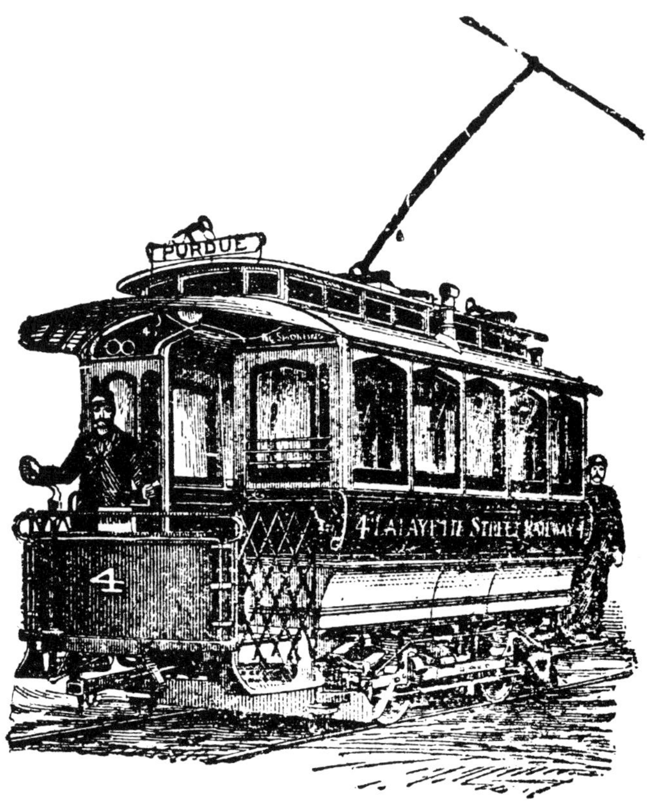

Lafayette is located in a pronounced valley, with fairly steep banks, created by the Wabash River. The older section of the city lies in the old river bottoms and is fairly level with gentle slopes toward the steeper banks. Coming out of this area requires surmounting some fairly steep ascending grades which caused the main line railroads to go through the city using some special routes to minimize the gradient. The new car line had to go up the steep grade, on the west side, to reach Chauncey, which was, essentially, out of the valley. This west side line had a six percent grade over 800 feet long with a sharp curve at the middle point in the hill. On the east side, a later car line had a 6.6% grade of nearly 800 feet with one portion in excess of seven percent. Long grades were notoriously hard on horses, required two-horse teams on the cars and, in some cases, additional "hill teams" to help pull the load. The "hill team" was stabled near State and River Road. In the building on the west side line, the Lafayette Street Railway had opposition about overloaded cars and the ability of the animals on the steep grade. This resistance to overloading the mules and horses must have had an effect on the owners who recognized that building of any additional lines would require solving the problem of steep grades out of the valley.

Mule-drawn streetcar 103 near Linnwood School.

Frank J. Sprague's new and successful electrification of the Richmond, Virginia car lines was important news. Although not the first electrified street railway, the Richmond line did prove to be a success...and it had steep grades. The Sprague system not only overcame the grades but it also seemed to be an efficient and economically sound operation. Clearly, the Sprague electrification was the most promising of the new electric railway systems and it might solve the Lafayette hill problems at a reasonable cost.

The company secured the passage of a new city ordinance on April 10, 1888 which allowed the company to change to electricity and extend its line. The owners also contracted with The Sprague Electric Railway and Motor Company to electrify the system. Work started in the summer of 1888 and wires and poles went up. The company had added new cars when they built the extension to the west side and now owned thirteen cars. Some would be electrified.

A trial trip was made on August 30, 1888 with electrified car 106. The car first ran two blocks north on Twelfth to the end of the line at Greenbush Cemetery and back in a trip that seems slow (by today's standards) but was far faster than the horses and mules. Regular service began on September 3, 1888. The power plant, located near the foot of Ferry Street, was designed for the operation of stationary motors as well as the streetcars so that the company could draw added revenues from industry. The electric cars easily made fifteen miles per hour, ran up the long grades, had pulled two loaded trailers on trial runs, and remained brilliantly lighted each night. Lafayette was now among the early, totally successful, electric railways and the earliest Sprague installation west of the Allegheny mountains. It was the first successful electric railway in Indiana.

On October 14, 1891, the company was reorganized with the Levering family of Lafayette taking an active interest. The Levering connections with their eastern relatives brought major Philadelphia investment capital into the Indiana electric railway scene. George E. C. Johnson became the president and treasurer and Thomas J. Levering was secretary of the company. The company was now operating nine electrified cars and three trailers. They still kept at least one team of horses for emergency purposes.

Improvements in the electric railway field came rapidly and new electric cars were ordered from J. G. Brill Company of Philadelphia. Although slightly larger and, perhaps, somewhat sturdier, they were little more than 16-foot closed car bodies of a traditional design delivered on special electric trucks. The older cars were withdrawn from regular service and some were used as trailers. The

To the left:** Cars 106 and 109 in the first run by electric trolley in Lafayette.* ***Tippecanoe County Historical Association Collection. Above: *The 103—one of the Sprague electrified, Jones built horsecars—heads west at the Court House in Lafayette in late 1888.* ***"The Electrical World."***

single car line on the west side was extended along the north gutter line of State Street, from Grant Street to the Main Gates of Purdue University during 1892. The Purdue Board of Trustees later authorized the tracks to be extended westward to form the West Lafayette (Purdue) loop. The line continued to State and Waldron Streets where it turned north to what is now Stadium Avenue (it then had three street names—W. 7th, Thornell and Harvey), east to Salisbury Street, and south to State Street. Service over this new line began on June 17, 1893. A group of eight-bench open cars also went into service that summer. T. J. Levering was now the company president. J. Levering Jones, of Philadelphia, was the attorney for the company.

Also, in Lafayette, another new line (Oakland) was built up Main Street, east from Ninth Street, to an area known as Oakland Hill. At the top of this steep grade is the "Five Points" intersection where the line turned east onto South Street for one block. It then proceeded over a rather unique route: southeast on Lincoln (paralleling Main Street) to Scott Street, northeast on Scott to the intersection of South, Park and Scott streets. The line then went east on South Street to 29th Street, south to Kossuth Street, westward on Kossuth Street to Ninth Street then north on South Ninth Street to Main Street. This line was completed in September, 1893. South Ninth Street also contained a long, steep grade extending from Columbia Street to State Street. Both of these steeply graded routes crossed the Wabash Railroad main line at level crossings, which presented a potentially serious hazard. A loop in the downtown area was built around the Courthouse by laying tracks on Third, Columbia and Fourth Streets. Also, another extension was built south on 18th Street, from Kossuth to the Tippecanoe County Fairgrounds.

As part of the expansion, the company completed, on December 30, 1893, a large car barn on Ferry Street, between Ninth and Tenth Streets. This barn as built could hold 34 cars. It served as the home base for the company throughout the trolley era and well into the bus era. A new powerhouse was built at the foot of South Street on the east bank of the Wabash River. The main portion was built in 1892 with an enlargement completed

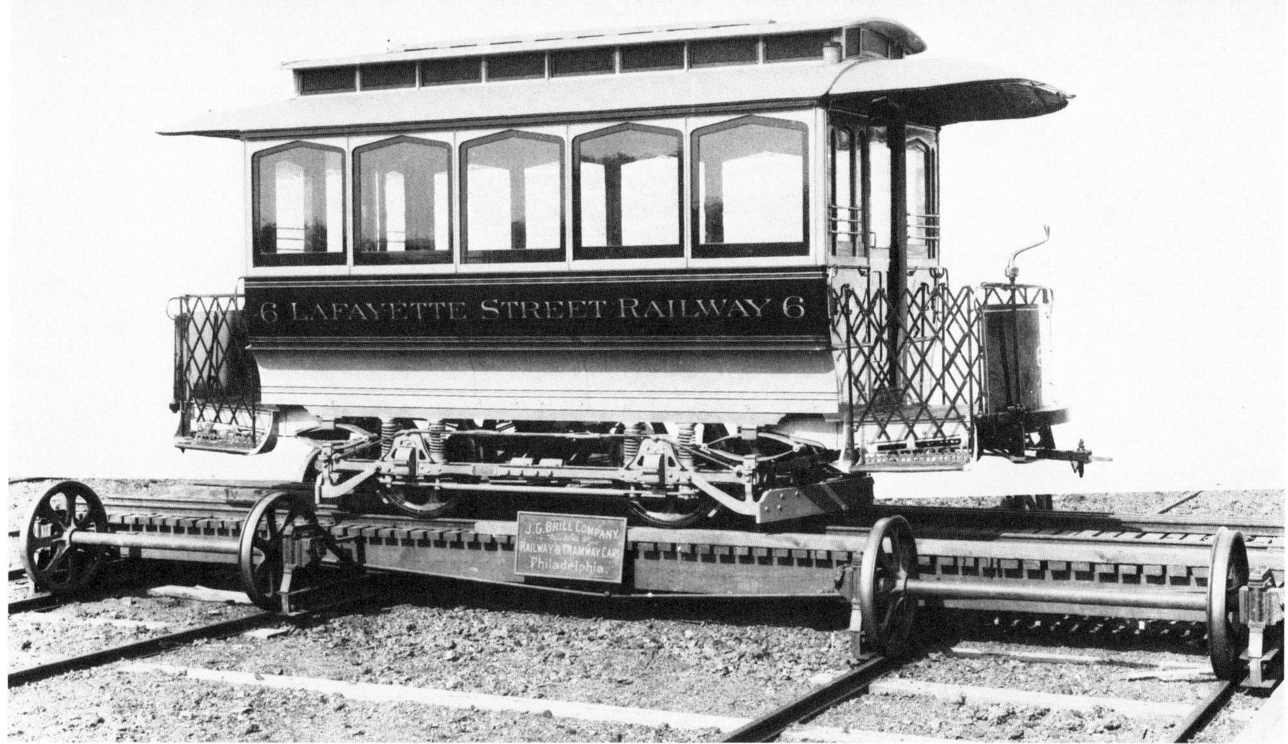

Above: *The J. G. Brill Company of Philadelphia supplied new closed cars to the company in 1891 and 1893.* ***Historical Society of Pennsylvania Collection. At the left:*** *The 1891 and 1893 Brill cars were equipped with enclosed platforms to conform to a new state law. This protected the motorman in cold and wet weather.* ***David W. Chambers Collection.***

The Purdue campus in 1893 with Brill built #6 on the north side of State Street at the old Main Gates. Only the center building, University Hall, still remains. ***Purdue University Photo.***

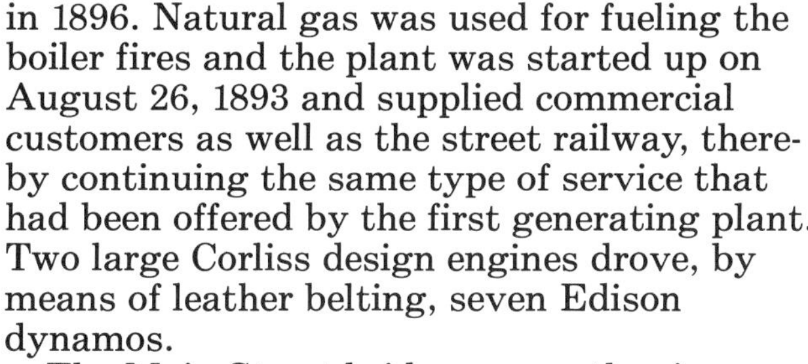
in 1896. Natural gas was used for fueling the boiler fires and the plant was started up on August 26, 1893 and supplied commercial customers as well as the street railway, thereby continuing the same type of service that had been offered by the first generating plant. Two large Corliss design engines drove, by means of leather belting, seven Edison dynamos.

The Main Street bridge across the river originally had the track located in the middle of the roadway. This earlier bridge was replaced with a new iron bridge and the railway used a through track on the north side of the bridge roadway. This was not considered safe by 1894 as the newer bridge had been designed for the first electric cars (converted horsecars) which were lighter than the new Brill built 1891 cars. The company stopped carrying passengers across the bridge in August. The people had to walk and a transfer car carried passengers from the public square to the bridge. Cars were kept on the west side. In 1895, the bridge was rebuilt with a special track on the north side and through service was restored.

As was the case with most electric street railways, the Lafayette company experienced tremendous good weather business on the

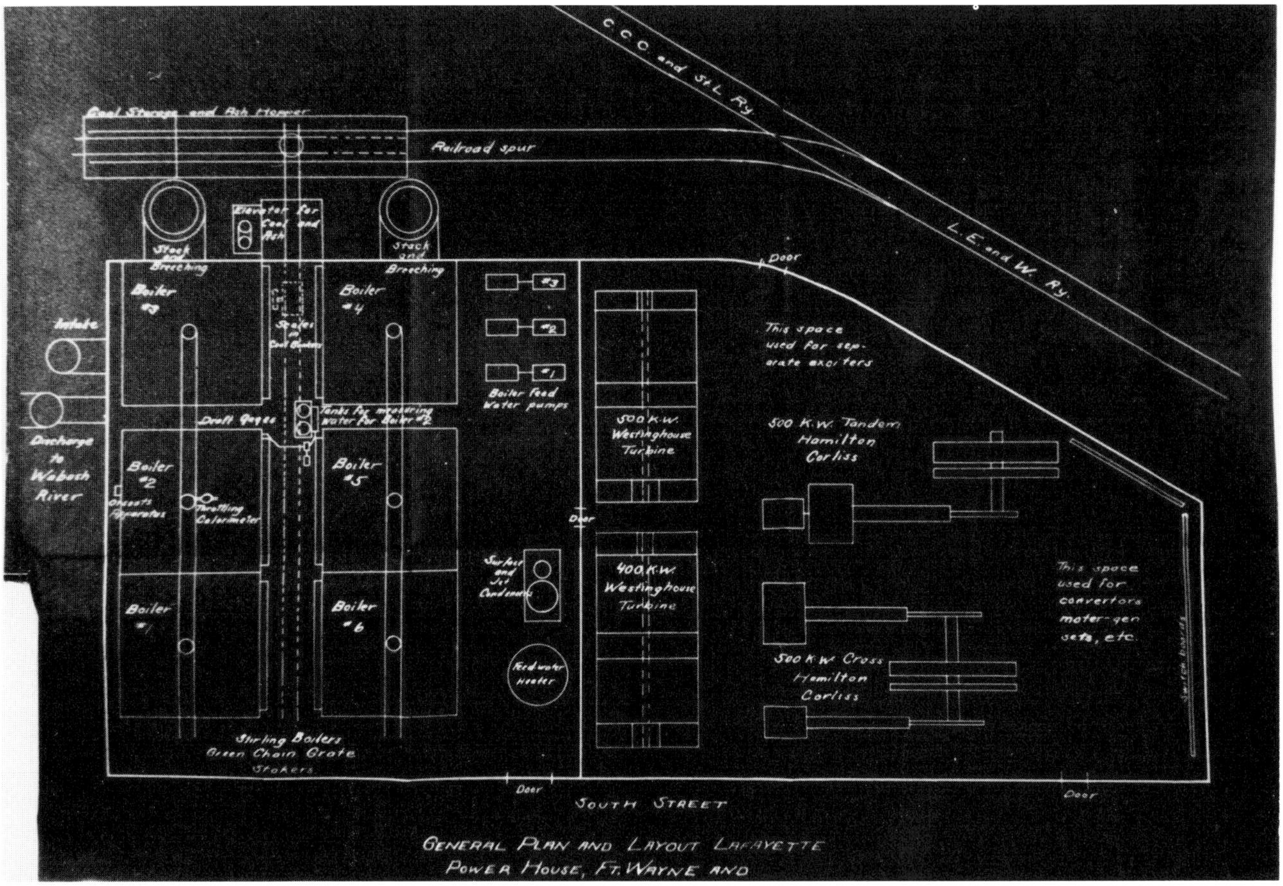

Above: *General plan and layout for the Lafayette Street Rwy. powerhouse c. 1911.* ***Tippecanoe County Historical Association Collection. To the right:*** *The first unit of the Lafayette Street Rwy. powerhouse at the foot of South Street, 1893.* ***David W. Chambers Collection.***

open streetcars. People rode for the pleasure of riding, the opportunity to be in the fresh air, to view the city, and, in some cases, to be seen by others. The city lines soon became too routine and in an attempt to preserve and enlarge on this unexpected business source of open air riding the company decided to build a special line. An extension of the tracks was built, on the west side of the river, northward on Salisbury Street from Stadium, to what is now Lincoln Street, west to Rose Street and then northward into an area with the intriguing name of "Happy Hollow." This was an area of rough terrain, part way up and along the high west banks of the Wabash River Valley where Happy Hollow Creek had cut a ravine. This 1896 pastoral setting was very picturesque and the meandering streetcar line was instantly popular. The same line also served as the base for a further extension to the new Indiana State Soldiers' Home. The tracks came up the valley side and ran along the top of the bluff to the Home. The Soldiers' Home was on the high bluff ground overlooking a long bend in the river and in a pleasant location. An inspection run was made on April 19, 1897 before regular service began May 11. Below the Home, along the river, the street railway company had already acquired the property of Tecumeseh Trail Park on March 12, 1896. The principal building was a large dancing pavilion. The wooded riverside area was laid out with trails which were ideal for strolling and picnics. The park was an instant attraction and required the company to add new cars to meet the crowd require-

Above:** Used from 1893 to 1974, the Ferry Street car barn was a "fresh air" operation providing little more than cover for the streetcars. Later, portions were closed off for buses. This 1930's view shows the southeast corner. **Ed Frank Photo.
Below:** Ft. Wayne & Wabash Valley 156 at Purdue University, West Lafayette, Indiana. This car was used in both Lafayette and Logansport. **David W. Chambers Collection.

The LSR's Ferry Street car barn built in 1893. This seven track barn housed most of the cars used in Lafayette. This photo was taken circa 1915. ***David W. Chambers Collection.***

ments. Cars started at the Courthouse Square in Lafayette. However, the car line ended at the Soldiers' Home, on the bluff, requiring the park patrons to walk through the grounds and down the long drives that brought vehicular traffic to the Home from the River Road, down in the valley. In pleasant weather, it was a delightful walk but it was a long hike if the weather turned to rain. An excursion boat also ran up the river from Lafayette.

Several changes and extensions were made to the city lines. The North Ninth Street line was extended via Greenbush and 18th Streets to reach the Monon Railroad Shops (further north on 18th)...The looping line in the Oakland Hill area was rebuilt in 1901 and split into two parts. Kossuth Street cars operated via South Ninth and Kossuth Streets ending near 26th Street with the remainder to 29th Street torn up. The trackage on South Street east from 25th (formerly Park) to 29th was kept in place. The trackage on 29th Street was abandoned in 1901. For the other route a sharp curve was placed at Scott and 25th where a car proceeding in a northeasterly direction abruptly turned and headed south on 25th to a connection at Kossuth Street. Another car line was built in 1903 south from Ninth and Kossuth to Owen Street, west to Fourth and south to Montefiore Street. This was a single-car feeder route.

On May 29, 1903, the Lafayette Street Railway Company was taken over by the Fort Wayne, Logansport, Lafayette and Lima Traction Company as the first property acquired in a major consolidation. The tie-in of the Levering family interests played an important part in this purchase as that family was closely allied with the Philadelphia-based Widener-Elkins-Dolan and Morgan financial interests. This new company became the Fort Wayne & Wabash Valley Traction Company on February 25, 1904.

The Murdock family of Lafayette, including James Murdock and his sons Charles and Samuel were connected with several electric railway enterprises. They were financially interested in the systems at Fort Wayne, South Bend and Evansville, plus having extensive gas and electric properties that had been consolidated as the Indiana Lighting Company. At the time of the merger of the Lafayette property into the Wabash Valley, the Murdock's because of their investment and financial alliances were publicly credited with being the major owners of the consolidating company. They were large scale investors and would continue their involvement with the Dietrich Syndicate and the Schoepf-McGowan Syndicate—mostly the latter—in years to come. The influx of new money changed the character of the Lafayette system from a local operation to a key property in a large system.

Scenic though it might be, the Happy Hollow line was not a practical operation. It was a remote route and immediately proved to be costly to maintain. Bridges, fills, and cuts over mountain goat type terrain required continual work. The easy and practical answer was a new line on the valley floor, following the route of the North River Road from State and Ellsworth Streets. During April 1902, the Happy Hollow Line was shut down, torn up, and moved to the new location. Service began again on April 29. The new route was not an "all-weather" route as it was prone to the Wabash River's flooding.

In 1905, the company extended the line north for another three miles from Tecumseh Trail Park to Battleground. Battleground was the site of General William Henry Harrison's victory over a major Indian alliance and their leader Tecumseh. Battleground was in 1905, a summer resort community, a sleepy small village, and a historic site. The line was fully operational on October 1, 1905. First service was furnished by a borrowed lightweight interurban car from the Indianapolis & Eastern Traction Company. Soon afterwards, two of the former Wabash River Traction's suburban, double-truck cars were sent to Lafayette and put into service, operating on a half hour schedule from the Court House square. The

At the right: The Happy Hollow streetcar headed south in West Lafayette between 1897-1902. ***Below:*** *The Happy Hollow line in 1897, looking southwest towards Grand View Cemetery (now located on the high bank behind the cars). The cars are on the biggest trestle over Happy Hollow Creek.* ***Both photos—Tippecanoe County Historical Association Collection.***

fare to the Soldiers' Home was ten cents and twenty-five cents to Battleground.

The original electrified closed cars and the newer Brill built closed cars in Lafayette quickly became too small and had to be replaced by larger cars on an "as available basis." A group of ten new cars came in 1904 (which were first split between Lafayette and Logansport) from the Cincinnati Car Company. These were all transferred to Lafayette to consolidate car classes.

Two interurban electric lines reached Lafayette and both were important lines of major systems. The first line was completed on December 1, 1903 and was built by the Indianapolis & Northwestern Traction Company. Entry into Lafayette, on this through line from Indianapolis, was gained by an extension of the tracks on Main Street from the Five Points intersection, at the top of Oakland Hill (at South Street), southward to the city limits. The Indianapolis & Northwestern was leased to the Terre Haute, Indianapolis & Eastern Traction Company in April 1907. The THI&E was a Schoepf-McGowan Syndicate property as was the Wabash Valley. The parallel trackage on Lincoln was taken up in 1904.

The second interurban line was the Wabash Valley's extension from Logansport to Lafayette which was built by the Wabash Valley's subsidiary, the Lafayette & Logansport Traction Company. This line ran its first car through on June 28, 1907 with through service beginning on July 4. The Wabash Valley's private car, Lawton, made the first 144-mile Fort Wayne-Lafayette through run in five hours. The interurban cars of both companies looped the Tippecanoe County Court House. The interurban station was located on Third Street between South and Columbia Streets. This station continued in use until February 11, 1923 when a new facility for freight and passengers was opened on Ferry Street west of the car barn.

In 1910, as part of the proposed Wabash Valley expansion plans, a large building at the southeast corner of 26th & Kossuth Streets was purchased for a proposed shop for heavy rail car repair work. The building had been built in the 1890's and had housed a carpet factory. After the great expansion plan was forgotten, the Fort Wayne & Northern Indiana Traction Company used the building as a storage car barn. Some active cars were based here and made their runs from the barn.

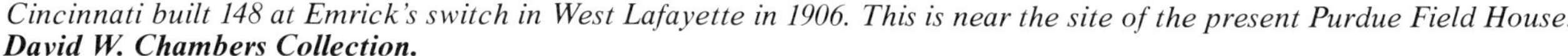

Cincinnati built 148 at Emrick's switch in West Lafayette in 1906. This is near the site of the present Purdue Field House. ***David W. Chambers Collection.***

Basically, it was a three-track storage barn for surplus cars.

The year 1913 was one of disaster and change for the company most of which was obvious but it also set the stage for a long range change in the company's future. Visible, however, was high water. Floods were common enough for the Lafayette system and they had even built special "high water" cars to tow trailers through the flooded low areas. But, the great flood of March, 1913 wreaked havoc throughout much of the midwest. Service stopped on March 24. The Main Street bridge which carried the main line between the two communities, as well as the Brown Street bridge (the other highway bridge) were severely damaged. Each lost one span to the swirling waters and the Main Street bridge's central pier had to be replaced. The levee area and the River Road tracks were completely under water when the river crested at 33 feet. At one point the water was 26 feet deep over the tracks. Streetcar service was suspended when water briefly entered the powerhouse which caused a shutdown for several hours. The receding water left a mess. No cars were on the west side when the Main Street bridge became impassable, and there was no immediate way to get them there, which caused a break in service. The ruined trackage, including the street paving, had to be rebuilt. A ferry boat was run by the company until a temporary streetcar bridge could be built later that spring. The temporary bridge was also an early winter victim of ice and water and the

At the right: *The 251 was one of the Wabash-Logansport Traction Company's cars. Two cars of this type were used on the Battleground line until 1922.* ***Below:*** *North River Road (looking south towards Lafayette) in 1913 before the flood reached its peak. At peak, the water was 8-10 feet higher at this location. An eight-bench open car is being towed by work car 7; the 7 is a rather poor rebuild of an old passenger car.* ***Both photos—Tippecanoe County Historical Association Collection.***

"The Village" of West Lafayette in 1912; the car shown is about to head down the long hill toward Lafayette. ***Tippecanoe County Historical Association Collection.***

Nearside car 226 was one of several built for use in Lafayette by the J. G. Brill Company. These cars were true "nearsides" built to the patents of the Nearside Car Company. These cars were also among the early street railway cars bought on an equipment trust financing plan; the trust company's plate can be seen on the platform knee below the first window. ***Historical Society of Pennsylvania Collection.***

ferry had to be restored. In December 1914 the new concrete bridge was finally available for use. The bridge was welcomed by the riders but the company was assessed for their "share" of the cost at an annual fee of $5,000.

As part of their continuing promise to improve service, the company bought a group of single-truck, "Nearside" cars in 1913. These cars, numbered 221-227, were built especially for service in Lafayette. They were a great improvement because of their higher speed loading.

The 26th and Kossuth storage barn was destroyed in a $75,000 fire at 4:30 a.m. on May 20, 1915. This was a severe loss with a total of 16 cars burned. These included eight closed cars, five open cars, a sweeper and a sand car plus a special brake test car, "Louise," that belonged to the THI&E. There was no electric power in the building but the fire

Third Street on the Square in 1915 with a city car making a loop around the Court House square. ***Tippecanoe County Historical Association Collection.***

department saved seven cars. The loss of the open cars was not of great concern, as they were seeing little use and few were now needed in Lafayette.

In 1916, a study of a typical street railway property—Lafayette—was written by Dr. Dressel D. Ewing of Purdue University. This study dealt with loading and unloading times for streetcars in regular service. Two car types were involved which showed the near-side cars accomplished their design aim of rapid loading and unloading through the elimination of bulkheads and the use of large folding doors. The other cars were older single-truck, double-end cars with longitudinal seats. The Nearsides were used on main routes in Lafayette and the older deck-roof were used on the west side (Purdue) line and the Battleground line. The advantages of the newer cars were very evident, especially since they carried a farebox, which aided the conductor in collecting fares, and were pay-as-you-enter cars. The other cars had high entrance steps and required the conductor to hand-collect and register the fares. These cars were slow loaders, except at Purdue, where Dr. Ewing noted, "a group of college students can get aboard a car in a phenomenally short time if the spirit moves them to do so."

At the time of Dr. Ewing's article, single-truck cars were being used on the long Battleground line. This note is unique because the long Battleground line normally used large double-truck cars which were faster and better riding.

Cars on hand and in use varied throughout the years. In 1908, the Lafayette property had 34 closed and open cars and used an average of twelve cars in daily service. By 1918, the number of available cars had been depleted and twenty-five cars were available with nineteen being closed cars plus a snow sweeper and a work car.

The Lafayette property was only one part of the Fort Wayne & Northern Indiana Traction Company but it was a troublesome operation. Jitney buses (motorists picking up passengers for a fare) were virtually unregulated, following World War I, and the Lafayette city government unfairly let the jitneys continue this unregulated competition with the streetcars. The company also had a high outstanding debt including the bridge assessment. Costs were high and revenues were down.

Another loss, which the company really did not miss was the destruction of the Tecumseh Trail Park pavilion and buildings by fire. Since the company was giving up its parks, this was not a true loss.

The FW&NI was sold and reorganized at the end of 1919. The new Indiana Service Corporation did not bid on the acquisition of the Lafayette lines. ISC did retain the Tecumseh Trail Park to Battleground trackage as it had

Fort Wayne & Wabash Valley's 250, used on the Battleground line, at the Ferry Street car barn in Lafayette, Indiana. ***Purdue University Photo/David W. Chambers Collection.***

been built by the Wabash Valley and was not an asset of the old Lafayette Street Railway. The city system was, in effect, turned loose to fend for itself as an independent. It emerged as the Lafayette Service Company.

On October 17, 1921 a foreclosure suit was filed against the company by the Real Estate Trust Company, Philadelphia, representing the owners of $225,000 in bonds. R. W. Levering was appointed receiver and filed a financial report showing, in addition to the bonds, another security claim of $7,952 plus a balance of about one-half of the company's indebtedness for the construction of the Main Street bridge. There was also an operating deficit of $11,060 for the 1921 operation of the 18.66 miles of track.

Levering wanted to restore the property to good condition through the abandonment of the Owen Street and Fairground lines, the purchase of 21 one-man cars and a rehabilitation of the remaining trackwork. The old power plant, which had also reverted to the property, was to be sold and electric power would be purchased. The proposed modernization would have cost an estimated $165,000. Some cash would be raised through the sale of the power facility and the land of the old Tecumseh Trail Park. Also, the city would be asked to enact an anti-jitney ordinance.

The federal court declined the plan because it was opposed by the bondholders. This group pushed for foreclosure because they did not see the property as being able to earn a fair return. Several questions of financial stability had been raised and the management had not been able to secure any support from the Lafayette City Council. This body had earlier adopted a policy of opposition to the Fort Wayne based company and seemingly would

The 503 at the Third Street station in Lafayette. The "Democrat" was a Lafayette newspaper. **George Krambles Collection.**

not budge to help the independent, but outside owned, Lafayette Service Corporation.

The company, forced to the wall by the repudiation of the bondholders and the negative local political forces, was offered for sale on March 1, 1922. It went out of existence in piece meal bits.

The tracks and carhouse went for $75,000 to Julius Berlovitz, who, stated after the sale, that if the proper co-operation was extended by the cities of Lafayette and West Lafayette the street railway would be continued and rehabilitated. What he did not say was that the alternative would be to scrap the system for its salvage value.

The power station was sold to the Northern Indiana Gas & Electric Company, the only bidder, for $120,000. The Tecumseh Trail Park property was sold to the Indiana State Soldiers' Home for $6,310. The total sale of the property netted $201,300 for the $225,000 held by the bondholders. Overall they did not do too badly as they had spent little and had had a reasonable return on the investment. Although not a matter of record, they probably had originally purchased the bonds at a discount.

Above: *Work car 3 was built from an old ISC-owned city car left at Lafayette.* ***David W. Chambers Collection.*** ***Below:*** *Car 52 alongside the Ferry Street car barn on tracks once used by the interurban cars for freight unloading.* ***Van Dusen-Zillmer Collection.***

LAFAYETTE STREET RAILWAY, INCORPORATED 1922-1940

Berlovitz and his associates proceeded to set up a new company. However it was almost as though they really expected not to be successful or that their decision to place an offer on the railway assets was a last minute effort. It was nearly three weeks after the purchase that articles of incorporation for the Lafayette Street Railway, Incorporated finally were filed with the state. This formal action took place on March 24, 1922. The capitalization was placed at $300,000 and a new bond was issued and held by a few local Lafayette business people.

The city, for its selfish action, was fairly lucky. They issued Berlovitz's company a new franchise which allowed certain route changes, excepted the company from further payments on the bridge or similar fees, and granted protection from jitney buses. Just how these City Council concessions, unobtainable for the Lafayette Service Corporation, came about has never been explained in print. Besides these advantages, the company proceeded to ignore an arrangement (or promise) that Berlovitz had made to build new trackage on Eleventh Street and a new car barn-terminal on Eleventh Street. As another part of the deal, the Fairgrounds line was abandoned and the Owen Street line was shortened by some four blocks.

However, the new Lafayette Street Railway, Inc. was given a very free hand to act with the City Council's protection and the company set out to improve, rebuild trackage and modernize the system. They also announced that they would buy new cars immediately.

The new company did well and greatly improved the city system. Streetcar service continued unbroken through the change from one company to the other. The new company leased cars from the ISC until the new cars were delivered. For the most part the transition period saw the same cars in use that had been used earlier. Almost all of these cars were scrapped soon after they were taken out of service.

The trackage east from Ninth and Main, up Oakland Hill, had not been used since February 24, 1921 because it was in bad condition. By May 13, 1922, the new company had replaced the old trackage and traffic was restored

Car 19 on a "Purdue Only" run at the Monon shops end of the line. **David W. Chambers Collection.**

on East Main Street to Five Points. During this period, the inbound THI&E interurban cars had turned west onto Kossuth Street and then north on South Ninth Street to reach the downtown. New trackage was built on South Street east from Main Street to Scott Street where it connected to existing track. The Scott Street tracks were taken up with the exception of a short stretch from Main Street to hold extra cars for events at Columbian Park. The trackage on Park Avenue between South and

Above: *Main Street in a snowstorm between Third and Fourth Streets.* ***Below:*** *Seven cars stalled in a snowstorm on State Street at Purdue.* **Both photos —David W. Chambers Collection.**

Car 12 at the end of the Salisbury Street line. ***David W. Chambers Collection.***

Kossuth was also removed. Also removed was a switch at the south end of Park which turned eastward into Bryce Street scrap yard previously used for dumping street railway paving rubble.

On the west side, much of the track was renewed or replaced. The Purdue loop was split into two parts in 1922. Trackage in the boulevard center of Waldron Street was torn up and replaced by new trackage a block east on University Street. The tracks on Stadium between Waldron and Grant were also torn up but not replaced. This change created the University Street line ending at University and Stadium, the "Purdue Only" line which ended on State Street a short distance west of Russell Street and the Salisbury Street line ending at Grant and Stadium. Salisbury Street was repaved in 1928 and new track was laid. During the summer of 1929, the Salisbury Street line was extended north on Grant from Stadium to Meridian. (This was the last track extension built in Lafayette). The three new west side lines were through routed with the Lafayette lines, eliminating the need to loop around the Court House. The Court House loop was used only for special services.

The rebuilding included special work at Ninth and Main Streets, the main intersection for the street railway system. Electric switches were located at that intersection to control the traffic. The University and State intersection also used an electric switch. The rest were spring operated (at turnouts) or hand-thrown. The twisting route of the Monon Shops line was shared with interurban cars and used signals to regulate the traffic. These automatic block signals were installed in 1922.

New cars came from J. G. Brill Company in two orders, as Lafayette Street Railway, Inc. continued improvements. These cars included a total of 18 four-wheel Birney style cars. They were delivered on the Monon Railroad to the Battleground coal siding and brought into Lafayette over the Indiana Service Corporation's isolated Tecumseh Trail Park-Battleground line. The cars were painted a bright orange below the windows, cream colored above. Roof, doors and sashes were painted maroon. Three secondhand, double-truck cars were purchased from the Chicago, South Bend & Northern Indiana Railway (South Bend) for the Soldiers' Home Route. The 21 cars bought in 1922 allowed the company to stop renting

Unloading a new LSR Brill-Birney car from a Monon R.R. flatcar along the North Ninth Street road near Battleground, May 1922. ***David W. Chambers Collection.***

LSR car 15 at the Ferry Street car barn. ***Van Dusen-Zillmer Collection.***

city cars from the Indiana Service Corporation. The 1922 cars were the last bought by the Lafayette company.

Indiana Service Corporation disposed of the Battleground line as quickly as possible. No cars ran through after April 1, 1922 and the line was not used for delivery of coal to the Soldiers' Home power plant after September. The tracks were torn up in 1923. The Soldiers' Home line remained in service as a marginally economic line until January 3, 1930 when flood waters and a sleet storm forced the Lafayette Street Railway to suspend service. A petition for abandonment was granted on January 11 and service was never restored on this line that had outlived its usefulness.

Lafayette may have been fortunate as the locally owned street railway lines lasted longer than they might have survived under the Indiana Service Corporation's control. The THI&E interurban line from Indianapolis died on November 1, 1930. The ISC's Wabash Valley line from Logansport expired on May 21, 1932. Had the ISC local control continued after 1920, the Lafayette City lines would have been isolated in 1932, and they might have been abandoned when the connecting interurban was abandoned as happened with the Logansport city lines. As an independent company, the Lafayette lines lasted longer.

Following the modernization period, the company settled into a daily work routine.

Car 27 on the Owens Street line (Ninth and Owens) in July 1937. ***Van Dusen-Zillmer Collection.***

Above: *Cars 17 and 10 sun themselves at the Ninth and Ferry Street car barn.* ***David W. Chambers Collection.*** ***At the right:*** *Car 28 at State and Russell, the end of the Purdue Only line, December 18, 1937.* ***Van Dusen-Zillmer Collection.***

The five cent fare was adequate since the company was protected from competition and free transfers allowed easy access to different areas of the city. The car routes were easy to identify by day or night. At night, illuminated route signs were augmented by colored lights above the windshields. In many cities these were used as markers, but Lafayette used a color code system by substituting colored lights for two white lights. Two green lights indicated the University Street-Kossuth Street line, and red and green lights were used for Salisbury Street-South Street and two red lights for the Purdue Only-Monon Shops lines. White lights were for extra cars used on South and Owen Street. The six main lines plus the South and Owen lines comprised the total runs. Headways were on a 12-minute basis on the heavier lines. Some streets such as Main and State Streets, had a continuing procession of cars as all routes, except Owen and South used the main thoroughfare. The main transferring point was Ninth and Main where car routes went off to the four points of the compass. The north route was the Monon Shops lines.

Monon Shops was the principal car line and a real bread and butter route. North Ninth was an old area and one that had been served by the first street railway company. This line, the first built by the second company, had been extended from its early day terminal on north 12th Street to a new route on 13th to Greenbush in 1891. At this time, the city of Lafayette, after much manuevering, secured the Monon Railroad Shops for the city. It would be a great source of employment and an asset to the city. The city voted $130,000 for the Shops. Forty acres of land north of the Linwood area near the Monon tracks were also donated. The shops were completed by 1895 and changed the character of the North Ninth Street line. This created the Monon Shops line which was completed in 1900 by building to 18th and Schuyler. The interurban to Logansport later connected to the city line at this point. In 1928, the Lafayette Street Railway built track one block north to Monon Avenue at the shop gate. (Interestingly enough, the first street railway had built south on Third Street to reach, besides the Purdue Agricultural Works, the junction of the rail lines, their local yards and the local shop and train facilities...one of them being the Monon's predecessor. This early horsecar line had failed while thirty years later the other line became a great success.)

Lafayette Street Ry. 51 at the Kossuth Street yard just after service ended in 1940. The three cars, which came from South Bend, were actually third-hand. They may have been part of a group built for the Central Market Street Railway Company (Columbus, Ohio) by Laconia Car Company in 1902. ***David W. Chambers Collection.***

Trackage remained static until 1935 when the old (1903) trackage on East Main between South and Kossuth was torn up as the city repaved the street with State help. The change eliminated the South Street connecting car by moving the East Main Street line from East Main and Kossuth straight out South Street. The Kossuth Street line was then extended over the Kossuth end of the former East Main line.

The long lines to West Lafayette always attracted a heavy Purdue University traffic load. As a result, these routes were the target for almost every imaginable kind of student prank and mischief. Car rocking was a popular stunt on the four-wheel cars that often led to derailments; groups of students would gather on both end platforms of a car and jump in unison on alternating ends. And the cover of night provided its own sport when students discovered that a car, nearing the end of University Street, could be thrown into total darkness by merely pulling the trolley pole. If the car's air brake supply was low, this prank and the resulting confusion could run the car off the end of the track...and did, frequently, as was evident in the street's concrete pavement.

University Street along the west side of the Purdue campus also saw many special car movements. The passing track just north of State was planned to hold extra cars for activities at the gym (later Women's Gym) and the Armory. Purdue Football games required extra cars and the big double-truck cars were regularly used for these occasions. Seven or eight cars would be lined up on University Street south of Stadium Avenue to handle the crowds from a Big Ten football game at Purdue's Ross-Ade Stadium. The new (1937) fieldhouse was located at the end of University Street and also supplied extra traffic.

As might be found in any city, many lesser special service operations occurred during the era of the Lafayette Street Railway. Numerous special interurban train movements were made

The Ninth and Main intersection looking east about 1937. ***Ed Frank Photo.***

Above: *The end of University Street with the Purdue Fieldhouse in the background.* ***David W. Chambers Collection. Top photo at right:*** *Car 20 on the State Street hill at the Salisbury Street junction.* ***Bottom photo at right:*** *Car 17, southbound up the Ninth Street hill, crosses the Wabash RR tracks.* ***Both photos —Ed Frank Photo / David W. Chambers Collection.***

but runs to the Purdue campus were practically nullified by the track rebuilding program. The single-end interurban cars could not be turned on the west side and had to run backwards to Lafayette. Proper turning facilities were located at the interurban station next to the Ferry Street car barn. The city trackage was planned almost exclusively for double-end cars.

By 1939, the street railway system was again in need of repair and rebuilding. The "T" rail trackage on the main lines, a legacy from the earlier companies, was less expensive to build but, because of auto and heavy truck traffic, appears to have required a great amount of preventive maintenance. Movement of paving blocks allowed rails to go out of alignment particularly when heavy vehicles chose to drive down the tracks.

The good car maintenance program continued year after year until the mid-thirties. By 1938, some cars began to look like the expected coat of paint hadn't been applied, yet they did not look rundown and were almost always clean. Mechanically, the cars were beginning to falter. They had had hard use and the Birney design was not an indestructible car design. Service and schedules were still kept except when Monon trains running

Seven cars line up for the football crowds at Purdue at the end of University Street. ***David W. Chambers Collection.***

through town, on Fifth Street, upset the service by five or more minutes. Train speeds were restricted. Streetcar schedules were loose enough to allow the streetcars to run a little faster and pick up the time.

On May 18, 1939 the company publicly announced a plan to replace the streetcars with motor buses. At this point, further maintenance, other than that required for day-to-day operation, ended. Early in 1940, the Ferry Street barn was remodeled as a motor bus repair shop and garage facility. New ACF gasoline motor buses (Model 26-S) were ordered and these began to arrive early in 1940. At this same time, the company, on March 14, 1940 changed its name to Lafayette Transit Company. Nineteen of the new silver and green buses were soon on hand and they began break-in runs. As soon as drivers were trained and the buses considered ready, they moved into service. Car lines were changed rather quietly and quickly as the buses became available. Wires came down on each line soon afterwards. On April 22, 1940, a "Last Streetcar Ride" was made using big car 50. This West Lafayette High School Senior Hi-Y event came from North Grant through to 30th and Kossuth Street. It was car 50's last run and it was sent to the 23rd and Kossuth storage yard. Kossuth Street was already motorized and the wires were coming down. The yard was stripped of its wires by the end of April although the old streetcars were still shoved into the area. All the cars were sent here for eventual scrapping.

On May 11, 1940 the last streetcars were run on the Salisbury Street-Monon Shops lines. There was no special announcement. Everyone overlooked the fact that the Monon Shops (North Ninth Street) line had been the first line of both street railway companies. Now it had been the last. At 11:20 p.m. car 26 pulled into the Main and Kossuth yard.

As the city cars stopped and the power was shut off, an era at Purdue University also ended. The Purdue test car which used an electrified stretch of the campus rail line depended on the street railway for power and was also stopped from its occasional trips. The car had once run on the local car lines and the interurban lines. It had been confined to the campus since 1923.

LAFAYETTE BUS SERVICE 1940-1982

The Lafayette Transit Company extended and changed several routes to broaden the service base although the basic route pattern remained unchanged until after the war. One useful and practical change restored the equivalent of the old Purdue University loop with buses running in both directions over the University, Stadium and Grant Streets. The company's initial fleet of 19 ACF 26-S buses was nearly overwhelmed by the wartime loads and was supplemented by one more 26-S, two new Yellow Coaches and two old White buses. Two new Ford buses came in 1944. After the war more Fords and four ACF C-36 buses were purchased...the last new buses bought by the system as a private company.

In 1953 the company was reorganized as the Greater Lafayette Bus Company. The original bus fleet was virtually all gone by 1959 and the company went into the secondhand market buying twelve TDH 3207 GMC buses from Kansas City. By 1963 the ownership had changed again with the new owners operating from Indianapolis. A steady procession of secondhand GMC buses flowed through the city, were used until they collapsed, and then replaced with more of the same. Good maintenance might have preserved them longer. Although this appears to be a poor way to do business, small bus companies—and some big ones—found it very hard to survive in the sixties. At least Lafayette had bus service when the state finally passed enabling legislation allowing municipalities to take over the local systems.

The Greater Lafayette Public Transportation Corporation acquired control in 1971 and started turning the situation around. The system has 27 buses as of January 1, 1982 and covers a large service area in Tippecanoe County.

At the right: *1940 ACF bus 34 at South Ninth and Kossuth Streets in Lafayette.* ***David W. Chambers Collection. Below:*** *Car 52 on Ninth Street at the switch to Ferry Street and the car barn.* ***Van Dusen-Zillmer Collection.***

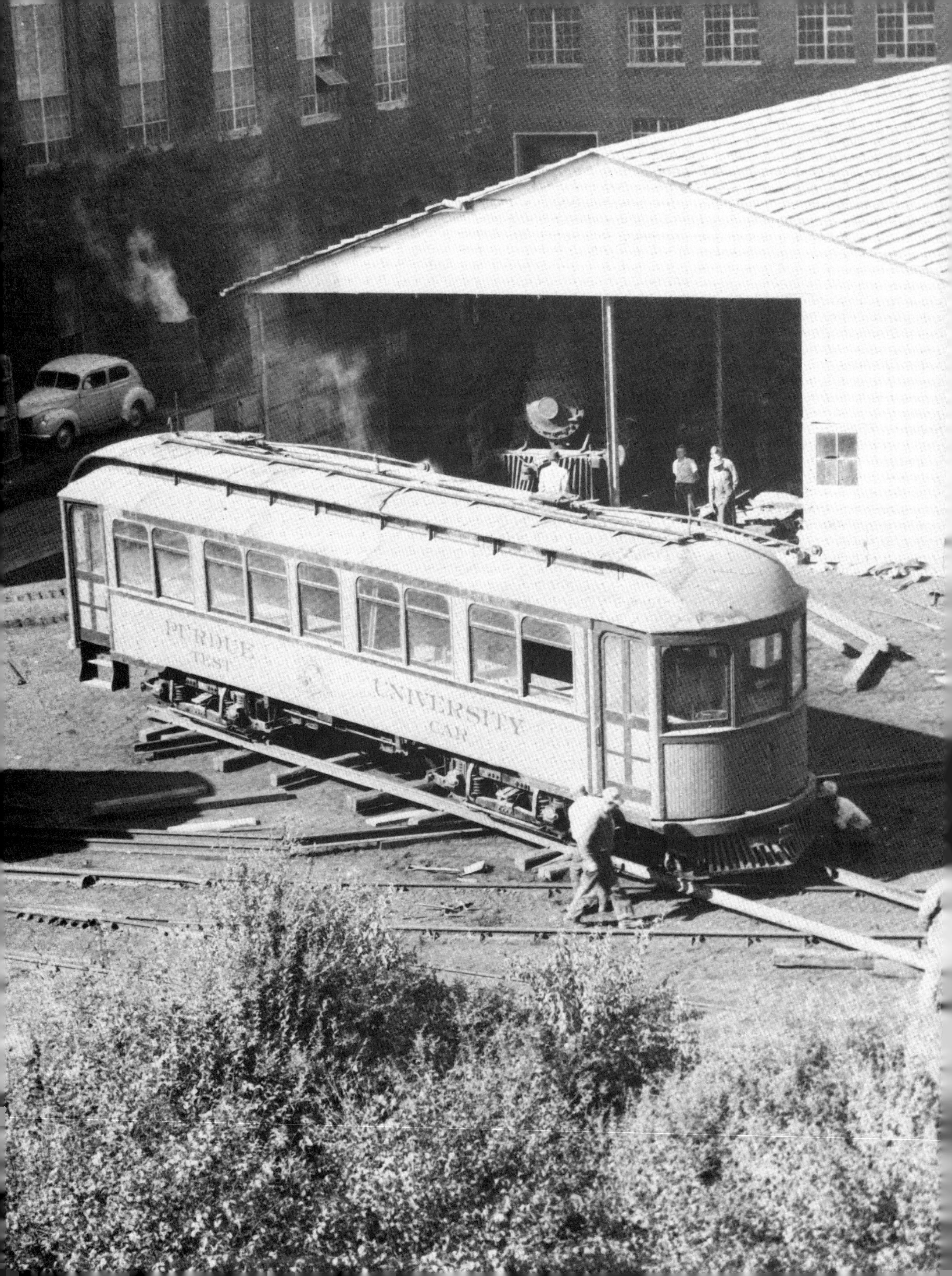
PURDUE
TEST
UNIVERSITY
CAR

CHAPTER 18

Purdue University & Electric Railway Engineering

John Purdue's university made its appearance in the 1870's, high above the Wabash River, west of Lafayette. Purdue grew rapidly due largely to two dynamic presidents who knew how to build a university, attract an excellent faculty and gather in an eager student body. From this base would come one of the fine engineering schools of the world. Emerson E. White laid the foundation that James H. Smart then built upon. Under President Smart, Purdue became noted for enthusiasm and nearly incredible accomplishments.

As the university grew Electrical Engineering became a separate school in 1888 and moved into its own building in 1889. This became the first home of what was quickly recognized as a first-class, well equipped school. At this same time, W. F. M. Goss, who had become the Dean of Engineering, developed at Purdue an interest in railroading and among the railroad companies an interest in Purdue. Goss in 1891 was granted $8000 with which he bought a $4000 locomotive and used the rest to build and equip the world's first stationary locomotive testing station. This first test plant was opened in January 1892 and was part of the shops which were later attached to and became part of the new Heavilon Hall (perhaps the finest engineering college building in the United States when that building was dedicated on January 19, 1894). Four days after the building's dedication a boiler room gas explosion ignited a fire that destroyed the building and adjoining shops—including the locomotive test plant. Heavilon Hall, in a spirit of "we refuse to be beaten," was rebuilt following Smart's ringing announcement, "...it shall be rebuilt and the tower shall be one brick higher." A second and separate locomotive test plant was built...all a part of the enthusiastic student, faculty and public response to the loss. From the test plant effort and contacts came the Purdue Locomotive Museum, assembled in the early 1900's to collect representative pieces of railroad equipment.

Purdue's Electrical Engineering school continued its growth and was well represented at the Louisiana Purchase Exposition held in St. Louis in 1904. Professor Winder E. Goldsborough, head of the Electrical Engineering school, served as Chief of the Department of Electricity at the St. Louis Fair. Goldsborough obtained some unique electrical equipment for Purdue after the exposition ended as well as a special testing car that had been used in connection with the exposition's scientific studies and experiments. The car was one of several rail vehicles connected with the exposition that carried the name "Louisiana."

Goldsborough, after the exposition had ended, joined a commercial engineering firm and resigned his professorship and as head of Electrical Engineering at Purdue. However, Goldsborough and Goss' interest in rail operation had already extended to the electric railway industry. In May 1898, the two had received three electric railway trucks from the J. G. Brill Company of Philadelphia. These were a No. 27 truck, a very early form of the later 27-E design (order 8452), a No. 22 truck (order 8453) and a No. 21-E truck (order 8454) for study and display at the university. Goldsborough had helped set the stage to keep the interest in electric railways moving ahead. Acquiring the "Louisiana" was a logical step forward.

This "Louisiana" was a unique and strange piece of equipment and the precursor of the "windsplitter" car designs used for a variety of electric interurban and self propelled railcars. This test car was one of the early scientific attempts to study the effects of wind resistance on a moving vehicle. The "Louisiana" was a special design dynamometer car which was assembled at the Anderson shops of the Union Traction company.

Essentially the test car was an interesting assembly of contributed parts. The Pressed Steel Car Company provided a standard steel flat car which was mounted on Baldwin MCB high speed trucks with four 75hp No. 85 Westinghouse electric motors. The flat car was equipped with special rollers and tracks to allow the free and measured movement of a car body riding on them. This car, built by the J. G. Brill Co., was a 32 foot, wooden, light interurban car body with only one fixed (rear) vestibule. Apparently no vestibule came with the other end. Special design parabolic wedge and blunted ends were provided or built at Anderson. The car was run at speeds up to 70 mph on the interurban lines near Anderson to test measure the side, front and roof wind resistance of the body. To aid in the

Above and below: *Test Car "Louisiana" equipped with a "parabolic wedge" movable vestibule.* ***Both photos — William D. Middleton Collection.***

free motion, the two L-4 electric controllers were mounted on the flat car through holes in the car body floor. The trolley stand was also fixed to the flat car floor with the trolley base mounted on the stand below the roof line, inside the car, with the trolley pole extended through a hole in the car body roof.

This car was completed late in 1904 and was used in a series of tests from January 15 to March 16, 1905. The final results showed the sharp wedge forward design to be effective in reducing wind resistance and a number of later cars adopted this design.

The whereabouts of the "Louisiana" following the 1905 tests and its next surfacing in the record annals are conjectural. It apparently came to Purdue in 1905 or 1906.

Dr. Charles Francis Harding became the head of Electrical Engineering in 1908. Electric Railway Engineering, begun in the 1890's was now to be strengthened by the addition and practical use of the former "Louisiana." In March and April of 1908 Harding approached Purdue's President W. E. Stone for money to lay a special connecting track, for a special berth in the Electrical Engineering Building, from the Purdue Railroad tracks at the power house. The Lafayette city system had already electrified part of the campus trackage in 1901 for cars going to the ball games. They had also installed a switch on State Street where the Purdue tracks crossed the streetcar tracks. In September Stone advised Harding to proceed and by the end of the year Stone had authorized at least $2500 for the project.

Harding acted and, in September, the "Louisiana" started through a change, apparently, at the local streetcar shops. The Brill built body was the key to the new car. The other parts disappeared although one of the Baldwin trucks is believed to have been the truck that was in the engineering lab for many years.

The car body was rebuilt to a full 44 foot overall length with a new standard design front vestibule. The floor and roof were rebuilt and the modified car body was mounted on a set of new Brill No. 27-E-2 high speed interurban trucks built on Brill order 16508. (The order for the car body is not known and doesn't appear on the Brill list.) The interior had no seats. A bench ran along one side of the car to hold a wide variety of electrical testing devices and instruments. The car was given four WH 56, 50hp motors, two GE K-35C controllers and Allis Chalmers air brakes.

The Purdue Test Car operates on the South Campus. ***Above:*** *The Test Car is near the north end of the overhead wire area on one of its traditional "last of the spring" Electrical Engineering School outings.* ***Below:*** *The car was photographed making one of its last trips ever under its own power.* ***David Chambers Collection.***

What a pleasant surprise to rediscover three steam locomotives and the interurban Test Car in the old "museum" building on the Purdue campus in 1950. All had been gathering dust for years with the Test Car having been the most recent arrival. ***Bradley-Harnish Collection.***

The Purdue Electric Test Car, painted in Purdue's old gold (yellow) and black embarked on a thirty year career as the prime attraction of Electric Railway Engineering. The car became a very familiar sight on the campus and in the surrounding area. Test runs were regularly made on the local Battleground line. Other runs were made on the Lafayette to Indianapolis, Lafayette to Fort Wayne and the Indianapolis to Crawfordsville line of the nearby interurban companies. One early trip sent the car to Indianapolis to have it weighed because, upon the completion of the conversion of the Brill body to the Test Car, no one had any idea of its total weight of 54,060 pounds.

The car was moved to the new Electrical Engineering Building in 1924 where a new special berth was built, complete with an inspection pit, at the south end of the main laboratory. This treatment was interesting because the fortunes of the electric railways had fallen on bad times and the need for a test car was lessening. The previous year the switch from the city streetcar line was removed and the overhead wire removed from the north campus. During the years 1924-1926 there was no operation of the car and it was a static display in its new berth. In 1927 a portion of the Purdue Railroad, south from State Street, was equipped with overhead wires. The 1650-foot electrified stretch received power from the Lafayette Street Railway and was energized as needed. The Test Car had to be towed from its new location to the south campus. The university's self propelled Orton crane was used for towing. This infrequent operation was usually in the spring of the year giving seniors in the Electrical Engineering school a chance to operate the car. May 1940 saw the end of the car's trips when the Lafayette Street Railway converted to buses and power was no longer available. The Test Car was now a useless white elephant and scrapping seemed inevitable.

The Goss collection of locomotives had become the Purdue Locomotive Museum but it fell on hard times after Goss left in 1907. There was never enough money to take good care of it so it was quietly closed up and forgotten until 1930 when the building was to be razed for the new Mechanical Engineering Building. The metal building produced an official surprise when the collection was rediscovered. The building was moved and re-erected behind the power plant and the locomotives were shoved into it. No public access was made available. In 1939 some of the engines were reclaimed by the railroads that had loaned them. The missing engines left open space in the three track museum building.

Dr. Dressel D. Ewing had been chief professor of Electric Railway Engineering since 1912 and as Harding's chief assistant considered the Test Car too personal and valuable to scrap. In late 1940 the south wall of the museum building was again opened and the Test Car was shoved onto one of the empty tracks...and forgotten. "Forgotten" was fortunate for the museum pieces. Because it was remembered, the test plant locomotive was patriotically scrapped.

In 1950, several members of the Purdue Railroad Club told new member George K. Bradley about the Test Car and the remaining locomotives. One volunteered to take Bradley there if they could get through the gates. What was not easily seen upon entry into the building was the collection as it was nearly buried under vast quantities of building materials and surplus steel window frames. Bradley, with Railroad Club help, local news articles by David Chambers, and several sympathetic professors secured over 2000 names on a petition to re-open the museum. Ewing, by then head of Electrical Engineering, offered his support in whatever way possible. Purdue's president Hovde did not know the collection existed or that the Test Car was there. He believed the building to be no more than a warehouse.

Hovde asked the Dean of Engineering, A. A. Potter, to seek a solution to the problem of the collection. Potter wanted to keep one locomotive and place it on display at some prominent spot on the campus. Although Hovde was sympathetic to the idea, he did not want to scatter the collection. The two resolved that further retention by Purdue was not in the best interests of the equipment, and the reopening of the museum with its limited collection was not practical. Potter formally contacted several major museums expecting at least one to respond favorably. Potter also asked Bradley if he had any suggestions. Bradley suggested the Museum of Transport at St. Louis although he knew nothing about them beyond an article in a magazine. He was told to contact them and tell them of the availability of the collection. Dr. John P. Roberts, then the president of the St. Louis museum, indicated a very positive interest in the entire collection. The museum had made a

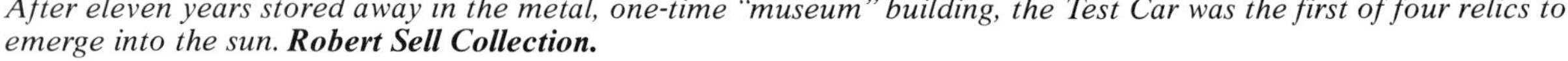

After eleven years stored away in the metal, one-time "museum" building, the Test Car was the first of four relics to emerge into the sun. ***Robert Sell Collection.***

Loaded and blocked, the Test Car awaits tie-downs in preparation for shipment from Purdue to the National Museum at St. Louis in October 1951. ***Robert Sell Collection.***

blind alley approach to some Purdue official at an earlier date and had been ignored. Strangely enough, the museums contacted by Dean Potter were extremely slow to respond and none wanted the entire group.

Bradley was asked if he would care to visit the Museum of Transport as an unofficial observer and then report his opinions to Dean Potter. The report was favorable and Potter sent it to Hovde with the suggestion that Dr. Roberts be invited to appear before the University's Board of Trustees. Roberts made a formal request for the collection plus offering to move the collection at no cost to Purdue. The Board of Trustees approved and approval was also secured from the Baltimore & Ohio Railroad who technically owned one of the engines. The Trustees did ask that the three locomotives and the electric test car be designated as coming from Purdue. Dr. Roberts asked Bradley to act as official representative of the museum during the movement. Loading was handled on the Purdue South Campus by the combined wreck trains' crews from the Monon and Nickel Plate railroads using two huge wreck cranes for loading. The collection travelled over the Wabash Railroad to St. Louis and to the museum on the Missouri Pacific Railroad. The latter railroad sent in its wreck train crew to unload the equipment. The transfer took place in October 1951 when the Purdue collection was fifty years old. The Purdue Electric Test Car is now part of the "Purdue Collection" and is a major exhibit at the National Museum of Transport.

The Purdue Locomotive Collection on the south Campus spur track in October 1951. ***Bradley-Harnish Collection.***

127

Rolling Stock

CHAPTER 19

There is no accurate or detailed document of the company rolling stock prior to the 1919 Deed of the Company to the ISC and the ISC 1920 Railway Utility Inventory. However, there are several excellent, official early records that provide large enough pieces of the story to allow a reasonably complete picture of the total number of cars owned at most times and frequently a numerical list of the cars. In 1899, Fort Wayne Traction Company established a uniform numbering system which was continued by the successor companies. Some cars from companies acquired after 1904 and scrapped prior to 1919 are the lost or obscure cars of the post-1900 period.

The McNairy & Claflen Company (also known as Cleveland Bridge & Car Works) of Cleveland, Ohio built Fort Wayne's first horse cars. Cars 10 and 12 were delivered to the Citizens' Street R.R. Co. in the last days of 1871 and were on hand for the opening day. The Cleveland company delivered four more cars in the spring of 1872. They were numbered 14, 16, 18 and 20. The McNairy & Claflen cars were apparently 14-foot "box" bodies with a very distinctive clerestory roof. The company bought or built a flat car for work service and fitted it with a detachable snow plow during the 1872-73 winter.

During 1874, three more box (closed passenger) cars were acquired. These were apparently given number 1, 2 and 3, but this has not been verified. The source of these cars is not known. In the next year, 1875, an open summer car was added to the roster.

By January, 1885, the company had added more cars and now owned 11 closed and two excursion (open) cars. These included two new closed cars bought in 1884 and a new open excursion car which was built in the company shops. All of the cars were double-end and numbered 1 through 7 plus 10-20 (even only). The open cars may have been number 6 and 7. No more new cars were added by the Citizens' company; and an 1887 list shows 11 two-horse and two one-horse cars, plus 41 horses.

Fort Wayne Street Railroad is difficult to chronicle because of Indiana & Michigan Electric Company's thoughtless destruction of the old records which had been carefully preserved for upwards of 100 years. The records of Fort Wayne Street Railroad, Fort Wayne Electric Railway, Fort Wayne Consolidated Railway and some of the Fort Wayne Traction Company were among those destroyed. Efforts on the part of outsiders and the Public Library belatedly convinced some officials to allow the salvage of at least part of these valuable and irreplaceable historic records. Meanwhile the Indiana & Michigan Electric's Public Affairs Department continued to maintain the records did not now exist and never had existed.

The horsecars can be partly followed from piecing records, but the sharp break from horse cars to electric cars is very difficult—nearly impossible—to reconstruct. The only records are one Cash Account book and seven original J. M. Jones' Sons invoices. These show that 13 Citizens' cars were sold to the new company for $6500 ($500 each). In November, 1887 the Fort Wayne Street Railroad bought 14 new Jones-built closed cars, which the **Street Railway Journal** described as 12-foot, 4-window cars. The 1887 cars, which came in groups of six, three, two and three, cost $950 each. In reality seven of these were 12-foot cars, and the others were 14-foot cars. Four 14-foot cars were added in November, 1888 (these were numbered 30, 31 and 41, 42). These four cost $925 each. They were bought for the new Belt Line and the Wallace Street Line.

The 31 cars required 131 horses, and Superintendent L. D. McNutt employed fifty-three drivers and transfer men to run the system.

The C. L. Centlivre Street Railway started service in August, 1887 and may have bought some of its rolling stock locally from the Fort Wayne Street Railroad. A photo shows car number 5 to be very similar to the old Citizens' McNairy & Claflen cars. This type had a "duck back" design roof with a small "eyebrow" window at each end. This may have been Citizens' car 5. The original McNairy & Claflen cars had an interesting modified monitor roof of a curving type which followed the basic roof line...a unique design.

The McNairy & Claflen cars retained their original Citizens' paint and lettering as long as they were in service on the Fort Wayne Street Railroad. One of them was used in M. M. M. Slattery's Jenny Electric Light Company 1891 battery car experiment. L. D. McNutt arranged to make the car available for experimentation as well as to use it in

The 14 was one of the original Jones built electric cars shown here in Ft. Wayne Traction's colors. All of these cars were retired by the early 1900's. ***John A. Rehor Collection.***

trial revenue service.

By the end of 1891, Fort Wayne Street Railroad owned 28 closed cars, two open cars and 160 horses. This includes the five box and two open ex-Citizens' cars still left, the fourteen 12-foot and 14-foot cars, of 1887, four 14-foot 1888 cars and five cars bought in 1889 and 1890. Most of these cars had a monitor deck roof although two or three had the so-called "Bombay" roof. The cars do not represent any consecutive numbering system. They carried the route names painted on the sides and ends which created permanent assignments. The car numbers may have been related to the several lines. This is the only explanation for the number assignments. Numbers 16, 30, 31, 41, 42 are four-window 12-foot cars. The 33 is an 1890 or 1891, 14-foot car with six windows. The 23 and 28 are not known other than by numbers.

In June, 1892, three new electric cars—the first of many—arrived on the Nickel Plate and were unloaded at the Glasgow Avenue Barns. These included open and closed cars all reportedly built by J. M. Jones' Sons at Troy, New York. The closed cars had open platforms and were described as maroon (tuscan red) in color and rich in decoration. Known numbers of these sixteen-footers are 2, 4, 10, 12, 14, 24, 26, 28, 30, 32, 34, 36, 38, 40, 42, 54, 60 and 68. A sprinkler was added in 1895. At the time of the electrification, records show that a number of horses and their equipment were sold to F. DeH. Robison's Cleveland City Cable Railway Company in 1892.

The Lakeside Street Railway got its cars from the Fort Wayne Electric Railway Company, and they came right out of the new car series. These were eight-bench open cars numbered 1 and 3 at a cost of $600 each and closed cars numbered 2 and 4 at a cost of $925 each.

The company's publicity claimed the car fleet to be entirely new and this may have been technically true. There were a number of nearly new horsecars on the property which were either sent back to Jones or rebuilt locally. A large center window was added to these cars giving each car four 34″ and one 45″ window on each side which made this a sixteen-foot car. Two of these cars are known to be 60 and 68 and were painted maroon (tuscan red) and chrome yellow with black trim and gold lettering. These spliced cars served for several years.

The 1894 purchase of the Centlivre line brought some more horsecars into Fort Wayne Electric Railway's ownership. The bill of sale included twenty horses, three summer cars, five closed cars, thirty sets of harness, three extra car trucks and an assortment of horse collars, picks, bars and brooms. The closed cars were numbered 1 through 5. The horse cars were used for less than two months by the new owners.

The company, in 1894, operated fifty-seven motor cars and twelve trailers with most mounted on Dorner & Dutton No. 20 trucks. (Some of these No. 20 trucks were later replaced with No. 25 trucks from the same manufacturer.) The 16-foot cars, with five windows, seated twenty-four on longitudinal seats, and the eight-bench open cars seated forty. The number of trailers reported varied because of some of the horsecars still on the property. The Short Electric Railway Company's motors were used on all the powered cars. Two twenty-horsepower single-reduction motors were used on most closed cars and one twenty-horsepower motor on the open cars. The spliced cars had only one motor. Since the city routes contained no heavy grades, such motor power was sufficient. An average of twelve miles an hour was claimed for the new electric cars. Twelve miles an hour was more likely a maximum speed. None of the cars used fenders; these would not be used until the new century.

Sorting out the numbering system of the early electrics is difficult because, although all were built by Jones, the J. M. Jones' sons company records no longer exist. Official lists do not agree on the total number of cars, and contemporary news stories often omit or embellish the details. To piece together the story requires some conjecture that is based on the known data.

The closed cars were 16-foot box body type numbered 2 through 68 (34 cars). The cars through the forties were the new Jones cars while 60 through 68 were splice-built from five of the newer horse cars. The cars in the fifties may also have been five more 14-foot horsecars converted to 16-foot electric cars with the center addition. These converted cars did not prove to be the sturdiest cars.

The open cars were of the eight-bench design with no rigid bulkheads. This type had a tendency to destroy itself as the uprights developed "play" and became loose from the jerking action of starting and stopping. The weight and action of the trolley pole and base accelerated their deterioration. As cars developed this progressive weakness they were used as trailers which cut down the weight factor but caused more jerking as the trailers were only braked by the motor car ahead in train service. These Jones-built cars were 33 in number and carried odd numbers from 1 through 65.

All three seven-bench Centlivre cars were probably taken into service and at least one was electrified with a Dorner & Dutton No. 20 truck. Although not verified, these were probably given numbers 81, 83 and 85, because the next group of open cars started at the unlikely number 87.

In mid-1896, Fort Wayne Consolidated bought twenty-five nine-bench open cars, numbered 87-135 (odd numbers). These cars went through the court in 1899 and became well identified bits of history. These Jones-built cars were mounted on Dorner & Dutton No. 25 trucks with two motors. These cars regularly pulled from one to three eight-bench trailers in Robison Park service.

Open car 59 heads east on East Creighton, captured in time by the Bowser Company's official photographer. The Bowser offices were located on E. Creighton just east from this spot. ***Bradley-Harnish Collection.***

Nine-bench open car 123 built in 1896. ***Bradley-Harnish Collection.***

An Indiana state law of 1895 ordered the enclosing of vestibules on all closed cars to provide some protection for motormen against inclement and cold weather. Some of these cars, as modified, had only one end enclosed and equipped for single-end operation. Some were also re-equipped with the No. 25 truck, new motors and controls.

By 1899, the "new" closed electric cars, although only a few years old, were victims of a high mortality rate. Sixteen-foot cars were much too small to be practical and they were not easily modernized...and most were not. The total dropped to 26, by 1901 to 18, and by 1904 only four were left. These ended their days in work service. The open cars fell, too. By 1901 twenty-five eight-bench opens were left along with all twenty-five of the nine-bench cars. No new open cars were bought by the company, but the car numbers were changed on two occasions.

The Consolidated Company's failure to buy new closed cars forced the new Fort Wayne Traction Company to invest in new larger equipment. Their first order was placed with the Jackson & Sharp Company for eight 22-foot double-end deck-roof cars in December 1899. These cars were numbered consecutively 101-108. While at the builders, and perhaps after they were delivered, the cars were mounted on a Lord Baltimore truck. Some, if not all, ended their years on a Peckham truck and in work service. They all seem to have been removed from passenger use by the mid-teens. Even with these new cars it is evident that the company enjoyed a tremendous summertime increase in business as the number of open cars was nearly double that of the closed fleet.

The next new cars came from Jones in 1902. These, with some minor differences, were near duplicates of the Jackson & Sharp cars. These were delivered on Peckham Metropolitan Special trucks. The two similar groups, starting at number 101, are the starting point for tabulation in the car roster.

Some of these cars lasted into the 1920's with the last one retired in 1923. Recorded numbers for these Jones-built cars range from 109 to 120. What at first appeared to be a stray car (number 133), an identical sister to the Jones cars, supports the record indicating that these cars came in two groups (109-120 and 132-137) with the company-built 121-131 in between. The company's Ledger for 1903 carries entries for "6 New Cars Lot #2," 6 Peckham trucks and GE-1000 motors. The two groups of Jones cars were the last bought from Jones by the Fort Wayne companies and broke a long-standing relationship which had seen only one small group of cars come from a different builder. The change of ownership

The 107 was one of eight 22' cars ordered for Ft. Wayne in 1899 from Jackson & Sharp (order no. 1604-1611). ***Above:*** *As viewed here, the car is merely sitting on a Lord Baltimore truck and is not secured to it. This truck also appears to be damaged or partly dismantled. These cars may have been mounted on Peckham trucks upon delivery in Ft. Wayne.* ***Below:*** *The interior of the 107 at Jackson & Sharp in 1899. The car was outfitted with drop window pockets, rattan seats, window shades and standee hand straps. The ceiling lamps have not been installed.* ***Both photos —State of Delaware, Division of Historical & Cultural Affairs, Dover, Delaware.***

at Fort Wayne and the syndicate's ownership interest in the new Cincinnati Car Company would dictate buying cars there.

The Baker Street (Chestnut Street) Shop produced the 121-131 series of 22-foot deck-roof cars. These cars were a straight-sided version of the Jackson & Sharp and Jones-built cars. As built all of these cars had only two entryways, for rear entrance use, and used folding gates instead of doors. This meant the motorman was left in the cold with one side of the platform open to the weather. All of the cars in the 101-137 series received folding doors later. None were used in one-man service.

During the Fort Wayne Traction days all newly acquired cars were numbered into sequence starting with the next available number. This practice was continued by the Wabash Valley for both city and interurban cars and is the reason that car series numbers start at what appear to be odd numerical positions. In 1917, the company changed to a "car series" or group (class) approach to numbering.

By mid-1904 the Wabash Valley began renumbering the cars acquired from those companies outside of Fort Wayne. There were many number overlaps with some car numbers used as many as four times. The closed city cars were numbered into the existing numbering sequence. These cars are not all known but some guesses can be made from the car lists on hand in 1904 and those cars and numbers that survived until later listings. At least ten new 20-foot cars came from Cincinnati in November 1904 and were probably numbered 147-156. The gap of 140-146 may be seven older 20-foot cars. The Barney & Smith-built cars fall into this category. Cars 137-139 may have been 18-foot cars and may also have been Cincinnati-built. Numbers 157-166 may be the remaining ten 18-foot cars on the property at Logansport and Lafayette. Six of these 18-foot cars were from the LR&N.

The new 1904 Cincinnati cars were bought for use in Lafayette and Logansport to supplement and replace older cars. These big 20-foot cars had five large windows on each side. They originally had a Dorner truck which was replaced by a Curtis truck in 1911. These cars lasted into the 1920's.

Car 169 was a stray built, according to some reports, by St. Louis Car Company or built "in St. Louis." Cars 167 and 168 are unknown but are most likely leftover cars from an underlying property prior to 1907 when cars 170-175 appeared. It is possible that these three cars are the Wabash River Traction's two

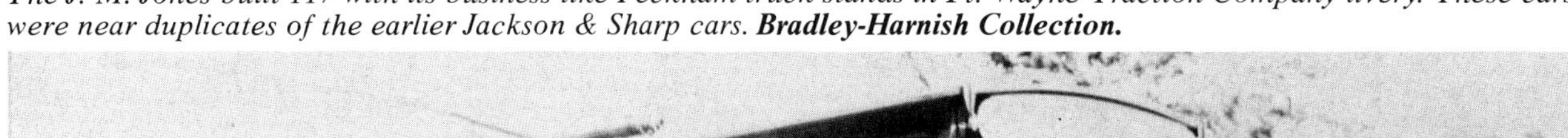
The J. M. Jones built 117 with its business-like Peckham truck stands in Ft. Wayne Traction Company livery. These cars were near duplicates of the earlier Jackson & Sharp cars. ***Bradley-Harnish Collection.***

small, January, 1902, city cars and the Wabash-Logansport's new Erie Street car of 1902 which came from "St. Louis."

The company continued the addition of new cars in 1907. Six semi-convertible cars arrived in May 1907. The 170-175 were mounted on a Peckham truck and apparently came in two groups. They may have been from two different orders and constructed as "add ons" to other Cincinnati Car Company orders. Cars 174-175 are described as having rattan cross seats. The inventory valuation, in 1920, listed these two as having a different original cost. Externally they all appear to be identical.

The arrival of the 170-175 provided for the release of six cars which were shifted from Logansport to Lafayette (probably six of the 1904 Cincinnati-built cars). When thoroughly overhauled, they standardized the fleet at Lafayette. The new 170-175 apparently were sent to Logansport for use on the city lines.

Twenty-six deck-roof semi-convertible cars with longitudinal rattan seats and Curtis trucks came in 1909. These 20-foot cars (176-201) were very similar to the earlier 170 group but had longer platforms.

No new city cars were added for several years but the fleet was reduced by the condemnation of sixteen older cars at Lafayette and Logansport. The new FW&NI company looked into the "Nearside" car idea and made two purchases.

Home-built 123 drifts along on a spring day in 1902 sporting the ornate paint designs used by Ft. Wayne Traction Company. ***Bradley-Harnish Collection.***

A contract was made with the E. H. York Company of Philadelphia for nineteen 32′4″ single-truck cars to be built by Cincinnati Car Company. The 202-220 were single-end cars built in 1913 to a modified nearside pattern. These cars had platforms somewhat

Cars, like the Ft. Wayne built 127, were very bulky and clumsy-looking streetcars, though the straight sides did allow for more interior room. The 127 carries no name and its number appears only in the clerestory. ***Bradley-Harnish Collection.***

Cincinnati Car Company built the 172, a 20' semi-convertible, in 1907. **Bradley-Harnish Collection.**

different than the patented design of the Nearside Car Company. They were limited to car lines that had turnaround facilities. Most of the turning wyes were removed by 1920 and these cars were rebuilt to a double-end configuration. In the rebuilding, the stubby rear platform was made the same size as the front. As rebuilt, these cars provided many years of good service.

The 221-227 were built in 1913 by the J. G. Brill Company through a contract with the Nearside Car Company. These "muzzle loaders" were built specifically for use in Lafayette and, in particular, on the long line that crossed

The 191 was a typical car built by Cincinnati Car Company in 1909; many of the Schoepf-McGowan properties had cars that were nearly identical. **Bradley-Harnish Collection.**

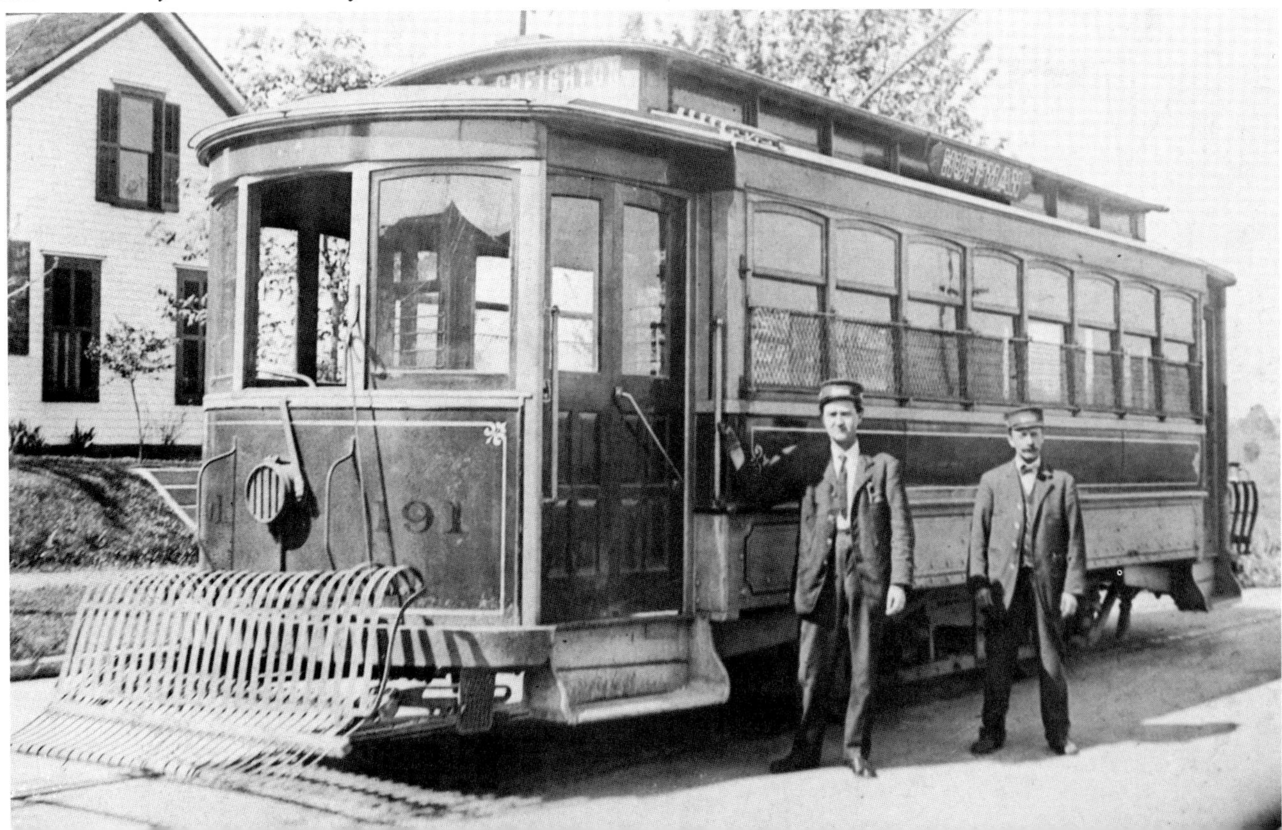

the river to West Lafayette and looped through the Purdue University campus. After the Lafayette system became an independent company, the nearsides came back to the Fort Wayne company. One of them was rebuilt in the same manner as the Cincinnati-built cars and put on a Curtis truck. (The reasoning behind this rebuilding is unknown as the company had more than enough cars, especially single-truck cars.) Apparently only the 225 was rebuilt as all the rest are shown as having been scrapped by 1922. The double end 225 worked on the Fort Wayne city lines for several years until 1928 when it was run up to the Vandalia interlocking plant, south of Garrett, where it replaced the old interlocking tower. Still mounted on its Curtis truck it sat on a couple of short rails by the interurban tracks for a number of years.

On May 26, 1915 the Lafayette Kossuth Street car barn burned with fifteen cars lost. These included eight closed cars, five open cars, one sweeper, one sand car and the THI&E's electric brake test car "Louise." In the 1919 Deed, the inventory showed many of the cars from the second generation 101-227 group were gone including some of the newer cars. In the 1909 series cars 183, 189, and 195 had disappeared and the 203 was gone from the 1913 nearsides.

The open car fleet underwent significant changes over the years and the total number owned is elusive. By 1902, the census reports showed 87 single-truck cars and two double-truck opens. One of the Fort Wayne eight-bench cars was sold to Angola Railway and Power Company (Angola, Indiana) in mid-1904 for $200. Seventeen opens were at Lafayette, sixteen opens were at Logansport (six on the Logansport Railway and ten on the LR&N) and six opens were at Wabash (two double-truck powered and four single-truck trailers). Fort Wayne had 50 eight- and nine-bench opens.

By 1907 the number of opens, including the two big cars, dropped to 60 and the cars were renumbered into a new grouping. The 300 series, known to run from 330 upwards seemed to hold part of the group. The Logansport and Lafayette nine- and ten-bench cars became the 350 series, and the WRT 15-bench cars became 370-371. Apparently due to numerical conflicts the other eight- and nine-bench cars, still surviving (in 1917) but with thinning ranks, were renumbered 600-638. Eighteen of them (610-611, 613-615, 622, 624-628, 631-632, 634-638) were trailers, with the rest being motor cars. Which of these were eight or nine bench and whether these were the original Jones cars is not known. The change of ownership to the Indiana Service Corporation and the closing of Robison Park spelled the end of all but two opens (370-371). By deed, the open cars were conveyed to the ISC by FW&NI but they were immediately scrapped. Only the 370-371 survived for special

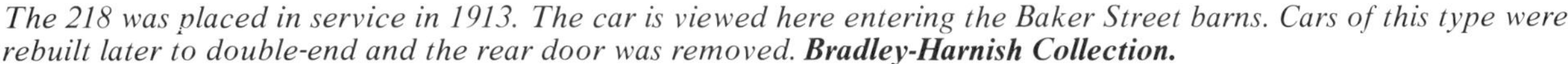
The 218 was placed in service in 1913. The car is viewed here entering the Baker Street barns. Cars of this type were rebuilt later to double-end and the rear door was removed. ***Bradley-Harnish Collection.***

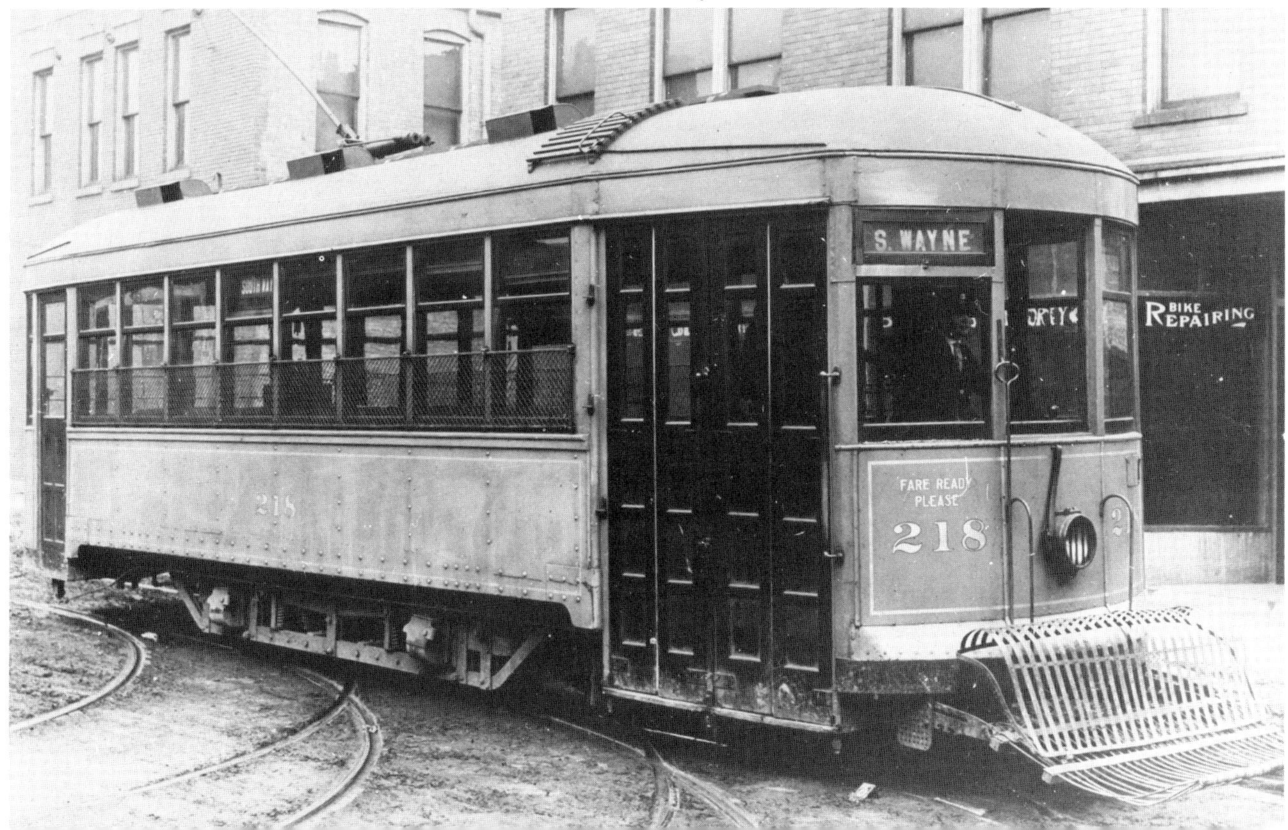

Double-trucker 254, posed on the Robison Park line, was built as car 12 of the Wabash River Traction. These cars were not used often in Ft. Wayne service except during the winter months and then only on the Park line. ***Bradley-Harnish Collection.***

use, until December 31, 1925.

The third generation of cars began quietly with the purchase of ten large double-truck cars in 1917 from St. Louis Car Company. The 240-249 were two-man rear-entrance arch-roof cars, very modern in design. These and later cars frequently described as "steel" cars had steel underframes and sides with a wood superstructure. They also introduced the new sand yellow (Tan) with black striping paint scheme. These popular, comfortable cars had the large capacity needed for the heavier lines. Big cars meant fewer cars were needed on some lines and rising labor costs could be cut accordingly.

In 1918 the company began the change to one-man operation. Part of Feustel's plan to turn the company around into a more profitable posture envisioned the purchase of new equipment rather than investing large sums in rebuilding antiquated cars. Twenty-five single-truck one-man cars were delivered by St. Louis in 1918. These were numbered 275-299 with the 291-299 arriving first and being sent to Logansport in response to the promise of new equipment. The oddity of these cars was the re-use of some Curtis trucks taken from older cars. These old trucks did not ride well and were later replaced with St. Louis 113B trucks as used under 275-290.

The modified double-end nearside design proved popular and economical. As a result, in 1919, the nearly identical 400-434 were built by St. Louis. These cars were equipment trust purchases and were not the property of the FW&NI as shown by the transfer to ISC in 1920. These cars, the 240 series and the 275 series were the cornerstones for Fort Wayne's third and last generation of streetcars.

Sixty improved double- and single-truck cars, following the basic design of the recent purchases, were added over the next five years (1921-1925). These were the 510-554, double-truck cars and the 435-449, single-truck cars. The 240-249 were rebuilt in October 1923 to conform to the 510-series design, and the 275-290 and 400-449 had single-door rear exits added. The 510-554 closely approximate an industry-suggested design for an ideal "standard" car.

One hundred and thirty modern city cars now served the system. All but ten of these operated in Fort Wayne. By 1926 over ninety old closed cars and the last two opens were retired from service. Only the older updated 202 series remained active as spares until 1931, with the 209 lasting until 1937.

The streetcars saw few changes until the depression days. The 290-series cars were brought to Fort Wayne when Logansport and Peru service ended but were never used again. In 1936 the old sand-yellow color with black striping and lettering gave way to

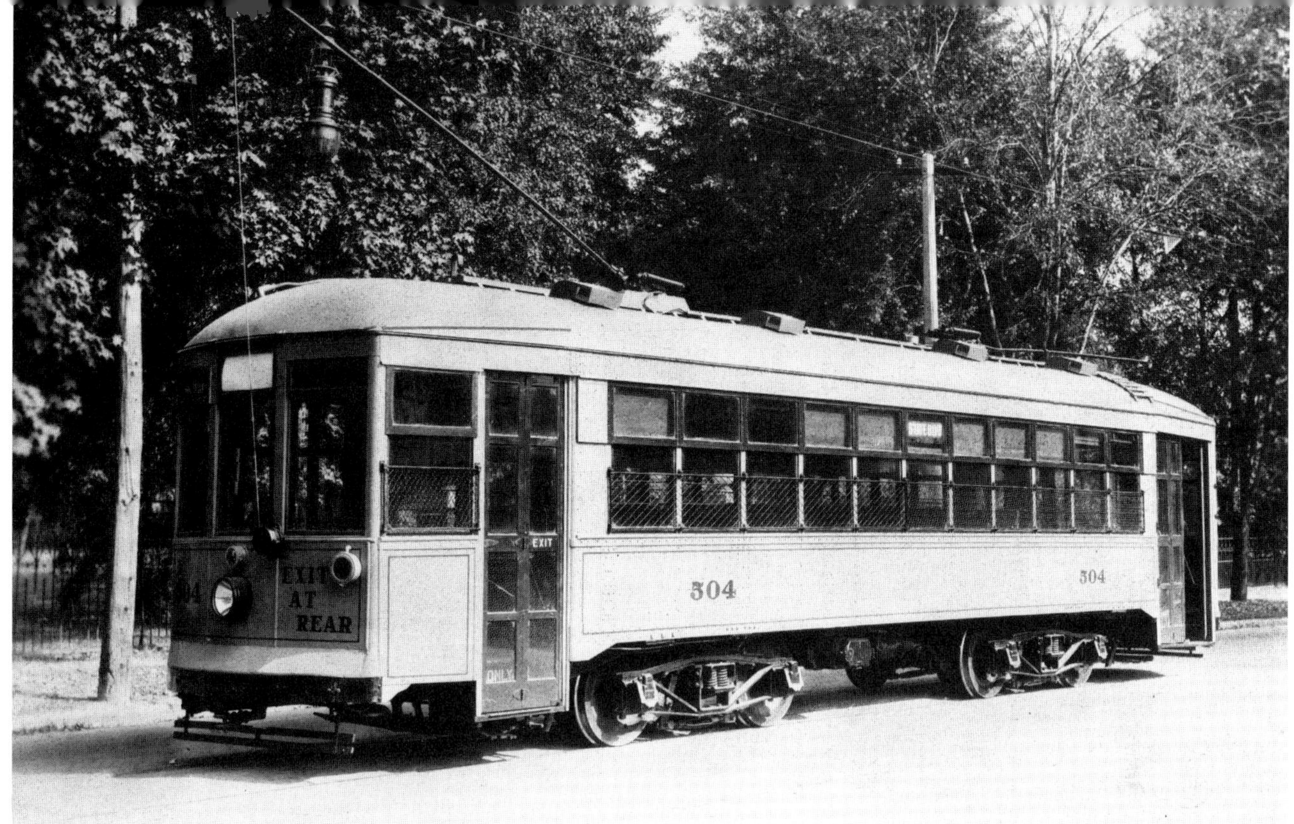

Above: *The 504 was rebuilt to one-man operation in October 1923. Posed here on East State Boulevard in Ft. Wayne, the car sports the sand yellow color scheme.* ***M. D. McCarter Collection. Below:*** *The 288 was from the first group of single-truck cars to appear in 1918 built by the St. Louis Car Company.* ***Bradley-Harnish Collection.***

maroon and cream. This color scheme was applied to most active double- and single-truck cars. In 1940, the new trolley coaches arrived with a color design modification for higher visibility. The company name also appeared after nearly a thirty year absence. This design change was followed as the double-truck cars came in for painting. The single-truck cars never carried this newer (1940) paint scheme. The surplus four wheelers started to the Spy Run Shop and McKinley Yard scrap line in 1936. By late 1940 or early 1941 all of them were gone. Usable equipment, controls and motors were salvaged as they could be used on the fifty-five double-truck cars. Even these remaining cars were supposed to be retired by mid-1942 when the new trolley coaches would be in service and replacing them.

Two cars, 506 and 507, were sold to St. Petersburg, Florida in early 1942. As 118 and 119 in their new home, they presented a smooth-riding pleasing contrast to the wooden-seat double-truck Birney cars used in St. Petersburg. Both were scrapped soon after the war when buses were substituted.

The remaining fifty-three 500 series were used more heavily than ever from 1942 through 1945. After December, 1942, eight could be allowed for spares. However, the original idea

All but nine of the 275 and 400 series cars had rear exits added; all were one-man operated. ***Above:*** *The 404, before a rear exit was added, sits on the outside pits of the Baker Street yards in 1919.* ***Below:*** *The interior of the modified 428 after being rebuilt with a rear exit.* ***Both photos—Bradley-Harnish Collection.***

The brand new 513, signed for the "#4 line," stands at the end of South Calhoun Street on October 20, 1923. These were very handsome, comfortable and utilitarian cars. **Bradley-Harnish Collection.**

Two unsuccessful experiments...**Above:** The 514 (April 1925) was given a one-side-only, cardboard-covering of the upper windows to test the look. The appearance-change was not approved and the idea was dropped for the moment. **Below:** The 523 was used to test Timkin-Detroit, Model 51, lightweight trucks in 1930; all new cabinet-mounted controls were added also. The experiment proved unsuccessful, however, as the brakes reportedly set the car on fire. Afterward the car was converted back to its standard appearance. **Both photos—Bradley-Harnish Collection.**

The 510-554 all were nearly identical. ***Above:*** *The 536 was one of the third group of 500 series cars.* ***Below:*** *The interior of double-truck 535. The car's rattan seats were fairly comfortable when compared to the wooden slat seats used in many other cities.* ***Both photos —Bradley-Harnish Collection.***

The 290's from Logansport never had rear exits added; they were stored after their Peru service ended. ***Van Dusen-Zillmer Collection.***

The 286 still displays the old paint scheme as it stands at the Spy Run shops in August 1936. ***Van Dusen-Zillmer Collection.***

504 appears much in need of paint in this 1936 view. ***Van Dusen-Zillmer Collection.***

of putting the remaining 500-505 and 508-509 out to permanent pasture was forgotten in the war years, as all were needed because of the frequent breakdowns from the earlier lack of maintenance. Except for the heavy use, the streetcars were in better condition, due to the rehabilitation effort, at the end of the war than before. Some were good enough for resale.

Cornwall Street Railway, of Cornwall, Ontario, purchased two 500's in 1945. For some reason they selected two cars from the two different car groups. The older 508 was unique as it was the only car with the experimental plating over the upper side windows.

538 enters Spy Run yards from Randolph Street in 1941; the car wears the new 1940 colors and paint scheme. ***R. O. Dingley Photo / W. A. Steventon Collection.***

Above: *551 at the end of the Broadway line with Foster Park and St. Mary's River in the background. The company's color scheme was modified to this design in 1940 and the company name was carried again on the car sides.* ***Bradley-Harnish Collection. Below:*** *550, on the Spy Run yard storage lead track, has just turned from Randolph Street and is passing the Fare Box House. The seldom used "Route 2" sign was used for cars turning short at Main and Calhoun.* ***R. O. Dingley Photo/W. A. Steventon Collection.***

(The experiment, done in 1940, had been tried in cardboard on one side of 514 in 1925.) It was not considered as worth repeating. The 508 was joined by 516 and although they basically looked the same, there were many small differences because 508 was from the 1917 group rebuilt to conform to the 510 (1923) design. The two became 33 and 37 and retained the same basic color scheme in Cornwall. There is some indication that Cornwall planned to drop the third digit and make these nos. 50 and 51. Both were scrapped when Cornwall abandoned streetcars.

Atlantic City Transportation Company had modernized its fleet with single-end, streamlined Brilliners before the war and disposed of most of its old double-end cars. This company was unique because it had only one, but extremely long, car line serving several adjoining shore communities. Atlantic City was a great convention center and frequently conventioneers' parades completely disrupted schedules as there were few looping facilities for short-turning the single-end Brilliners. The company decided that medium-size double-end cars could maintain traffic at each end of the route whenever a parade broke the line in two. To meet this need the Atlantic City company bought six cars from Fort Wayne in 1945. These cars were the ideal size, they were available in good condition, and the price was right as ISC was eager to dispose of some of its

Above: *Newest of the single-truckers, 449 sits in the Spy Run yards in 1941. This was the last of the small cars and in 1941 its useful days were over; it will soon be scrapped.* ***R. O. Dingley Photo /W. A. Steventon Collection. Below:*** *Streetcars were not immune from accidents; the 524 was the victim of a severe collision. This car would be rebuilt and back in service during war time when every car was needed.* ***Bradley-Harnish Collection.***

St. Petersburg (Florida) Municipal Railway's 118 and 119, ex-Ft. Wayne 506 and 507, at work in 1942. ***W. C. Janssen Photo.***

Cornwall Street Railway's 37 was Ft. Wayne's 516 bought in 1945. There is some indication that Cornwall planned to drop the last digit (making this car 51). The 508 would have been 50 instead of 33. ***Van Dusen-Zillmer Collection.***

surplus cars. The cars sold were 527, 537, 540, 546, 550 and 552, and after some modifications they became Atlantic City's 294-299. They were not heavily used and, with one exception, were scrapped by the mid-fifties. They outlived their sister cars by several years. One car outlasted all Atlantic City cars and was not junked until 1958, although it had been out of service for some time.

The end of wartime restrictions on the company operations, the end of gas rationing, plus new automobiles brought about an end to the regular use of streetcars on all but the Taylor line. Streetcars filled in as trippers on the other routes, but their use declined with a decline in passengers. The company started scrapping cars in 1946. After 543's "last run" on June 27, 1947 the remaining cars were quickly sold for scrap.

ROLLING STOCK INTERURBAN CARS

Wabash River Traction's and the Fort Wayne & Southwestern's first cars arrived at almost the same time with the WRT's cars being unloaded on July 10, 1901, slightly less than three weeks earlier than the arrival of the Southwestern's cars, on July 29. The cars of the two companies were as different as the construction philosophy of each.

The WRT bought four 28-foot body double-end closed cars from the American Car Company of St. Louis. The 10, 12, 14 and 16 were mounted on McGuire trucks with four motors. Two 15-bench double-truck opens, numbered 11 and 13 and mounted on McGuire trucks also had four motors and were built by American as double-end cars (later changed to

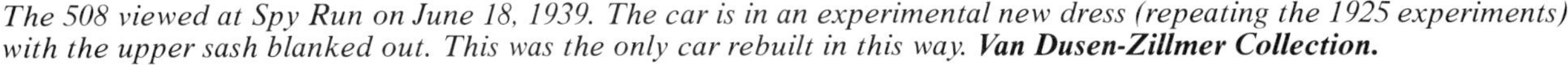

The 508 viewed at Spy Run on June 18, 1939. The car is in an experimental new dress (repeating the 1925 experiments) with the upper sash blanked out. This was the only car rebuilt in this way. ***Van Dusen-Zillmer Collection.***

The Cornwall (Ontario) Street Railway Light & Power Company 33, formerly ISC 508, displays its blocked-off upper sash (a change made experimentally in Ft. Wayne). The company liked Ft. Wayne's maroon and cream color scheme and adopted it as Cornwall's fleet colors. The car was photographed at the Water Street car barn on August 27, 1947. **John D. Knowles Collection.**

At the left: *Six of the Ft. Wayne 510-554 series cars were sold to Atlantic City in 1945. The 552 is in the Atlantic City car barn with its old name painted out.* ***M. D. McCarter Collection. Below:*** *Atlantic City Transportation Company's 298 was Ft. Wayne's 550. Several exterior changes were made.* ***Van Dusen-Zillmer Collection.***

Above: *The 301, in dead storage at McKinley yard, was among the last wooden cars in service and repainted following a minor accident in April 1930.* ***Below:*** *The 302 in storage awaits scrapping at McKinley yard in 1932.* ***Both photos — George Krambles Collection.***

single-end and renumbered 370-371). All of the cars were painted a bright yellow. Four old second-hand single-truck opens were also acquired for trailers. They were reported as coming from New York.

Two smaller closed city cars arrived in January 1902 from Worcester, Massachusetts. If new, they may have been from Osgood Bradley Car Company, which was located in that city. All of the cars used were city/suburban cars and typical of what might be found on a New England rural trolley line. They had no place in the Midwest interurban scheme of things. All the big cars were rough riding and incapable of any speed. They were out of place in the Wabash Valley.

The Fort Wayne & Southwestern cars were a complete contrast to the WRT cars. These cars were designed for intercity service and were both faster and more comfortable than the WRT cars. The first group of five cars was built by Jackson & Sharp Company at their Delaware Car Works (acquired in 1901 by American Car & Foundry). These were of what might be described as a "contractor's design," with nearly identical cars being built for the Erie Rapid Transit (Erie, Pa.), the Hampton, Va. interurban line and the Indianapolis & Shelbyville. The five Southwestern cars were a straight coach type, and named (Indiana, Ohio, Kentucky, Illinois and Iowa) instead of numbered. The cars were painted green with the company name and the car name on the sides. These cars had a distinct liability in their relatively weak underframes with only four reinforced sills running the length of the car. The builder believed that, since these cars were intended for single unit operation, the only bumps and jars that might be expected would occur at low speeds in the shop or car barn. In practice this was not true because all of the Southwestern's cars were subjected to frequent jarring bumps in a continuing series of minor head and rear-end collisions. These were usually from misjudged speeds.

The five cars arrived on July 29, 1901, at Huntington. They were unloaded and sat east of the city for several months until the company's Erie Railroad underpass was completed. The first trip was made on September 30, 1901, with one of the new cars being pulled to Fort Wayne by a steam engine. On December 11, the cars were moved into the Huntington shop under their own power. On the same day the "Indiana" made the first trip from Huntington to Fort Wayne and return.

On July 30, 1902, four 26-ton John Stephenson-built interurban combines numbered 301-304 joined the five original cars. These were bought for the new Huntington-Wabash extension. Both car groups seated 46 passengers. The Stephenson cars had very sturdy underframes.

The record of these early cars became confused as early as 1905. The abbreviation letters "J & S" were easily confused for either Jackson & Sharp or John Stephenson. The shop people also confused the names of American Car Company (St. Louis) and the American Car & Foundry Company (the Jackson & Sharp Works). The Southwestern's cars were very hard to distinguish in written descriptions because of their many similarities and the fact that they were only one inch different in length.

The Southwestern also had an express car from Jackson & Sharp, first numbered 1 and then 12. It was apparently a typical box motor, with a 30′ body and electric equipment similar to the passenger cars. It was ordered in April 1901.

All of these cars were used very hard and given minimal repairs. When the Wabash Valley took over the operation, the cars were found to be in poor physical condition. Two were not even operable. The cars were repaired and then repainted from the Southwestern's light green to the standard Schoepf-McGowan syndicate's olive green (Pullman green). They were also renumbered into the Wabash Valley System's numbering scheme. The Jackson & Sharp cars became 201-205, and the four Stephenson cars became 206-209.

During 1905 the cars were rehabilitated with some of the Southwestern's cars receiving new trucks and electrical equipment. Car 202 exceeded the 65 mph mark in a start-to-stop run of nine minutes over a rebuilt stretch of track near Roanoke.

The Peru-Logansport extension of the Wabash-Logansport Traction Company required better cars than the line between Wabash and Peru possessed. The earlier cars had short-wheelbase McGuire streetcar trucks. Their average speed was less than fifteen miles per hour and the limited-stop express took forty-six minutes to cover the eighteen-mile Wabash-Peru stretch. The Jewett Car Company delivered four large deck-roof double-end suburban cars. These 41-foot cars weighed in at 20 tons. The cars, numbered 22, 24 (August 1902) and 26, 28 (February 1903), which were longer than the 1901 cars, were also painted the Wabash River Traction yellow. Sometime after the merger of these lines into the Wabash Valley, it is believed that all these double-truck deck-roof closed cars may have been first renumbered (briefly) into the 400 series. This is

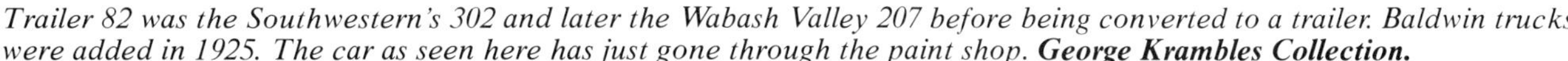

Trailer 82 was the Southwestern's 302 and later the Wabash Valley 207 before being converted to a trailer. Baldwin trucks were added in 1925. The car as seen here has just gone through the paint shop. ***George Krambles Collection.***

hard to establish as two of the eight cars were used for other service prior to the later renumbering of the remaining six passenger cars in the 250-255 series.

In the spring of 1905 one of the Wabash & Logansport Traction Company's Jewett-built cars was brought to the Fort Wayne Baker Street car shops and transformed into a gem of a private car named "Lawton." According to the **Journal-Gazette** the car was "fitted with tapestries, easy chairs, tables and other conveniences. The car is finished in natural woods and is decorated in olive green and gold." It made its first long-distance journey on July 8, going to Wabash and back.

In the modification, much of the yellow deck-roof 41′3″ car was reconstructed. The body segment, believed to have been a basic 30′8″ box body, was salvaged and the old interior was stripped. The short and narrow vestibule ends were removed. New, longer (6′6″) full-width vestibule ends with raised floors, to eliminate the drop platforms, and three large full-length windows were added to each end. The old end sills were modified for support of the longer, raised ends. The car's basic steel-plate-reinforced all-wood frame remained. The deck-roof was extended and curved down into the "railroad roof" style. The Lawton, still numbered 402, (later 800), was now over 43 feet long. However, it still retained its streetcar body appearance which made it appear lighter in weight than some other private cars. It acquired an excellent legacy from its early days in the form of the 6′4″ wheelbase, Peckham 26 D-3 trucks, with 33-inch wheels and the four GE 67, 50-hp motors. The Lawton was well known for its easy ride and for its ability to run at fairly high speeds allowing very fast times over several midwest routes with low-speed time schedules. It was used as a "special" car into the early 1920's.

The Lawton was also used as the Pay Car—a popular assignment—and, although "officially" retired in 1922 may have survived for another ten years.

The other deck-roof cars became 250-252 (the 3 Jewetts) and 253-255 (the 3 Americans) and were used in service over the entire system. The 250, 252 and 253 were retired in 1919 with the rest retired in 1923. The fourth American deck-roof car became overhead line car 41 in 1905.

The Fort Wayne, Van Wert & Lima Traction Company officially opened on November 1, 1905 using new, large type 55-foot interurban cars numbered 1-3. These cars were built by Cincinnati Car Company. As built they had drop platforms at both ends and an entrance door and steps at the right front corner. The steps were later removed.

During 1906, Cincinnati Car Company also delivered a large number of 55-foot combination baggage-passenger interurban cars to Schoepf-McGowan properties. The first were the Lima line's cars 4-7, which arrived in January 1906. These had fairly flat ends, with only a gentle curve, which left several inches of siding between the front corner posts and the baggage doors. The Wabash Valley's 301-302 were duplicates, which arrived in March after the Bluffton line opened. Later Lima line cars, 8 through 11, delivered in mid-1906 were also duplicates of 4 through 7. The next five Wabash Valley cars, 303-307, had rounder ends which placed the corner posts at the immediate front of the baggage doors. The Lima-

The last of the big cars built at Ft. Wayne, 322 served successfully until its active service as a passenger car ended at Roanoke in 1924. ***George Krambles Collection.***

The new 304 of Wabash Valley was built for the subsidiary Lafayette & Logansport Traction Company. These cars had a single window in their baggage compartment. ***George Krambles Collection.***

Toledo 77-78, built in early 1907, and a large order for the Terre Haute, Indianapolis & Eastern were very similar. Three more similar cars turned up in California, in 1906, as Northern Electric Railway Company's 203-205 (later Sacramento Northern's 103-105). The Wabash Valley 303-307 had one distinctive different feature as built. Each had a single window centered between the baggage door and the first pair of windows on either side. These windows were removed after 1910 when all the Wabash Valley's wooden cars were rebuilt to eliminate, among other features, the drop platforms.

The "lightning fast" palace cars came to the Wabash Valley in the spring of 1906. The Syndicate's ownership of a vast amount of interurban through routes set the stage for a new, higher standard of service. The existing 55-foot cars, divided into baggage, smoking and coach sections, already provided a higher grade service than the older coaches commonly used on steam railroad local trains. The Syndicate felt it was now time to go one step further and offer an even finer service.

The new palace cars provided first class services. These cars were used on special "limited" trains which began Fort Wayne-Indianapolis service on May 1, 1906 over the route via Peru.

Through service over the Bluffton line was delayed for over a year because the big cars could not pass through a low bridge at Hartford City.

Seven of these palace cars were built as part of a Wabash Valley order to the Cincinnati Car Company. Each had a special parlor—buffet section with individual leather-covered barrel-style chairs and facilities for light meals. The rear observation vestibule was enclosed by two large, nearly full-length windows, and the passenger entrance doors were also largely glass to provide the best view. The Wabash Valley numbered their four deluxe 61′6″ cars 501-504 and gave them individual names—"Kenilworth" (501), "Ivanhoe" (502), "Talisman" (503) and "Woodstock" (504). Union Traction's part of the delivered order was for only two identical cars for the service. These were 297 and 298 and were named "Kokomo" and "Peru" after two of the cities on the route. The seventh car was built as 101 of the Lima & Toledo for Fort Wayne-Lima service. This car, named "Van Wert" was delivered and

Above: *"Talisman" (504) was the fourth of the great palace cars built by Cincinnati Car Company and placed in service in May 1906.* ***Below:*** *In 1933, the 354 (formerly 504 and much rebuilt) moves off storage track 21 at the Spy Run car yards. Curtis trucks have been substituted for Baldwin trucks.* ***Both photos —George Krambles Collection.***

placed in service in June 1906. The 101's great length allegedly created continuing troubles in negotiating several tight radius curves on the Lima line, and it was soon removed from service. On January 7, 1907, the 101 was sold to Union Traction to become their 296 (first named "Muncie" and then "Bluffton") and placed in the car pool.

The seven cars were among the finest of the interurban car builders' art. They were designed for the public's use and were both graceful and tasteful in the height of the prevailing wooden car building style. At the same time they were practical and utilitarian in their design. The cars were widely hailed in the trade press and were a delight to many electric railway officials, especially to one group from Ohio and Indiana who rode the "Kenilworth" from Lima to Indianapolis to the March 1906 Central Electric Railway Association meeting. The heavy car raced through a severe Indiana snowstorm with ease. **The Street Railway Journal**, in describing this run, generously called the big "Kenilworth" a "magnificent new 62 ft. parlor buffet car."

The other area companies bought a variety of rolling stock and favored the Niles Car

Company of Niles, Ohio with most of the car orders. Two of these lines used alternating current to power their cars.

The Toledo & Chicago Interurban Railway Company opened service with two 45-foot double-truck double-end interurban coaches for local service. The two cars had Peckham No. 40 MCB trucks. Car 1 had a baggage compartment and doors added by the end of 1907. These 1906 Niles built cars were soon followed by six more from the same builder. The six newer cars were 52-foot double-truck single-end interurban combines, seating 46, with the graceful semi-elliptical arch windows which were very characteristic of the Niles company. Two of these cars (3-4) rode on Peckham MCB trucks while the rest (5-8) had Baldwin MCB trucks. All had heavy reinforced I-beam frames. Two double-truck double-end 52-foot freight motors (50-51), a work motor car and a trailer freight car (101) rounded out the roster. The passenger cars had motors and controllers for operation on both A.C. and D.C. segments. Speeds were from 40 to 50 mph.

The Fort Wayne & Springfield's ambitious plans envisioned a fairly long route and anticipated many benefits from their 6600-volt A.C. power system. Slow starts in building the line caused delays in acquiring cars. Niles Car Company was finally able to deliver them in late 1906. The three passenger cars (1-3) were of the combination baggage-passenger design with three compartments. They were very similar to the Toledo & Chicago's cars except for their 53-foot length and doors at the front corners. A 44-foot baggage car, numbered 50, also came from Niles.

All of these cars had 6′10″ wheelbase Baldwin trucks equipped with four single phase motors. These cars used 6600 volts A.C. on the main line, 500 volts A.C. in Decatur and 550 volts D.C. in Fort Wayne. These voltage changes required clumsy electrical switching arrangements.

The bow-trolley, as a current-collecting device, was originally applied to the front end of the Decatur line cars. They were soon replaced with conventional trolley poles. Both current collecting device types were mounted on heavy-duty insulators to protect the rest of the car from the high voltage. The big cars of both of the A.C. lines were excessively heavy, inefficient and costly to operate.

The crew of this T&C car relaxes for the camera while the passengers wait. ***George Krambles Collection.***

Marion & Bluffton 340, used as a reserve car, stands at the Spy Run shops about 1930. **George Krambles Collection.**

At the left: *The interior of Marion & Bluffton 202 as the car stands in storage at Spy Run in 1937.* ***James F. Cook Photo. Below:*** *Marion & Bluffton's one-man 202, in storage at Spy Run, is lettered for the ISC. The entrance doors have been changed from their original configuration.* ***George Krambles Collection.***

The more conventional Marion & Bluffton also used Niles-built cars. These were short, 45-foot combination cars mounted on Taylor MCB trucks. Two large, center-aisle open cars were an oddity of this company as compared to most Midwestern interurban lines. They were used principally on short-distance excursion trains at Marion. The related Bluffton to Geneva line owned one Jewett-built car and used the M&B cars as needed.

In 1909 the Wabash Valley added four Cincinnati-built 55-foot combines numbered 308-311. These were very similar to the earlier 300's but used heavy Curtis trucks. The additional cars displaced the small Southwestern cars used for local service. Some of these little cars had already been demotorized and used as passenger trailers which solved a capacity

Above:** The 308 was one of the 1909 group of 55-foot cars. By 1932 it had joined the McKinley yard scrap line.* ***Below (top photo): *The 309 was painted in the ISC's red in 1924 and stayed in that color until taken out-of-service; Union Traction also utilized the same red. The 309 was photographed in August 1932 much in need of paint.* ***Below (bottom photo):*** *311 rolls off track 21 in the Spy Run Avenue car yards in 1933 faced with no further duties except to stand in the inevitable scrap line.* ***All photos—George Krambles Collection.***

problem but caused slower schedules. The company really needed additional large, fast limited cars and had less need for the small cars.

In November 1909, the Jackson & Sharp-built 202 was brought to the Chestnut Street Shop for lengthening and structural reconstruction. This car was to be one of two company carbuilding experiments. The car was taken apart and virtually built as new with the underframe being lengthened and strengthened in the reconstruction process. The "new" car, as completed, was 63-feet long and rode on new, seven-foot-wheelbase Baldwin trucks (the company's new standard truck for better riding, eventually added to most of the big cars). The 202 became the 321 in the transformation. It used Westinghouse HL control with four Westinghouse motors. Seven months later, in June 1910, the Jackson & Sharp-built 201 was brought to an adjoining bay at the shop and taken apart and treated the same as sister car 202. As in the case of 202, little more than the basic side framing and window layout of 201 survived. The underframe and roof were completely reconstructed and extended. The result of this transformation was the "new" 320. The 320, as first rebuilt, had one small window between the seven paired windows and the baggage doors. Initially the two cars were similar in appearance. The 320 was given GE type M control and four Westinghouse motors. The company wanted to fully test the two cars and the controls before proceeding with any more. The 320 and 321, now three-compartment, baggage-passenger cars, were placed in service in 1910. The two big cars became very popular with train crews and passengers because they were powerful, fast and comfortable.

The Wabash Valley planned to follow the same plan with at least two more cars until the Kingsland wreck in September upset the idea. The 303, as rebuilt at Chestnut Street, resembled the design of the 320 and 321. Certainly the reorganization of early 1911 held up any action on new cars. The new company did decide to continue the program for one more car based on the two test cars. The 322 was built in 1912 using the same car design, the

Ever popular, the big 321 was modernized to a limited extent and painted in the last ISC "Indiana Central Lines" color scheme of sand yellow and olive green. ***George Krambles Collection.***

Rear of the Fort Wayne terminal (Pearl Street) showing the loading dock. ISC bus 454 (built by ACF), the rebuilt 303, and a taxi offered three forms of transportation. ***Bradley-Harnish Collection.***

Westinghouse HL control, and Baldwin 73 trucks. However, the 322 had eight pairs of windows placed somewhat differently than the earlier two. The disappearance of 203 and 204 is probably explained in the 322 emergence. Apparently parts of one or both of them were used in assembling the new car. Both cars 203 and 204 came off the list at this same time.

The Stephenson cars (206-209) were remodeled to trail passenger cars, converted to an all-coach configuration. Three were renumbered 81 (ex 206), 82 (ex 207) and 83 (ex 209). The remaining Jackson & Sharp car (205) also became a trailer. The 81-83 had fairly extensive use, with two of them (82-83) lasting into the thirties. The 205 and 208 were junked in the summer of 1920.

The parlor-buffet services were not particularly successful or practical and were suspended at an early date, but the 500-series cars were great favorites with the company officials and continued to hold down the

The Fort Wayne bus depot was located on Berry Street west of Harrison before 1930. The depot is behind the ISC intercity coaches (L to R: 121, 110, 111, 112, 202, 300, 205). ***Bradley-Harnish Collection.***

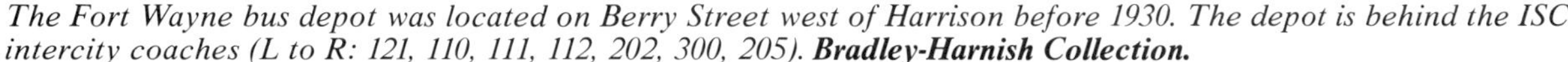

limited runs. The numbers were changed to the 351 series in the late teens, and the cars were converted to a more standard three-compartment seating configuration. In subsequent shop visits the observation section was replaced by a standard vestibule. The 503 was the last altered and retained its original appearance until 1920. The 501 was completely reconditioned as 351, partially steel plated and painted the briefly used red paint. It was involved in a head-on collision with Union Traction's steel 409 on June 3, 1925. The 351 was destroyed and the 409 wrecked beyond repair in the collision and subsequent fire. The 322 and 306 were wrecked at Roanoke on May 19, 1924 and both were retired.

With the exception of the 322 and 351, the remaining five cars of the 320 and 351 series proved to be most successful. They were regularly overhauled and modernized to meet the most current conditions and were excellently maintained. All limited trains used these fast and comfortable cars until the steel 375 series arrived in 1926 and, even then, they continued in regular Fort Wayne-Lafayette use. Far more popular and useful than the 300's, the five sixty-plus footers survived well into the steel car era on ISC mainline assignments until the Indiana Railroad's lightweights rendered them surplus in the latter part of 1931.

The Decatur line, in 1916, produced the next series of interesting cars. These were a cross between a light and heavyweight car design with a relatively light (50,000 lbs.) body on heavy high-wheeled Baldwin trucks. The three steel combines were painted "Pennsylvania R.R. red," numbered 101-103 and were quite successful in service. A new wooden baggage-express car, numbered 110, painted yellow, was also placed in service. They had Westinghouse HL controls and motors equipped for 600 and 1200 volts D.C. and remained in service until 1927.

Arthur Redderson, Superintendent of Motive Power, designed the Decatur line's St. Louis-built cars. Feustel invited him to work with St. Louis again, in late 1923, to design and build a new lightweight car series for use on the ISC and Lima lines. They were to be joined by a comparable group of cars on the Union Traction for the Indianapolis-Fort Wayne through services. The joint effort was so final in its plans that all of the new cars were to be painted a brilliant red with gold trim later adopted by the Union Traction for all of its cars. ISC extended the red paint beyond the ten cars to some of its wooden cars—309 and 351 in particular.

The first of the new cars arrived in mid-April, 1924. They weighed in at 51,700 pounds, and were 52′8″ long. Each was powered by four motors mounted on Commonwealth Steel, low-frame trucks with 28″ wheels. The cars cost $18,000 each. The cars were good performers.

But then catastrophe struck both Union Traction and the ISC in the form of head-on collisions. In both cases several cars were involved. The earlier Union Traction collision at Fortville, on February 2, 1924, was very frightening—thirteen died—and memorable to

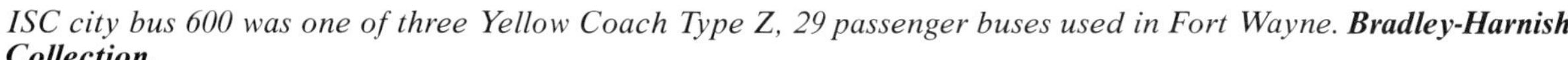

ISC city bus 600 was one of three Yellow Coach Type Z, 29 passenger buses used in Fort Wayne. ***Bradley-Harnish Collection.***

The Ft. Wayne-Decatur 102 poses at the Kendallville barn in October 1935. At this time, the car had been partly relettered for the ISC with its old name painted out. There is, however, no record of the 101-102 being used in revenue service; both were leased to Indiana Railroad for possible conversion to one-man operation, but neither left the ISC property.
Glen Nicely Photo /George Krambles Collection.

all concerned because the two wrecked trains caught fire and were destroyed. The cars in this train had floor heights that were approximately close but telescoping of cars, crushing those in the middle, was severe. At Roanoke, the 322 collided head on with 306 and 307 on May 19, 1924. Six died as a result. Telescoping was not as bad but the heavier 322 destroyed the 306 even though floor heights were nearly identical.

Both companies did not need a third reminder when they studied these two collisions and recalled the tragedy at Kingsland where a heavy car practically ran completely through a lighter low-floor car. To their credit they both decided the heterogenous car assignments were a serious hazard. Later, Indiana Railroad, with operating staffs from both companies pursued the same policy. It was out of the question in 1924 to reequip a main line with cars like the new ones unless you could eliminate all the high floor cars.

The new lightweight cars stayed off the main Indiana lines. However, six cars (90-95) went into Fort Wayne-Lima service as planned. On this route they replaced all of the wooden passenger cars then in regular service. The other four (323-326), however, had little use until the Northern Division was acquired in late 1924, and they were then assigned to run in comparative safety where there would be little chance of encountering heavy wooden cars. The four were overhauled and altered in 1928. Each car was turned end-for-end, received new interiors and bucket seats, and made one man. The former Decatur line's 103 was also extensively altered, changed to one-man operation, placed on Commonwealth trucks and numbered 327. The 327 was actually the pilot model for the recycling experiment and was considered to be expendable. The Decatur 101-102 remained unused and in storage because the rebuilt 323-326 and the 327 were sufficient for the Northern Division service.

The 323-327, although very successful in service, were scrapped after the Northern Division passenger service ended. Apparently they were unsuccessfully offered for sale by

Above: *The brand new, bright red ISC 323 photographed April 12, 1924 on East State Boulevard.* ***Below:*** *The interior of ISC 323 viewed as originally built.* ***Both photos —Bradley-Harnish Collection.***

ISC. None was leased to the Indiana Railroad as the Northern Division did not run as part of the Indiana Railroad System after the receivership. However, the 323-326 were repainted and relettered in the Indiana Railroad Traction orange with green trim colors. The 327 was never repainted for IRR and, as the orphan car of the group, kept as a spare. It was, however, used by IRR on the Muncie-New Castle run in the Indiana Railroad System early days.

The Lima line's 90-95 remained unchanged as two-man cars until their retirement in 1932. Eventually, four of the six were sold to Oklahoma Railway Company (221-224), in 1938, where they served until after World War II. For use in Oklahoma these four were also one-manned, apparently by ISC's shop force, on a much simpler basis than the 323's by just reversing everything. The old seats were kept in these cars.

In 1926, ISC purchased seven large and

Top photo:** The 325 stands ready at the Ft. Wayne station for a run to Waterloo in 1933.* ***George Krambles Collection. Center photo:** The 325 working on the Northern Division in October 1935. By this time, the 325 had been converted to standard C-50-PL plate frame trucks. The reason for this conversion as well as the success of the experiment is not known.* ***Glen Nicely Photo /George Krambles Collection. Photo at left:** ISC's 325 and other 323's are being dismantled behind the Spy Run shop on August 20, 1938.* ***Van Dusen-Zillmer Collection.

very heavy (101,000 lbs.) interurban cars. This began implementing the decision made two years earlier to use only heavy, high-floor cars on the longer interurban routes. Five of these were combines and along with the two parlor cars were among the finest and heaviest interurban cars ever built. Parlor cars "Anthony Wayne" and "Little Turtle" were teamed up with combines for the WABASH VALLEY FLYER. The two parlor cars (390-391) were not mere trailers going along for the ride as both were powered and capable of operation by themselves. The first regular runs using these two car trains were made August 11, 1926. The parlor cars were used for only five years before going into storage and eventually scrapped in 1939. The combines 375-379 were leased to and extensively

Above: *Oklahoma Railway's 223 pictured in 1947 at Norman, Oklahoma. Four of the Ft. Wayne-Lima 90 series cars went to Oklahoma in 1934 and were used until 1947.* ***Van Dusen-Zillmer Collection. Below:*** *The 378 (August 1933) awaits a call for another run on the coach storage tracks at the old Pearl Street freight station.* ***George Krambles Collection.***

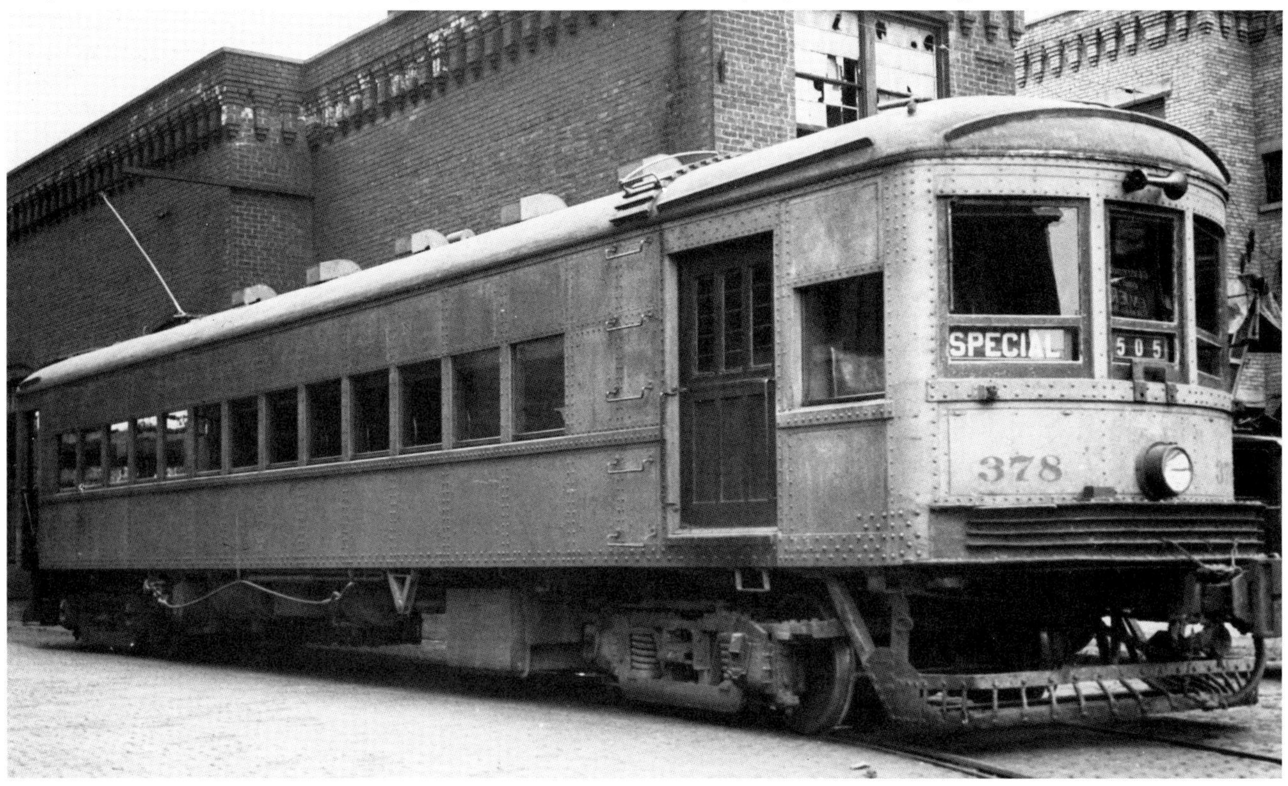

used by Indiana Railroad, and three still survive in different garb today. The 375-377 were converted to Railway Post Office (R.P.O.) combination passenger cars. The three were returned to ISC in January 1941 when IRR ended passenger service. ISC sold the three R.P.O. cars to the South Shore Line. The 376 still retains much of its original body appearance although extensively modified (especially the roof) and runs as the South Shore's line car 1100. The 375 and 377 were rebuilt by the South Shore to express trailers 503 and 504 respectively. The 378-379 were converted to one-man operation as cars 458-459 of Indiana Railroad. By 1938 IRR apparently had enough cars of its own and these two leased cars could be considered surplus. Returned to Spy Run, they were also scrapped.

The new steel cars introduced the final ISC color scheme for interurban cars. Colors had

Above: *378 and parlor car 390, "Little Turtle," pose near the end of the Broadway line. When built in 1926, these were probably the finest and best interurban cars in the country.* ***Below:*** *The interior of 378 (from the rear) shows the coach section; the smoker and baggage sections were forward.* ***Both photos —Bradley-Harnish Collection.***

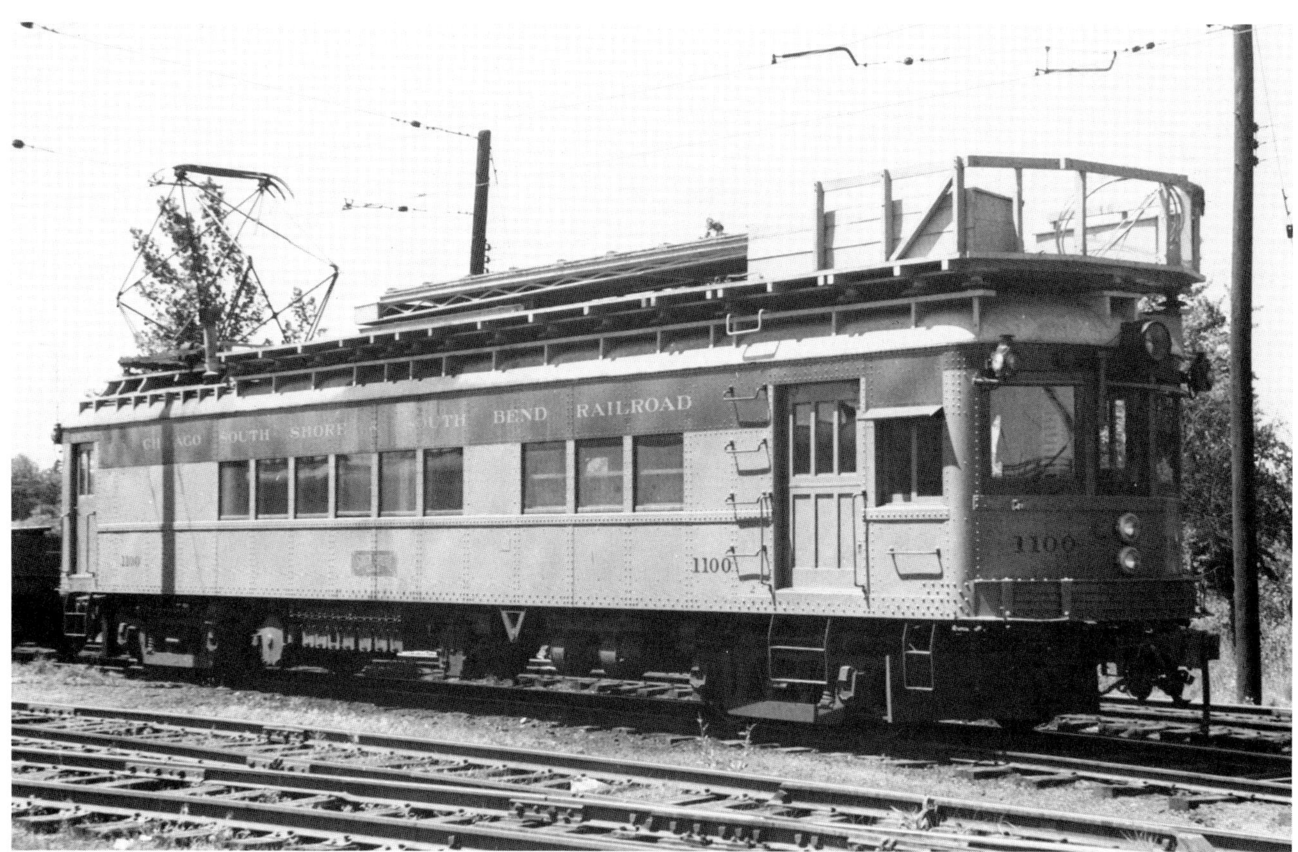

The Chicago, South Shore & South Bend R.R. line car 1100 was originally the ISC's 375. The car was sold by the ISC to South Shore in 1941 after cars 375-377 were returned from service on the Indiana Railroad. The 1100 is still in service today (1982) on the South Shore. ***Bradley-Harnish Collection.***

Top photo at left: *The ISC 390 stands idle in the Spy Run yard in August 1939, shortly before it was scrapped along with IRR 457-458 (the former 378-379).* ***R. O. Dingley Photo/W. A. Steventon Collection. Bottom photo at left:*** *A Ft. Wayne-Lima car stands at the Lima station on April 27, 1932. The red paint is now as faded as the hopes of the Lima line which would last for only two more months.* ***George Krambles Collection.***

changed during the 1920's as the company turned away from Pullman green. Tan, (sometimes described as sand yellow) was first used on the city cars in 1917 on the 240 series cars. Tan began to appear on interurban passenger cars after 1920. A brilliant red paint was briefly used on a few cars. The red and tan cars carried only the letters "ISC" and the car numbers. The 375 series introduced a new trim scheme with the cars having extensive green stripping and lettering. The cars had an olive green roof, black undercarriage and maroon hardware. All interurban passenger cars painted after mid-1926 received the new paint scheme. Freight and service cars were also painted in the tan but with less trim paint. Those pieces of interurban and city service equipment, picked for continued use

The 47 was a classic Cincinnati Car Company 61-foot car built in 1910 for the Ohio Electric and given to the Ft. Wayne, Van Wert & Lima line in the break-up of the big system. The 47, here, has been involved in an accident. Both the 47 and 48 were used for work trains on the Lima line. ***George Krambles Collection.***

Top photo at right: *It's the end of the line for parlor car 391 on August 11, 1939 as Spy Run shop crews cut apart this fine example of the 1920's builders' art. Sister cars 378, 379 and 390 suffered the same fate.* ***R. O. Dingley Photo /W. A. Steventon Collection. Bottom photo at right:*** *Portable substation 1000 at the end of the Pontiac-Harvester line.* ***Bradley-Harnish Collection.***

after 1936, were painted in the new city colors of maroon and cream. These included nos. 1, 3, 4, 5, 7, 13, 817, 818, 826, 827 and 848. The last two cars in use—remaining into the 1950's—were 817 and 848. They were painted a dark green color by Indiana & Michigan Electric Co.

Many of the surplus wooden passenger cars were stored at McKinley Avenue yard after 1925 with most retired by 1931. The 301, for example, remained active into 1932 because it had a rear drawbar and could pull an express trailer. It was used on the Lima line as a substitute because the 90 series could not pull trail cars. A few were rebuilt into freight motors, as the sound bodies were the basis for an excellent freight unit. By the early thirties McKinley Yard was full of surplus wooden cars in various states of repair. More came in as IRR retired the leased equipment and returned it to Fort Wayne. Most were scrapped at McKinley Yard. Some car bodies were sold for other uses such as "diners" and sheds.

The freight and service fleet was large, varied and diverse. Some of the cars were bought new from the carbuilding companies, but the bulk were company reconstructions from something else and then, in some cases, reworked again. A roster identity problem arises from the fact that the company frequently dated its work and freight equipment from the latest year it was passed through the shop for reconstruction. For the most part, ISC engineers developed a fairly standard and distinctive design for their rebuilding work, particularly those cars that were extensively modified. The identity of lesser rebuilds often showed through. Most of the work and service fleet is nearly impossible to trace unless some of the early records turn up which, fortunately, in some cases, has happened.

The line wagon and crew in the early 1900's before special rail cars were built. For repair purposes, this arrangement would have been more flexible than a fixed rail car. ***Bradley-Harnish Collection.***

Very few work cars were needed or in use prior to the advent of the interurban lines. The city systems were small and, besides a snow sweeper or plow and a few other small work cars, had little need for many special cars.

A great many specialty cars were in use for the system operation, the four small city operations and the Fort Wayne city lines. One large line car and several smaller service cars were regularly assigned to each city. Until 1911 the freight cars were painted Pullman green like the passenger cars. Yellow was then adopted for the freight cars. At least in later years, the roof was dark gray and trucks, underbody, hardware and lettering were black. ISC had more than fifty such cars and over seventy-five freight cars.

Wing Plow #1 was a reconstruction of old city car 125, built to comply with a city order to keep the tracks clear of snow without dumping it on the roadway. The #1 was built for the interurban lines and assigned to the interurban division though it also was kept in city use in Ft. Wayne. The car is pictured on Baker Street. ***Bradley-Harnish Collection.***

Above:** Freight motor 57 and four new trailers (63-66), all with the Wabash Valley's "good luck" logo, was built new in 1910. It was rebuilt and shortened in 1928, later becoming IRR's 734.* ***George Krambles Collection. Below: *IRR's 731 (ex-854, ex-54) was bought new as a freight motor in 1907. It stands for this photo at the Indianapolis freight terminal on July 4, 1938.* ***Van Dusen-Zillmer Collection.***

Work and freight equipment for the interurban lines developed as the lines were built and the system was pieced together. The Fort Wayne system's freight and service equipment, over the years, was directly parallel to that used throughout the electric interurban industry. Initially new cars had to be purchased while, in later years, older cars were converted or downgraded to work on freight operations.

The Southwestern purchased box motor 1 in April 1901 from Jackson & Sharp. The number was changed to 12 and it retained that odd number designation when it came into the Wabash Valley roster. One car was not enough, so Cincinnati Car Company delivered two large double-truck freight motor bodies in August 1905. The two bodies were taken to Boyd Park barn and temporarily stored. When the Wabash Valley re-equipped some of the 200-series passenger cars, the older Peckham 14 trucks and electrical equipment were put on these two. Freight motors 10 and 11 went into service in October 1905. Within a few months the company realized that it had too many cars with the same numbers and these cars were renumbered with 10 and 11 becoming 51 and 52 while the 12 became 53. The 51 and 53 were destroyed in an unidentified fire in 1917. The 52 was extensively reconstructed in the 1920's.

Through 1917, the major car builders delivered three more sets of two each, numbered 54-55, 56-57 and 58-59. The last two had

***Above:** The 32 had been Ohio Electric's 767. The arch roof is actually the old clerestory roof with its center dropped to be nearly flush with the rest of the roof.*
At the left:** Ft. Wayne, Van Wert & Lima Traction Company's 34 was a reconstruction of passenger car 42. In this photo, the 34 has reached the end of the line and is being scrapped.* ***Both photos —Dr. Reed C. Prugh Collection.

Box cars 67 and 70 were built at the Huntington shop in 1922. ***Bradley-Harnish Collection.***

arch roofs. These were adequate until the aggressive growth of the freight business in the 1920's.

As the system matured in the 1920's, ISC discovered two factors. One was an insufficiency of good freight equipment in the face of increasing traffic. The other was a lack of first class work and service equipment. Much of the latter was old, converted single-truck equipment which was both inefficient and

Ft. Wayne-Lima Traction Company's freight motor 35 stands ready at the Ft. Wayne freight terminal in the late 1920's. The 35 was formerly passenger car 43 reconstructed for freight service. ***Bradley-Harnish Collection.***

slow. Post-World War I labor costs had increased considerably and more efficient equipment was needed.

In 1924 the ISC acquired the FtW-L 41-46 and put these former passenger cars into freight and work service. The six were reconstructed into five cars: 30, 34 and 35 for FtW-L and 45 and 46 for ISC. Parts of 44 were used in the second reconstruction of 853 in 1929.

The second 53 was a result of the Roanoke collision which left the 322 with a crushed front. A modest reconstruction shortened the old 322 and removed the windows plus adding side freight doors. The 53 had the misfortune of becoming a near total loss in August 1929 when it was involved in a collision. Virtually the entire upper body works were demolished. The remains plus salvaged parts and the body of FtW-L 44 were used to build another 53, later renumbered 853.

In late 1924 ISC purchased the Fort Wayne

Trailer car 101 served a variety of uses including the transporting of prize draught horses. ***Bradley-Harnish Collection.***

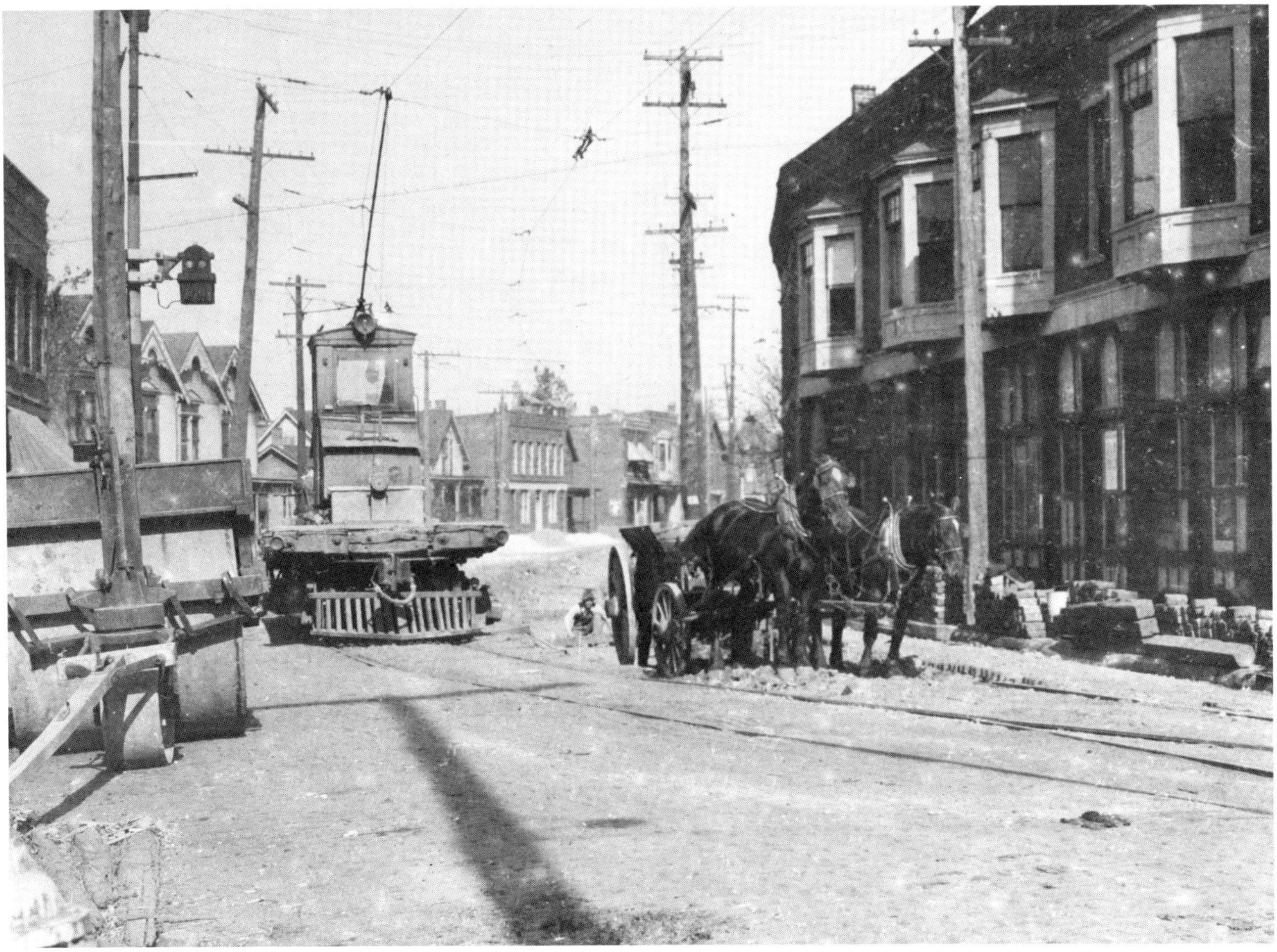

Above: *Work motor 21, as it appeared in 1921, already had been reconstructed more than once; it would change again in 1929. Here it works on Wells Street in 1921.* ***Bradley-Harnish Collection. Below:*** *ISC freight motor 845 was a reconstruction of FW-L 45. It later became IRR 726. Russ Powell is the motorman in this 1935 scene in Indianapolis.* ***George Krambles Collection.***

Above: *IRR 730 (ex-ISC 853, ex-53, ex-passenger 322) was the last of three reconstructions that the old passenger 322 (a reconstruction in itself) underwent. The 730 poses at the Wabash passenger station on August 3, 1936.* ***Van Dusen-Zillmer Collection. Below:*** *The 28 (later 828) had been Ft. Wayne & Northwestern 7 before being rebuilt to the ISC Tool and Equipment car. This 1927 view shows the 28 and 1102 in the Spy Run yards.* ***Bradley-Harnish Collection.***

& Northwestern and acquired six wooden passenger cars and two wooden freight motors. The two freight motors moved easily into the ISC roster and even retained their numbers (50-51). The two were shopped and put in good repair but were little changed. The passenger cars went into a variety of freight, work and service vehicles. All were extensively reconstructed and became 17, 18, 27, 28, 48 and 130, with no two alike.

In ISC operation these freight motors usually stayed on their own lines or the through joint routes with the Union Traction. The Ft. Wayne-Lima operated by ISC occasionally used ISC equipment, but it went no further into Ohio. The company's wide variety of freight trailers, flat cars, gondola and dump cars traveled all over the Midwest in interchange with other lines.

In 1928 or 1929 all of the freight and work motors in interurban service were given an 800 prefix. This appears to have been part of a master plan (perhaps sponsored by the Central Electric Railway Association's traffic

IRR 1153 had been Ft. Wayne & Northwestern's freight motor 51 built in 1906 and absorbed by ISC as their 51 (later 851). When photographed it was on the scrap line at McKinley yard. ***M. D. McCarter Collection.***

Coke car 130 was the shell of a Ft. Wayne & Northwestern passenger car (either car 4 or 6). Here, it stands at Spy Run in 1937. ***Van Dusen-Zillmer Collection.***

Above: *The 794 was assigned a new number, 821, by Indiana RR; though they never used the car. This was the final form for the 21 (821) shown here in August 1936.* ***Van Dusen-Zillmer Collection. Below:*** *Line motor 827 was reconstructed from Ft. Wayne & Northwestern #1 and repainted in the new colors; it had a rear train door. The 827 ended its duties and was scrapped in 1941.* ***Dr. Reed C. Prugh Collection.***

committee) to avoid numerical registry problems when freight and other equipment was through-run over more than one company's lines. Several other interurban railways instituted freight car series in other groups, such as 1200's on the Indiana, Columbus & Eastern, 1700's on the THI&E and 3000's on the Cincinnati, Hamilton & Dayton. The Indiana Railroad eventually renumbered the cars into the company's uniform roster (based on the Union Traction's system). The Indiana Railroad owned the Union Traction cars, and the "system" (later leased) cars were renumbered for operating convenience and uniformity. At first the ISC cars had the old number painted out and a new one added until they could be fully repainted and relettered for the Indiana Railroad System. Some cars that received the new numbers were never used by the Indiana Railroad, especially after the receivership required formal leases. Other ISC cars were assigned IRR numbers which were never painted on the cars.

The cars turned over to the Indiana Railroad came back over a period of years and all were scrapped or returned by mid-1941. Most were useless after January 1941 and those that came back to Fort Wayne were joined by

Above: *ISC's 859 poses on the south side through track (headed toward Commerce Drive) at the new Ft. Wayne freight terminal on June 3, 1929.* ***Bradley-Harnish Collection. Below:*** *The 820 (ex-20), later to be IRR's 793, stands ready for work at the Wabash station on August 3, 1936.* ***Van Dusen-Zillmer Collection.***

Center cab ISC 818 became Indiana RR 792. It was built from Ft. Wayne & Northwestern passenger car 5. This line motor was returned to ISC in 1940 (the only IRR car ever returned to ISC service), restored to its old number 818, repainted and used as the Northern Division snow plow until 1945. ***Van Dusen-Zillmer Collection.***

Above: *Line car 41 about 1906 at Peru. This car was originally Wabash River Traction's car 14 modified about 1904. Later it was reconstructed again to a different style eventually becoming 825.* ***David Chambers Collection. Below:*** *Line car 825 (ex-25, ex-41) stands at McKinley yards on August 7, 1937.* ***Van Dusen-Zillmer Collection.***

surplus cars, in use in and around Fort Wayne, at McKinley yard where they were scrapped. In an interesting switch ISC 818 had been used by IRR as 792 and in 1941 this car reverted to its old number of 818 and served as the Northern Division snow plow until 1945. Several pieces of interurban work and freight equipment were repainted in the new "maroon (tuscan red) and cream." The 827 was either repainted by mistake or else it was decided that the 818 would be more suitable, as 827 was scrapped in 1942.

In addition to the freight equipment the system, over the years, acquired a variety of special service cars. The Wabash Valley assembled four heavy line cars for interurban service in 1910. Originally numbered 40-43, at least one had an earlier career and had been a Wabash River Traction passenger car (probably the 14). These four cars were based at

Line car 42 at Huntington about 1910 became the 23 (later 823) before becoming IRR 764. **George Krambles Collection.**

Above: *The 43 was built as the Ft. Wayne Division line car; it became the 24 (later 824). The car was scrapped about 1932. It is shown here at the Baker Street barn.* ***Bradley-Harnish Collection. To the left:*** *The 829 (later IRR's 767) was a line motor reconstructed in 1929 from Ft. Wayne-Decatur Traction Company's 110. It was photographed at the Peru passenger station on August 3, 1936.* ***Van Dusen-Zillmer Collection.***

Fort Wayne, Huntington, Logansport and Lafayette. The four were renumbered 23-26 (later 823-826). The 27 (827) and 29 (829) were added later giving the company six main-line overhead line motors. The 829 became Indiana Railroad 767. The 826 and the 827 remained in ISC service with the others retired by 1932. The 827 was ISC's best, crew carrying, main

Above: *The 826 started as line car 40; it was refurbished in 1939 and given Baldwin trucks to replace its old Peckham trucks. Repainted in the new maroon and cream, the 826 became the Northern Division line car until 1945.* ***Bradley-Harnish Collection. Below:*** *Ft. Wayne-Lima 33 had been Ohio Electric's 769 and originally was identical to the 32.* ***George Krambles Collection.***

line interurban, overhead service car. The #2 end had a train door. The 826 continued in use as the Fort Wayne city and Northern Division line car until 1945.

ISC and FtW-L used the old 61-foot Cincinnati passenger cars (47 & 48), retired by FtW-L, in work service with no modifications. The 47 was used to pull dump cars in building the fill work that replaced the Lima line's Monroeville and Delphos trestles. Apparently they were scrapped sometime in the late 1920's.

The 49 is an unknown quantity as no description exists. It appears only in a 1926 notation that it was a fire loss that year. However, in

Freight and express motors 264 and 278 were used jointly by the MB&E and the BG&C lines. The 264 may have become ISC's 49. ***Bradley-Harnish Collection.***

At the right: *A Jaeger concrete mixer was mounted on an old Peckham truck and towed to the job.* ***Below:*** *One of the 1942 Brill 44 SMT trolley coaches painted for Fire Prevention. Trolley coaches were painted for public service use and one was annually painted as the Christmas "Candy Cane" coach. The special coach would be switched to different routes for maximum exposure.* ***Both photos — Bradley-Harnish Collection.***

Above: *At the Spy Run yards in 1941, the snow fleet included plow 1 (on the left); sweepers 3, 4 and 5 (all in this line-up); plus sweeper 7. The 3, built in 1895, was the oldest piece of equipment for many years.* ***Below (top photo):*** *Sweeper 5, shown here at Spy Run yards, was built in 1905. Its design was nearly standard for all McGuire-Cummings sweepers.* ***Below (bottom photo):*** *Sweeper 7 was built by the company in 1915 and looked very similar to the older sweepers. It may have been built from an old unpowered sweeper.* ***All photos —R. O. Dingley Photo /W. A. Steventon Collection.***

Wreck car 13 carried re-railing and towing gear to rescue city cars. ***Van Dusen-Zillmer Collection.***

Above: *Sand car 14 was retired by 1937.* ***Below:*** *Work car 19 was considered surplus in 1937 as it stood at the McKinley yards. This car was used last in the 1920's track reconstruction.* ***Both photos — Van Dusen-Zillmer Collection.***

1926 ISC acquired control of the Marion & Bluffton which had a freight motor (264)similar to the 50 and 51 of the Ft. Wayne & Northwestern. The latter cars were directly absorbed into the roster and the 264 may have come in as the 49 as it was part of the sale of the M&B to the ISC.

The city lines had a variety of equipment in use at various times. These included the snow plows and sweepers. The city equipment kept after 1940, was repainted the new tuscan red and cream and kept in use. Plow 1 and sweepers 4 and 5 were kept until the end of the streetcar service in 1947.

The 817 and 848 were retained after 1945 to do switching for the NYC interchange to the power plant and on Spy Run Avenue. The 848 was kept as a spare and was rarely used except to see that it could operate. The open platform 817 was the regularly used motor. When it shunted its last car on October 1, 1952 it brought down the curtain on electric rail operations in Fort Wayne.

Car No.	Car Type	Builder	Year Built	Truck	Motor	Control	Year Retired	Notes
Horsecars								
Citizens' Street Railroad (1871-1887)								
10, 12	14′ Horsecars	McNairy & Claflen Co.	1871	Pedestal	—	—	After 1887	14′ "Box" body double-end, closed horsecars. Delivered in Dec. 1871. First used Jan. 6, 1872.
14, 16, 18, 20	14′ Horsecars	McNairy & Claflen Co.	1872	Pedestal	—	—	After 1887	Same as 10 and 12. Delivered Spring 1872. One of these cars used in the 1891 battery car experiment.
One car	Flat	Citizens' St. RR Co.	1872	Pedestal	—	—	?	Used for moving supplies. Later fitted with a detachable snowplow. Probably built locally.
1, 2, 3 (?)	Closed Horsecar	?	1874	Pedestal	—	—	After 1887	Purchased new, double-end horsecars.
6 (?)	Open	?	1875	Pedestal	—	—	After 1887	Open summer horsecar for two horses. Bought new, builder not known.
4, 5 (?)	Closed Horsecar	?	1884	Pedestal	—	—	After 1887	Purchased new, double-end horsecars. Bought in 1884.
7 (?)	Open Horsecar	Citizens' St. RR Co.	1884	Pedestal	—	—	After 1887	Open summer, 7-bench, 2 horse car.

Notes: Closed cars normally pulled by one horse. Under predictable heavy load conditions or winter weather all cars were pulled by two horses.

Car numbers one through seven were used. The exact sequence is not known.

Fort Wayne Street Railroad (1887-1892)

Accurate information is not complete for the cars bought by this company. Cars (13) of the Citizens' St. RR Co. were acquired, plus new cars from J. M. Jones' Sons (at least 18 closed twelve and fourteen foot cars). See text for information.

C. L. Centlivre Street Railway Co. (1887-1892)

This company acquired five closed cars and three open cars. All sold to and briefly used by Fort Wayne Electric Railway. See text for information.

Car No.	Car Type	Builder	Year Built	Truck	Motor	Control	Year Retired	Notes
Electric Cars								
Lakeside Street Railway (1892-1900)								
2, 4	16′ Closed Box	J. M. Jones' Sons	1892	Dorner & Dutton #20	2-Short 20 hp	?	Between 1900 and 1904	Bought new from Fort Wayne Electric Railway. Bought back by Fort Wayne Traction in 1900.
1, 3	8-Bench Open	J. M. Jones' Sons	1892	Dorner & Dutton #20	2-Short 20 hp	?	After 1900	Bought new from Fort Wayne Electric Railway. Cost $600@. Bought back by Fort Wayne Traction in 1900.
Fort Wayne Electric Railway (1892-1895) Fort Wayne Consolidated Ry. Co. (1895-1899)								
2-48 Even Nos.	16′ Closed Box	J. M. Jones' Sons	1892	Dorner & Dutton #20	2-Short 20 hp	?	By 1904	Five-window cars. Vestibules closed. Some changed to Dorner & Dutton 25 truck. Cars 2 and 4 sold in 1892 to Lakeside St. Ry. (same numbers) and reacquired in 1900. Most others vestibuled in 1895-1896. Almost all retired by 1904. Four cars in work service. 14 last known car in use.

Car No.	Car Type	Builder	Year Built	Truck	Motor	Control	Year Retired	Notes
50-58 Even Nos.	16′** Closed Box	J. M. Jones' Sons	1888 1892	Dorner & Dutton #20	1-Short 20 hp	?	By 1902	Believed former 14′ closed horsecars. Spliced with new center section in 1892. Five windows. Probably the 1887 horsecars.
60-68 Even Nos.	16′** Closed Box	J. M. Jones' Sons	1888 1892	Dorner & Dutton #20	1-Short 20 hp	?	By 1902	Spliced 14′ ex-horsecars, built in 1888. Rebuilt with a fifth large center window added in 1892 to approx. 16′ car body length.
1-65 Odd Nos.	8-Bench Open	J. M. Jones' Sons	1892	Dorner & Dutton #20	1-Short 20 hp*	?	By 1920	Cost $600@. Some lasted in service until 1920 but renumbered into the 300 series and then the 600 series. Cars 1 and 3 sold in 1892 to Lakeside St. Ry. (same numbers) and reacquired in 1900.
81, 83, 85	7-Bench Open	?	1889?	Dorner & Dutton #20	?	?	By 1910	At least one seven-bench open is verified. The Centlivre Co. had three and would explain the odd numbering of the next group. Converted from Centlivre's horsecars.
87-135	9-Bench Open	J. M. Jones' Sons	1896	Dorner & Dutton #25	?	?	1920	Built for Fort Wayne Consolidated Ry. Co. and bought for Robison Park service. Pulled up to three trailers in service.
1-4	Sweepers	McGuire Mfg. Co.	1895	McGuire	?	?	—	Snow sweepers.
?	Sprinkler	?	1895	?	?	?	—	Recorded only as a purchase. No other details.

Notes: In addition to the cars listed, five closed horsecars acquired with the C. L. Centlivre St. Ry. were briefly used until electrification was completed.

*Not all were motorized. Trailers and motor cars were identical except for electrical equipment.

**Rebuilt dimension length is an approximation.

Fort Wayne Traction Co. (1899-1904)
Fort Wayne & Wabash Valley Traction Co. (1904-1911)
Fort Wayne & Northern Indiana Traction Co. (1911-1920)
Indiana Service Corporation (1920-1947)

City Passenger Cars

Car No.	Car Type	Builder	Year Built	Truck	Motor	Control	Year Retired	Notes
101-108	ST, DR 22′ Cars	Jackson & Sharp Co. Serial #1604-1611	1899	Lord Baltimore	?	?	By 1917	Fort Wayne Traction's first new cars, changed to Peckham 8-B truck. Retired to scrap or work service. One became 17.
109-120	ST, DR 22′ Cars	J. M. Jones' Sons	1902	Peckham Metropolitan Special	2-GE-1000 or 2-GE-67	2-K-10	By 1923	Nearly identical to 101-108.
121-131	ST, DR 22′ Cars	Ft. Wayne Traction	1902	Peckham Metropolitan Special	2-GE-1000	2-K-10	By 1925	Straight side version of the 101-108 series. 125 rebuilt as plow 1.
132-137	ST, DR 22′ Cars	J. M. Jones' Sons	1902	Peckham Metropolitan Special	2-GE-67 or 2-GE-1000	2-K-10	By 1923	"Lot #2" on company records (1903). Identical to 109-120.
138-139	?	?	?	?	?	?	?	Believed to be some of the six Logansport, Rochester & Northern's 18′ closed cars.
140-146	ST, DR 20′ Cars	Barney & Smith	?	?	?	?	By 1927	Believed to have been bought for Lafayette. Changed to a Curtis truck with 2-GE-216 motors and 2-K-36 or 2-K-10 controllers.

Car No.	Car Type	Builder	Year Built	Truck	Motor	Control	Year Retired	Notes
147-156	ST, DR 20′ Cars	Cincinnati Car Co. (Order #225)	1904	Dorner	2-GE-216	2-K-36 or 2-K-10	By 1923	Large window cars. Changed to Curtis truck in 1911.
157-166	ST, DR 18′ Cars	?	?	?	?	?	?	Ten cars at Logansport and Lafayette. Originally six at Logansport (LR&N) and seven at Lafayette.
167-168	?	?	?	?	?	?	?	May have been Wabash River Traction's two, Jan. 1902, closed cars from Worcester, Mass.
169	?	?	1905	Curtis CS 58-96	2-GE-216	2-K-36	By 1922	May have been the Wabash-Logansport's Erie Street car for Logansport (1902). May have been built by American Car Co.
170-173	ST, DR 20′ Semi-convertible	Cincinnati Car Co.	1907	Peckham Metropolitan Special	2-GE-216	2-K-10	By 1930	Longitudinal seats. Bought May, 1907.
174-175	ST, DR 20′ Semi-convertible	Cincinnati Car Co.	1907	Peckham Metropolitan Special	2-GE-216 or 2-GE-80	2-K-36 or 2-K-10	By 1924	Same as 170-173, cross seats.
176-201	ST, DR 20′ Semi-convertible	Cincinnati Car Co. (Order #1110)	1909	Curtis CS 58-96	2-GE-80	2-K-10	Last in 1934	Longitudinal seats.
202-220	ST, AR 32′4″ Nearside	Cincinnati Car Co. (Order #1685)	1913	Curtis CS 58-96	2-GE-216	2-K-35	1937 (209)	Originally single-end. Rebuilt to one-man, double-end.
221-227	ST, AR Nearside	J. G. Brill Co. (Order #18712)	1913	Brill 21-E	2-GE-216	1-K-36	1928 (225) By 1922 (others)	Built for Lafayette. 225 rebuilt to double-end and changed to Curtis truck.
240-249	DT, AR 2-Man Rear-entrance	St. Louis Car Co. (Order #1152)	1917	Baldwin 68-18-C	4-WH-506 C2	2-K-12A	1947	249 had St. Louis 119B trucks. Rebuilt 1922-23. See 500-509.
250-252	DT, DR 30′8″ Box Body	Jewett Car Co.	1902-1903	Peckham 26-D-3	4-GE-67	2-K-6	Last in 1924	Built for Wabash-Logansport Traction Co. as 22, 24, 26, 28. Suburban cars with an overall length of 41′3″. Believed renumbered 400-403. 402 became 800 (the "Lawton"). Renumbered 250-252 in 1907. Usually used in Lafayette.
253-255	DT, DR 25′ Semi-convertible	American Car Co. (Order #379)	1901	McGuire 39A	4-GE-1000	2-K-6	Last in 1924	Built as Wabash River Traction Co. 10, 12, 16. Overall length 39′6″. Sister car 14 reconstructed to line car 41 at an early date. Renumbered in 1907 to 253-255. Used in Fort Wayne and Lafayette.
275-290	ST, AR Nearside	St. Louis Car Co. (Order #1179)	1918	St. Louis 113B	2-GE-258C	2-K-63B	By 1940	Steel safety cars, rear doors added in 1924.
291-299	ST, AR Nearside	St. Louis Car Co. (Order #1179)	1918	Curtis CS-58-96	2-GE-258C	2-K-63B	By 1934	Same as 275-290. Built for Logansport. Changed to St. Louis 113C truck. No rear doors added.
370-371	DT, DR 15-Bench Open	American Car Co. (Order #378)	1901	McGuire 39A	4-GE-67	1-K-6	1924	Built for Wabash River Traction Co. as 11, 13.
350-354	ST, DR 10-Bench Open	Cincinnati Car Co.	?	?	?	?	1915	Ten-bench open cars with enclosed front ends.

Car No.	Car Type	Builder	Year Built	Truck	Motor	Control	Year Retired	Notes
355-359	ST, DR 10-Bench Open	?	?	?	?	?	Last in 1920	Ten-bench open cars.
1st 400-403	—	—	—	—	—	—	—	See 250-252.
400-434	ST, AR Nearside	St. Louis Car Co. (Order #1195)	1919	St. Louis 113C	2-GE-258	2-K-36B	1940	Steel safety cars. Rear door added in 1924. Same as 275-290, except for 400 which became a sand-car (1936).
435-449	ST, AR Nearside	St. Louis Car Co. (Order #1283)	1922	St. Louis 113D	2-GE-258	2-K-36BR	1940	Same as 400-434. All 32 passenger.
500-509	DT, AR	St. Louis Car Co. (Order #1152)	1917	Baldwin 68-18-C	4-WH-506 C2	2-K-35	1947	Rebuilt from 240-249. 508 had upper sash plated over; sold to Cornwall in 1945. 506-507 sold to St. Petersburg 1942.
510-524	DT, AR 1-Man Cars	St. Louis Car Co. (Order #1309)	1923	St. Louis AM64	4-GE-264A	2-K-35J	1947	Forty-four passenger cars with both St. Louis and Baldwin arch bar trucks.
525-539	DT, AR 1-Man Cars	St. Louis Car Co. (Order #1334)	1924	St. Louis AM64	4-GE-264A	2-K-35J	1947	Same as 510-524. 543 last car used in Fort Wayne. 516 sold to Cornwall in 1945.
540-554	DT, AR 1-Man Cars	St. Louis Car Co. (Order #1378)	1925	St. Louis AM64	4-GE-264A	2-K-35J	1947	Repeat of 510-524. 527, 537, 540, 546, 550, 552 sold to Atlantic City in 1945.

Fort Wayne, Van Wert & Lima Traction Co. (1905-1906)
Lima-Toledo Traction Co. (1906)
Ohio Electric Ry. (1906-1921)

Wooden Cars—all double-truck.

Car No.	Car Type	Builder	Year Built	Truck	Motor	Control	Year Retired	Notes
1-3	SE RR Roof 55′ 3 Compartment Combines	Cincinnati Car Co. (Order #260)	1905	Taylor	4-WH 85	Type M	1925*	Built in Nov. 1905. Became Ohio Electric 76, 87, 88. Returned to FWVW&L and numbered 41, 42, 43. Changed to Baldwin trucks by 1920. Totally reconstructed by ISC to work and freight motors 30, 34, 35.
4-7	SE RR Roof 55′ 3 Compartment Combines	Cincinnati Car Co. (Order #370)	1906	Baldwin MCB	4-WH 121	Type M	1925*	Delivered Jan. 1906. 6 & 7 delivered and painted for Lima-Toledo Tr. Co. Became O.E. 79-82. 82 wrecked and destroyed at Convoy, Ohio 3/27/10. 79-81 became FWVW&L in 1920 and numbered 44, 45, 46.
8-11	SE RR Roof 55′ 3 Compartment Combines	Cincinnati Car Co. (Order #485, Repeat of #370)	1906	Baldwin MCB	4-WH 121	?	c. 1929	Delivered in mid-1906. Became L&T then OE 83-86. Sent to Columbus, Newark & Zanesville in 1920 by OE. Scrapped by CN&Z.
101	SE RR Roof 61′6″ 3 Compartment Combines	Cincinnati Car Co. (Order #315)	1906	Baldwin MCB	4-WH 121	1-L4	1928	One car of an order of seven deluxe inter-urban parlor-buffet cars placed by FW&WV. Traded to Union Traction Co. in 1907, became 296. Wrecked in 1928.

Car No.	Car Type	Builder	Year Built	Truck	Motor	Control	Year Retired	Notes
201	RR Roof Express Motor 4 Doors	Cincinnati Car Co. (Order #360)	1906	?	?	?	1927*	201 became L&T and OE 760. 760 became FWVW&L 31. Reconstructed 12/27 with only two side doors. Used as line car and renumbered 31.
202	RR Roof Express Motor 4 Doors	Cincinnati Car Co. (Order #475)	1906	?	?	?	c. 1938	The 202 became L&T 761 later C&LE 761.
50	?	?	1906	?	?	?	c. 1930	50 became L&T 713 and stayed on L&T after 1920.
51	Work Car	?	1906	?	?	?	1907	Wrecked in a collision with 85 in 1907.

Note: *Reconstructed for other service.

Fort Wayne, Van Wert & Lima Traction Co. (1921-1926)
Fort Wayne-Lima R.R. (1926-1933)

Wooden Cars—all double truck.

Car No.	Car Type	Builder	Year Built	Truck	Motor	Control	Year Retired	Notes
41-43	SE RR Roof 55′ 3 Compartment Combines	Cincinnati Car Co. (Order #260)	1905	Baldwin MCB	4-WH 85	Type M	1925*	Returned by OE in 1921. These cars had had several changes; rebuilt to 30, 34, 35 for FW-L by ISC.
44-46	SE RR Roof 55′ 3 Compartment Combines	Cincinnati Car Co. (Order #370)	1906	Baldwin MCB	4-GE205	2-HL	1925*	Returned by OE in 1921. Salvage and parts of 44 used in ISC 853. 45, 46 used for ISC 845, 846 (freight motors).
47-48	SE RR Roof 60′ 3 Compartment Combines	Cincinnati Car Co. (Order #1095)	1910	Taylor MCB	4-WH	?	c. 1930*	OE Cars 295 and 297 turned over to the FWVW&L in 1921 to replace original equipment no longer available. Used in work service after 1924. Scrapped about 1930.
90-95	SE Arch Roof Combines	St. Louis Car Co. (Order #1314)	1924	Commonwealth	4-GE275	1-K35	1933 1947	Six two-man lightweight steel cars. Four were one-manned and sold to Oklahoma Ry. in 1934, scrapped 1947. Others scrapped in 1935 at Fort Wayne. Part of the ISC order for ten cars.
30	DE Center Cab Work Motor	ISC	1925	Baldwin MCB	?	?	1933	Originally planned as a line car. Very similar to ISC 818. From 41.
31	DE RR Roof Freight Motor	Cincinnati Car Co. (Order #360)	1906	Baldwin MCB	?	?	1933	OE 760 returned to FWVW&L 1921. Reconstructed from 4 door to 2 door configuration in 1927. Used as a line car.
32-33	DE RR Roof Freight Motor	Cincinnati Car Co. (Order #1090)	1910	Baldwin MCB	?	?	1933	Former OE 767 and 769 turned over to FWVW&L to replace lost cars. The 32 had an arch roof built by dropping the clerestory and lowering that roof portion.
2nd 34	SE RR Roof Freight Motor	ISC	1928	Baldwin MCB	?	?	1933	Reconstructed from 42 and 43.

Car No.	Car Type	Builder	Year Built	Truck	Motor	Control	Year Retired	Notes
2nd 35	DE RR Roof Freight Motor	ISC	1928	Baldwin MCB	?	?	1933	Same as 34.
34-39	Box	?	?	?	—	—	1933	Listed in 1924 **Interurban Railway Equipment Register (IRER).**
114-119	Box	?	?	?	—	—	?	In 1928 **IRER**. May have been 34-39.
120-129	Box	?	?	?	—	—	1933	Listed in 1924, 1928, 1931 **IRER**.

Notes: All cars of wooden construction except 90-95.
*Cars 41-48 were surplus after 1925. Used as spares until reconstructed for other service.

Toledo & Chicago Interurban Ry. Co. (1906-1913) Fort Wayne & Northwestern Ry. Co. (1913-1924)

Wooden Cars—all double truck.

Car No.	Car Type	Builder	Year Built	Truck	Motor	Control	Year Retired	Notes
1-2	DE, DT RR Roof 45′ Coaches	Niles	1906	Peckham* No. 40 MCB	4-GEA605** 75 hp	GE, T-33	1924	Delivered as double-end and changed to single-end almost immediately. No. 1 converted to a combine (1907), rebuilt to ISC 27 in 1924. No. 2 became a trailer in 1912 and was retired in 1921.
3-4	SE, DT RR Roof 52′ 3 Compartment Combines	Niles	1906	Peckham* No. 40 MCB	4-GEA605** 75 hp	GE, T-33	1926	No. 3 rebuilt to 848 in 1926. No. 4 was destroyed in 1916 or became coke car 130.
5-8	SE, DT RR Roof 52′ 3 Compartment Combines	Niles	1906	Baldwin MCB*	4-GEA605** 75 hp	GE, T-33	1925	Same as 3-4. No. 5 rebuilt to 818. No. 7 rebuilt to 828. No. 8 rebuilt to 817. No. 6 either destroyed in 1916 or became coke car 130.
50-51	SE, DT 45′ Express Motor	Niles	1906	Peckham No. 40 MCB	4-GEA605** 75 hp	GE, T-33	1939	Freight motors. Side door configuration changed on 50. Both repaired and modified. Became ISC 50-51.
101	40′ Freight Trailer	?	1906	Arch Bar	—	—	?	Freight and stock trailer. End doors.
102-103	Box Trail	?	By 1912?	?	—	—	?	Listed in 1920, 1924 **Interurban Railway Equipment Register (IRER).** 102 may have had end doors.
104	Box Trail	?	?	?	—	—	?	Listed in 1920, 1924 **IRER**, had end doors.
—	Work Motor	T & C	1906	Brill 27	?	?	?	Off-center cab on a flat car. Also used as plow. This may be the car listed as "A" in **Interurban Railway Equipment Register** in 1920.
237	45′ Passenger Trailer	Barney & Smith	?	Barney & Smith	None	None	?	Former Indiana Union Traction Co. passenger combine used by construction crews as a work trailer. Probably returned to IUT.
10-12	Flat Cars	?	?	?	—	—	?	Listed in 1920 **IRER**.
20-25	Ballast Cars	?	?	?	—	—	?	Listed in 1920 **IRER**.

Notes: *Truck listed to show original trucks as delivered.
**Motors and control were originally for 3300 volts AC, changed to 600 volts DC. Motors and controls were changed.

Car No.	Car Type	Builder	Year Built	Truck	Motor	Control	Year Retired	Notes
Fort Wayne & Springfield Ry. Co. (1903-1916)								
Wooden Cars—all double truck.								
1-3	SE, DT RR Roof 53′ 3 Compartment Combines	Niles	1906	Baldwin	4-WH 106A (75 hp)	West. Electric pneumatic AC & DC	1918 Out of service	These cars were equipped for 6600 volt AC operation with 500 volt AC in Decatur and 550 volt DC in Ft. Wayne, wt. approx. 90,000. As built, had a front bow trolley collector, soon changed to standard trolley pole. One or more of these cars was severely damaged while in the Kamm Street barn fire Sept. 11, 1917.
50	SE, DT RR Roof 44′ 4-Door Baggage Car	Niles	1906	Peckham	4-WH 106A (75 hp)	West. Electric pneumatic AC & DC	1917	The fate of this car plus 1-3 is not known. There is no indication that they were involved in the 1916 fire at Decatur. They do not reappear as "rebuilds" on ISC.
51	RR Roof Refrigerator Car	FW&S Decatur Shop	1908	5-ft. MCB	—	—	?	Placed in service Feb. 13, 1908.
?	Snow Plow	?	?	?	?	?	?	Shown only in 1907 census. Apparently used motors from one of the other cars.
—	Flat Cars	?	?	?	—	—	?	14 cars listed in 1914.
—	Steam Locomotive	?	?	?	—	—	?	Second hand construction locomotive.
—	Steam Shovel	?	?	?	—	—	?	May have gone to ISC.
Fort Wayne & Decatur Traction Co. (1916-1927)								
101-103	SE, DT Arch Roof 48′ 3 Compartment Combine	St. Louis Car Co. (Order #1110)	1916	Baldwin MCB-73-18K	4-WH 307CV 600-1200 Volt DC	1-West HL	1936 (101-102) 1937 (327)	Medium weight cars, 59,000 lbs. 103 rebuilt to 327 in 1928. 101-102 not regularly used after 1927. Leased to Indiana Railroad but not used.
110	SE, DT Arch Roof 40′ Wooden Express Car	Cincinnati Car Co. (Order #2160)	1916	Baldwin MCB-73-18K	4-WH 307CV 600-1200 Volt DC	1-West HL	1929	Rebuilt to ISC line car 829 in 1929; to IRR 767. Scrapped in 1938.
111	Box Trail	?		?	—	—	?	Listed in 1920, 1924 **IRER**.
120	Flat Car	?		?	—	—	?	Listed in 1920, 1924 **IRER**.
Marion, Bluffton & Eastern Traction Co. (1906-1914)* Marion & Bluffton Traction Co. (1914-1926)								
Wooden Cars—all double truck.								
150	DT Box Trail	?	?	Taylor	None	None	To ISC	Acquired or renumbered from 154 between 1920 and 1924.
152-153	DT Flat Trail	?	?	?	None	None	1929	Acquired 1907.
154	DT Box Trail	?	?	?	None	None		Acquired 1909 or 1910. Retired or renumbered to 154 between 1920 and 1924.
201-202	DT, AR Passenger	Cummings (Order #9785)	1925	Cummings 62	4-GE?	?	To ISC 1931	One man lightweight cars ISC retained in service until M&B abandoned.
264	DT, RR Roof Express Motor	Niles (Order #258)	1906	Taylor	4-WH93A	?	To ISC	Put in service for ISC. May have been 49.

Car No.	Car Type	Builder	Year Built	Truck	Motor	Control	Year Retired	Notes
278	DT Work Motor	Niles	1906	Taylor	4-WH??	?	To ISC	May be the car listed as a derrick in 1908-09 and later (in 1920) as a box motor.
325, 330, 335, 345	DT, RR Baggage Motor	Niles	1906	Taylor	4-WH93A	K-14	To ISC	Car 330 wrecked 7/7/12.
340	DT, RR Smoker Motor	Niles	1906	Taylor	4-WH93A	K-14	To ISC	Used as spare car to back-up 201-202 after 1926.
350	DT Open, Motor 18-Bench	Cincinnati (Order #935)	1908	Taylor	4-WH93A	K-14	1922	Sides not open. Actually enclosed to the belt rail. Wrecked 7/7/12 and repaired.
355	DT Open, Motor 18-Bench	Cincinnati (Order #1230)	1910	Taylor	4-WH??	K-14	To ISC	Reported as a convertible car.
400	DT Passenger-Baggage, Motor	Jewett	1910	Taylor	4-GE87	K-14	Sold 1921	From Bluffton, Geneva & Celina. Reported as owned by M&B but not recorded as such. Sold to Union Traction in 1921. Became 416.

Notes: On August 1, 1926, ISC took control of the M&B and its equipment. The only cars kept in active use were the 201-202. Both of these received some modifications at Spy Run Shop in 1928 with the principal physical feature being the reduction of the front entrance door size and moving the headlight to the dash. Neither car was used after 1931. Stored at Spy Run and then scrapped. The wooden passenger cars were virtually retired before ISC took over and most were scrapped in the late twenties. One or two were kept as spares with the 345 known to have been relettered for ISC service.

*The Marion & Bluffton data was furnished by Roy G. Benedict.

Bluffton, Geneva & Celina Traction Co. (1910-1917)*

Wooden Cars—all double truck.

Car No.	Car Type	Builder	Year Built	Truck	Motor	Control	Year Retired	Notes
400	Passenger-Baggage Motor	Jewett	1910	Taylor	4 GE87	GE K-14	Sold 1917	See Marion & Bluffton roster.
One car	Box Motor	Interstate	1910	Taylor	4 GE87	?	1917	
Two cars	Box Trail	?	?	?	—	—	See note	Purchased 1911 or 1912. One retired 1914 or 1915, the other 1917.
Five cars	Ballast	?	by 1911	?	—	—	1917	Rodger ballast cars.
One car	Portable Substation	?	1910	?	—	—	1917	

*The BG&C data was furnished by Roy G. Benedict.

Wabash River Traction Company (1901-1904)
Wabash-Logansport Traction Company (1902-1904)

Closed Passenger Cars*

Car No.	Car Type	Builder	Year Built	Truck	Motor	Control	Year Retired	Notes
10, 12, 14, 16	DT, DE, DR 28′ Closed Body	American Car Co. (Order #379)	1901	McGuire 39A	4-GE-1000	2-K-6	See notes	In 1905, car 14 was converted to line car 41 (later 24, still later 824). The other three cars were renumbered to FW&WV 253-255.
18 ?, 20 ?	ST, DE Closed City	?	?	?	?	?	?	Received Jan. 1902, reportedly from Worcester, Mass.
22, 24, 26, 28	DT, DE 41′3″ Overall Closed Body	Jewett	1902-1903	Peckham 26D3	4-GE-67 (50 hp)	2-K-6	See notes	22, 24 received Aug. 1902; 26, 28 received Feb. 1903. In 1905, one car (402) converted to private car "Lawton," later renumbered to 800. The other three cars were renumbered to FW&WV 250-252.

Car No.	Car Type	Builder	Year Built	Truck	Motor	Control	Year Retired	Notes
Open Passenger Cars								
11, 13	DT, DE 15-Bench Open	American Car Co. (Order #378)	1901	McGuire 39A	4-GE-67	1-K-6	See notes	Later made single-end. Became FW&WV 370-371.
Four cars	ST Open	?	?	?	—	—	—	Secondhand, reportedly from New York.

Note: *One additional closed city car was purchased for the Erie Street line in Logansport. This may be the additional car appearing in one 1903 list.

Fort Wayne & Southwestern Traction Company (1901-1904)

Car No.	Car Type	Builder	Year Built	Truck	Motor	Control	Year Retired	Notes
"Indiana" "Ohio" "Kentucky" "Illinois" "Iowa"	43′ RR Roof Passenger Coach	Jackson & Sharp Serial #2142-2148*	1901	Peckham 14AX	4 Lorain 34, 50 hp	Lorain	See notes	Cars not numbered. Became FW&WV 201-205, Body 34′5″ long.
301-304	43′ RR Roof Passenger-Baggage Combination	John Stephenson	1902	Peckham 14AX	4 Lorain 34, 50 hp	Lorain	See notes	Same design as cars used on the Muncie, Hartford & Ft. Wayne. Became FW&WV 206-209.
12	DT, AR 30′ (body)	Jackson & Sharp Serial #2199	1901	Peckham 14	?	?	See notes	Freight motor. Originally 1. Became FW&WV 12, later 53 (1st).
?	?	?	?	?	?	?	—	"Dinkey." One or two small passenger cars used in Huntington (?) or between Huntington and Wabash.

Notes: *Jackson & Sharp order books list the order as seven cars. The other two, if built, may have been diverted to another property.

There are discrepancies in the number of cars. The 10 listed plus one "dinkey" are the only cars recorded or mentioned in contemporary accounts. Powers' St. Ry. Directory for 1903 indicates 14 motor cars and 1 express with the builders being Jackson & Sharp, John Stephenson and St. Louis Car Co. Of these, 13 had 4-motor equipment and one had 2-motor equipment. Motors were 50 or 67 hp Lorain and General Electric. All trucks listed as Peckham.

Fort Wayne & Wabash Valley Traction Co. (1904-1911)
Fort Wayne & Northern Indiana Traction Co. (1911-1920)
Indiana Service Corporation (1920-1947)
Indiana & Michigan Electric Co. (1947-1952)

Wooden Interurban Passenger (All Double Truck)

Car No.	Car Type	Builder	Year Built	Truck	Motor	Control	Year Retired	Notes
81-83	—	—	—	—	—	—	—	See 206, 207, 209.
201	43′ RR Roof Passenger Coach	Jackson & Sharp	1901	Peckham 14AX	4 Lorain 34	Lorain	1910	201-205 from FW&SW state named cars. Cars reconditioned in 1904-1905. Trucks changed on some to a standard MCB type—probably Baldwin. 201 reconstructed 1910 to 321.
202	43′ RR Roof Passenger Coach	Jackson & Sharp	1901	Peckham 14AX	4 Lorain 34	Lorain	1910	202 reconstructed 1909-1910 to 320.
203-204	43′ RR Roof Passenger Coach	Jackson & Sharp	1901	Peckham 14AX	4 Lorain 34	Lorain	1912	Indications are that both 203 and 204 used in the construction of 322.

Car No.	Car Type	Builder	Year Built	Truck	Motor	Control	Year Retired	Notes
205	43′ RR Roof Passenger Coach	Jackson & Sharp	1901	Peckham 14AX	4 Lorain 34	Lorain	1920	Converted to a straight coach trailer. Scrapped 1920.
206	43′ RR Roof Passenger-Baggage Combine	John Stephenson	1902	Peckham 14AX	4 Lorain 34	Lorain	1927	206-209 were FW&SW 301-304. Converted to straight coach trailer 81. Body burned 6/4/27 at Huntington shop.
207	43′ RR Roof Passenger-Baggage Combine	John Stephenson	1902	Peckham 14AX	4 Lorain 34	Lorain	c. 1935	Converted to straight coach trailer 82. Changed to Baldwin 73 trucks in 1928. Assigned 1161 for IRR but not repainted or used by IRR. Retired by 1935.
208	43′ RR Roof Passenger-Baggage Combine	John Stephenson	1902	Peckham 14AX	4 Lorain 34	Lorain	1920	Converted to a trailer. Retired and scrapped 1920.
209	43′ RR Roof Passenger-Baggage Combine	John Stephenson	1902	Peckham 14AX	4 Lorain 34	Lorain	1930	Converted to a straight coach trailer 83. Retired by 1930.
301-302	SE RR Roof, 55′ 3 Compartment Combines	Cincinnati Car Co. (Order #550)	1906	Baldwin MCB	4 GE205	1-L4	1932	301 derailed by a cow in 1929 and rebuilt 8/29. Derailed 4/30 in Lafayette. Rebuilt. 302 changed to HL control.
303-307	SE RR Roof, 55′ 3 Compartment Combines	Cincinnati Car Co. (Order #700)	1906	Baldwin MCB	4 WH121	1-HL	1932	Similar to 301-302. Built for Lafayette & Logansport Tr. Co. 303 wrecked in 1910 and rebuilt to a different design. Changed to GE205 motors. 306 destroyed 5/19/24 at Roanoke.
308-310	SE RR Roof, 55′ 3 Compartment Combines	Cincinnati Car Co. (Order #1130)	1909	Curtis J-669	4 GE205	1-L4	1932	Similar to 301-307. 310 reconstructed to 47 (847) in 1927. 309 was painted Union Traction red.
320	SE RR Roof, 63′ 3 Compartment Combine	FW&WV	1910	Baldwin MCB	4 WH121	GE Type M	1932	Reconstructed from 202 at Baker Street Shop. Rebuilt several times.
321	SE RR Roof, 63′ 3 Compartment Combine	FW&WV	1910	Baldwin MCB	4 WH121	1 WH-HL	1932	Reconstructed from 201 at Baker Street Shop. Considerably modernized in 1928.
322	SE RR Roof, 63′ 3 Compartment Combine	FW&WV	1912	Baldwin 73	4 WH303	1 WH-HL	1924	Reconstructed at Baker Street Shop from 203 and 204. Wrecked 5/19/24. Reconstructed to 53 (853).
351-354	SE RR Roof, 61′ 3 Compartment Combines	Cincinnati Car Co. (Order #315)	1906	Baldwin MCB 7′ Wheelbase	4 WH121	1-L4	1932	Former 501-504. Rebuilt to baggage-coach 1918-1920. 351 destroyed 6/3/25.

Car No.	Car Type	Builder	Year Built	Truck	Motor	Control	Year Retired	Notes
501-504	SE RR Roof, 61′6″ 3 Compartment Combines	Cincinnati Car Co. (Order #315)	1906	Baldwin MCB	4 WH121 (90 hp)	1-L4	1932	Named Kenilworth (501), Ivanhoe (502), Talisman (503) and Woodstock (504). At least one car had WH 85 motors. Became 351-354.
800	SE RR Roof, 43′ Office or Business	FW&WV	1905	Peckham 26-D-3	4 GE67	1 K-35	1922*	"Lawton" was the company private car, first numbered 402. Reconstructed from one of the Wabash-Logansport 22-28 series. Also used as a pay car.
Steel Interurban Passenger Cars (All Double Truck)								
101-103	SE Arch Roof 48′ 3 Compartment Combines	St. Louis Car Co. (Order #1110)	1916	Baldwin MCB 73-18K	4 WH307CV	1 WH HL	1936	From FW-D. Probably never used by ISC. Leased to IRR (but never used) for possible conversion to one man cars. 103 became 327. 101 known relettered for ISC service.
201-202	SE, AR Passenger	Cummings Car & Coach (Order #9785)	1925	Cummings 62	4 GE	?	1936	Former Marion & Bluffton cars. Used as spare cars after 1931.
323-326, (90-95)	SE, AR 52′ 3 Compartment Combines	St. Louis Car Co. (Order #1314)	1924	Commonwealth	4 GE275	1 K-35	1937 (323-326)	Medium weight cars. Ten ordered for use on ISC and FW-L. ISC 323-326 turned end-for-end and rebuilt in 1928 for one-man. Four of 90 series sold to Oklahoma Rys. in 1938. Ends reversed by ISC and made one-man. Other two scrapped. 323-326 leased to IRR.
327	SE, AR 48′ Combine	St. Louis Car Co. (Order #1110) and ISC	1916/ 1928	Commonwealth	4 GE274	1 K-35	1935	Originally 103. The 103 was the pilot rebuilt for 323-326 in 1928. Leased to and used by IRR but never repainted to IRR colors.
375-379	SE, AR, 61′6″ 3 Compartment Combines	St. Louis Car Co. (Order #1389)	1926	Baldwin MCB	4 WH333VV6 (125 hp)	HL	1941	All leased to IRR. 375-377 had an RPO section added (1935). 378-379 made one man and numbered 457-458 (1936); retired in 1938. 375-377 returned to ISC and sold to CSS&SB (1941) (503, 376, 504 respectively).
390-391	SE, AR 61′6″	St. Louis Car Co. (Order #1390)	1926	Baldwin MCB	2 WH333VV6	HL	1930	Parlor-Buffet cars "Little Turtle" (390), "Anthony Wayne" (391). Stored until scrapped in 1939.
Freight and Service Cars								
1 (1st)	Sweeper	McGuire Mfg. Co.	1895	McGuire	?	?	?	Sweeper—Probably identical to 2-4.
1 (2nd)	ST Wing Plow	FW&NI	1918	Curtis CS 58-96	2-GE216	2-K35	1947	Wing snow plow built from city car 125 for clearing interurban tracks.
2	ST Sweeper	McGuire Mfg. Co.	1895	McGuire	2-GE1000	2-K10	1940	Sold to Lafayette Street Railway, Inc. Became LSR 1.
3	ST Sweeper	McGuire Mfg. Co.	1895	McGuire	2-GE1000	2-K10	1943	Sweepers 2-5 and 7 had one GE800 motor and one K10 Controller for broom operation. All similar in appearance.
4	ST Sweeper	McGuire Mfg. Co.	1895	McGuire	2-GE1000	2-K10	1947	
5	ST Sweeper	McGuire-Cummings	1905	McGuire-Cummings	2-GE1000	2-K10	1947	
6	ST Sweeper	McGuire-Cummings	?	McGuire-Cummings	?	?	1915	No. 6 is believed to be the sweeper destroyed in 1915 at Kossuth St. Remains to Lafayette St. Ry. and may have been used in LSR's 2.

*The official reported date. This car (and others ?) may have had some additional use before scrapping.

Car No.	Car Type	Builder	Year Built	Truck	Motor	Control	Year Retired	Notes
7	Sweeper	FW&NI	1915	McGuire-Cummings	2-GE1000	2-K10	1943	Probably a reconstruction of an earlier unpowered sweeper.
8	ST Sand Car	J. M. Jones' Sons	?	Dorner & Dutton	2-GE52	2-K10	1923	Probably an 1892 closed city car.
10 (1st)	—	—	—	—	—	—	—	See 51 (1st).
10 (2nd)	ST Wooden Gondola	ISC	1921	Curtis CS 58-96	None	None	1940	Trash car listed as former 1029.
11 (1st)	—	—	—	—	—	—	—	See 52.
11 (2nd)	ST Work Car	FW&NI	1912	Peckham Metropolitan	2-GE800	1-K2	?	Single truck closed car apparently retired by 1930.
12	—	—	—	—	—	—	—	See 53 (1st).
13	ST Wreck Car	FW&NI	1913	Curtis CS 58-96	2-GE216	2-K10	1943	Originally had Peckham truck and Lorain motors.
14 (1st)	Sand Car	J. M. Jones' Sons	1892	Dorner & Dutton	2-GE1000	2-K10	c. 1922	On the property in 1920. Former city passenger Car 14.
14 (2nd)	Line Car	Cincinnati Car Co.	1909	Curtis CS 58-96	2-GE 80	2-K10	c. 1934	Former city passenger car. Retired about 1934.
15	Sprinkler	McGuire-Cummings	1909	Pedestal	?	?	1923	3000 gallon sprinkler. No electric equipment listed in the 1920 inventory but was originally powered.
16	ST Bonding Car	Electric Railway Improvement Co.	1908	?	—	—	1923	This car was not powered.
17 (1st)	ST Work Car	Jackson & Sharp	1899	Peckham Metropolitan	2-GE1000	2-K10	1923	Single truck car from 101-108 class city car.
17 (2nd)→ 817	DT Switching Motor	Niles/ISC	1925	Baldwin MCB	4-GE205	2-HL	1952	Ex17 built from FW&NW 8 (built in 1906). Last electric car on Fort Wayne streets. Open end platforms.
18 → 818	DT Service Motor	Niles/ISC	1925	Baldwin MCB	4-GE205B	2-HL	1945	Ex18 built from FW&NW 5 (built in 1906). Center cab freight motor. Became IRR 792. Returned to ISC as 818 and became Northern Division snow plow.
19	ST Work Car	ISC	Prior to 1922	Curtis CS 58-96	?	?	Before 1935	Built by ISC before 1922 from a single truck city car.
20 → 820	DT Work Motor	FW&WV	1907	Baldwin MCB	4-WH121	2-L4	1938	Ex20, 820 renumbered to IRR 793 in 1936. Built as an end cab, flat work motor. Reconstructed 1912.
21 → 821	DT Work Motor	FW&NI	Prior to 1909	Peckham 26	4-W85	1-L4 (later 2-L4)	c. 1937	Known rebuilt in April 1909. Ex21. Built with a small center cab about the size of a phone booth. Completely reconstructed by ISC 1925. Changed to a different, boxy-looking body style, with Brill 27 trucks and in 1928 to Baldwin trucks. May have kept the same electrical equipment. Renumbered 794 for IRR but never used by IRR.
22 → 822	DT Service Motor	ISC	1921	Baldwin MCB	4-?	2-?	c. 1937	Ex22 similar in design to 818. Assigned to IRR as 795.

Car No.	Car Type	Builder	Year Built	Truck	Motor	Control	Year Retired	Notes
23 → 823	DT Line Motor	FW&WV	1910	Peckham 14	2-GE101	2-L4	c. 1938	Ex42, Ex23 (Note: 823-826 very similar in appearance. All originally carried a reel on one end) 823 became IRR 764.
24 → 824	DT Line Motor	FW&WV	1910	Peckham 14	2-GE201	2-K6	c. 1932	Ex43, Ex24 originally the Fort Wayne Div. Line Motor.
25 → 825	DT Line Motor	FW&WV	1910	Peckham 26	2-GE201	2-K6	By 1932	Ex41, Ex25 first built from a 1901 DT Deck Roof car, probably WRT 14. Reconstructed in 1910. First had McGuire short wheelbase trucks. As 41 this car was the Lafayette Div. line car.
26 → 826	DT Line Motor	FW&WV	1910	Baldwin 73	2-GE201	20K6A	1945	Ex40, Ex26. Was very similar to 825 and had Peckham 26 trucks. In 1939 this car was modified using Baldwin trucks. Assigned 765 for IRR—never renumbered or used by IRR. Retained in service by ISC until 1945.
27 → 827	DT Line Car	Niles/ISC	1924	Peckham MCB 40-A	4-GE214	2-K34	1941	Line car reconstructed as 27 from FW&NW 1. Assigned IRR 766 but not used or repainted for IRR.
28 → 828	DT Service Car	Niles/ISC	1924	Baldwin MCB	4-GE214	2-K34	1941	Ex28, "Tool and Equipment." This was FW&NW 7 and was changed largely by removing windows and modifying the vestibule ends. Remained unchanged 52′ in length. Assigned 1154 for IRR but never used by IRR or repainted.
29 → 829	DT Line Motor	Cincinnati/ISC (Order #2160)	1929	Baldwin 73-18K	4-WH307 CV6	1-K6A	1928	Built as FWD 110 in 1916. Assigned to IRR as 767.
40-43	—	—	—	—	—	—	—	See 23-26.
45 → 845	DT Freight Motor	ISC	1925	Baldwin MCB	4-GE205	2-HL	1940	Ex45, constructed from FW&L 45. Became IRR 726.
46 → 846	DT Freight Motor	ISC	1925	Baldwin MCB	4-GE205	2-HL	1940	Ex46, constructed from FW-L46. Became IRR 727.
47 → 847	DT Freight Motor	Cincinnati/ISC (Order #1130)	1927	Curtis Type J	4-GE205	1-L4	1938	Ex47, built by remodeling former passenger car 310.
48 → 848	DT Freight Motor	Niles/ISC	1926	Baldwin MCB	4-GE205	2-HL	1951	Ex48, remodeled from FW&NW 3. Retained in use by ISC and repainted. Used with 817 on Northern Division. Painted a dark green and carried no number after 1947.
49	DT Freight Motor	ISC (?)	1926 (?)	?	?	?	1926	The 49 had a brief life and little was recorded about it. It first appeared and was lost to fire in 1926. This may have been the former M&B 264 built by Niles in 1906.
50 → 850	DT Freight Motor	Niles	1926	Peckham MCB 40A	?	?	1932	Ex#50, in existence in mid-1932 and disappeared after that time. Was FW&NW 50.
51 (1st)	DT Freight Motor	Cincinnati (Order #550)	1905	Baldwin MCB	4-GE205B	2-L4	1917	This car was first given 10 and, in Oct. 1905 equipped with Peckham 14 trucks from the 200 series passenger cars. In early 1906 renumbered as first 51. It was destroyed by fire in 1917.

Car No.	Car Type	Builder	Year Built	Truck	Motor	Control	Year Retired	Notes
51 (2nd) → 851	DT Wreck Motor	Niles	1926	Peckham MCB 40A	4-GE214	2-K34	1939	Taken into ISC service from FW&NW. Was FW&NW 51. Became IRR 1153.
52 → 852	DT Freight Motor	Cincinnati (Order #550)	1905	Baldwin MCB	4-GE205B	2-L4	1939	Same as 51 (1st) originally 11. Renumbered to 52. Became IRR 729. Thoroughly reconstructed in 1927. Peckham trucks were installed in 1905 changed later to Baldwin.
53 (1st)	DT Freight Motor	Jackson & Sharp Serial #2199	1902	Peckham 14	?	?	1917	Built as FW&SW 1, changed to 12, retained same number on FW&WV. Renumbered 53 (1st). Destroyed 1917.
53 (2nd) → 853	DT Freight Motor	ISC	1924/ 1929	Baldwin 73	4-GE205	2-HL	1940	Reconstructed as 53 (2nd) from passenger car 322 (1913) in 1924. Almost totally destroyed at France Siding 8/21/29. Only trucks and frame salvaged. Totally rebuilt using parts of FW-L 44. Became IRR 730.
54 → 854	DT Freight Motor	Cincinnati (Order #710)	1907	Baldwin MCB	4-GE205	1-L4	1938	Built new as 54. Originally had Peckham 14 trucks. Became IRR 731. Bought for Lafayette & Logansport Tr. Co.
55 → 855	DT Freight Motor	Cincinnati (Order #710)	1907	Baldwin MCB	4-GE205	1-L4	1938	Same as 854. Built as 55. Became IRR 732.
56 → 856	DT Freight Motor	Cincinnati (Order #1140)	1910	Curtis J-669	4-W303	1-L4	1938	Built as 56. Rebuilt 1927 by ISC. Became IRR 733.
57 → 857	DT Freight Motor	Cincinnati (Order #1140)	1910	Curtis J-669	4-GE205B	1-L4	1939	Sister car to 856. Built as 57. Rebuilt and shortened in 1928. Became IRR 734.
58 → 858	DT Freight Motor	St. Louis (Order #1151)	1917	Baldwin MCB	4-GE205B	1-HL	1940	Built as 58. Became IRR 735.
59 → 859	DT Freight Motor	St. Louis (Order #1151)	1917	Baldwin MCB	4-GE205B	1-HL	1940	Sister to 858. Built as 59. Became IRR 736.
999	Portable Substation	McGuire-Cummings	1906	Arch Bar	—	—	1919	Acquired from Philadelphia Rapid Transit Co. Westinghouse equipped. Burned July 9, 1919.
1000	Portable Substation	McGuire-Cummings	1910	Arch Bar	—	—	1945	Last used on the Pontiac line. Westinghouse equipped.
Freight Trail Cars								
118	Box Freight	?	?	Arch Bar	—	—	?	Railroad roof, square ends, off-center end doors.
130	Coke Car	Niles/ISC	1906	Arch Bar	—	—	1937	Shell of a FW&NW passenger combine (either 4 or 6).
144	Box Freight	?	1917	Arch Bar	—	—	?	144 used as the freight house at Garrett. Came from FW-D (may have been their 111). Arch roof, end doors, round ends.
145-149	Box Freight	?	?	Arch Bar	—	—	?	Information on 145-158 is limited. Not on the property in 1924, but in a 1928 list. Several Builders. Most cars reconstructed several times. Roof designs varied.

Car No.	Car Type	Builder	Year Built	Truck	Motor	Control	Year Retired	Notes
150-154	Box Freight	?	?	Arch Bar	—	—	?	
155-158	Box Freight	?	1920?	Arch Bar	—	—	?	
70 → 159	Box Freight	ISC	1922	Simplex/ Arch Bar	—	—	1941	Built at Huntington shop as Car 70, renumbered prior to 1925 to 159, again renumbered between 1935, 1938 to IRR 2nd 625.
60 → 160, 61 → 161	Box Freight Automobile Cars	St. Louis (Order #696A)	1906	Arch Bar	—	—	1940	160 retired before 1928. 161 arch roof, end opening doors. May have been first rebuilt in 1909.
62 → 162	Box Freight	FW&NI	1910	Peckham	—	—	1940	
63 → 163 thru 66 → 166	Box Freight	Cincinnati (Order #1145)	1911	Arch Bar	—	—	1940	Square end, these were built with end train doors. Described as "express trail cars."
67 → 167	Box Freight	ISC	1922	Simplex/ Arch Bar	—	—	1941	Built at Huntington shop as car 67, renumbered prior to 1925 to 167. Stripped to flat car about 1932.
68 → 168, 69 → 169	Box Freight	ISC	1922	Simplex/ Arch Bar	—	—	1941	Built at Huntington shop as cars 68-69, renumbered prior to 1925 to 168-169 respectively, again renumbered between 1935, 1938 to IRR 628-629 respectively.
1001-1010	Gondola Flat Bottom Side Dump	Haskell & Barker	1909	Arch Bar	—	—	1940	Some used by IRR. 1005 retired between 1924, 1928. 1001-1002 retired between 1928, 1931.
1011-1017	Gravel Cars	Haffner-Thrall Co.	1924	Arch Bar	—	—	1945	1011, 1014, 1015, 1017 survived until 1945 in use by ISC.
1029	—	—	—	—	—	—	—	See car 10 (2nd).
1030-1033	Hopper Dump	Differential Steel Car Co.	1923	Arch Bar	—	—	1945	1032 survived until 1945. Steel bottom dump.
1034-1045	Side Dump	Differential Steel Car Co.	1923-1925	Arch Bar	—	—	1945	The first six may have been a 1923 order. 1043-1045 survived until 1945. Capacity 80,000 lbs. Steel electric side dump.
1046-1055	Side Dump	Differential Steel Car Co.	1929	Arch Bar	—	—	1945	1049, 1052, 1055 survived until 1945. Steel electric side dump.
1051-1053 (1st)	Gondola	?	?	Arch Bar	—	—	1928	1053 was a flat bottom gondola. 1051-1052 were side dump gondolas, retired in 1923.
1055-1056	Gondola	?	?	Arch Bar	—	—	1928	Flat Bottom. Both retired by 1928.
1101-1110	Flat Cars	?	?	Diamond/ Arch Bar	—	—	?	Only 1101, 1106 and 1108 by 1924. These may have been the flat cars first numbered in the 500 series.
1115-1117	Flat Cars	?	?	Diamond/ Arch Bar	—	—	1930	The company inventory indicates they lost the record of the builder of flat cars 1101-1110 and 1115-1117.
1118-1121	Flat Cars	?	?	Arch Bar	—	—	?	These numbers are shown on a 1931 equipment roster. Also see 1119.

Car No.	Car Type	Builder	Year Built	Truck	Motor	Control	Year Retired	Notes
1122	Flat Car	—	?	Arch Bar	—	—	?	
1123-1125	Flat Car	ISC	1938	Arch Bar	—	—	1941	Rebuilt from salvage of older cars in 1938. These may have been used to carry rails salvaged from the Peru line.
1128	Flat Car	ISC	?	Arch Bar	—	—	1941	Probably same as 1123.
Maintenance & Service Equipment								
1119	Boom Derrick	?	?	Arch Bar	—	—	1926	Double truck, 10 hp vertical boiler, steam powered, boom derrick car. Frame and boom of wood, reinforced with steel. Machinery to 1140 in 1926.
1140	Boom Derrick	Body only on St. Louis (Job #1406)	1926	Arch Bar	—	—	1940	Double truck, steel frame derrick body. Equipped by ISC with a new all-steel boom derrick rig. Steam machinery from boom derrick 1119.
14 (3rd)	Clam-Shell Crane	Orton & Steinbrenner Co.	1913	Rigid Frame Type 4-Wheels	?	?	1962	Originally a self-propelled electric boom crane for coal handling at the Spy Run power plant. The last electric powered equipment on the property, seldom, if ever, used after 1953.
?	Clam-Shell Crane	Orton	?	Arch Bar	—	—	1941	Double truck steam crane.
—	Steam Shovel	Thew Steam Shovel Co.	1912	Rigid 4-Wheel	—	—	?	
—	Steam Shovel	?	?	Rigid 4-Wheel	—	—	?	
—	Weed Burner	Wayne Co.	1911	4-Wheel	—	—	?	
—	Tank for Weed Burner	?	1911	4-Wheel	—	—	?	
—	Rail Grinder Car	Kerwin Co.	1911	4-Wheel	—	—	?	Also used as an electrically-powered circular "buzz" saw and other power take-off for on-site use.
—	Cement Mixer Car	Jaeger Co.	1920	Peckham Metropolitan	—	—	?	Portable mixer for street cement. Probably older than recorded "1920."

Also—3 Mudge motor section cars, 8 section hand-pump cars and 13 section push cars...and a significant and vast array of miscellaneous equipment which varied throughout the years. All retired by 1945.

In 1907, the company owned 2 secondhand steam locomotives for construction trains.

ROLLING STOCK
LAFAYETTE

J. M. Jones' Sons built the horsecars used by the second Lafayette street railroad. (The builder for the first company's six cars is unknown.) Six cars were on hand for the 1884 opening of the new company's line. These cars, numbers 100-105, were five window, 14 foot cars and were virtually identical to the cars bought the previous year for use in Logansport. At least two more groups were acquired as cars 106 and 109 have been identified. These two cars each have a different body style. There are some reports that as many as 13 cars may have been acquired and that the numbers may have run as high as 112. All of these double-end cars had the popular "bombay" roof style with a raised clerestory and eyebrow window ends.

When the Sprague engineers arrived they electrified seven of the Jones built cars with two motors. Car 106 was the first one used on trial runs. An eighth car was electrified in 1889 and was reportedly equipped with Sprague No. 6 motors.

In 1891 the J. G. Brill Company delivered four 14 foot, No. 2, motor car bodies (order 3829) mounted on Brill No. 13 motor trucks with a six foot wheelbase and 33 inch wheels (order 3829-1/2). Although approximately the same size as the electrified horsecars these cars (1-4) were much heavier, and created a problem as the Wabash River bridge was believed too weak to carry the extra weight.

The company went back to Brill for several more car orders (orders 4001, 4002 and 4002-1/2 for car no. 5 and two trucks). However, there is an apparent error or a change of order reflected in Brill Order 4921 of 1893 for four "16 foot cars." These cars are, in appearance at least, duplicate sister cars to the 14 foot cars.

A number of open cars were also built by Brill with six cars (10-15) delivered on Order 4922. These eight bench cars were mounted on Brill No. 21 trucks (order 4922-1/2). Three more (16-18) came on Order 5136. Order 6417 was for five No. 21C trucks and was the last placed with the Brill works by the company. However, the reputation would hang on for Brill.

After 1895 the car record becomes confused because later purchases came from builders whose records have not survived and reflect lapses in the company inventory records. By 1898 the Lafayette Street Railway boasted 14 open cars and 12 closed cars with all but two powered. By the turn of the century the electrified horsecars must have been gone.

By 1902 the company claimed 15 closed body cars with most of them "small and old" and 17 open cars. With the rapid advances in closed car design the 1891-1892 closed electric cars were very out-of-date. Some of them may have been retired. New cars were added as some records indicate an increase of three closed cars by 1900 and three more by 1902. The open cars increased in like amounts at the same time. However, the sources for this car information are not necessarily accurate for two reasons. The reports were based on questions asked of the company and the actual reporting date is not defined. Also the questions request information in general terms which leaves room for further error through the interpretation of the official supplying information.

The six newer closed cars may have become the Wabash Valley's 140-146 (a seven car series even though the increase may have been reported as only six). Nowhere is there any recorded indication of a decrease in the cars. The 140 series cars, the 1904 Cincinnati built cars (147-156) and the 1913 Brill Nearsides were the principal closed cars in use until 1920. It is interesting to note that the system bought Brill built Nearside cars exclusively for Lafayette use when at the same time similar cars were being built by Cincinnati Car Company for Fort Wayne use. These few Brill built cars in a sea of Cincinnati built cars are an enigma. The fact that the Brill name enjoyed a good reputation in Lafayette may be the reason.

The company's additional six open cars are not known by number or style. No one seems to know whether these were new or second-hand cars. Also at the turn of the century the company had two flat cars and two snow plows (one was an 1895 McGuire built sweeper).

In 1920 the Lafayette Street Railway claimed to own only two cars—closed car 169 and open car 359. In 1921 R. W. Levering reported to the State of Indiana, "The company owns but three cars: One single truck flat car and two open passenger cars which are absolutely unfit for service and are only awaiting a rise in the scrap metal market to be junked." The company leased 20 cars from the ISC plus one snow sweeper, two work cars and one sand car.

The new Lafayette Street Railway continued to lease cars as needed and purchased the work and service equipment. In addition the new company built, or reconstructed, a second sweeper in 1925. Since sweepers 2 and 6 are missing from the Fort Wayne roster these are the logical source for Lafayette's 1 and 2. Work car 3 may have been the old 359.

...and the new firm went back to Brill for its fleet of Birney cars. The cars were built at the Brill plant in Philadelphia instead of in St. Louis at Brill's American Car Company subsidiary.

The Birney cars were delivered in two groups during 1922. The first came in the spring and were numbered 10 through 25 with the number 13 omitted. Most reports state that a car 13 was delivered but soon renumbered to 25. Three more Birneys came late in 1922. These were identical and were numbered 26 through 28. The cars were built on Brill order 21481 and 21615. Both orders were filled from order 21384-9/21 which was for 30 cars for stock.

Three more cars were also added in 1922 from the secondhand market. These were for the Battleground line to replace cars of the 250 series which were returned to the ISC. The three were from the Chicago, South Bend & Northern Indiana Railway in South Bend and had been that company's 218-220 built by the Laconia Car Company. The cars were secondhand when the Northern Indiana bought them about 1904. They may have been part of the Laconia car group purchased by Central Market Street Railway (Columbus, Ohio) in 1901. These cars were used for large crowds such as football games and other activities at Purdue.

All the cars were scrapped in 1940.

ROLLING STOCK LOGANSPORT

The Logansport cars are a source of confusion because of the large number in use in that city in the early 1900's. The Logansport Street Railway started out modestly enough with nine 14 foot horsecars, numbered 1 through 9. These were built by J. M. Jones' Sons in 1883 and were of a standard Jones design seen also in Fort Wayne and Lafayette. All but one were destroyed in a May 20, 1891 fire. Replacement cars were purchased, according to some accounts, "from St. Louis." This has not been verified, although seven-bench open car number 6 was mounted on a St. Louis Car Company truck. However, in the rush to acquire cars the company may have purchased some sound secondhand car bodies and equipped them for electric operation. This would partly explain a 1902 newspaper comment about the then older cars having come from the Cincinnati streetcar system some years earlier. The company had to be short on cash and the surviving Jones built horsecar was probably electrified also. By 1897 the company was reporting nine motor and three trail cars.

By 1900 the quality of the reporting varies considerably but, for tax purposes, only 11 cars were reported. The report also stated that the company had six sets of electrical equipment indicating the company engaged in the then common practice of switching electrical equipment from open to closed cars on a seasonal basis.

At the end of 1902 the Logansport Street Railway reported to the U.S. Census Bureau that they owned eight closed and six open cars plus one work car. All but two were powered. Some of the cars were on Dorner trucks or so was claimed in an advertisement of Dorner Truck & Foundry of Logansport (Dorner also claimed truck deliveries to Fort Wayne and Wabash River Traction). The open cars included with the property were five seven-bench cars. Only a few random car numbers are known. These are 1, 6, 11, 13, 15, 20 and 30 but no sequence is known.

Apparently some, probably four, of the cars were converted from narrow to standard gauge trucks. These were used as the track was being rebuilt and then continued in use after the last narrow gauge track was replaced in November 1903 and were taken into the Wabash Valley's numbering system. They were among the early car scrappings and, therefore, little is known about them.

The Erie Street (Boyd line) had two cars. The first was an old car supposedly, according to a news note, secondhand from Cincinnati. This car was replaced by a new car in November, 1902 that came "from St. Louis." Both of the Erie Street cars were standard gauge and painted the Wabash River Traction yellow color. The new car stayed in service in Logansport after the Wabash Valley System took over.

These cars were joined by the Logansport, Rochester & Northern cars to provide the local service after 1903, so there were plenty of cars for the small system. The fleet might have remained static for a few years but new cars were added.

The Logansport, Rochester & Northern acquired its small car fleet in 1902. This included six 18-foot closed single truck cars as well as ten open cars probably mixed as six nine-bench and four eight-bench. The open car listing does not indicate how many of the opens were powered after they arrived. It should also be noted that one newspaper account indicates the opens as ten-bench cars.

Regrettably, although these cars made a grand impression on the Logansport newspapers, none of the reporters mentioned the car numbers or the builders. One happy clue was a report in one newspaper that the open cars, at least, were not new. It was noted that they had been thoroughly reconditioned, carefully repainted and relettered. These cars arrived on the Panhandle (Pittsburgh, Cincinnati, Chicago & St. Louis Railroad—part of the Pennsylvania system) and most likely from Cincinnati. It is entirely possible that these cars had been rebuilt by the then new Cincinnati Car Company which was in the control of the Schoepf-McGowan Syndicate interests. The source for the cars could have been the Cincinnati Traction Company but this is not verified.

All of the LR&N cars came into the Wabash Valley's car roster and were numbered accordingly. The 350 series of ten-bench open cars may have been bought for the LR&N or the Lafayette lines. They may have been "add-ons" to an Indiana Union Traction Co. order built by Cincinnati Car Co.

In later years the car fleet at Logansport went through a number of changes. The 140 series cars was first split between Lafayette and Logansport and then sent to Lafayette. The new 170-175 cars were sent to Logansport in 1907.

The car fleet changed somewhat and a 1918 report would indicate nine closed cars in use and stationed in Logansport. Five of these would appear to have been the older Jones and Barney and Smith cars. The other four would probably be from the 170-175 group. There were also ten motorized open cars including four eight-bench, one nine-bench and five ten-bench cars. The ten-bench cars were the 350 series cars with the semi-enclosed front vestibules. A snow sweeper and work car completed the city car collection. Also, based at the Logansport barns was a heavy line car for city and interurban lines.

Logansport had a good barn for light repair work and had plenty of good indoor and outdoor storage for extra cars. This allowed extra cars to be kept on the local scene, a nice luxury for the far ends of a long, strung-out rail system.

Additional cars came in 1918 when the new 290-299 cars came on the scene allowing the existing closed cars to be kept as spares for a few years. Most were scrapped by the early twenties. Even the ten 290's were soon more than the local lines needed. They were the last local cars used.

ROLLING STOCK WABASH AND PERU

After the Wabash Valley took control both Wabash and Peru each had two cars for local use. Storage was at the Boyd Park barn although the cars in use may have spent their few idle hours sitting in the street...a situation that would hardly be practical when autos became more common.

The early Wabash cars may have been the two Wabash River Traction single-truck cars. Peru had a succession from the Jones built 109 series then, by 1918, the 174-175. Both cities then received cars from the 176-201 series and then the 202-220. Although not regularly used, open cars for seasonal service were available from the Boyd Park barn. Peru, from 1932 to 1934, as the sole survivor of the ISC controlled small city lines used cars from the 290 series group.

ROLLING STOCK FORT WAYNE BUSES

Motor buses came to Fort Wayne in 1917 when four bus/truck chasis were purchased from the Studebaker company. The local shops built bodies for the buses. Only two were in use at one time. Not successful, the chasis were used for service vehicles.

During the 1920's up to 23 intercity buses were in use and city buses again made their appearance. The intercity buses ranged from fairly plain types through fancy Fageol parlor coaches. All of these intercity buses were sold by 1932. Some of the city buses were sold and others were scrapped. Only one of these older buses survived into the forties. This was the single bus salvaged from parts of the three "scrapped" Fargos. Somewhat unique, the Fargos had identical numbers to a series of active streetcars even though there was a wide range of vacant numbers.

In 1940 the company bought seven ACF and two Ford buses. However, the conversion plans were based on the trolley coach and 28 J. G. Brill 40SMT trolley coaches were put in service. Forty Brill 44SMT (added in 1942) and ten Brill TC-44 (added in 1946) trolley coaches completed the acquisition of electric vehicles. The last group was sold to Indianapolis in 1953 and later sold to Dayton. The rest with some early retirements remained in service until 1960. One is preserved (157).

Following the war, ISC started modernizing and expanding the motor bus fleet by buying the new model Twin Coach 38-S gasoline powered bus. During the sale conversations, which ended in purchase by Fort Wayne Transit, Inc., the question of diesel buses came up in the proposals of some potential buyers. Resistance to the diesel bus fumes made the bid from one national bus line operator virtually unacceptable. The same operator also

Bus No.	Make	Model	Serial No.	Capacity	Year	Purchase Year (if used)	Notes
Trolley Coaches (1940-1960) ISC and FWT							
100-127	J. G. Brill	40 SMT	549-576	40	1940	—	Last one retired in 1959.
128-167	J. G. Brill	44 SMT	270-309	44	1942	—	Out of service 6/10/60. 157 at National Museum of Transport.
168-177	ACF-Brill	TC-44	226-235	44	1946	—	Sold to Indianapolis Rys. in 1953 as 781-790. Resold to Dayton in 1958 as 48-57. Reitred circa 1966.
Fort Wayne City Buses—Twin Coach purchased by ISC and FWT from 1947 through 1960.							
12-26	Twin Coach	38-S	532B-546B	38	5/1947	—	Bought new by ISC. Sold to FWT 5/1/48. 20 wrecked 5/53 beyond repair. 12, 14-19, 21-23, 26 sold to PTC—Retired 1969.
27-31	Twin Coach	41-S	1206B-1210B	41	10/21/48	—	Bought new by FWT. 27-28, 30-31 sold to PTC—Retired 1969.
32-36	Twin Coach	41-S	1295-1299	41	9/22/50	—	Bought new by FWT. 32-36 sold to PTC—Retired 1969.
37-41	Twin Coach	41-S	1329-1332	41	5/11/51	—	Bought new by FWT. 37-41 sold to PTC—Retired 1969.
42-45	Twin Coach	41-S	861-864	41	1947	8/1953	Bought from Co-Operative Transit, Inc., Wheeling, WV, were 97-99, 180. 42 and 45 sold to PTC—Retired 1969.
46-48	Twin Coach	41-S	866-868	41	1947	8/1953	Were Wheeling 181-183. 46-48 sold to PTC—Retired 1969.
49	Twin Coach	34-S	62	34	1946	9/24/57	Bought from Hannibal, MO, was 28. Sold to PTC—Retired in 1969.
50-51	Twin Coach	34-S	182-183	34	1946	9/24/57	Were Hannibal 30-31. 50 sold to PTC—Retired 1969.
52-53	Twin Coach	34-S	350B-351B	34	1946	9/24/57	Were Hannibal 32-33.
54	Twin Coach	41-S	929B	41	1947	3/5/59	Bought from Niagara Frontier Transit, Buffalo, NY, was 5113. Sold to PTC—Retired 1969.
Note: Buses no. 12-54 used propane fuel.							
201-213	Twin Coach	41-S	?	41	1947	3/5/59	Bought from Niagara Frontier Transit, Buffalo, NY. Sold or retired by 1962 (no data available).
214	Twin Coach	41-S	576	41	1947	3/5/59	Was NFT 5055. Retired by 1967.
215	Twin Coach	41-S	570	41	1947	3/5/59	Was NFT 5049. Retired by 1967.
216	Twin Coach	41-S	545	41	1947	3/5/59	Was NFT 5024. Retired by 1967.
217	Twin Coach	41-S	130	41	1947	3/5/59	Was NFT 5020. Retired by 1967.
218	Twin Coach	41-S	543	41	1947	3/5/59	Was NFT 5022. Retired by 1967.
219	Twin Coach	41-S	547	41	1947	3/5/59	Was NFT 5026. Retired by 1967.
220	Twin Coach	41-S	548	41	1947	3/5/59	Was NFT 5027. Retired by 1967.
221	Twin Coach	41-S	568	41	1947	3/5/59	Was NFT 5047. Retired by 1967.
222	Twin Coach	41-S	549	41	1947	3/5/59	Was NFT 5028. Retired by 1967.
223	Twin Coach	41-S	125	41	1947	3/5/59	Was NFT 5015. Retired by 1967.

Bus No.	Make	Model	Serial No.	Capacity	Year	Purchase Year (if used)	Notes
224	Twin Coach	41-S	559	41	1947	3/5/59	Was NFT 5038. Retired by 1967.
225	Twin Coach	41-S	560	41	1947	3/5/59	Was NFT 5039. Retired by 1967.
226	Twin Coach	41-S	?	41	1947	3/5/59	Was NFT ?. Retired by 1961.
227	Twin Coach	41-S	564	41	1947	3/5/59	Was NFT 5043. Retired by 1967.
228	Twin Coach	41-S	571	41	1947	3/5/59	Was NFT 5050. Retired by 1967.
229	Twin Coach	41-S	577	41	1947	3/5/59	Was NFT 5058. Retired by 1967.

Note: Three buses in above series were resold to Evansville, IN in 1962—serial nos. 128, 566 and 574. 201-229 had gasoline-powered engines. 229 was converted to propane in 1964.

Bus No.	Make	Model	Serial No.	Capacity	Year	Purchase Year (if used)	Notes
230	Twin Coach	41-S	536	41	1947	3/26/60	Bought from Dept. of Street Railways, Detroit, MI. Was DSR 4756. Sold to PTC—Retired 1969.
231	Twin Coach	41-S	739	41	1947	3/26/60	Was DSR 4854. Retired by 1967.
232	Twin Coach	41-S	?	41	1947	3/26/60	Was DSR ?. Retired 1961.
233	Twin Coach	41-S	510	41	1947	3/26/60	Was DSR 4730. Retired by 1967.
234	Twin Coach	41-S	498	41	1947	3/26/60	Was DSR 4718. Retired by 1967.
235	Twin Coach	41-S	665	41	1947	3/26/60	Was DSR 4780. Sold to PTC. Retired 1969.
236	Twin Coach	41-S	485	41	1947	3/26/60	Was DSR 4705. Retired by 1967.
237	Twin Coach	41-S	489	41	1947	3/26/60	Was DSR 4709. Retired by 1967.
238	Twin Coach	41-S	727	41	1947	3/26/60	Was DSR 4842. Retired by 1967.
239	Twin Coach	41-S	523	41	1947	3/26/60	Was DSR 4753. Retired by 1967.
240	Twin Coach	41-S	715	41	1947	3/26/60	Was DSR 4830. Retired by 1967.
241	Twin Coach	41-S	694	41	1947	3/26/60	Was DSR 4809. Retired by 1967.
242	Twin Coach	41-S	722	41	1947	3/26/60	Was DSR 4837. Sold to PTC. Retired 1969.
243	Twin Coach	41-S	724	41	1947	3/26/60	Was DSR 4843. Retired by 1967.
244	Twin Coach	41-S	749	41	1947	3/26/60	Was DSR 4864. Retired by 1967.
245	Twin Coach	41-S	730	41	1947	3/26/60	Was DSR 4845. Retired by 1967.
246	Twin Coach	41-S	540	41	1947	3/26/60	Was DSR 4760. Retired by 1967.
247	Twin Coach	41-S	764	41	1947	3/26/60	Was DSR 4879. Retired by 1967.
248	Twin Coach	41-S	678	41	1947	3/26/60	Was DSR 4793. Retired by 1967.
249	Twin Coach	41-S	750	41	1947	3/26/60	Was DSR 4865. Sold to Evansville, IN 1962.
250	Twin Coach	41-S	?	41	1947	3/26/60	Was DSR ?. Retired in 1961.
251	Twin Coach	41-S	?	41	1947	3/26/60	Was DSR ?. Retired in 1961.
252	Twin Coach	41-S	648	41	1947	3/26/60	Was DSR 4763. Sold to Evansville, IN 1962.
253	Twin Coach	41-S	702	41	1947	3/26/60	Was DSR 4817. Sold to Evansville, IN 1962.
254	Twin Coach	41-S	765	41	1947	3/26/60	Was DSR 4880. Sold to Evansville, IN 1962.
255	Twin Coach	41-S	528	41	1947	3/26/60	Was DSR 4748. Sold to Evansville, IN 1962.
256	Twin Coach	41-S	671	41	1947	3/26/60	Was DSR 4786. Sold to Evansville, IN 1962.
257	Twin Coach	41-S	?	41	1947	3/26/60	Was DSR ?. Retired 1961-62.

Bus No.	Make	Model	Serial No.	Capacity	Year	Purchase Year (if used)	Notes
258	Twin Coach	41-S	?	41	1947	3/26/60	Was DSR ?. Retired 1961-62.
259	Twin Coach	41-S	?	41	1947	3/26/60	Was DSR ?. Retired 1961-62.

Note: One additional bus (serial no. 496) sold to Evansville, IN. Buses 230-259 used gasoline fuel. Serial nos. for 249, 252-256 may not be in exact order.

Fort Wayne City Buses—GMC Diesels purchased by FWT. All sold to PTC.

Bus No.	Make	Model	Serial No.	Capacity	Year	Purchase Year (if used)	Notes
101-102	GMC	TDH 4512	2232-2233	45	1957	9/6/61	From MK&O (Tulsa, OK) 747-748. First diesel city buses in Ft. Wayne. 101 was sold to the Boy Scouts in 1976. 102 was sold to to Greater Lafayette PTC in 1976.
103-106	GMC	TDH 4512	2234-2237	45	1957	6/11/62	Were MK&O 749-757 sold to Greater Lafayette PTC 1976.
107	GMC	TDH 4512	2242	45	1957	7/13/63	Was MK&O 757 sold to Greater Lafayette PTC 1976.
108-110	GMC	TDH 4512	1568-1570	45	1956	9/3/64	From Ohio Valley Bus Co. sold to Greater Lafayette PTC 1976.
111-112	GMC	TDH 4512	1566-1567	45	1956	9/3/64	Same as 108-110. Original numbers of 108-112 are not known. Sold to Lafayette in 1976.
131-136	GMC	TDH 3612	314-319	36	1950	8/31/62	Bought from Bibb Transit Co., Macon, GA. Were 500-505, retired by 1970.
137	GMC	TDH 3207	257	32	1947	6/4/63	Built for Twin City Lines, Fort Smith, AK. FWT bought from Sheridan (?), retired 1969.
261-262	GMC	TDH 4008	814-815	40	1947	1/12/67	Bought from Indianapolis Rys. (IRys), were 840-841, retired by 1974.
263-270	GMC	TDH 4008	806-813	40	1947	3/28/67	From IRys, 832-839, retired by 1974.
271-275	GMC	TDH 4008	816-820	40	1947	3/28/67	From IRys, 842-846, retired by 1974.

Fort Wayne City Buses—PTC (1968 to present)

Bus No.	Make	Model	Serial No.	Capacity	Year	Purchase Year (if used)	Notes
151-152	GMC	TDH 4519	903-904	43	1965	1968	GMC "new look" bought by FWT. Only non-air conditioned PTC buses.
153-158	GMC	TGH 4521A	210-215	43	1968	—	First new buses bought by PTC, 153-220, air conditioned.
159-178	GMC	TGH 4521A	462-481	45	1969	—	
179-198	GMC	TGH 4521A	570-589	43	1970	—	
199-202	GMC	TGH 4523A	757-760	45	1974	—	
203-204	GMC	TGH 4523A	905-906	45	1974	—	
205-220	GMC	TGH 4523A	1883-1898	45	1976	—	
101-128	GMC	T70604	741-768	35	1981	—	Newest style GMC bus delivered in June 1981. Cost extra because of required handicap accessibility equipment. Air conditioned.
401-404	(Twin Coach Highway Products Co.)	T-23	25739-25742	23	1974	—	PTC's only non-GMC buses. Sold in 1976 to Walt Disney World Co.

Bus No.	Make	Model	Serial No.	Capacity	Year	Purchase Year (if used)	Notes
Ft. Wayne Buses for Intercity Charter Service							
301	GMC	PDA 3702	471-5145	—	1944	1959	301-303 bought in Indianapolis and retired by 1967.
302	GMC	PDA 3702	471-5525	—	1945	1959	
303	GMC	PD-4104	4104-1380	—	1955	1/23/62	Was Indiana Motor Bus Co. 156. Sold in 1974 by PTC.
304-305	Aerocoach	P-46	371811-371812	—	1947	1962	304 from Transit Service Co. (Indianapolis) and 305 from the Eli Lilly Co. Both sold to Memphis, TN 1/75 by PTC.
306	GMC (Yellow Coach)	PDG-4101	4101-087	—	1940	7/12/62	From Eastern Greyhound Lines (E-4047). Retired before 1967.
Lafayette Transit Co. (1940-1956) Greater Lafayette Bus Co. (1956-1971) Greater Lafayette Public Transportation Corp. (1971-present)							
31-49	ACF Motors Co.	26-S	90-108	27	1940	—	New. Last (33 and 39) retired 1959.
50	ACF Motors Co.	26-S	136	27	1940	—	New. Retired 1958.
60-61	Yellow Truck & Coach Co.	TG-2706	294-295	27	3/1942	—	New. Retired 1950.
70-71	White Motor Co.	?	196525 (70), 195340 (71)	?	1936	9/26/42	Retired before 1948.
80-81	Ford Motor Co.	29-B	581041, 581042	27	1944	—	Built by War Prod. Bd. 1942. Delivered 1944 by O.D.T. order. Retired 1954 (80) and 1955 (81).
82-83	Ford Motor Co.	69-B	1176107-1170901	27	1946	—	Retired by 1958.
84-85	Ford Motor Co.	69-B	952234, 952119	27	1946	—	84 retired by 1958, 85 retired by 1957.
86-87	Ford Motor Co.	69-B	1212202, 1033558	27	1946	—	Retired by 1958.
51-54	ACF-Brill Motors Co.	C-36	1189-1192	36	2/1948	—	New. All retired by 1958.
55-58	ACF-Brill Motors Co.	C-36	386, 385, 538, 539	36	1947	6/1957	From Gary Railways 65-84 series. All retired by 1960.
1001-1012	GMC	TDH 3207	131-142	32	4/1947	4/1958	Kansas City Public Service 1001-1012. All retired by end of 1958.
1013-1014	GMC	TDH 3207	232, 239	32	1947	1960	Retired 1966 (1013), 1967 (1014).
1015-1016	GMC	TDM 4507	1903, 1917	45	1948	1960	Retired 1969. Were Great Lakes Greyhound Lines G6763, G6777.
1017	GMC	TDH 3207	247	32	1947	1961	Retired 1969. Was Twin Cities Motor Coach Lines 220, Benton Harbor, MI.
1018	GMC	TDH 3207	062	32	1947	1961	Retired 1969. From Suburban Bus Co. #?, Nashville, TN.
1019-1020	GMC	TDH 3609	006, 104	36	1946	1962	Retired by 1969. Were Great Lakes Greyhound Lines G6718 and G6730.

Bus No.	Make	Model	Serial No.	Capacity	Year	Purchase Year (if used)	Notes
102-132 (1st) came from several sources and all were retired by 1976.							
102-104	GMC	TDH 3612	1877, 1878, 1879	36	1953	1963	Retired before 1976. Were Leppert Bus Lines, Inc. 102-104, Columbus, IN.
105-107	GMC	TDH 3714	051, 052, 053	37	1953	1963	Retired before 1976. Were Leppert 105-107.
108	GMC	PD 4103	704	?	1951	1963	Retired before 1976. Was Eastern Greyhound Lines E5162.
109-110	GMC	TDH 3612	1700, 1699	36	1952	1963	Retired before 1976. Was Savannah Transit 448, 449.
111	GMC	TDH 3612	?	36	1952	1963	Information missing. Was Savannah Transit #?.
112-113	GMC	TDH 3612	1697, 1698	36	1952	1963	Retired before 1976 (112), retired 1971 (113). Were Savannah Transit 446, 447.
114	GMC	TDH 3610	149	36	1948	1968	Retired by 1976. Was Charleston, W. Va. 947.
115	GMC	TD 4008	164(?)	40	1948	1968	Information missing. Retired by 1976.
116-117	?	?	?	?	?	?	These numbers probably used but there is no record.
118	GMC	?	?	?	1947	1968	Retired 1969. No details.
119	GMC	TDH 4507	2625	45	1948	1968	Retired by 1976. Was Cincinnati Street Railway 829.
120	GMC	TDH 3501	010	35	1946	1968	Retired by 1976. Was Savannah Transit 488.
121-123	GMC	TDH 4008	822, 823, 824	40	1947	1968	Retired by 1976. Were Indianapolis Ry. 848-850.
124	GMC	?	?	?	1950	1968	Retired 1969. No record. Was Indianapolis Transit, Inc. #?.
125	GMC	TDH 4509	2102	45	1952	1968	Retired by 1976.
126-128	GMC	TDH 4507	113, 115, 109	45	1946	1968	Retired by 1976. Were Louisville Ry. 501, 505, 507.
129-132	GMC	TDH 4507	?	45	1948	1971	Retired by 1976. Were Louisville Ry. #?.
102-112 (2nd) purchased from Ft. Wayne Public Transportation Corporation.							
102-107	GMC	TDH 4512	2233-2237, 2242	45	1957	1976	From Ft. Wayne PTC 102-107. 102, 103, 105 and 106 in use 1/82.
108-112	GMC	TDH 4512	1568-1570, 1566-1567	45	1956	1976	From Ft. Wayne PTC 108-112. 109 and 112 in use 1/82.
201-216	Twin Coach	TC-25	25346-25361	25	1973	—	New from Highway Products, Kent, OH 205 and 207 in use 1/82.
218-222	Flxible	35096-6-1	59913-59917	40	1975	—	New.
301-305	Flxible	45096-6-0	63620-63624		1978	—	New.
401-410	GMD	T6H 4523N	3500369-3500378		1981	—	New. Built by GM Diesel Division of Canada.

GENERAL ARRANGEMENT OF CITY CARS

ST. LOUIS DOUBLE TRUCK

8 cars—nos. 500-505 inclusive, 508 and 509.

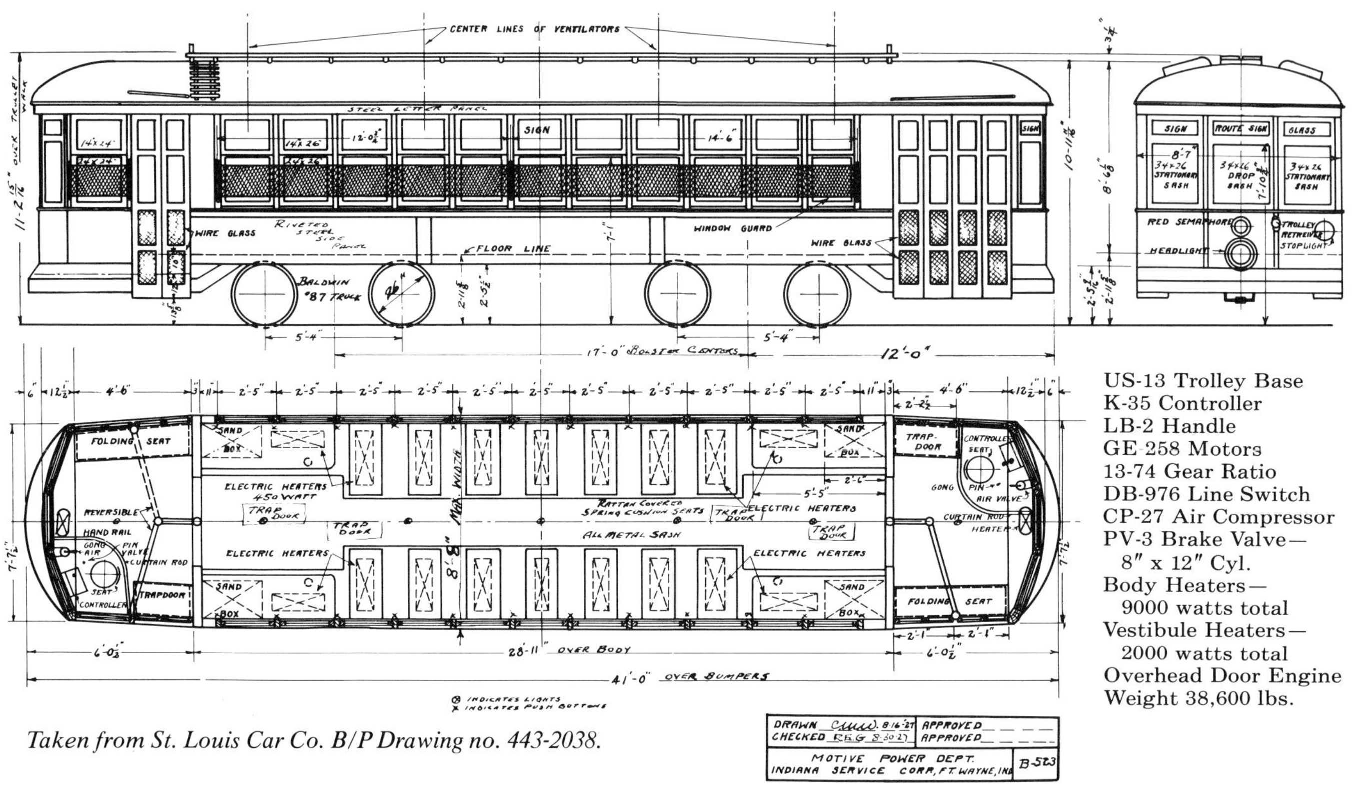

US-13 Trolley Base
K-35 Controller
LB-2 Handle
GE 258 Motors
13-74 Gear Ratio
DB-976 Line Switch
CP-27 Air Compressor
PV-3 Brake Valve—
8″ x 12″ Cyl.
Body Heaters—
9000 watts total
Vestibule Heaters—
2000 watts total
Overhead Door Engine
Weight 38,600 lbs.

Taken from St. Louis Car Co. B/P Drawing no. 443-2038.

ST. LOUIS DOUBLE TRUCK

45 cars—nos. 510-554 inclusive.

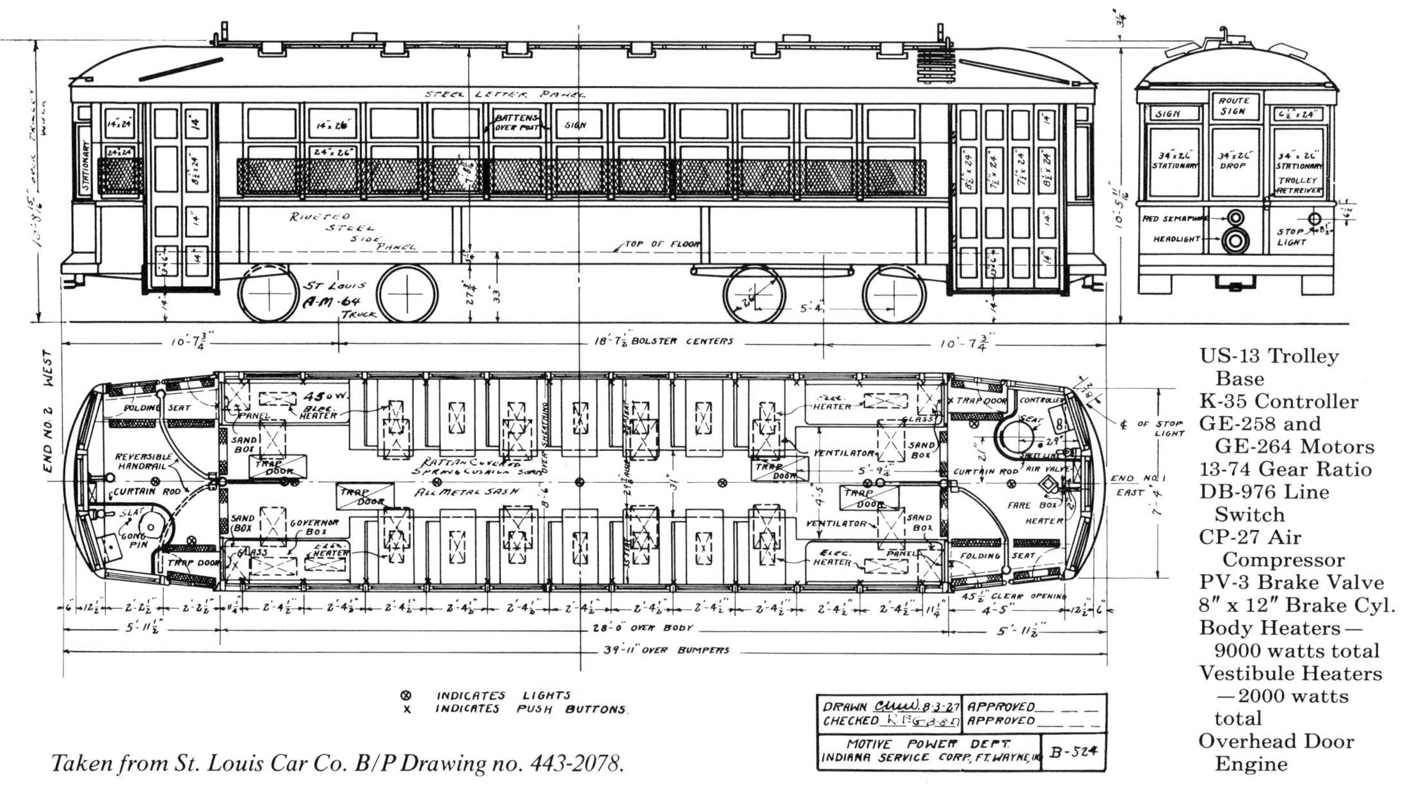

US-13 Trolley
Base
K-35 Controller
GE-258 and
GE-264 Motors
13-74 Gear Ratio
DB-976 Line
Switch
CP-27 Air
Compressor
PV-3 Brake Valve
8″ x 12″ Brake Cyl.
Body Heaters—
9000 watts total
Vestibule Heaters
—2000 watts
total
Overhead Door
Engine

Taken from St. Louis Car Co. B/P Drawing no. 443-2078.

GENERAL ARRANGEMENT OF CITY CARS

ST. LOUIS SINGLE TRUCK

16 cars—nos. 275-290, 45 cars—nos. 400-444.

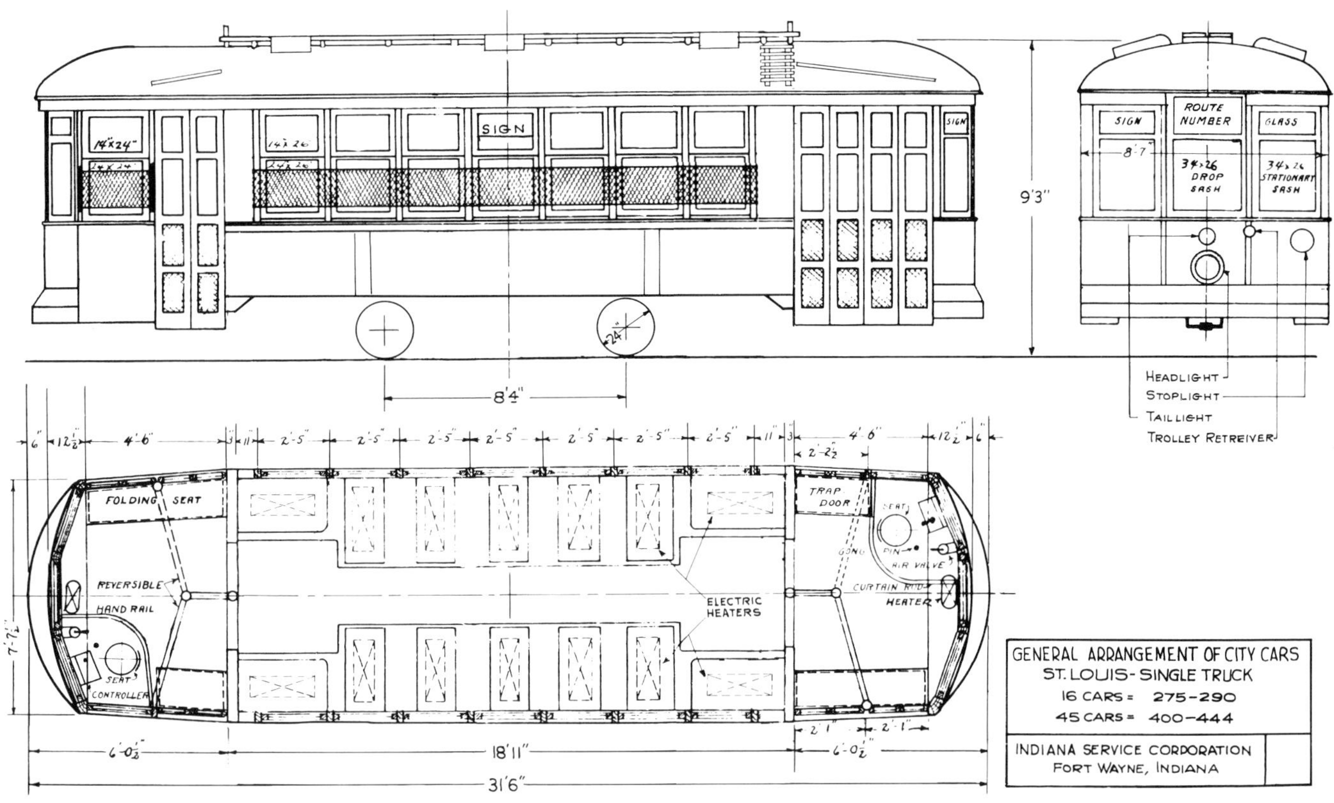

DIAGRAM OF SNOW PLOW—CAR NO. 1

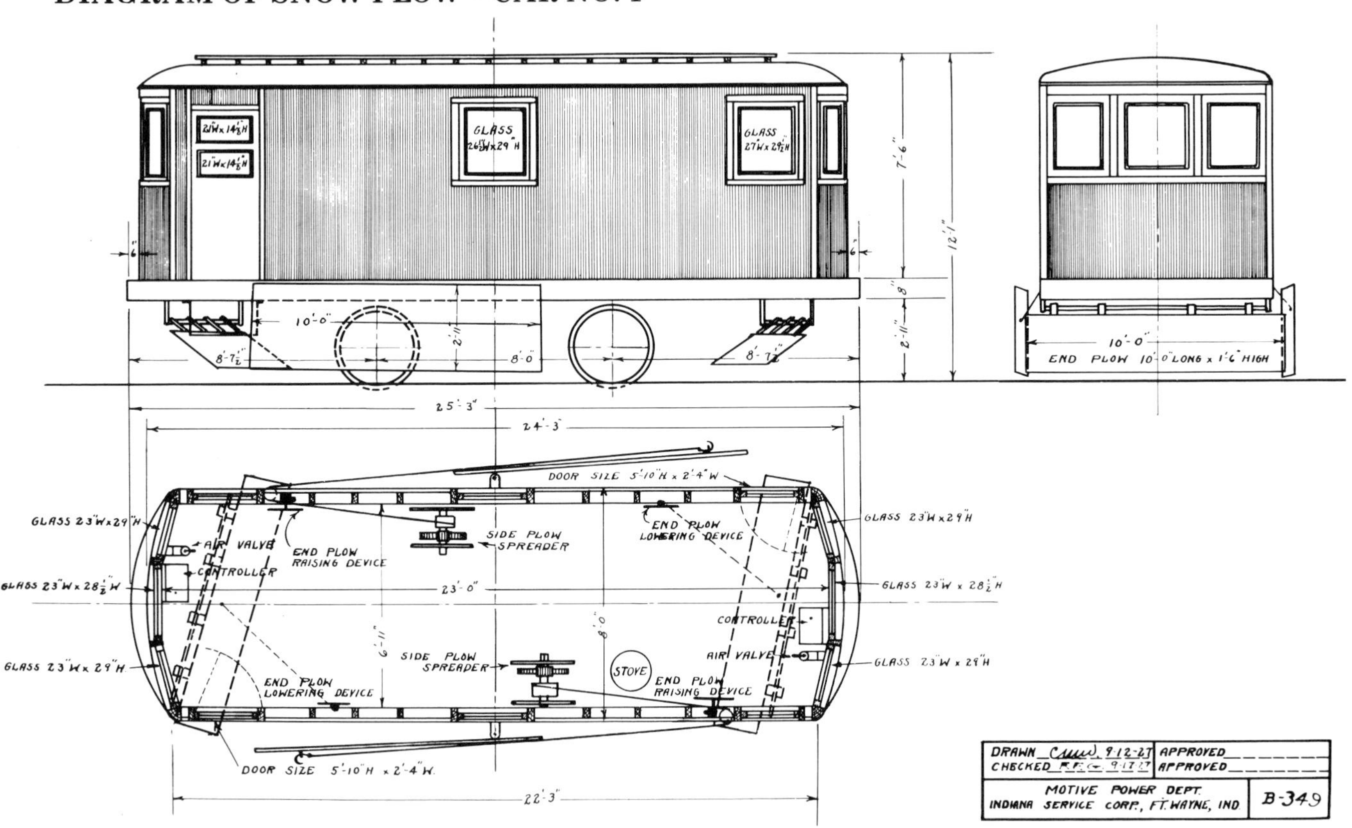

FT. WAYNE & SOUTHWESTERN TRACTION COMPANY

JACKSON & SHARP CARS 5 cars—nos. 201-205.

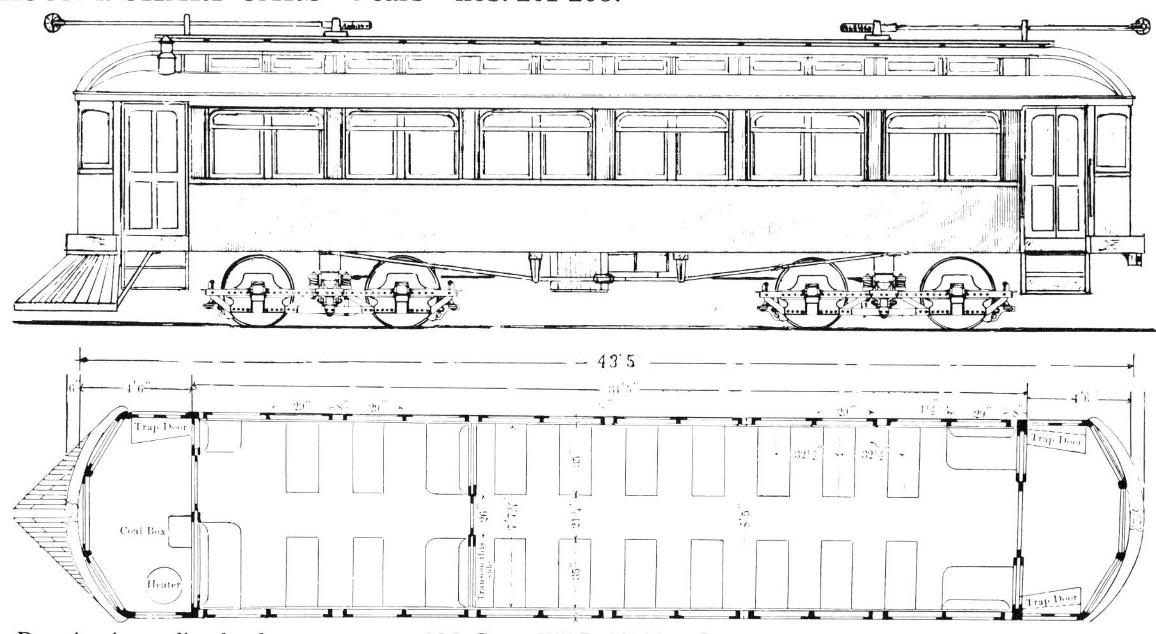

Drawing immediately above courtesy of McGraw-Hill Publishing Company.

JOHN STEPHENSON CO. CARS

4 cars—nos. 301-304 (later renumbered 206-209 by Wabash Valley).

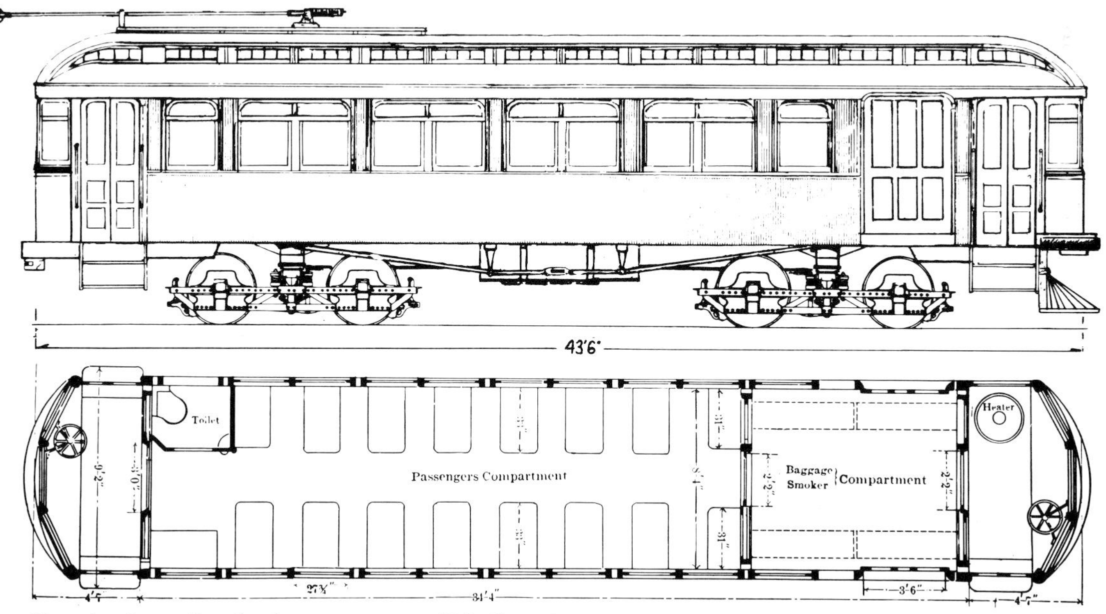

Drawing immediately above courtesy of McGraw-Hill Publishing Company.

CAR 321

Built in 1910 using two of the older Southwestern Jackson & Sharp 200 series cars.

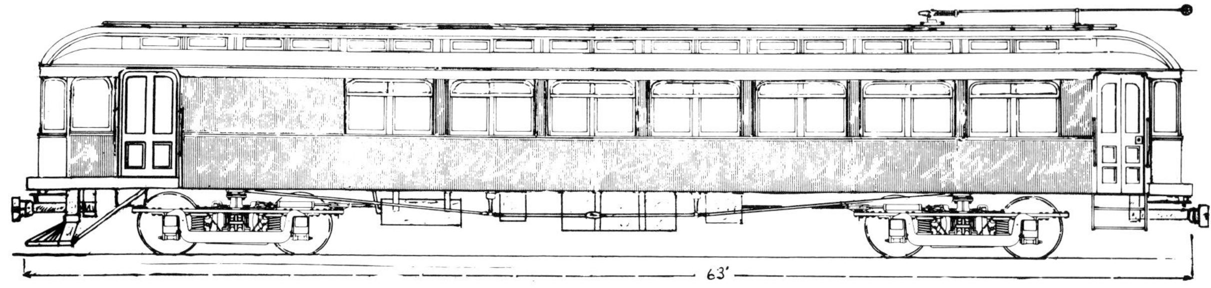

FT. WAYNE & WABASH VALLEY TRACTION COMPANY

CINCINNATI CAR CO. CARS
11 cars—nos. 301-311.

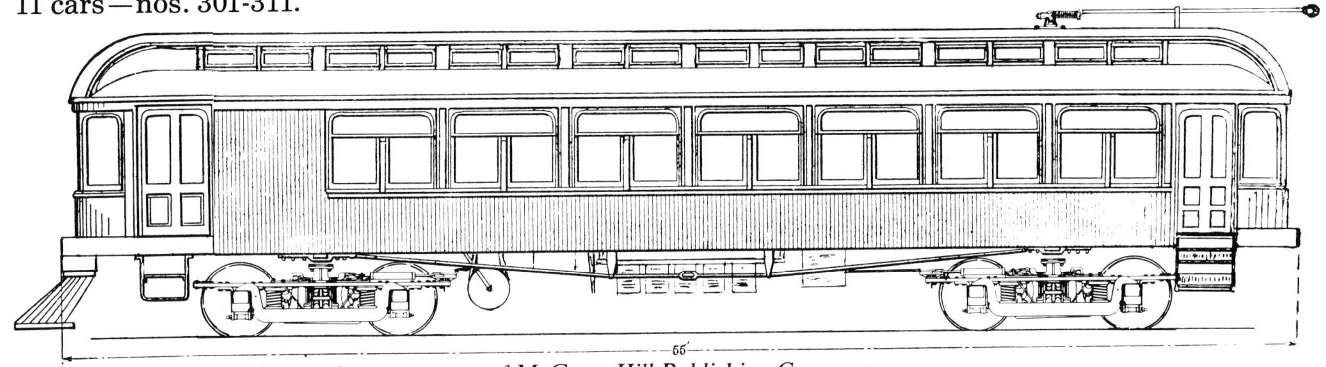

Drawing immediately above courtesy of McGraw-Hill Publishing Company.

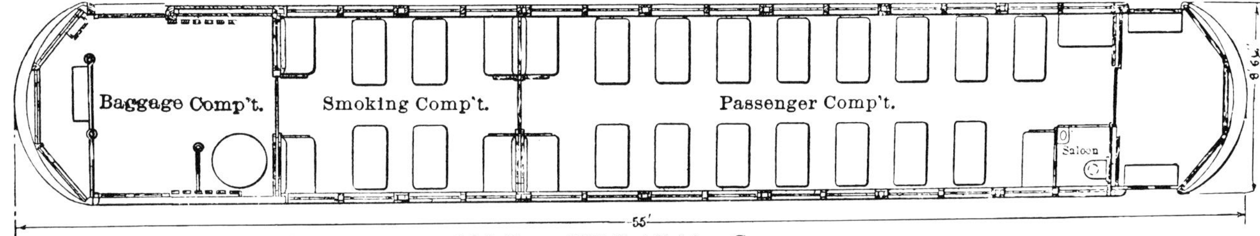

Drawing immediately above courtesy of McGraw-Hill Publishing Company.

CARS 301-302

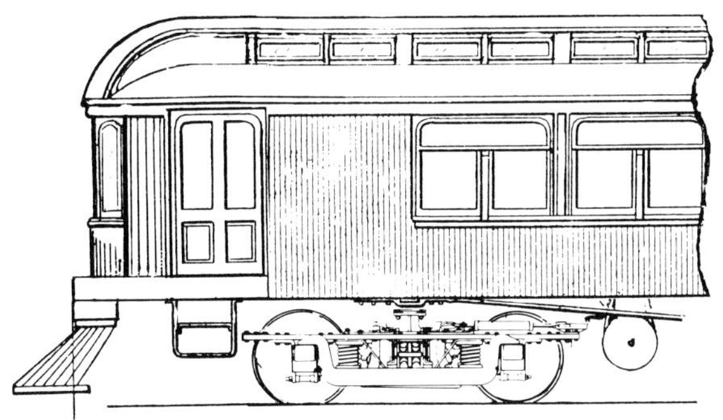

CARS 303-307 (as built)

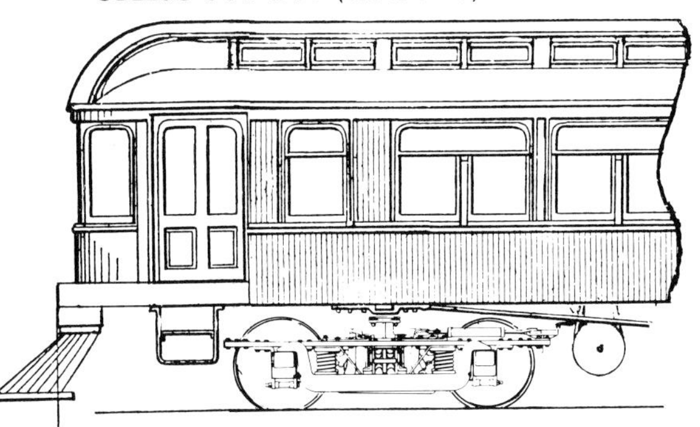

CINCINNATI CAR CO. DELUXE PARLOR-BUFFET CARS
4 cars—nos. 501-504.

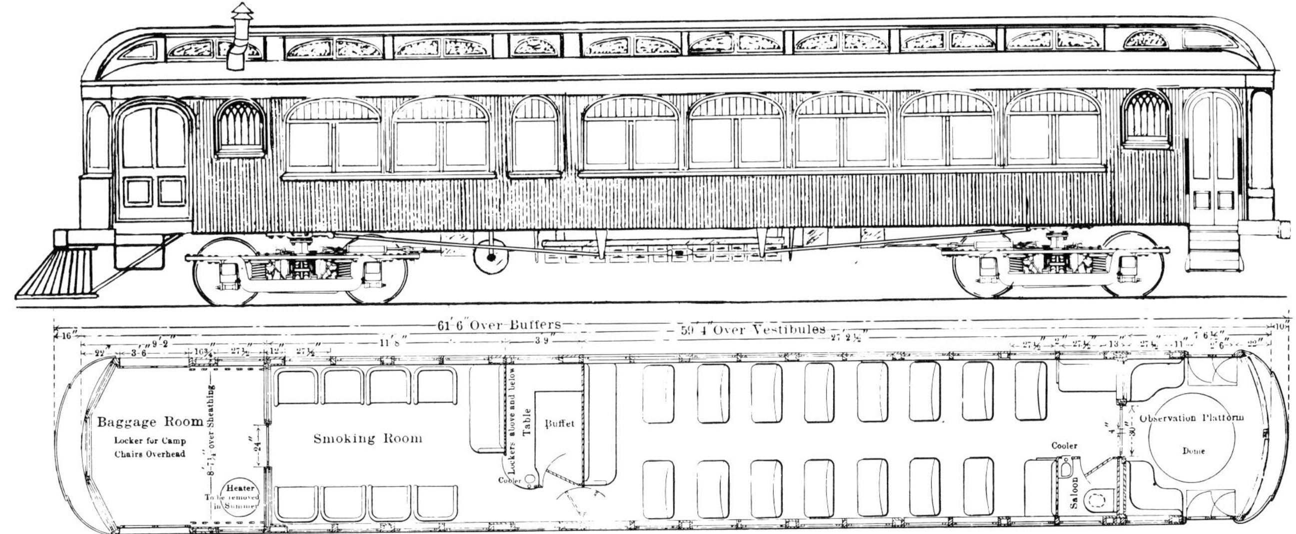

Drawing immediately above courtesy of McGraw-Hill Publishing Company.

PURDUE UNIVERSITY TEST CAR

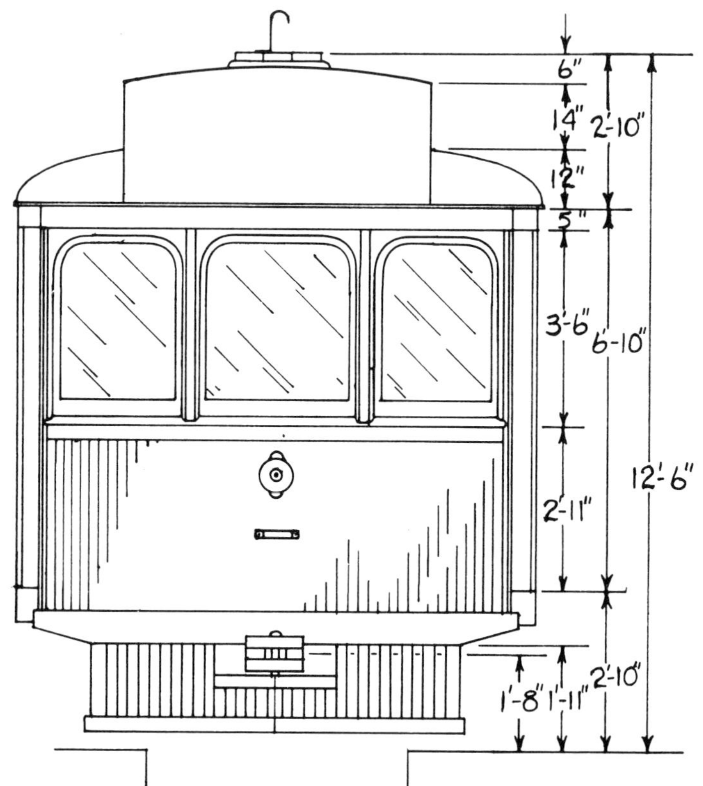

Purdue University Test Car: Body built in 1904 by the J. G. Brill Company as test car body "Louisiana." Modified and rebuilt as shown in 1908. Operated by Purdue from 1908 until 1940. Stored until 1951 and then sent to the National Museum of Transport in St. Louis.

Drawn by William J. Clouser

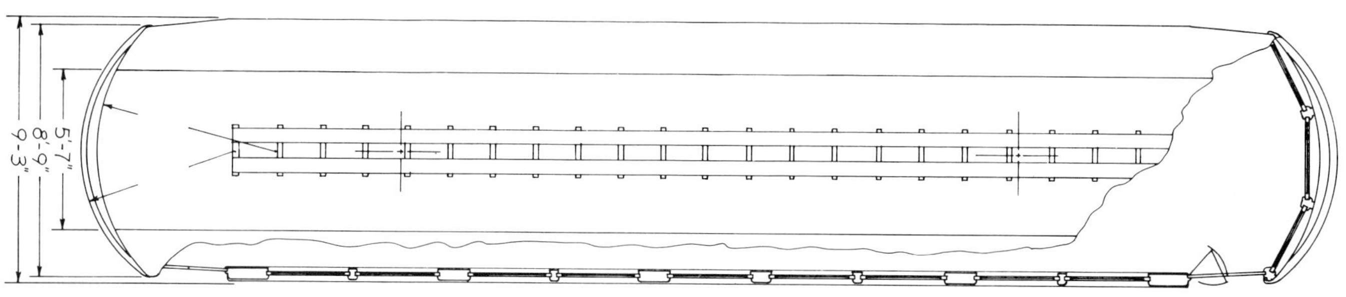

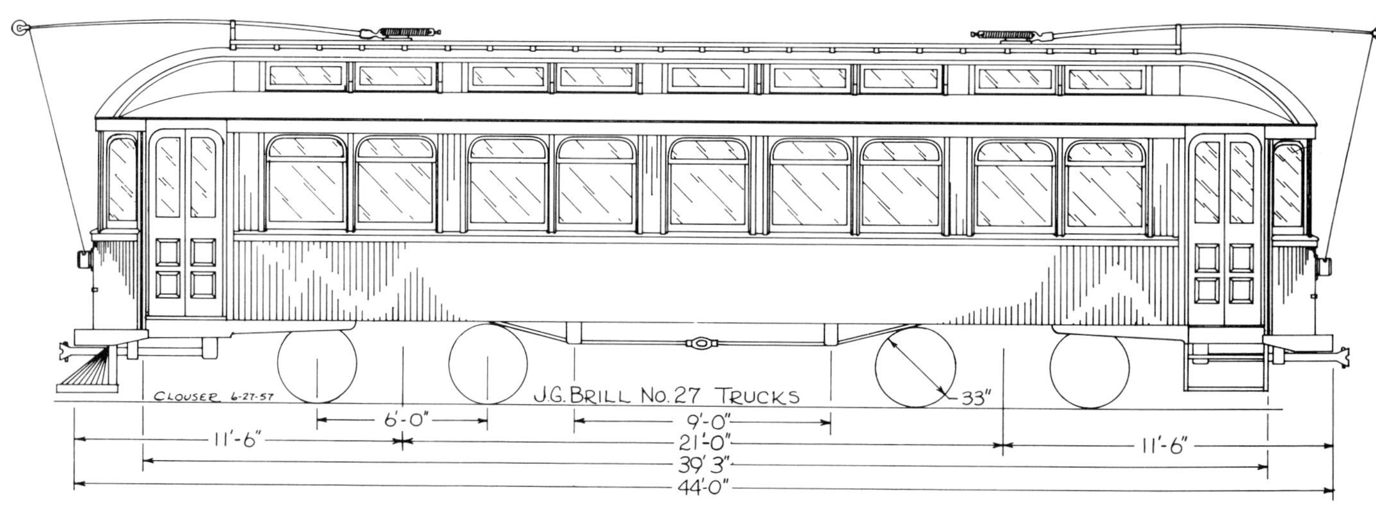

GENERAL ARRANGEMENT OF INTERURBAN CARS

ST. LOUIS CAR COMPANY—INTERURBAN PASSENGER AND BAGGAGE CAR

5 cars—nos. 375-379. All leased to IRR. 375-377 modified in 1935 with an RPO section. 378-379, with ends reversed, changed to one-man service, renumbered 457-458 (1936), returned to ISC and scrapped (1938). 375-377 returned to ISC (1941) and sold to CSS and SB.

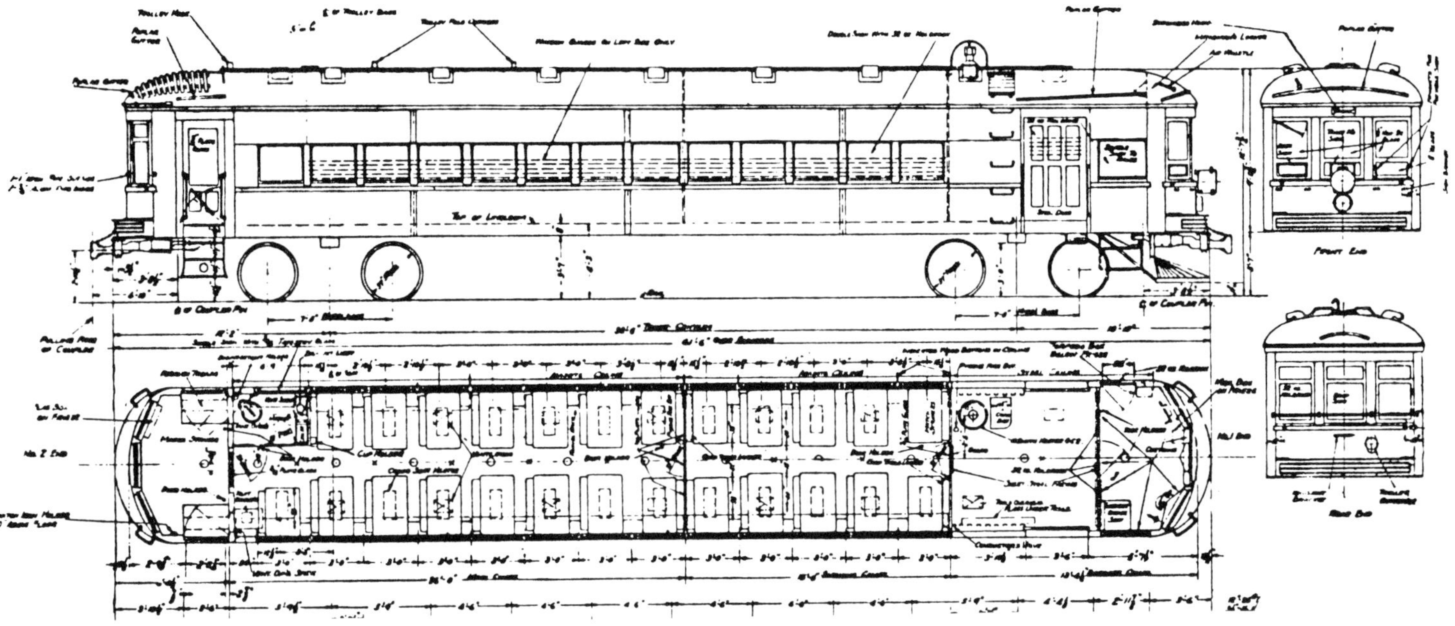

Taken from St. Louis Car Co. B/P Drawing no. 443-1055 (dated 11/17/25).

ST. LOUIS CAR COMPANY— INTERURBAN PARLOR CAR

Parlor-buffet cars "Little Turtle" (390) and "Anthony Wayne" (391) were used briefly in IRR System service. Stored at Spy Run and scrapped (1939).

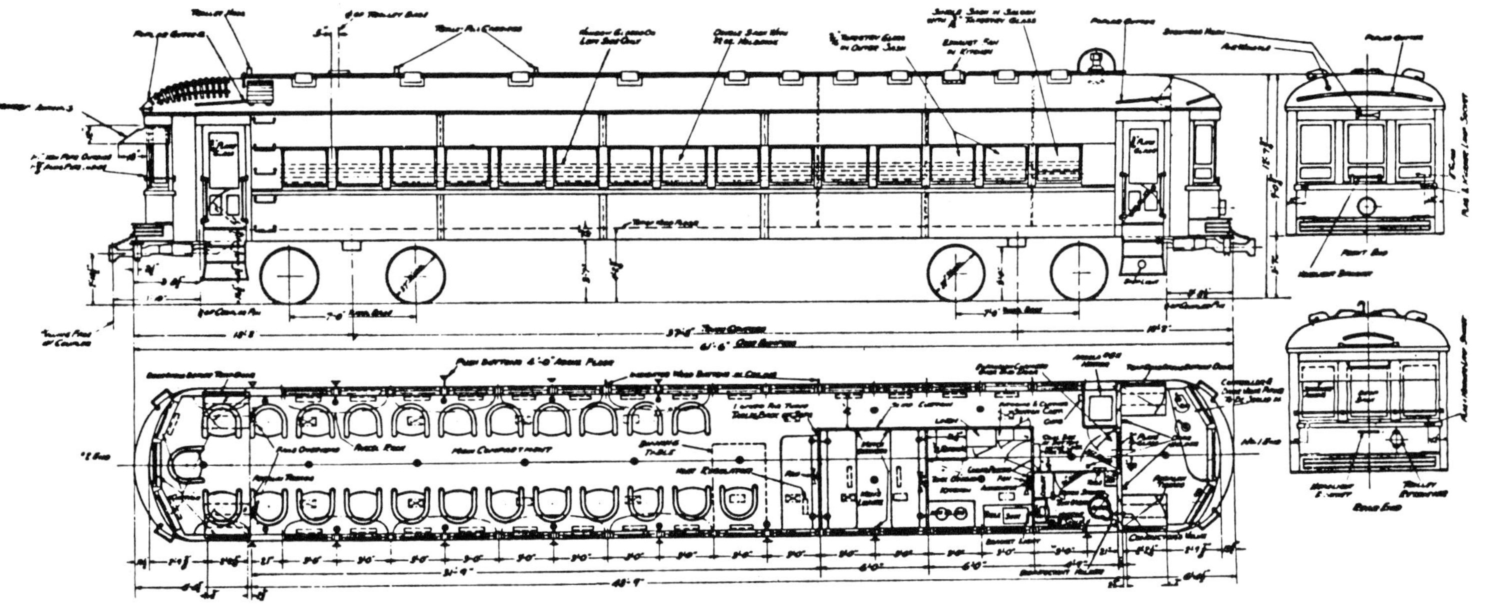

Taken from St. Louis Car Co. B/P Drawing no. 443-1056 (dated 2/5/26).

Bibliography

Section I—Books and Pamphlets

R. M. Bates, *Interurban Railways of Allen County Indiana,* (Fort Wayne: Public Library, 1958).

R. M. Bates, *Robison Park 1896-1919,* (2nd Edition), (Fort Wayne: Old Fort News Vol. XIX, No. 2, Allen County-Fort Wayne Historical Society, 1956).

R. G. Benedict, *The Bluffton, Geneva and Celina Story,* (Chicago, 1981).

R. G. Benedict, *The Interurban from Marion to Bluffton,* (Chicago, 1980).

G. K. Bradley, *Fort Wayne's Trolleys,* (Chicago: Owen Davies, 1963).

D. W. Chambers, *Lafayette Street Railway,* (Chicago: Bulletin #32 of the Electric Railway Historical Society, 1958).

E. H. Charlton, *Electric Railway Car Trucks,* (Forty Fort, PA: Harold E. Cox, 1967).

B. J. Griswold, *History of Fort Wayne and Allen County,* (Chicago: Robert O. Law Co., 1917).

G. W. Hilton, *The Cable Car in America,* (Berkeley: Howell-North, 1971).

G. W. Hilton and J. F. Due, *The Electric Interurban Railways in America,* (Stanford: Stanford University Press, 1960).

H. B. Knoll, *The Story of Purdue Engineering,* (W. Lafayette: Purdue University Studies, 1962).

A. R. Lind, *From Horsecars to Streamliners,* (Park Forest, IL: Transport History Press, 1978).

F. McDonald, *Insull,* (Chicago: University of Chicago Press, 1962).

J. Marlette, *Electric Railroads of Indiana,* (Indianapolis: Council for Local History, 1959).

D. H. Mitchell, *Northern Indiana Public Service Company,* (Princeton: Newcomen Society in North America, 1960).

F. W. Rowsome, Jr., *Trolley Car Treasury,* (New York: McGraw-Hill, 1956).

Brill Magazine (various issues), (Philadelphia: J. G. Brill Co.).

Electric Railway Dictionary, (New York: McGraw, 1911).

The Fort Wayne Code of 1931, (Fort Wayne: City of Fort Wayne, 1931).

Fort Wayne Up-To-Date, 1874-1894, (Fort Wayne: Twentieth Anniversary of Fort Wayne Daily News, 1894).

Indiana Railroad System, (Chicago: Bulletin 91 of the Central Electric Railfans' Association, 1950).

Indiana Service Corporation, (Fort Wayne: ISC Booklet, 1926).

Moody's Manual of Investments—Public Utilities, (New York: Moody's Investment Service, Inc., 1920-1948).

Report of the Electric Railway Test Commission, (St. Louis: Electric Industries and Research Section, Louisiana Purchase Exposition, 1904).

Street and Electric Railways—Bureau of Census Special Report, (1902 and 1907), (Washington: Government Printing Office, 1905 and 1907).

Union Traction Company of Indiana, (Chicago: Bulletin 62 and 63 of the Central Electric Railfans' Association, 1945).

Section II—Company and Private Papers

Fort Wayne and Northern Indiana Traction Company; Deed-Feustel, Receiver, to Indiana Service Corporation Dated April 21st, 1920.

Fort Wayne and Northern Indiana Traction Company—Operating Statistics, 1904-1918, (A detailed study of why the company was failing and about to go into receivership).

Fort Wayne and Northern Indiana Traction Company, Inventory and Appraisal of Railway Property as of January 1, 1918, (The complete record of the interurban and street railway line in detail).

R. M. Feustel, Fort Wayne and Northern Indiana Traction Company—Report of the Operating and Investment Data, 1918, (A detailed report by the company president).

Fort Wayne Transit Annual Reports, 1947-1968.

Fort Wayne and Wabash Valley Traction and Terminal Company Consolidation Proposal, 1910.

Fort Wayne & Wabash Valley Traction Company—Ordinances and Other Records 1906, Vol. 1, (A compilation of legal documents prepared by the General Counsel. This is a typed record, several copies made, of all deeds, court actions, City Council proceedings and County Commissioners records, from their several records, of all action pertaining to the company and its predecessors from 1870-1906).

Indiana Service Corporation Memorandum Report on Abandonment of Interurban Lines, Indianapolis: Earl L. Carter, 1939.

Indiana Service Corporation, Operating and Investment Data—City Lines, 1919.

Indiana Service Corporation, Annual Reports, 1920-1947.

Inventory and Appraisal May 1, 1920—Railway Utility, Indiana Service Corporation, Fort Wayne, Indiana, (The complete inventory and valuation. The copy used by the author had been in the mechanical department and carefully annotated with additional dates and information until late in 1926).

Inventory 1926—Railway Utility, Indiana Service Corporation, Fort Wayne, Indiana.

Section III—Newspapers and Periodicals

Fort Wayne Journal-Gazette.

Fort Wayne News-Sentinel.

Huntington Daily News Democrat.

Huntington Evening Herald.

Lafayette Journal-Courier.

Logansport Daily Reporter.

Logansport Morning Journal.

Logansport Pharos.

Peru Evening Journal.

Wabash Plain Dealer.

Indiana Service News, Vol. 1-3.

Transit Journal and its predecessors, *Street Railway Journal* (1894); *Street Railway Review* (1891), later *Electric Railway Review* (1906) and *Electric Railway Review* with *Street Railway Journal* as *Electric Railway Journal* (1908). Name changed to *Transit Journal* in 1932 and discontinued in 1942. Published by McGraw-Hill.

Mass Transportation and its predecessors; *Interurban Railway Journal* (1905) became *Electric Traction Weekly* (1906), then *Electric Traction* (1912), then *Electric Traction and Bus Journal* (1932), with the last name change to *Mass Transportation* (1935). Last published by Kenfield-Davis.

The following track maps illustrate the Wabash Valley System lines, its connections and the principal cities.

BASE MAP

INDIANA SERVICE CORPORATION AND CONNECTING ELECTRIC RAILWAYS

Kendallville
Waterloo
Garrett
I.S.C.
Robison Park
FORT WAYNE
New Haven
DEFIANCE
O.E.Ry.
(C.& L.E.) To Toledo
O.E.Ry. To Findlay
Ft.W.&D.T.Co.
Decatur
Monroeville
Ft.W.VW.&L.T.Co.
Convoy
Van Wert
Middlepoint
Delphos
LIMA
O.E.Ry.
W.O.R.R. To Dayton
To Springfield
INDIANA
OHIO
WINONA R.R. To Warsaw
HUNTINGTON
I.S.C.
WABASH
PERU
LOGANSPORT
Bluffton
B.G.&C.T.Co.
Geneva
U.T.Co.
MARION
N.I.P.Co.
KOKOMO
Delphi
Battle Ground
Soldier's Home
LAFAYETTE
TH.I.&E.T.Co.
FRANKFORT
T.H.I.& E.T.Co. To Lebanon
U.T.Co. To Indianapolis
U.T.Co. To Anderson
U.T.Co. To Muncie

Lines covered in this Bulletin
Indiana Service Corporation
Ft. Wayne, Van Wert & Lima Traction Co.
Ft. Wayne & Decatur Traction Co.
Bluffton, Geneva & Celina Traction Co.
Connecting electric lines
not covered in this Bulletin

Drawn by Max A. Zink

Rail lines not otherwise identified in this Bulletin

Railroads

A.C. & Y.R.R. Akron, Canton & Youngstown Railway
B. & O. R.R. Baltimore & Ohio Railroad
C. & O. R.R. Chesapeake & Ohio Railway
C.C.C. & ST.L.R.R. Cleveland, Cincinnati, Chicago & St. Louis Railway later New York Central lines.
N.Y.C.R.R. New York Central Railroad Company
N.Y.C. & ST.L.R.R. New York, Chicago & St. Louis Railroad Company (Nickel Plate Road), later Norfolk & Western Railway
Penn R.R. Pennsylvania Railroad (and subsidiary lines)
T.ST.L.&W.R.R. Toledo, St. Louis & Western Railroad (Nickel Plate Road), later Norfolk & Western Railway
Wabash R.R. Wabash Railroad, later Norfolk & Western Railway

Electric Railways

C. & L.E.R.R. Cincinnati & Lake Erie Railroad
N.I.P.Co. Northern Indiana Power Company
O.E.Ry. Ohio Electric Railway
T.H.I. & E.T.Co. Terre Haute, Indianapolis & Eastern Traction Company
W.O.R.R. Western Ohio Railway
U.T.Co. Union Traction Company of Indiana

MAP 1

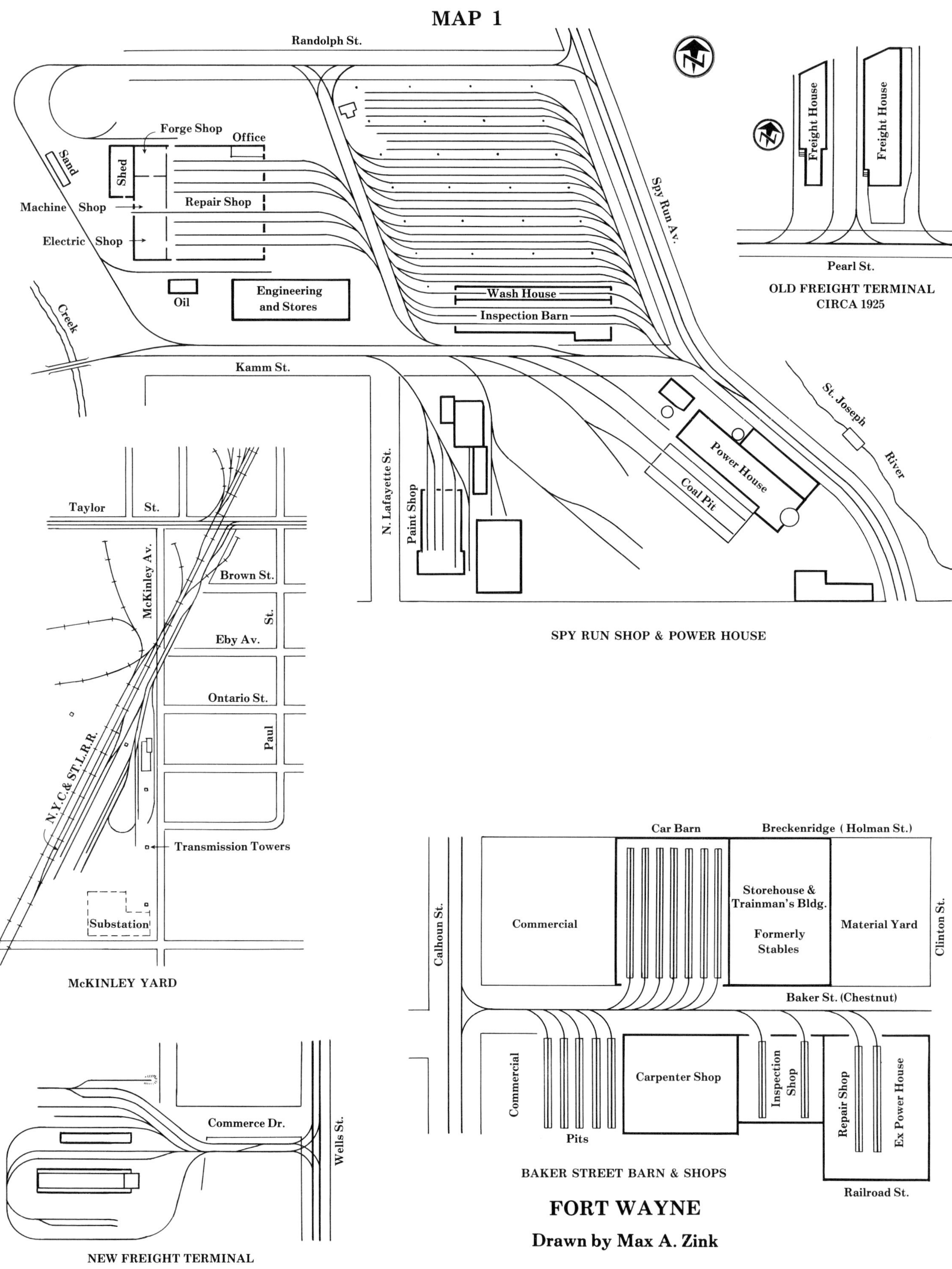

FORT WAYNE

Drawn by Max A. Zink

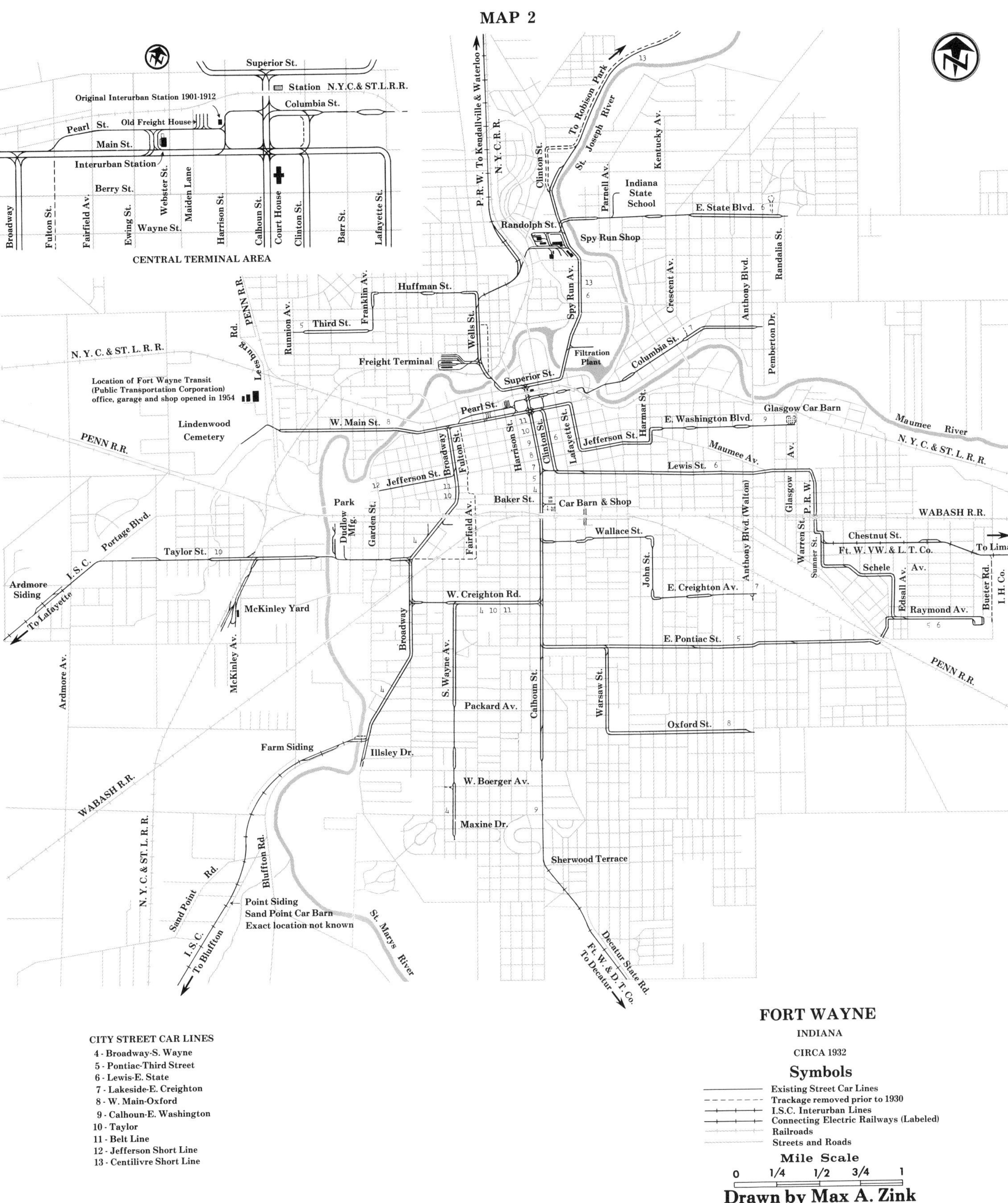
MAP 2
Superior St.
Station N.Y.C.& ST.L.R.R.
Original Interurban Station 1901-1912
Columbia St.
Pearl St.
Old Freight House
Main St.
Interurban Station
Berry St.
Wayne St.
Broadway
Fulton St.
Fairfield Av.
Ewing St.
Webster St.
Maiden Lane
Harrison St.
Calhoun St.
Court House
Clinton St.
Barr St.
Lafayette St.
CENTRAL TERMINAL AREA
P. R. W. To Kendallville & Waterloo
N. Y. C. R. R.
Clinton St.
To Robison Park
St. Joseph River
Parnell Av.
Kentucky Av.
Indiana State School
E. State Blvd.
Randolph St.
Spy Run Shop
Huffman St.
Franklin Av.
PENN R.R.
Lees burg Rd.
Runnion Av.
Third St.
Wells St.
Spy Run Av.
Crescent Av.
Anthony Blvd.
Randalia St.
Pemberton Dr.
N. Y. C. & ST. L. R. R.
Freight Terminal
Filtration Plant
Columbia St.
Location of Fort Wayne Transit (Public Transportation Corporation) office, garage and shop opened in 1954
Superior St.
Pearl St.
Glasgow Car Barn
Maumee River
W. Main St.
Lindenwood Cemetery
E. Washington Blvd.
Harmar St.
Jefferson St.
N. Y. C. & ST. L. R. R.
PENN R.R.
Maumee Av.
Lewis St.
Jefferson St.
Broadway
Fulton St.
Harrison St.
Clinton St.
Lafayette St.
Park
Baker St.
Car Barn & Shop
Glasgow Av.
P. R. W.
WABASH R.R.
Portage Blvd.
Dudlow Mfg.
Garden St.
Fairfield Av.
Wallace St.
Anthony Blvd. (Walton)
Warren St.
Chestnut St.
To Lima
Ft. W. VW. & L. T. Co.
Taylor St.
I. S. C.
Ardmore Siding
To Lafayette
Sumner St.
Schele Av.
John St.
E. Creighton Av.
Edsall Av.
Bueter Rd.
I. H. Co.
W. Creighton Rd.
McKinley Yard
Raymond Av.
E. Pontiac St.
Broadway
PENN R.R.
Ardmore Av.
McKinley Av.
S. Wayne Av.
Calhoun St.
Warsaw St.
Packard Av.
Oxford St.
Farm Siding
Illsley Dr.
W. Boerger Av.
WABASH R.R.
Maxine Dr.
Sherwood Terrace
N. Y. C. & ST. L. R. R.
Bluffton Rd.
Sand Point Rd.
Point Siding
Sand Point Car Barn
Exact location not known
St. Marys River
I. S. C.
To Bluffton
Decatur State Rd.
Ft. W. & D. T. Co.
To Decatur
FORT WAYNE
INDIANA
CIRCA 1932
CITY STREET CAR LINES
4 - Broadway-S. Wayne
5 - Pontiac-Third Street
6 - Lewis-E. State
7 - Lakeside-E. Creighton
8 - W. Main-Oxford
9 - Calhoun-E. Washington
10 - Taylor
11 - Belt Line
12 - Jefferson Short Line
13 - Centilivre Short Line
Symbols
Existing Street Car Lines
Trackage removed prior to 1930
I.S.C. Interurban Lines
Connecting Electric Railways (Labeled)
Railroads
Streets and Roads
Mile Scale
0 1/4 1/2 3/4 1
Drawn by Max A. Zink

MAP 3

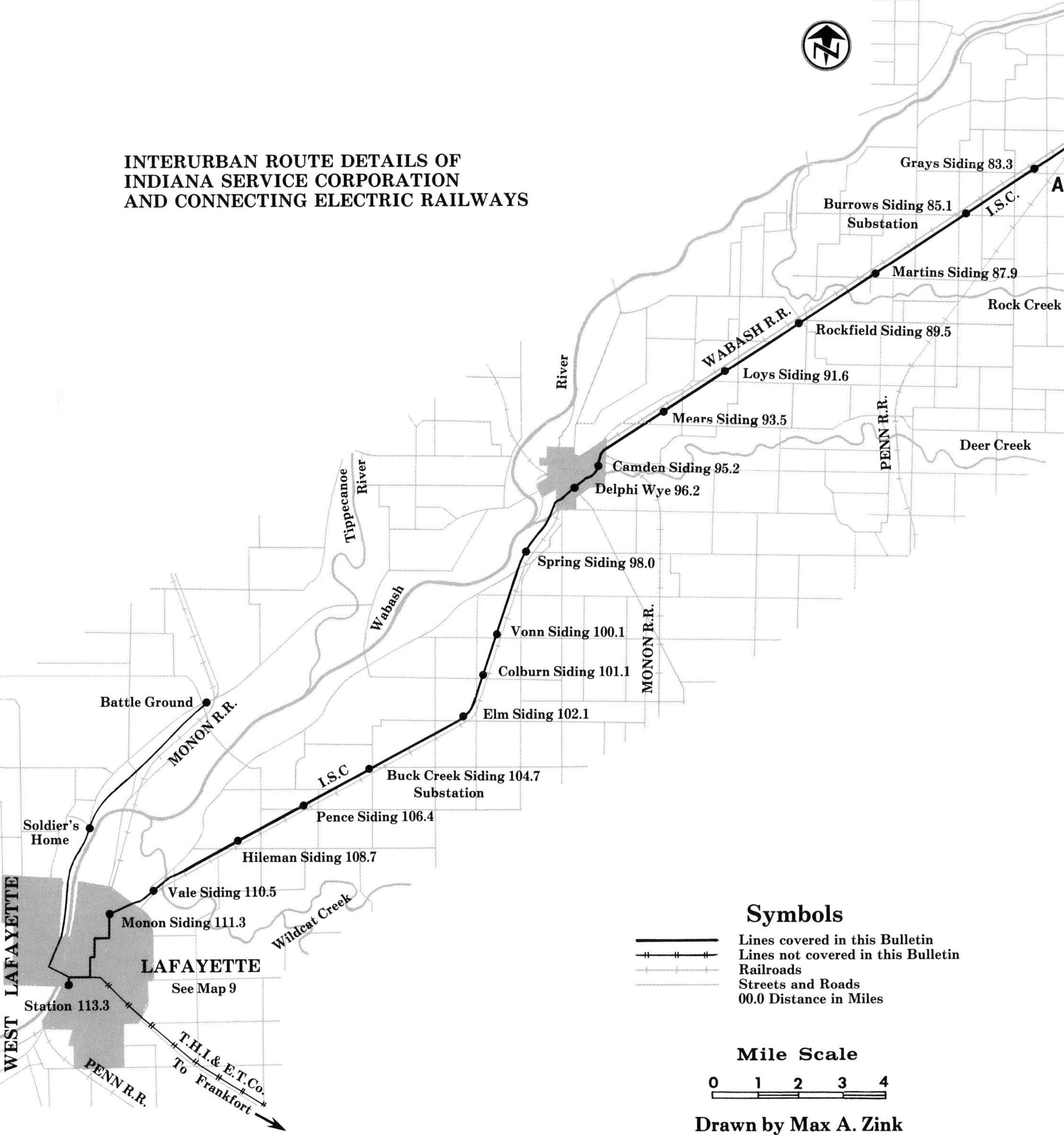

INTERURBAN ROUTE DETAILS OF
INDIANA SERVICE CORPORATION
AND CONNECTING ELECTRIC RAILWAYS
Grays Siding 83.3
A
Burrows Siding 85.1
Substation
I.S.C.
Martins Siding 87.9
Rock Creek
WABASH R.R.
Rockfield Siding 89.5
Loys Siding 91.6
River
Mears Siding 93.5
PENN R.R.
Deer Creek
Camden Siding 95.2
Delphi Wye 96.2
Tippecanoe
River
Spring Siding 98.0
Wabash
Vonn Siding 100.1
Colburn Siding 101.1
MONON R.R.
Battle Ground
MONON R.R.
Elm Siding 102.1
I.S.C
Buck Creek Siding 104.7
Substation
Soldier's
Home
Pence Siding 106.4
Hileman Siding 108.7
Vale Siding 110.5
Wildcat Creek
Monon Siding 111.3
LAFAYETTE
See Map 9
WEST LAFAYETTE
Station 113.3
T.H.I.& E.T.Co.
To Frankfort
PENN R.R.
Symbols
Lines covered in this Bulletin
Lines not covered in this Bulletin
Railroads
Streets and Roads
00.0 Distance in Miles
Mile Scale
0 1 2 3 4
Drawn by Max A. Zink

MAP 4

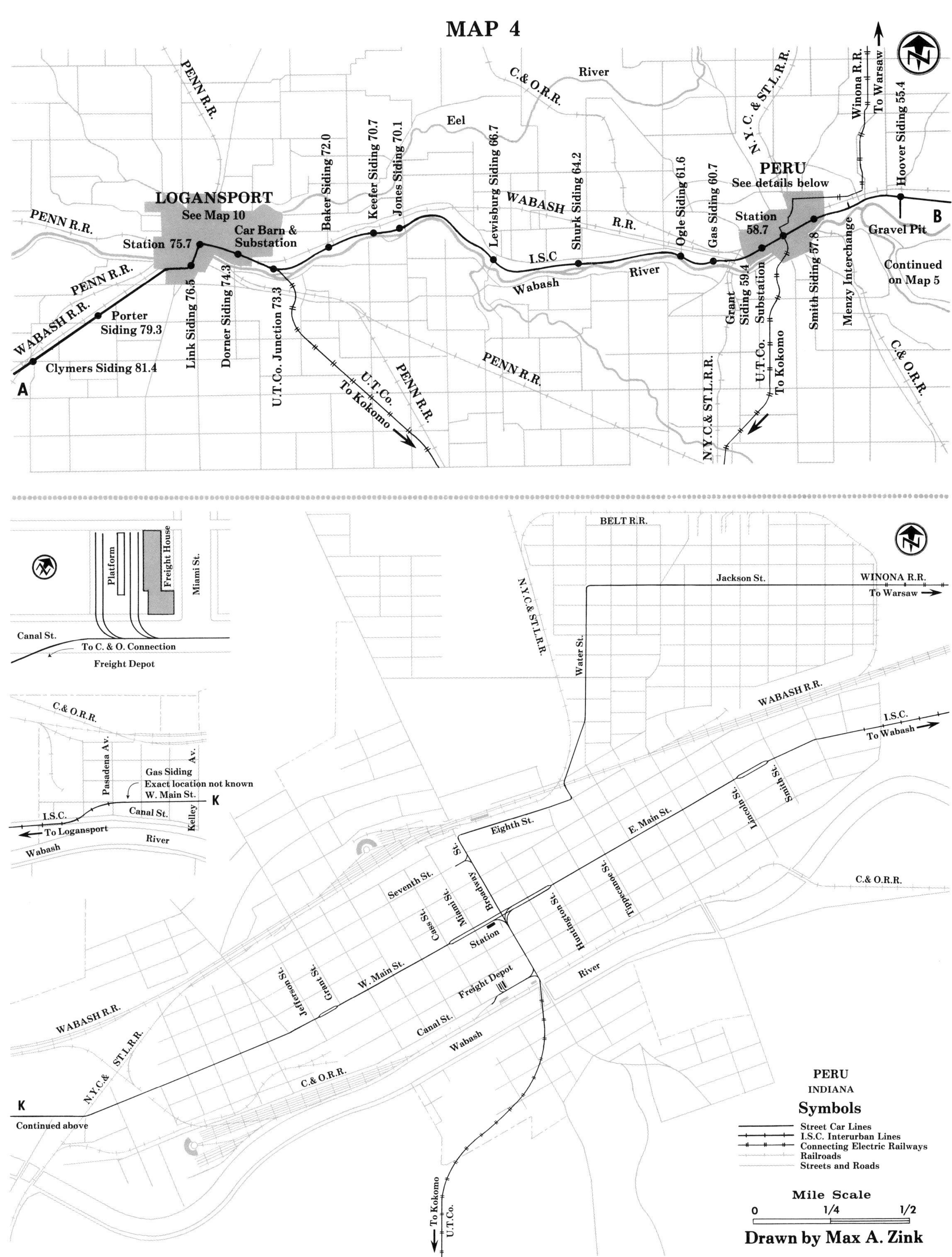

LOGANSPORT
See Map 10
Station 75.7
Car Barn & Substation
PENN R.R.
WABASH R.R.
Porter Siding 79.3
Clymers Siding 81.4
A
Link Siding 76.5
Dorner Siding 74.3
U.T.Co. Junction 73.3
U.T.Co. To Kokomo
Baker Siding 72.0
Keefer Siding 70.7
Jones Siding 70.1
Eel
River
C.& O.R.R.
Lewisburg Siding 66.7
WABASH R.R.
I.S.C
Wabash
River
Shurk Siding 64.2
Ogle Siding 61.6
Gas Siding 60.7
N.Y.C. & ST.L.R.R.
PERU
See details below
Station 58.7
Grant Siding 59.4
Substation
U.T.Co. To Kokomo
Smith Siding 57.8
Menzy Interchange
Winona R.R.
To Warsaw
Hoover Siding 55.4
Gravel Pit
B
Continued on Map 5
Platform
Freight House
Miami St.
Canal St.
To C. & O. Connection
Freight Depot
Pasadena Av.
Av.
Gas Siding
Exact location not known
W. Main St.
K
I.S.C.
To Logansport
Canal St.
Kelley
River
Wabash
BELT R.R.
N.Y.C.& ST.L.R.R.
Jackson St.
WINONA R.R.
To Warsaw
Water St.
WABASH R.R.
I.S.C.
To Wabash
Eighth St.
E. Main St.
Lincoln St.
Smith St.
St.
Broadway
Seventh St.
Cass St.
Miami St.
Huntington St.
Tippecanoe St.
C.& O.R.R.
Station
W. Main St.
Jefferson St.
Grant St.
Freight Depot
River
Canal St.
Wabash
C.& O.R.R.
N.Y.C.& ST.L.R.R.
K
Continued above
To Kokomo
U.T.Co.
PERU
INDIANA
Symbols
Street Car Lines
I.S.C. Interurban Lines
Connecting Electric Railways
Railroads
Streets and Roads
Mile Scale
0
1/4
1/2
Drawn by Max A. Zink

MAP 5

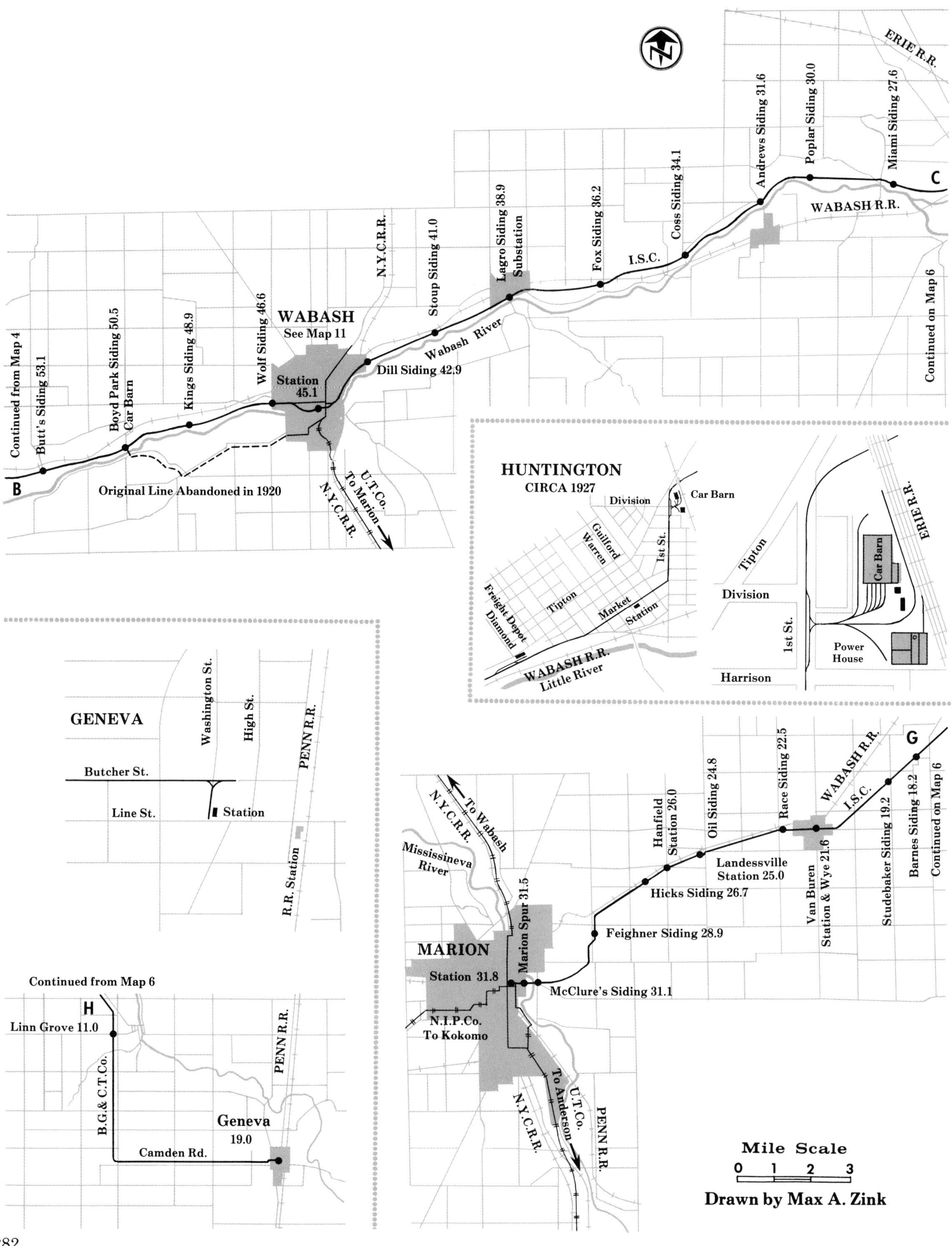

ERIE R.R.
Andrews Siding 31.6
Poplar Siding 30.0
Miami Siding 27.6
C
WABASH R.R.
Coss Siding 34.1
I.S.C.
Fox Siding 36.2
Lagro Siding 38.9
Substation
Stoup Siding 41.0
N.Y.C.R.R.
Continued on Map 6
WABASH
See Map 11
Wabash River
Dill Siding 42.9
Station
45.1
Continued from Map 4
Butt's Siding 53.1
Boyd Park Siding 50.5
Car Barn
Kings Siding 48.9
Wolf Siding 46.6
B
Original Line Abandoned in 1920
U.T.Co.
To Marion
N.Y.C.R.R.
HUNTINGTON
CIRCA 1927
Division
Car Barn
Guilford
Warren
1st St.
Freight Depot
Diamond
Tipton
Market
Station
WABASH R.R.
Little River
Tipton
Division
1st St.
Harrison
Car Barn
ERIE R.R.
Power
House
GENEVA
Washington St.
High St.
PENN R.R.
Butcher St.
Line St.
Station
R.R. Station
G
WABASH R.R.
I.S.C.
Race Siding 22.5
Oil Siding 24.8
Hanfield
Station 26.0
Landessville
Station 25.0
Hicks Siding 26.7
Van Buren
Station & Wye 21.6
Studebaker Siding 19.2
Barnes Siding 18.2
Continued on Map 6
N.Y.C.R.R.
To Wabash
Mississineva
River
Marion Spur 31.5
MARION
Station 31.8
Feighner Siding 28.9
McClure's Siding 31.1
N.I.P.Co.
To Kokomo
To Anderson
U.T.Co.
N.Y.C.R.R.
PENN R.R.
Continued from Map 6
H
Linn Grove 11.0
B.G.& C.T.Co.
PENN R.R.
Geneva
19.0
Camden Rd.
Mile Scale
0 1 2 3
Drawn by Max A. Zink

MAP 6

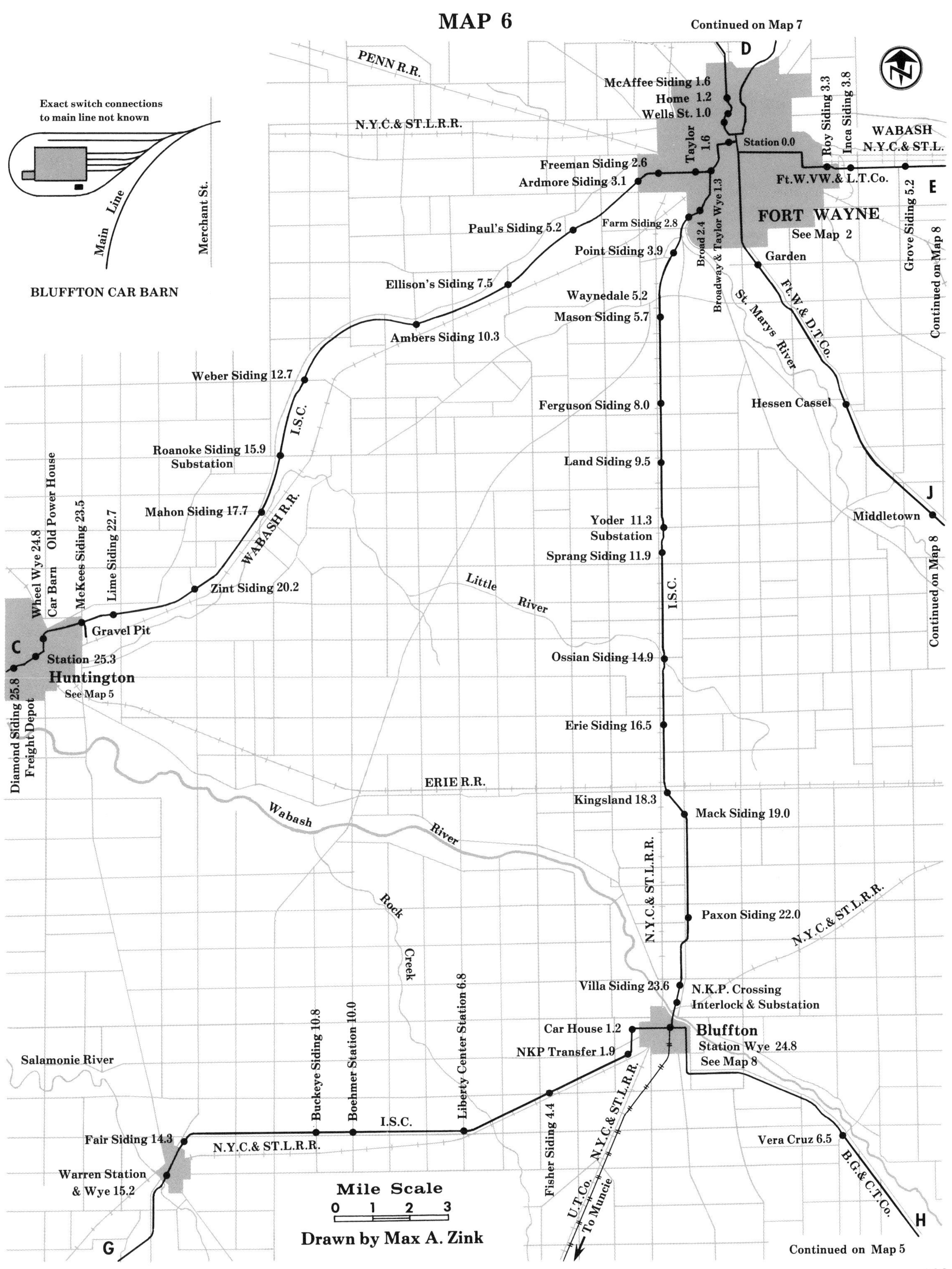

Continued on Map 7
PENN R.R.
N.Y.C.& ST.L.R.R.
Exact switch connections
to main line not known
Main Line
Merchant St.
BLUFFTON CAR BARN
D
McAffee Siding 1.6
Home 1.2
Wells St. 1.0
Taylor 1.6
Station 0.0
Roy Siding 3.3
Inca Siding 3.8
WABASH
N.Y.C.& ST.L.
Freeman Siding 2.6
Ardmore Siding 3.1
Ft.W.VW.& L.T.Co.
E
Broadway & Taylor Wye 1.3
Broad 2.4
Farm Siding 2.8
Paul's Siding 5.2
FORT WAYNE
See Map 2
Grove Siding 5.2
Continued on Map 8
Point Siding 3.9
Garden
Ellison's Siding 7.5
Waynedale 5.2
Mason Siding 5.7
St. Marys River
Ft.W.& D.T.Co.
Ambers Siding 10.3
Weber Siding 12.7
Ferguson Siding 8.0
Hessen Cassel
I.S.C.
Roanoke Siding 15.9
Substation
Land Siding 9.5
J
Mahon Siding 17.7
WABASH R.R.
Yoder 11.3
Substation
Middletown
Old Power House
Wheel Wye 24.8
Car Barn
McKees Siding 23.5
Lime Siding 22.7
Sprang Siding 11.9
Zint Siding 20.2
Little River
I.S.C.
Continued on Map 8
Gravel Pit
C
Station 25.3
Huntington
See Map 5
Ossian Siding 14.9
Diamond Siding 25.8
Freight Depot
Erie Siding 16.5
ERIE R.R.
Kingsland 18.3
Mack Siding 19.0
Wabash River
N.Y.C.& ST.L.R.R.
Rock Creek
Paxon Siding 22.0
N.Y.C.& ST.L.R.R.
Villa Siding 23.6
N.K.P. Crossing
Interlock & Substation
Buckeye Siding 10.8
Boehmer Station 10.0
Liberty Center Station 6.8
Car House 1.2
Bluffton
Station Wye 24.8
See Map 8
NKP Transfer 1.9
Salamonie River
I.S.C.
Fisher Siding 4.4
N.Y.C.& ST.L.R.R.
Fair Siding 14.3
N.Y.C.& ST.L.R.R.
Vera Cruz 6.5
Warren Station
& Wye 15.2
B.G.& C.T.Co.
Mile Scale
0 1 2 3
U.T.Co.
To Muncie
H
Drawn by Max A. Zink
G
Continued on Map 5

MAP 7

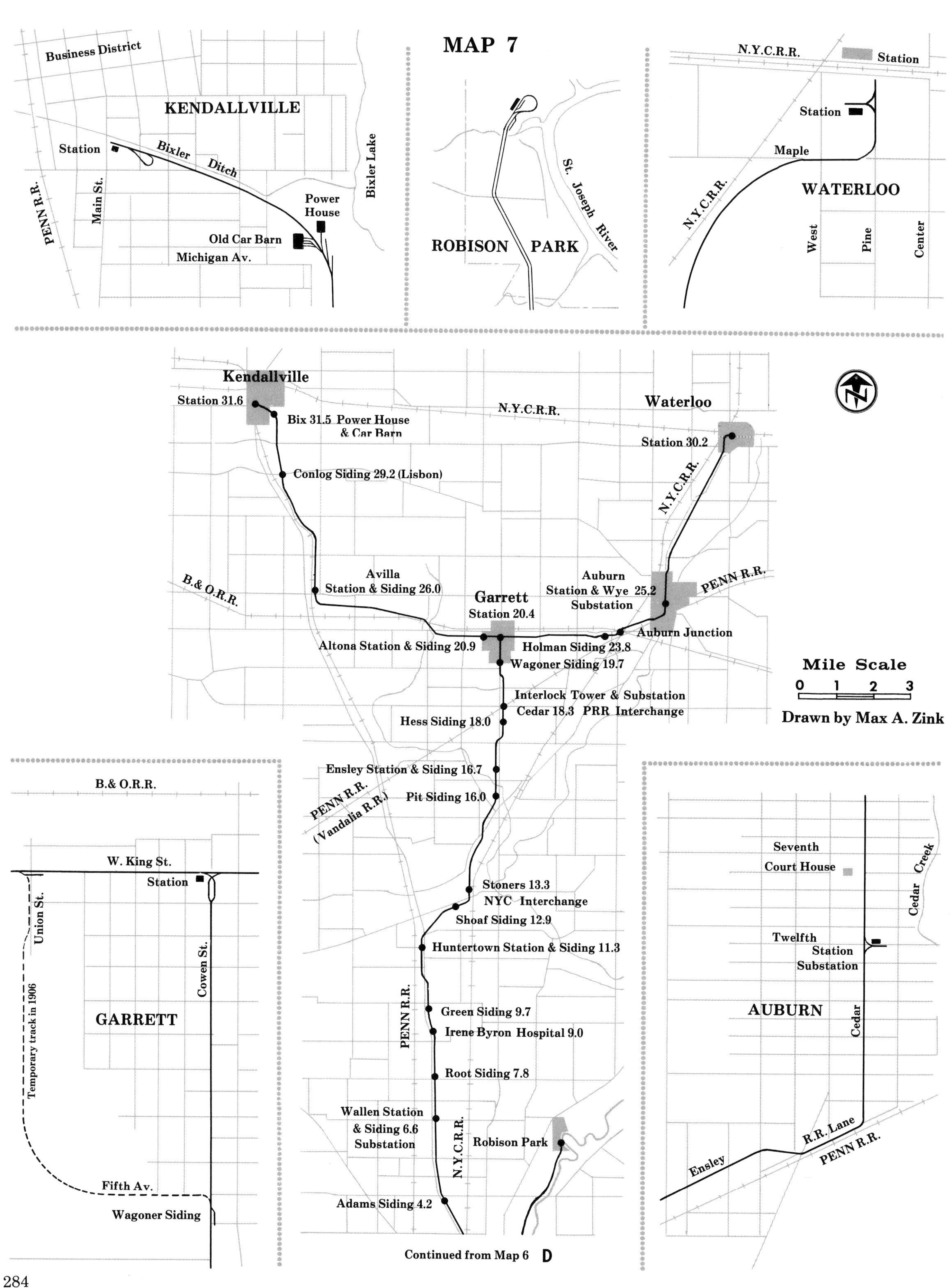

Business District
KENDALLVILLE
Station
Bixler
Ditch
PENN R.R.
Main St.
Power House
Bixler Lake
Old Car Barn
Michigan Av.
ROBISON PARK
St. Joseph River
N.Y.C.R.R.
Station
Station
Maple
N.Y.C.R.R.
WATERLOO
West
Pine
Center
Kendallville
Station 31.6
Bix 31.5 Power House & Car Barn
N.Y.C.R.R.
Waterloo
Station 30.2
Conlog Siding 29.2 (Lisbon)
N.Y.C.R.R.
B.& O.R.R.
Avilla Station & Siding 26.0
Garrett
Station 20.4
Auburn Station & Wye 25.2 Substation
PENN R.R.
Auburn Junction
Altona Station & Siding 20.9
Holman Siding 23.8
Wagoner Siding 19.7
Mile Scale
0 1 2 3
Interlock Tower & Substation
Cedar 18.3 PRR Interchange
Hess Siding 18.0
Drawn by Max A. Zink
Ensley Station & Siding 16.7
PENN R.R. (Vandalia R.R.)
Pit Siding 16.0
Stoners 13.3
NYC Interchange
Shoaf Siding 12.9
Huntertown Station & Siding 11.3
PENN R.R.
Green Siding 9.7
Irene Byron Hospital 9.0
Root Siding 7.8
Wallen Station & Siding 6.6 Substation
N.Y.C.R.R.
Robison Park
Adams Siding 4.2
Continued from Map 6 D
B.& O.R.R.
W. King St.
Station
Union St.
Cowen St.
Temporary track in 1906
GARRETT
Fifth Av.
Wagoner Siding
Seventh
Court House
Cedar Creek
Twelfth
Station
Substation
AUBURN
Cedar
R.R. Lane
Ensley
PENN R.R.

MAP 8

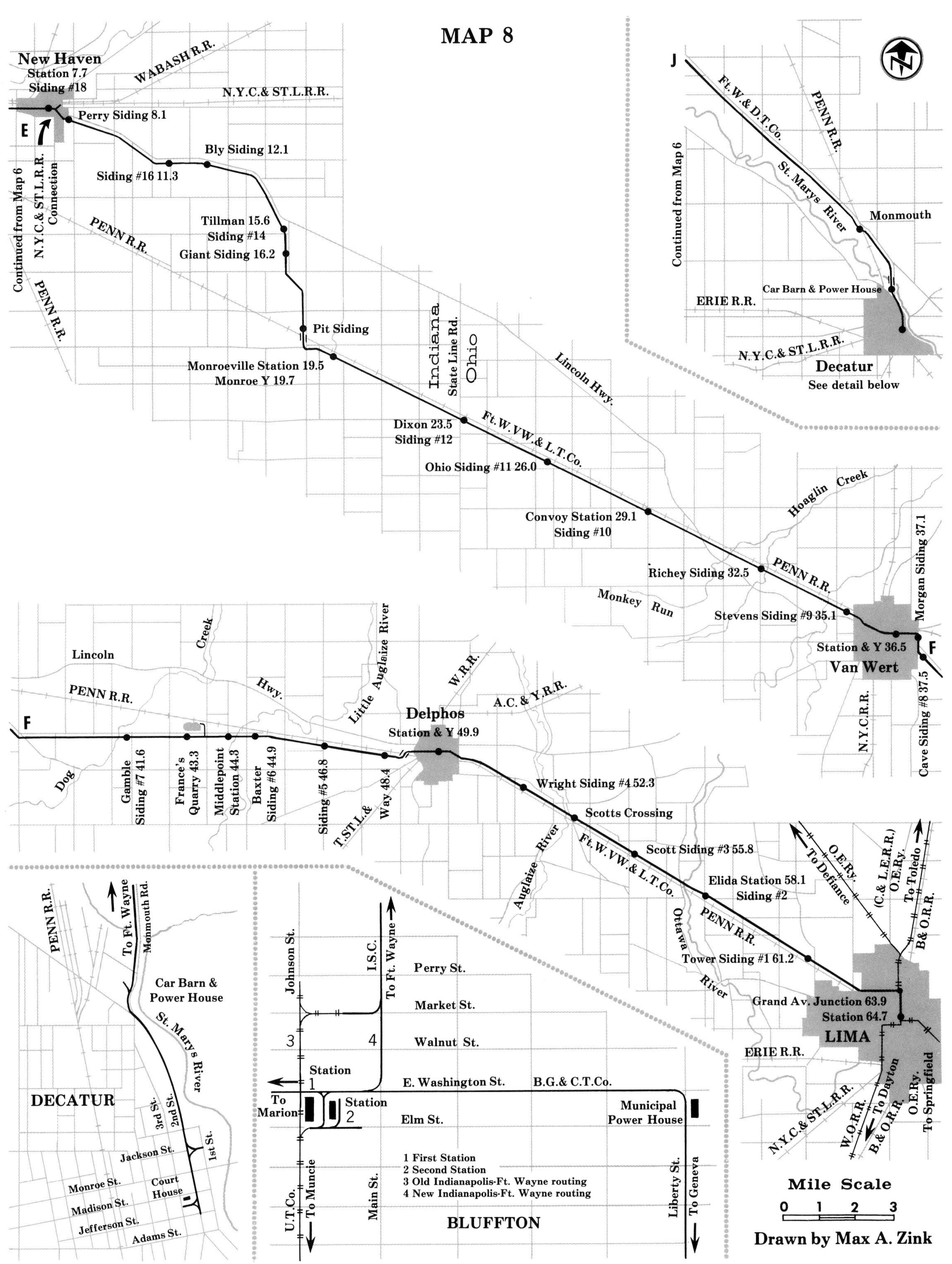

New Haven
Station 7.7
Siding #18
WABASH R.R.
N.Y.C.& ST.L.R.R.
Perry Siding 8.1
E
Bly Siding 12.1
Siding #16 11.3
N.Y.C.& ST.L.R.R. Connection
Continued from Map 6
PENN R.R.
Tillman 15.6
Siding #14
Giant Siding 16.2
PENN R.R.
Pit Siding
Monroeville Station 19.5
Monroe Y 19.7
Indiana
State Line Rd.
Ohio
Lincoln Hwy.
Dixon 23.5
Siding #12
Ft. W. VW. & L.T.Co.
Ohio Siding #11 26.0
Convoy Station 29.1
Siding #10
Hoaglin Creek
Richey Siding 32.5
PENN R.R.
Monkey Run
Stevens Siding #9 35.1
Morgan Siding 37.1
Station & Y 36.5
F
Van Wert
N.Y.C.R.R.
Cave Siding #8 37.5
J
Ft. W. & D.T.Co.
PENN R.R.
St. Marys River
Continued from Map 6
Monmouth
Car Barn & Power House
ERIE R.R.
N.Y.C.& ST.L.R.R.
Decatur
See detail below
Lincoln
Creek
Little Auglaize River
PENN R.R.
Hwy.
W.R.R.
A.C. & Y.R.R.
Delphos
Station & Y 49.9
F
Dog
Gamble Siding #7 41.6
France's Quarry 43.3
Middlepoint Station 44.3
Baxter Siding #6 44.9
Siding #5 46.8
T.ST.L.& Way 48.4
Wright Siding #4 52.3
Scotts Crossing
Auglaize River
Ft. W. VW. & L.T.Co.
Scott Siding #3 55.8
Elida Station 58.1
Siding #2
O.E.Ry.
To Defiance
(C.& L.E.R.R.) O.E.Ry.
To Toledo
B& O.R.R.
Ottawa River
PENN R.R.
Tower Siding #1 61.2
Grand Av. Junction 63.9
Station 64.7
LIMA
ERIE R.R.
N.Y.C.& ST.L.R.R.
W.O.R.R.
To Dayton
B.& O.R.R.
O.E.Ry.
To Springfield
PENN R.R.
To Ft. Wayne
Monmouth Rd.
Car Barn & Power House
St. Marys River
DECATUR
3rd St.
2nd St.
1st St.
Jackson St.
Monroe St.
Court House
Madison St.
Jefferson St.
Adams St.
Johnson St.
I.S.C.
To Ft. Wayne
Perry St.
Market St.
3
4
Walnut St.
Station
1
E. Washington St.
B.G.& C.T.Co.
To Marion
Station
2
Elm St.
Municipal Power House
1 First Station
2 Second Station
3 Old Indianapolis-Ft. Wayne routing
4 New Indianapolis-Ft. Wayne routing
U.T.Co.
To Muncie
Main St.
BLUFFTON
Liberty St.
To Geneva
Mile Scale
0 1 2 3
Drawn by Max A. Zink

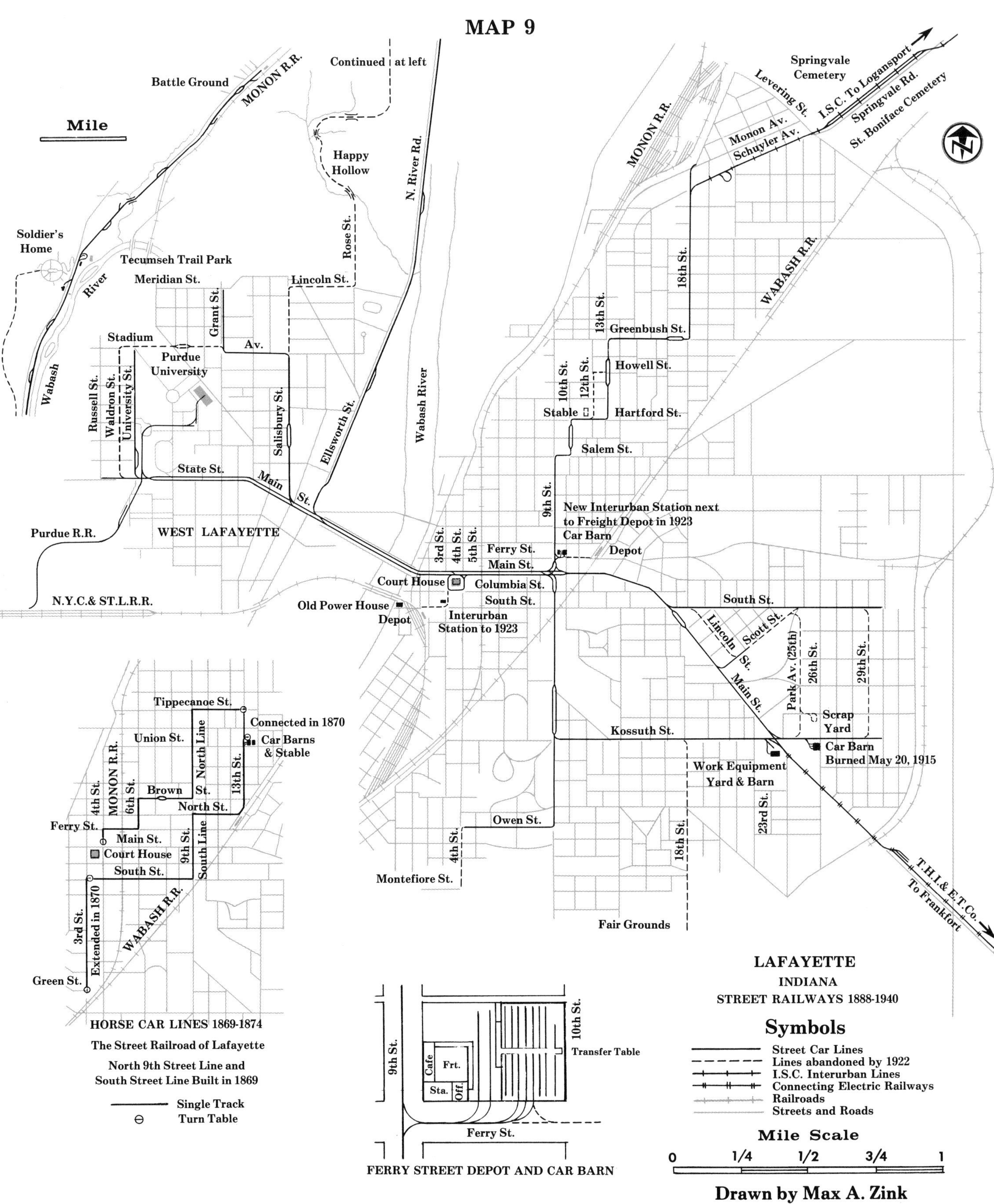
MAP 9
Mile
Battle Ground
MONON R.R.
Continued at left
Happy Hollow
N. River Rd.
Soldier's Home
Tecumseh Trail Park
River
Meridian St.
Rose St.
Lincoln St.
Grant St.
Stadium
Av.
Purdue University
Wabash
Russell St.
Waldron St.
University St.
Salisbury St.
Ellsworth St.
Wabash River
State St.
Main St.
Purdue R.R.
WEST LAFAYETTE
N.Y.C.& ST.L.R.R.
Springvale Cemetery
Levering St.
I.S.C. To Logansport
Springvale Rd.
St. Boniface Cemetery
Monon Av.
Schuyler Av.
MONON R.R.
18th St.
WABASH R.R.
13th St.
Greenbush St.
10th St.
12th St.
Howell St.
Stable
Hartford St.
Salem St.
9th St.
New Interurban Station next to Freight Depot in 1923
Car Barn
Depot
3rd St.
4th St.
5th St.
Ferry St.
Main St.
Court House
Columbia St.
South St.
Old Power House
Depot
Interurban Station to 1923
South St.
Lincoln St.
Scott St.
Park Av. (25th)
26th St.
29th St.
Main St.
Scrap Yard
Kossuth St.
Car Barn Burned May 20, 1915
Work Equipment Yard & Barn
23rd St.
Owen St.
4th St.
18th St.
Montefiore St.
Fair Grounds
T.H.I.& E.T.Co.
To Frankfort
Tippecanoe St.
Connected in 1870
Union St.
North Line
Car Barns & Stable
MONON R.R.
4th St.
6th St.
Brown
St.
13th St.
North St.
Ferry St.
Main St.
9th St.
South Line
Court House
South St.
WABASH R.R.
3rd St.
Extended in 1870
Green St.
HORSE CAR LINES 1869-1874
The Street Railroad of Lafayette
North 9th Street Line and South Street Line Built in 1869
Single Track
Turn Table
9th St.
10th St.
Cafe
Frt.
Sta.
Off.
Transfer Table
Ferry St.
FERRY STREET DEPOT AND CAR BARN
LAFAYETTE
INDIANA
STREET RAILWAYS 1888-1940
Symbols
Street Car Lines
Lines abandoned by 1922
I.S.C. Interurban Lines
Connecting Electric Railways
Railroads
Streets and Roads
Mile Scale
0
1/4
1/2
3/4
1
Drawn by Max A. Zink

MAP 10

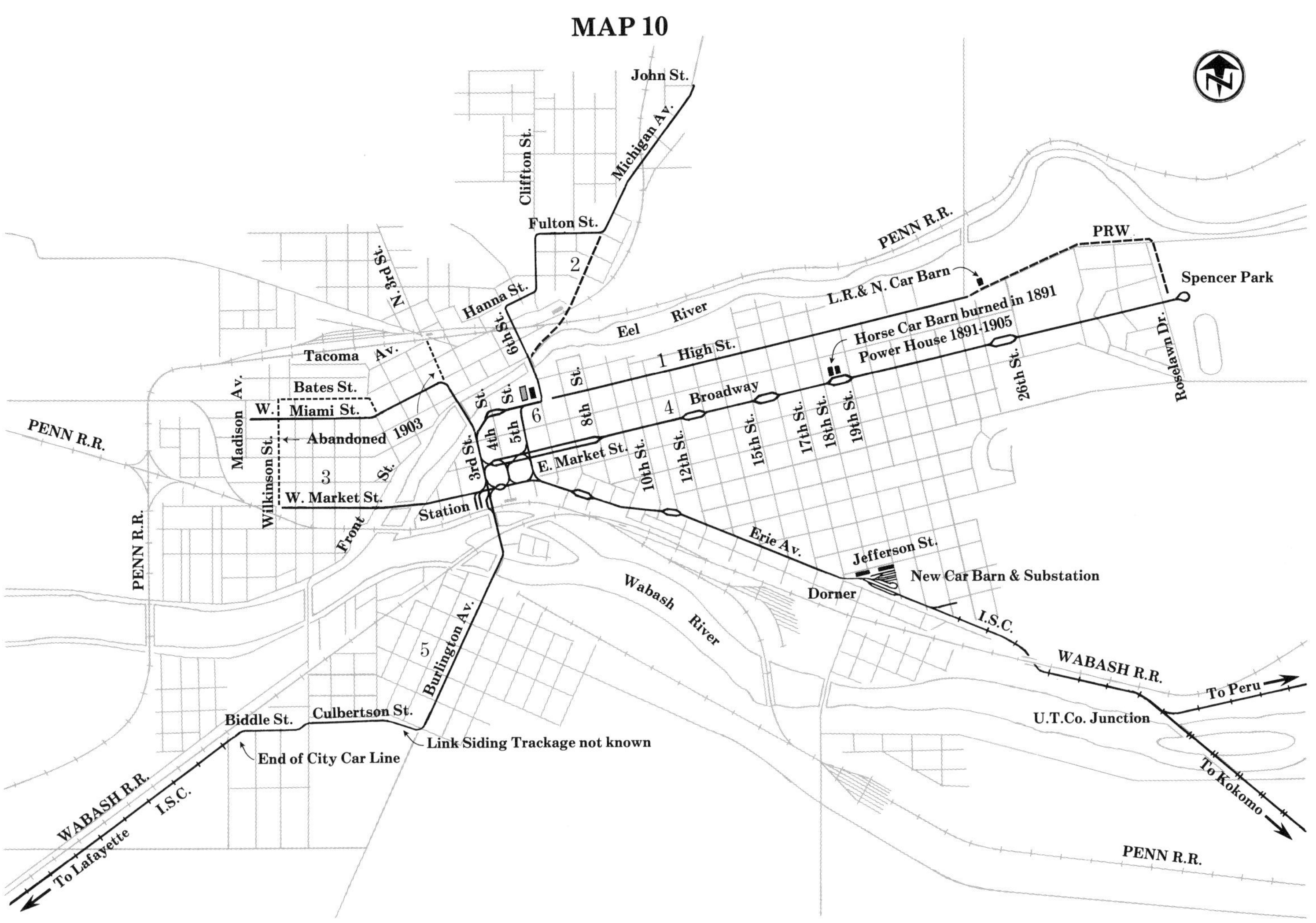

LOGANSPORT

INDIANA 1883-1932

DETAILS OF TRACK LAYOUT CIRCA 1920

Notes

1. High Street Line disconnected in 1918. Tracks in place in the street but removed from PRW and overhead removed.
2. Michigan Avenue trackage ordered retained in 1918 but removed in early 1920's.
3. Market Street Line disconnected in mid 1920's upon completion of a new bridge with no tracks. Overhead removed. Tracks remained in street.
4. Broadway Line and West Side Loop built as narrow gauge track. Others, standard gauge. West Side Loop replaced in 1903 by two separate standard gauge lines.
5. Burlington Avenue Line built in 1907.
6. L.R.& N. Power House is east of Columbia Brewing Co.

Symbols

Street Car Lines
Abandoned Car Lines
I.S.C. Interurban Lines
Connecting Electric Railways
Railroads
Streets and Roads

Mile Scale

0 1/2 1

Drawn by Max A. Zink

MAP 11

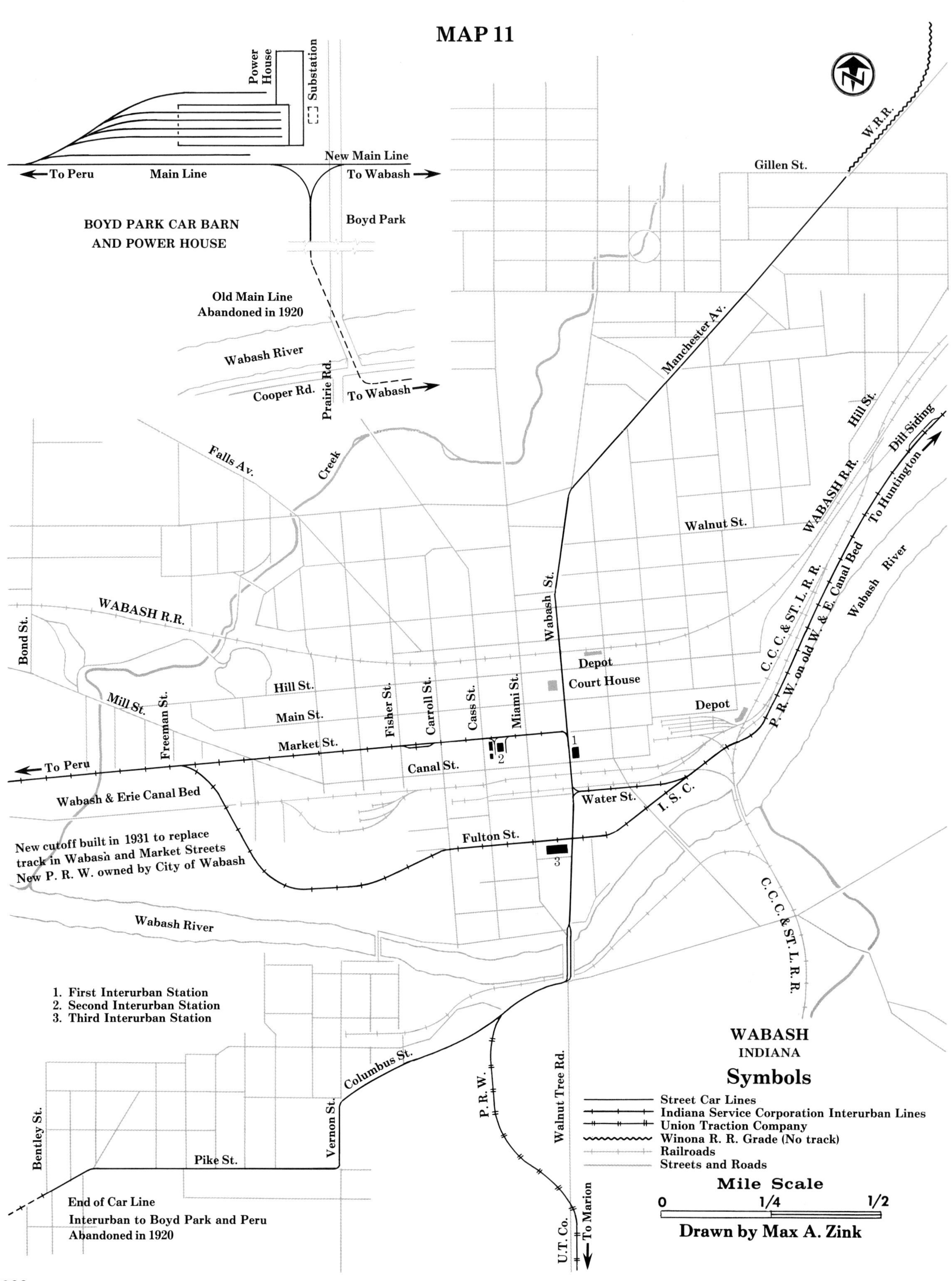

Power House
Substation
New Main Line
To Peru
Main Line
To Wabash
BOYD PARK CAR BARN AND POWER HOUSE
Boyd Park
Old Main Line Abandoned in 1920
Wabash River
Cooper Rd.
Prairie Rd.
To Wabash
W.R.R.
Gillen St.
Manchester Av.
Hill St.
Dill Siding
To Huntington
WABASH R.R.
Walnut St.
Falls Av.
Creek
Wabash St.
C. C. C. & ST. L. R.R.
P. R. W. on old W. & E. Canal Bed
Wabash River
WABASH R.R.
Bond St.
Depot
Court House
Hill St.
Mill St.
Freeman St.
Fisher St.
Carroll St.
Cass St.
Miami St.
Main St.
Depot
Market St.
To Peru
Canal St.
Water St.
I. S. C.
Wabash & Erie Canal Bed
Fulton St.
New cutoff built in 1931 to replace track in Wabash and Market Streets New P. R. W. owned by City of Wabash
C. C. C. & ST. L. R. R.
Wabash River
1. First Interurban Station
2. Second Interurban Station
3. Third Interurban Station
WABASH
INDIANA
Symbols
Street Car Lines
Indiana Service Corporation Interurban Lines
Union Traction Company
Winona R. R. Grade (No track)
Railroads
Streets and Roads
Columbus St.
P. R. W.
Walnut Tree Rd.
Bentley St.
Vernon St.
Pike St.
End of Car Line
Interurban to Boyd Park and Peru Abandoned in 1920
U.T. Co.
To Marion
Mile Scale
0
1/4
1/2
Drawn by Max A. Zink